T0295954

PROFITABLY HEALTHY COMPANIES

PROFITABLY HEALTHY COMPANIES

Principles of Organizational Growth and Development

W. Warner Burke and Michael O'Malley

Columbia Business School Publishing

Columbia University Press
Publishers Since 1893
New York   Chichester, West Sussex
cup.columbia.edu

Library of Congress Cataloging-in-Publication Data
Names: Burke, W. Warner (Wyatt Warner), 1935– author. |
O'Malley, Michael, 1954– author.
Title: Profitably healthy companies : principles of organizational growth and
development / W. Warner Burke and Michael O'Malley.
Description: New York : Columbia University Press, [2022] | Includes index.
Identifiers: LCCN 2021033318 (print) | LCCN 2021033319 (ebook) |
ISBN 9780231186902 (hardback) | ISBN 9780231186919 (trade paperback) |
ISBN 9780231546881 (ebook)
Subjects: LCSH: Success in business. | Organizational change—Management. |
Corporate culture. | Psychology, Industrial.
Classification: LCC HF5386 .B8895 2022 (print) | LCC HF5386 (ebook) |
DDC 658.4/09—dc23
LC record available at https://lccn.loc.gov/2021033318
LC ebook record available at https://lccn.loc.gov/2021033319

Columbia University Press books are printed on permanent
and durable acid-free paper.
Printed and bound by CPI Group (UK) Ltd, Croydon, CR0 4YY

Cover design: Noah Arlow

Contents

Introduction
1

CHAPTER ONE
Organization Development Basics
3

CHAPTER TWO
Organize for Change
32

CHAPTER THREE
Anticipate the Future
58

CHAPTER FOUR
Encourage Cooperation
81

CHAPTER FIVE
Remain Flexible
104

CHAPTER SIX
Create Distinctive Spaces
127

CHAPTER SEVEN
Diversify and Inclusify the Workforce
145

CHAPTER EIGHT
Promote Personal Growth
166

CHAPTER NINE
Empower People
192

CHAPTER TEN
Reward High Performers
213

CHAPTER ELEVEN
Foster a Leadership Culture
238

Notes
261

Index
319

PROFITABLY HEALTHY COMPANIES

Introduction

READERS WILL HAVE different reasons to pick up this book. Those reasons will dictate how you might use this information. Our preference, of course, is for you to read the book the way we intended. To paraphrase *Alice in Wonderland*, the best place to start is at the beginning and then stop when you get to the end. For general readers, that would be our recommendation.

Teachers and practitioners, however, may want to use the book a little differently. Teachers may want to use the book as a primary or supplemental text in organizational behavior, organization development, or human resource management. Because the book is structured by actions organizations should take to succeed, you can either rearrange existing notes to fit this new thematic setup or complement current texts with select chapters from the book.

We wrote the book with teachers in mind. The developmental principles we provide are connected to the questions students have when they first encounter organization development interventions: "What are we trying to achieve?" And "How do these fit into the entire organization as opposed to being one-off modifications?"

We start with and organize around the question "Why?" We give developmental tools and approaches a home with purpose. We believe those connections between the how's and why's will provide a stickier and more vibrant learning experience.

Practitioners or consultants on assignment may want to comb through the book for ideas related to a particular project. Potential approaches and change tactics are scattered throughout the book, and a change-agent may want to assemble ideas from different parts of the book as needed using the index as a guide. Certain chapters likely will be closer to some readers' interests than other chapters. For example, if you are looking for ways to enhance employee development, the chapters on personal growth (chapter 8) and empowerment (chapter 9) will contain most of the discussion and references you will be looking for. If you are trying to get teams to work more harmoniously, you will want to look to the chapter on cooperation (chapter 4). If, like most organizations, you are wanting to get the most out of your diversity efforts, our chapter on diversity and inclusion (chapter 7) as well as our discussions on systems throughout the book will be helpful.

And, finally, we are easy to find online. Write to us if you have a question or want to discuss an issue we examine in the book more fully. Our electronic pathway is always open and, if you are close to New York or New Haven, so are our doors.

CHAPTER ONE

Organization
Development Basics

EVERYBODY BELONGS TO an organization of some sort. Those who work within these organizations are responsible for making sure these organizations run smoothly and achieve their goals. The efforts of groups, however, frequently fall far short of expectations. Even in the best of circumstances when group members are full of goodwill and best intentions, results do not always turn out as hoped.

Groups often are weighed down by ambiguous objectives, poor communications, internal dissention, suspect decision-making procedures, and subpar execution. Slowly, group members' enthusiasm dissolves into frustration, fatigue, and despair. The embattled casualties of ruinous group dynamics either drop out or become discouraged, aloof observers. All but the mightiest and most resilient remain actively engaged and soldier on.

These tragically familiar outcomes of group processes are unfortunate because overcoming challenges and succeeding as a team can be an exhilarating experience. Exceptional group results do not arise easily, but they do occur. They occur in the arts, in sports, in charitable organizations, and in businesses. They should occur more frequently.

The purpose of this book is to ensure that they do occur . . . in your organization.

Our way forward relies on a compilation of concepts, tools, and techniques that together comprise organization development (OD). OD is a summary term that includes both the approach to, and realization of, organizational improvements. Think of it this way: say you want to remodel your kitchen. The contractor you hire for the work will begin with an idea of what makes kitchens practical, functional, and aesthetically pleasing. They will start their work with an overall conception of design that includes an understanding of kitchen layouts and materials, and how foundational elements such as structural supports, electrical wiring, gas lines, and plumbing influence the configuration of the space and eventual build-out. Equipped with the appropriate diagnostic gear and tools, carpenters, electricians, and plumbers implement the design according to the detailed blueprints and project plan. OD encompasses each of these phases from concept design, through the procedures followed, to the instrumentation and tools required to transform ideas into reality. It is a big undertaking that applies to organizations as large as multinational companies and as small as work groups.

This book offers a practical guide to what you can do to make the organization in which you work or consult more successful. Our focus is on action: on helping you as an organizational educator, adviser, team member, or leader realize the potential of the group. We will not encumber you with theory or esoteric distinctions among concepts argued over by academics. Rather, we will stick to the main path and provide you with what you need to make the changes you want. In the process, we will take a few illustrious excursions to highlight our points through exhibits, historical references, and case studies.

WHAT IS ORGANIZATION DEVELOPMENT?

The OD label stretches back to the mid- to late 1950s; however, the inception of OD predates that period by about twenty-five years. For aficionados of history, the OD term has been traced to work on group processes at Esso's Bayway Refinery and to culture change at General Mills under the direction of OD pioneers Herbert Shepard, Robert Blake, Douglas McGregor, and Richard Beckhard.[1] Nevertheless, once a name was affixed to the compendium of practices that became known as organization development, academics and practitioners tried to squeeze out the essence of OD by offering an assortment of definitions, despite the problems of shoehorning an immense field into a few words.

Not everyone completely agrees on the contours of OD. When you read the definitions in box 1.1, however, you can see that there are commonalities among them.[2] Despite variations in emphases, then, these snippets provide a good feel of what OD is all about. We have extracted a few of the key concepts and offer these as the basic tenants of OD, without asserting that we have at long last settled all differences of opinion. We have highlighted words from our summation that serve as the headings to the ensuing sections where we say more about each. This is not a survey chapter. Those of you who are

---

BOX 1.1
Sample Definitions of Organization Development

OD is . . .

. . . a planned, organization-wide intervention managed from the top and designed to increase an organization's effectiveness and health.
R. Beckhard

. . . a complex educational strategy intended to change beliefs, attitudes, values and structures of organizations so that they can better adapt to new technologies, markets, and challenges . . .
W. Bennis

. . . a process of fundamental change in an organization's culture.
W. W. Burke

. . . a systematic process for applying behavioral science principles and practices in organizations to increase individual and organization performance.
W. French and C. Bell

. . . a body of concepts, tools, and techniques used in improving organizational effectiveness and ability to cope with change.
N. Margulies and A. P. Raia

. . . about building and maintaining the health of the organization as a total system.
E. Schein

conversant in the field will have to have faith that the people and topics that you might have expected to encounter in an opening chapter will appear elsewhere in this book.

OD is:

- a **planned**,
- **collaborative** method of
- **organization change** that is
- designed to enhance the **health** of the organization
- through the application of **behavioral principles**.

Importantly, OD is a theory-governed, evidenced-based discipline. OD is the distillation of science into practical organizational actions involving the agreeable merger between town and gown.

Before we dissect our definition further, one matter demands some clarification. The tidiness of our description does not convey the true messiness of change. Plans and projections always look lovely on paper where progress marches uninterruptedly onward from the starting line to the goal. Substantive organizational improvements never work like that. People who you thought would support change, do not, and vice versa. Ideas you thought would work, do not; ideas that you thought would not work, do. And so on. In any creative endeavor you will feel, on occasion, like you are going in circles like those loop de loops shown in figure 1.1. The process can be extremely frustrating to those unacquainted with weighty change initiatives that seem like they are going nowhere. The practitioner's responsibility is to sensitize participants to the inevitable doubts that arise during a change effort and to ensure that temporary setbacks are natural parts of the process. Indeed, occasional setbacks and encounters with obstacles are the *sine qua nons* for innovation and progress.

PLANNED

In a sense, all change is planned in that it is goal-directed and intentional. Planned, in the hands of an OD practitioner, means having a holistic conception of a problem and an associated approach to change. "Planned" does not imply that all contingencies can be known in advance nor does it annul the fact that important changes

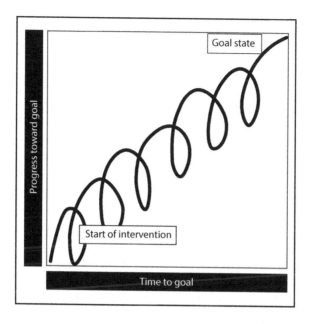

Figure 1.1 The ups and downs of change: two steps forward, one step back.

can spontaneously arise from the shop floor. Rather, planned means that when OD is called upon to intervene, it enters with a particular value orientation, understandings (e.g., of group processes), and perspective.

H. L. Mencken is said to have remarked that for every complex problem there is a solution that is quick, simple, and wrong. This adage is true because the right solution is seldom the one right next to the problem or because the solution creates new, unexpected problems. For example, societies may decide to reduce drug usage by effectively controlling the inflow of drugs into their countries; a successful program may reduce drug usage but the higher priced drugs resulting from scarcity may drive up users' need for cash and, consequently, crime rates. Incentivizing the recycling of plastics lowers costs, which in turn generates more plastics. Similarly, a pay-for-performance program may increase the desired productivity but also reduce quality and adherence to safety protocols given people's quest to hit quantitative goals. These results occur because most everything is connected to something else and disturbances in one place have effects in another.

For example, when two power lines failed in Oregon, eleven U.S. states and two Canadian providences—and seven million customers—subsequently lost electricity for sixteen hours.[3] If everything was simple, we would have found solutions to everything by now.

To plan interventions, an OD practitioner needs the equivalent of a global positioning satellite for guidance. In the case of organizations, the map used to navigate through problems to a resolution is a little fuzzy because it is ever changing: not so much in flux that the way forward is unrecognizable, but enough to remind us that we are not dealing with a static system. And "system" is the operative word. In contrast to mechanistic views of organizations in which pulling a problem-lever invariably, in gear-like fashion, leads straight to a solution-solved response, OD consultants' plans and approaches are based on the well-founded premise that organizations are complex systems.

A system is an interconnected set of elements that sensibly combine to perform a function or fulfill a purpose. Box 1.2 provides the kinds of questions that systems' thinking invites.[4] Look around and you will see systems everywhere. A city is a system with transit, residences, parks, businesses, schools, and arts centers organized to make it an attractive place to work, live, and play. The local football team is a system with people organized in a way to maximize its own team's points and minimize the points of an opponent. Organizations are systems in which structures, such as functional units, are linked together through internal processes. Our bodies, too, are systems.

Our bodies are composed of many components, or elements, each performing a unique function that, taken together, make us the living creatures that we are. The system falters when a part goes bad because of its intimate ties to other parts. The human body is a perfect example of a highly connected system because we have few internal parts that we can do without. For example, removing a problematic heart without a replacement is not a good option. Moreover, fixing a part may not be the solution because the real problem may lie elsewhere in the system. For example, an organization may attribute unusually high turnover rates to compensation that is too low but find that increased wages do not thwart turnover because the real causes have more to do with management styles and poor opportunities for employee growth.

We have provided a prototypical depiction of a system in figure 1.2. The illustration shows that systems have interconnected parts that are embedded in environments from which the system gives and takes. These exchanges with the external world may be things such as

Questions to Ask for Systems Thinking

1. What external forces affect the system of interest?
2. What does the system require to remain vital and operationally effective?
3. How are inflows into the system controlled?
4. What feedback mechanisms are in place to let you know if, for example, you are moving too fast (slow) or producing too much (little)?
5. Are the people and technologies well aligned?
6. Are internal connections among different parts of the organization weak or strong?
7. Is the way you are operating having any unexpected or unintended consequences?
8. How do you exchange materials, information, and goods with other systems?
9. What are the system's key outputs?
10. What aspects of the system are most vulnerable to breakdown, failure, and disruption?

A system is a set of connected parts working together to form a complex whole. For most systems to function properly, its interdependent mechanisms must be able to adjust to changes in the environment that envelops the system.

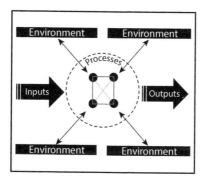

Figure 1.2 Basic elements of a system. Gap analyses often produce misleading information because they focus on a part of the system to the exclusion of the whole.

information, raw materials, and manufactured goods. We will explore several aspects of systems throughout the book, but the following principles are worthy of early mention.

- **The whole is greater than the sum of the parts:** This axiom means that something qualitatively different emerges when all the parts are combined. The whole behaves nothing like the individual parts themselves. Therefore, it is difficult to infer the essence of the whole by examining individual parts. We can liken this property of systems to the tale of the six blind men who are asked to describe an elephant only by touching one of its parts (e.g., tusk, trunk, leg). Naturally, the blind men disagree on what the elephant looks like. OD consultants, therefore, contemplate the whole of an entity and recognize that its effective operation depends on organizational parts, such as functions or departments, performing in a coordinated manner.
- **Systems can be open or closed:** An open system relates to its environment. It takes in information, energy, and materials and then transforms these inputs and returns them to the environment (usually to customers in the case of organizations) as useful outputs. Systems that are open change their behavior to regulate the balance between inflows and outflows based on the *all-important* guidance of feedback, as shown in figure 1.3. In contrast, closed

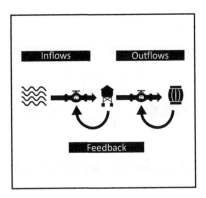

Figure 1.3 Simple model of system flows. Water levels in the tank are regulated by expanding or compressing inflows, or by expanding or compressing outflows based on feedback on water levels in the tank and barrel.

systems are not affected by influences outside of themselves. The system is relatively unresponsive to the environment because of the lack of communication. An uncommunicative system that is insensitive to changes in the environment cannot survive unless an external source, such as a benevolent government agency or good-hearted donor, are true believers in lost causes. The distinction between open and closed systems has been likened to throwing a lump of coal versus a live bird, even if the latter had identical chemistry and weight as the former. The trajectory of the coal is determined by its initial conditions, whereas the bird has an internal apparatus that will respond to external conditions once in flight.[5] Most organizations (systems) are never completely open or closed although, as Alan Turing observed a half century ago, new complex behavioral patterns will emerge only in systems that are knocked out of their equilibrium (i.e., are open).[6] Indeed, organizations will only be able to chart new directions when they have due appreciation of external realities and are aware of the necessities of change.

• **System solutions are indeterminate:** The general systems' literature calls this aspect of systems "equifinality." It means that there is more than one way to skin a cat and many roads that lead to Rome. More directly, complex problems have many possible solutions, several of which could reasonably qualify as "correct." The sorts of problems that have multiple, viable pathways to their resolution are called "wicked."

In the 1960s, following NASA's technical triumph of landing an astronaut on the moon, the University of California–Berkeley sponsored a seminar series that explored whether technology could be transferred and applied to resolve social issues such as the major urban disturbances that were occurring at the time. One professor, Horst Rittel, explained that certain kinds of problems are altogether different and unrelatable. Some, like a moon shot, follow a direct, predictable path to a destination that one could conclude is right or wrong or true or false: Did the astronauts land on the moon? In contrast, many large social problems, such as alleviating civil unrest, have no clear problem formulation without considerable deliberation and agreement, are open to several feasible routes of execution, and have no standard for right or wrong answers (just good or bad, better or worse).

Additionally, solutions to these wicked problems typically create new problems: in fact, some systems' experts would argue that every problem is the result of a solution.[7] The automobile helped to solve our need for accessible transportation at the turn of the twentieth century, but the decision to use gas versus alternative fuel sources (e.g., steam) contributed to the deleterious buildup of greenhouse gases in our atmosphere—a problem we were smart enough to create but have not been smart enough to fix. Most problems in organizations are wicked problems, and OD practitioners are looking for ways to make systems better rather than futilely searching for the one perfect mixture of a system's chemistry that will yield the optimal system-level results, now and for always.

- **Systems will not grow indefinitely:** Managers in organizations, analysts, and pundits speak about organizations as if they will go on forever, but systems reach capacities or limits beyond which the system becomes fallible (unless checked by a self-correcting mechanism as when we sweat to cool down when our bodies get too hot). Take a city, for example. If the most desirable city in the world attracted an unprecedented number of people, the beguiling elements of that system would start to lose their value because the increases in population may, for example, overload services, such as public transportation, and create new unforeseen problems, such as frustratingly scarce tickets at local attractions and events. Systems create their own limits if growth is unrestrained. Similar results occur in the natural ecosystem when, for example, the Canadian Lynx decimate the snowshoe hare population and then starve (the hares then return, and the cycle continues). Organizations, therefore, will sometimes set their own limits as W. L. Gore, a global manufacturer of polymer-based products, does; they believe that businesses become unduly bureaucratic when they reach a certain size and, therefore, break up units that become too large. Indeed, some think that unduly large organizations are fertile grounds for toxic bosses, personal indignities, internecine warfare, operational complacency, and strategic dogma. Therefore, growth can seed companies' decline.[8] Miller likens the dangers confronted by onetime high-flying companies to the fall of Icarus whose cleverly crafted wax and feather wings were both his salvation (from being imprisoned) and his demise when he flew too close to the sun and the wax on his wings melted. (This decline following a rise to preeminence is called the Icarus paradox.)

- **Systems exist within systems within systems:** The graphic in figure 1.3 omits an important feature of systems. Systems are nested within other systems. People are systems who belong to families; these families live in neighborhoods, towns, states, countries, and so on to the ends of the universe. There is no limit to how small or how large systems can be. You have to draw the line and establish a boundary somewhere, however, for your intervention. The nature of the issue and associated change effort likely will dictate the logical contours of the problem.

Organizations also have systems that overlay one another. Just as the human body has multiple systems (e.g., circulatory, endocrine), organizations have multiple systems as well. OD is concerned specifically with two major systems: the social and technical systems of organizations.[9] The social system consists of the people of the organization: what they know and can do, the relationships they have, and the culture they work within. The technical system is made up of those features of the organization that are associated with flows involving the tools, techniques, technologies, and processes that are used to store and transport goods and information.

The ideas behind sociotechnical systems, the combination of the two systems, had their origin in the coal mines of the United Kingdom. New automation involving longwall methods of mining (blocks of coal are cut and put on conveyor belts) were introduced that allowed work to be disaggregated and reconfigured. This automation provided researchers (Eric Trist and others) a chance to experiment with work arrangements that were more consistent with the new processes being introduced.[10]

Traditionally, work in the mines was highly specialized with each miner performing a certain task. Trist reorganized the work in a manner that we would describe today as autonomous work teams. This involved transferring decision-making authority for tasks, assignments, and schedules to newly formed units that became responsible for meeting production quotas. The central aim was to structure the work in a way that was responsive to the underlying technology and afforded miners the discretion to organize work and the flexibility to adjust routines and team roles in the manner they thought best.

The experiment was a success. Results showed increases in both productivity and worker satisfaction. These outcomes were replicated two decades later at the Rushton coal mine, a small, privately held mine located in central Pennsylvania.[11]

A goal of OD is to ensure that the social and technical systems of an organization are jointly optimized: they mix in a manner that satisfies human needs and delivers the best, workable organizational results. An illustration of incongruence between the social and technical systems is nicely portrayed in the famous chocolate scene from *I Love Lucy* in which a conveyor belt of chocolates exceeds Lucy's and Ethel's ability to keep pace in wrapping the candies.[12] The results would have been better—but less funny—if the plant had slowed the conveyor belt to levels that accommodated the number and skills of the people on the line. This scenario highlights another important point about systems. The best organizational results under given conditions are not necessarily achieved through the optimization of each individual system. Superior outcomes at the organization (system) level are products of the sober alignment of social and technical systems and not their separate and individual optimization.

Although the topic is outside the purview of this book, OD practitioners and policy makers increasingly will have to contend with the effects of automation on the labor force. Technology introduces new opportunities into the workplace, but it eliminates others. A recent analysis showed that of seven hundred jobs examined, almost half will be outdated within twenty years and be supplanted by automated systems.[13] The atrophying of skills coupled with increased automation may partly be responsible for a dwindling eligible labor pool. Currently, 37 percent of people sixteen years old and older in the United States have exited the workforce and are not looking for work. This withdrawal has been most acute among prime work-age individuals, twenty-five to fifty-four, especially men without college educations. Indeed, the decline in workforce participation over the past twenty years has been the steepest in the United States when comparing all member countries of the Organization for Economic Cooperation and Development.[14] Economists offer other reasons for the decline in addition to changes in automation, such as dramatically falling real wages and failing or unstable marriages that reduce familial incentives for work. Nevertheless, educational systems and organizations will need a cogent response to the persistent decrease of a skilled workforce.

COLLABORATIVE

It is impossible to trace the beginning of OD to a single person, place, or time. (Although, we have included an overview of key people and their associated works during the early days of OD in box 1.3).

BOX 1.3
Selected Works in the Formative Years of OD

1933 Elton Mayo
The Human Problems of an Industrial Civilization

1938 Chester Bernard
The Functions of the Executive

1939 Fritz Roethlisberger (with W. J. Dickson)
Management and the Worker

1947 Kurt Lewin
Frontiers in Group Dynamics

1951 Elliot Jacques
The Changing Culture of a Factory

1957 Alfred Marrow
Making Management Human

1958 Ronald Lippitt (with J. Watson)
The Dynamics of Planned Change

1959 Frederick Hertzberg (with B. Mausner and B. Snyderman)
The Motivation to Work

1960 Douglas McGregor
The Human Side of Enterprise

1961 Rensis Likert
New Patterns of Management

1961 Wilfred Bion
Experiences in Groups and Other Papers

1962 Chris Argyris
Interpersonal Competence and Organizational Effectiveness

1963 Eric Trist (with G. W. Higgin, H. Murray, and A. B. Pollock)
Organizational Choice

1964 Robert Blake, Jane Mouton, and Herbert A. Shepard
Managing Intergroup Conflict in Industry

1969 Richard Beckhard
Organizational Development: Strategies and Models

Rather, OD was a gradual outgrowth of working conditions during the period of industrialization from the latter part of the nineteenth century to the Second World War. The conditions were harsh, job security unstable, the wages low, and the hours long. Most of the larger factories at the turn of the century were in forbidding, highly physical industries, such as meat packing, railroad construction, and iron and steel. Today, we forget that the celebrated monuments of industrialization, such as the Hoover Dam (1931–1935), were sites to many work-related fatalities (ninety-six people died building the Hoover Dam) and considerable employer–employee strife.

As the need for labor reforms mounted and public opinion changed, organizations began to jettison the mind-numbing practices of scientific management pioneered by Frederick Taylor at Bethlehem Steel. Much of Taylor's projects involved the installation of piece-rate work and the maximization of output through the harmonization of movements between man and machine.[15] Inspired by the magnificent internal choreography of well-crafted machines, such as clocks, it was easy to envision a world of perfectly synchronized motions with employees playing the unflattering role of internal parts. The factory proved to be the ideal testing ground for the Clockwork Universe of René Descartes, Gottfied Leibniz, and others.

Proponents of scientific management sought to take much of the ferocity out of management–employee relations by appealing to objective, unbiased principles of science to guide and regulate the activities of the workforce, as opposed to relying on the more customary means of threats, coercion, and brute force. Because the application of the scientific principles and establishment of work standards really were under the control of management, the new methods of management remained solely production focused and failed to rescue managers and workers from their grim and unfriendly bonds. Productivity, in many factories, continued to languish.

By the early 1920s, major employers shifted their attention to how the work environment and quality of conditions affected employees' productivity. Consequently, organizations began to investigate ideal conditions in the workplace. The most famous of these studies began in 1924 at the Western Electric Hawthorne Plant in Cicero, Illinois— the makers of telephone system components for American Telephone and Telegraph.

Most people know of these studies through their legacy in textbooks, discussed as the Hawthorne effect. This effect is a reference to experimental artifacts that unintentionally influence results. Researchers at Hawthorne manipulated lighting conditions—and, subsequently, rest intervals, lunchtimes, refreshments, payment methods, and more—and found that productivity within both the experimental (treated) and control (untreated) groups improved regardless of what was done with working conditions. Although quite a bit has been written about these studies and what really happened, researchers seemed to have had ongoing dialogue with employees and the act of including employees in the change process may have been sufficient to increase productivity regardless of the modifications made in the workplace.[16]

A new, inclusive workplace blossomed between 1929 and 1932 when Elton Mayo, teaching at the Harvard Business School, convinced Western Electric's leadership to engage in a bold experiment in which he and many trained researchers would interview employees about their likes and dislikes of the workplace. They would use a nondirective questioning procedure—then being pioneered by Jean Piaget, Carl Rogers, and others—and deploy a new technology to capture employees' comments: audio recording. The information gleaned would be used to make changes in the workplace and to develop materials for supervisory training.[17]

This clinical approach used to probe employees' inner lives was directly related to the new human relations movement that valued the inherent worth of people, their capacity for personal growth, and their desire to be authors of their own lives. This was a significant change in the industrial mindset as workers no longer were conceived as simpleton members of the species homo sapiens or as malleable, instrumental components of the industrial apparatus, but rather were viewed as people with interests, needs, and capabilities who could—and should—have a voice in their organizational station.

Eventually the values of the human relations movement were assimilated into the OD framework.[18] Ever since, the practice of OD has been predicated on open, honest communications among all parties involved in the change effort and has remained faithful to a process in which members of the group participate in shaping the solutions that will affect them. More generally, OD adopted humanism's unwavering regard for human dignity, developmental objective of fulfilling human potential, and the belief in individuals' ability to diagnose their own problems, provide input into material matters, and aspire to a future of their creation.

ORGANIZATION CHANGE

The success of an OD consultant partly depends on his or her ability to transfer knowledge to organizational members to enhance the organization's long-term self-sufficiency. It is the OD consultant's task to plan for their own obsolescence by ensuring that the organization acquires the ability to continuously renew itself.

Although the consultant remains available when assistance is needed, one of the goals of OD is to build up the organization's capacity to revitalize—that is, to initiate its own change. For fans of the *Doctor Who* series, we could call an organization's ability to sustain itself through transformational change, regeneration: the sci-fi process allows a Time Lord who is old, wounded, or dying to acquire a new robust physical form and a slightly different character. Importantly, the new doctor does not become a younger, more vibrant version of him- or herself but a qualitatively different being who is more prepared to combat evil forces in the universe. In many instances, this form of transformation is the same kind of change organizations require.

The metamorphosis of an organization into a new competitive construction involves implementing what theorists have called double-loop learning. As shown in figure 1.4, the first loop is learning to fix problems according to standard goals and protocols. The second loop involves creating systems that permit organizations to reflect upon and question the purpose and efficacy of the first loop. Is the organization looking at issues or concerns in the right way, or does it need to reconceive how it thinks about the marketplace and its operations? This superordinate reflective capability is known as "metacognition," or thinking about thinking. Overall, metacognition refers to the overarching processes an individual or organization uses to plan, monitor, and assess self-understanding and performance. It is a critical aspect of learning that enables problem-solvers to think through a problem, select appropriate strategies, and make decisions about a best course of action.

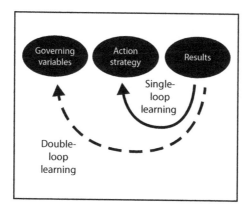

Figure 1.4 Single- and double-loop learning. If expected results are not achieved, double-loop learning suggests rethinking the entire problem rather than making additional attempts using similar approaches and expecting different results.

OD theorist Chris Argyris illustrates the difference between single- and double-loop learning using a thermostat: "A thermostat that automatically turns on the heat whenever the temperature in a room drops below 68°F is a good example of single-loop learning. A thermostat that could ask, 'Why am I set to 68°F?' and then explore whether or not some other temperature might more economically achieve the goal of heating the room to a comfortable temperature would be engaged in double-loop learning."[19] This latter mechanism of self-examination is a prerequisite for ongoing change; however, organizations still need to learn what to do and have the presence and fortitude to act.[20]

Writing within the OD tradition, Peter Senge reinvigorated and popularized the notion of a learning organization that he described as one that is able to take effective action and continually recreate its future.[21] Learning organizations, for example, can avoid repeat mistakes and meet new challenges because of their capacity to acquire and apply new relevant information. A pedestrian example of this adaptiveness is learning what it feels like to be wet and grabbing an umbrella before going outside on a cloudy day. Similarly, organizations that learn more and more about their relationship to the world outside its walls are putting themselves in a position to adjust in response to, or in anticipation of, new conditions.

Many organizations serve as poster-organizations for adaptive successes and failures. One great success in the past twenty-five years has been the rebound of the faltering behemoth, IBM. Observers once believed this moribund bureaucracy was destined for the mainframe graveyard along with obsolete Digital Equipment Computers (DEC) and Control Data until Lou Gerstner, Jr. reignited IBM's service culture and introduced new markets through technology solutions.

In contrast, during the 1960s, the anchor supermarket at our local strip mall belonged to the Great Atlantic and Pacific Tea Company (A&P). As teens, we would walk that strip mall and quench our thirst at the fountain counter inside Woolworth's (later to become Footlocker). If Woolworth's was busy, we would cross the street to S. S. Kresge's (which became Kmart). We developed finger strength by producing school reports on a Remington typewriter, patched clothes on a Singer sewing machine, lifted jokes from grandma's *Reader's Digest*, developed pictures from Kodak film, captured moments with a Polaroid, and watched our three channels of programming on a Zenith television that was as big and heavy as a baby grand piano. Recently, it was revealed that future teenagers will never know the exhilaration of discovering discarded *Playboy* magazines in the neighbor's trash (one man's trash is a teenager's treasure) as *Playboy* has become yet another casualty to the internet age. Many people living today have never heard of these companies. The people born today probably never will. Although it once took a company a lifetime or two to go poof, a company today can go from the apex of the market to the nadir within a decade (e.g., Netscape, Napster). Given the speed of market transitions and the rapidity of potential organizational decline, organizations no longer have much time to fiddle while they dwindle. OD is more important now than ever.

We all can think of organizations that aptly could be described as "smart" or "dumb"—the bright and profound versus the dull and shallow. Before we discuss how organizations become one or another (or one, and then the other) later in this book, we take up the leitmotif of a learned organization and what general capabilities intelligent companies seem to have that allow them to convert resources into usable outputs, that is, the capabilities that dumb companies do not possess.

Intelligence is believed to have at least two parts, metaphorically illustrated as the difference between five tall people and a championship basketball team. Intelligence is not simply a matter of having native abilities; a second mechanism that makes wise deployment and use of those talents is needed as well. In the same way, organizational intelligence is not scored by tabulating what individuals in the organization know. Until the organization can demonstrate that it is able to use what its employees know, it will remain an organization with smart people versus a smart organization. Therefore, having a thorough understanding of the business environment, the competition, industry trends, and unique technologies is critical but constitutes only half of smartness. The distinction between knowing and sound judgment and efficacious doing is captured by statements like, "For a smart guy, he sure is dumb."

The learning in organizations, then, generally has two phases. The first phase of leaning mainly pertains to an organization's ability to gather, integrate, and distribute meaningful information, including the following:[22]

- **Knowledge acquisition:** A means of scanning for, appraising, and gathering vital and timely information
- **Knowledge sharing:** A means of processing and making reliable information readily accessible
- **Knowledge synthesis:** A means of integrating and interpreting the meaning of information

The second part of intelligence is akin to executive functioning that enables people and institutions to break free of entrenched and rote patterns of behaving by inhibiting impulsive actions, maintaining focus, monitoring and adding relevant information to one's knowledge base, and flexibly reconceiving one's notions in light of new facts. Executive functioning means developing a collective mindset that inhibits organizational tendencies to concentrate on irrelevant information and take automatic action when, instead, the situation calls for new outlooks and behavioral repertoires. This added cognitive sophistication is what allows people to set goals, make plans, and see their goals through to the end, altering course if necessary.[23]

Much of what organizations do is guided by hardwired, overpracticed, and overlearned actions that have been successful in the past. An extreme example of behaviors frozen in time is recounted in a time and motion study conducted on British artillery crews during the Second World War as reported in Alan Kantrow's book, *The Constraints of Corporate Tradition*.[24] In it, he recounts a story told by technology historian Elting Morison from the early days of the Second World War. Investigators were hopeful they could find ways to increase the speed of operation of cannon fire. Upon observing the five-person crews, the researchers noticed that as the gun was loaded, two men stood at attention for three seconds before returning to action in preparation for the next round. There was no immediate explanation for the seemingly useless three-second pause; the crews maintained that was what they were taught in gunnery school. The researchers showed pictures of these practices to a long-retired artillery officer who, after some puzzlement, realized that the two men were holding the horses: they were positioned precisely where the men once stood in the First World War to keep the horses still during canon fire.

When circumstances change, the organization must be able to modify its behavior and follow through on revised plans to achieve its goals. For that, the organization requires a well-developed frontal cortex that will save it from habitually flying into the proverbial flame. Specifically, organizations need well-developed and disciplined decision-making mechanisms to prudently guide them forward at critical choice points.

HEALTH

The idea of wanting an organization that is "healthy" may seem odd because most organizations would be quite happy to grow profitably—verbum sap. Although the idea of market potency and financial success are increasingly in vogue as interventionists' goals under the caption of "organizational effectiveness," business outcomes alone miss the more encompassing, holistic perspective of OD. For OD practitioners, goals solely directed at conventional business outcomes are incomplete portrayals of an organization's true state of well-being. For this reason, "health," which denotes a broader conception of physical and mental welfare and a future orientation to remain fit, is preferred over the ersatz synonym, "effectiveness." The American Psychological Association embraces this broader conception of health in describing the healthy workplace as one that supports health-promotion practices such as employee assistance programs, flexible benefits, and amenable working conditions and that underwrites programs dedicated to the development, safety, and emotional welfare of employees.[25]

The idea of a healthy organization seems to have its genesis in the work of M. B. Miles who conceived of health as durability: the ability of organizations to survive despite obstacles and setbacks.[26] The concept of a healthy company became more expansive when a MacArthur Foundation–sponsored report itemized the dimensions of healthy companies in the late 1980s. These included such dimensions as open communications, employee involvement, learning and renewal, and economic security.[27] Since then, many other taxonomies have been developed, but all embody a common theme: A healthy organization is one that is able to achieve positive economic growth while preserving the human-ness of the actors, the social purposes of the organization, and the ability of the institution to continuously renew itself. These many components, in addition to those financial results that are found on income statements and balance sheets, need to be attended to for a consultant's work to fall within the bailiwick of OD.

That history notwithstanding, OD always has had a therapeutic, introspective dimension to it and never was singularly focused on organizations' financial objectives. During the Second World War, Wilfred Bion and other members of the psychodynamically oriented Tavistock Institute in the United Kingdom created what might be loosely construed as the forerunners to Training Groups (T-groups) that formed in the United States under the auspices of the National Training Labs in Bethel, Maine.[28] Both transatlantic institutions held that the healthy development of a group required an ability to look at itself, reflect on its effectiveness as an operating unit, and openly address difficult subjects. As with individuals, self-awareness and self-analysis were viewed as indispensable ingredients for organizational vitality and change.

Bion's early work concerned group therapy with battle-fatigued soldiers. Bion thought that the progress of groups could be facilitated or forestalled by the degree to which members managed the underlying emotional dynamics of the groups. Until a group can recognize and remedy unhealthy tendencies and unresolved affective undercurrents among members, the group will never be able to move forward and engage in productive work.[29]

Those of us who have spent considerable time on teams probably have noticed that many teams operate as two groups in one. One group operates on the surface, diligently working on the task at hand. Another shadow group works beneath the surface at an emotional level, silently aggressing against or fleeing from the work to be done.

Because members of a team can discuss a task rationally does not mean their attitudes are consistent with the interests of the group and that their behaviors will conform to their voiced commitments once the meeting is adjourned. The consultant's job is to get the group to examine its internal machinations more closely and to identify how each of the members may be contributing to or interfering with the advancement of the team's objectives. Thus, sound interpersonal relations and group dynamics are integral parts of healthy organizations: key developmental attributes that are best achieved in culturally rich environments of openness, trust, cooperation, common purpose, and personal security.

T-groups operated with the same core assumption as the Tavistock groups. By learning about the behavior patterns within the group, and especially about one's own behavior, the group would be able to diagnose its problems and change itself for the better. Healthy organizations with the competence to improve, then, were predicated on perceptive, self-aware group members and internal relationships of quality and depth.

T-groups (sometimes referenced as sensitivity groups) are leaderless, nondirective groups that instruct by providing little structure in a controlled (laboratory) setting, allowing members of the group to explore their own and one another's behavior in an unconstrained social situation. Given that powerful social norms and task demands are absent, group members' personalities—blemishes included—are prominently put on display, exposing the emotional underbelly of groups that frequently is hidden from view. (Encounter groups, spearheaded by Romanian psychologist Jacob Moreno, also were developing at the same time and held the same underlying principles as T-groups—that is, that freedom from social constraint allows for more honest and forthright exchanges among group members to take place and affords individuals a rare unadulterated glimpse at their own behavior.[30])

Many groups believe they can think their way through any problem and resolve any issue not realizing the extent to which their solutions are influenced by unseen personal agendas, underlying emotions, and the divergent unexpressed preferences of members. No group regardless of size will be able to continually make good decisions or take prudent actions if the silent killers of group processes are left undisturbed to do their destructive business.

It is unfortunate that T-groups, once frequently used, fell into disrepute as an indicted management fad. This may have been due to the entry of untrained charlatans into the T-group frenzy as well as a propensity of legitimate practitioners to overgeneralize results too far beyond the work of the group to broader more complex issues to which teambuilding alone did not completely apply. Although T-groups may not have directly produced the systemic results organizations had hoped to see, they offered valuable insights to those who made the pilgrimage to the National Training Laboratory in Maine and returned to their workplaces with greater self-awareness.

BEHAVIORAL PRINCIPLES

The formative years of OD occurred in the troubling times surrounding the Second World War, and OD partly was conceived by those such as Kurt Lewin, who had front row seats. Working as a professor at the University of Berlin, Lewin was particularly concerned about anti-Semitism and the plight of the disadvantaged—topics that were not high-priority issues within the burgeoning Nazi Party. With the proliferation of discrimination, intergroup conflicts, and the naming of Hitler as chancellor, Lewin emigrated to the United States in 1934 where he completed a highly influential academic career.

Lewin was one of the forerunners of a general methodology for change called action research that, in its original instantiation, might be thought of as a social movement.[31] The aims of the original practitioners were to solve social and organizational problems using scientific methods and principles from diverse fields. Much of OD's seminal work ambitiously concentrated on big societal concerns of social equality and justice.[32] For example, in his relatively short research career, Lewin sought ways to end interpersonal and intergroup strife involving racism, discrimination, prejudice, destructive conflicts, war, and other issues of elevated importance. The field of OD aimed high.[33]

With action research, OD practitioners are not the white-labcoat types who are playing the role of inquisitive, impartial bystanders sterilely doing research on people at arm's length. Rather, they are interested participants who are doing research with and for people and who have normative leanings toward social welfare and the common good. OD consultants have a point of view. Although job creation, increases in national productivity, and improvements in our living standards are laudable business goals, they would not be worthwhile pursuits if they could be attained only at the expense of employees, the communities that host organizations, or the broader ecosystems of which organizations are a part. For example, a change effort designed to increase corporate sales ("turbocharge") of the highly addictive painkiller, oxycontin, without aggressive precautions against the potential abuse of the substance would be anathema to an OD practitioner.

Although the methods used in the course of change may vary, action research adheres to a uniform pattern. The research follows an evidence-based cyclical pattern of problem diagnosis and identification, planning, action, and evaluation and interpretation. The warehouse of knowledge generated by the research is used to refine plans and actions with organizational phenomena more precisely understood over time and more effectively addressed. Action research is a blend of the pragmatic with the theoretical in which action is informed by theory, and theory is advanced by action.

Several aspects related to action research highlight additional features of OD. Four features stand out:

- **Based on evidence:** From the very beginning, OD theorists have insisted upon solutions to social and organizational problems that were grounded in data. Theorists were duly aware that complete understanding of collective behavior was untenable but that research within the social sciences offered the best way forward and, with accumulated experience and findings, would progressively move us closer to the truth and a more congenial and tolerant society. Among some, OD has developed a reputation of being "soft"; this perception likely is due to exposure to practitioners who used the OD moniker without adhering to the discipline's behavioral and evidence-based decrees.
- **Reflects meaningful change:** OD is not terribly concerned about helping people inside organizations check off boxes on their annual to-do lists. Fulfillment of certain goals may be nontrivial to those who are accountable; however, simply completing goals that do not have evident beneficial impact on the lives of people, the performance of an organizational unit, and, in some instances, the community at large does not constitute an OD intervention. Routine objectives insulated from the wider

implications of the work are tasks to be accomplished, not to be associated with change efforts that are designed to improve a system's functioning and make a difference in people's lives. OD extends the customary ideas of organizational success to employee development and healthy group dynamics, sound decision making, and socially responsible action.

- **Concerns culture change:** OD invariably is about influencing collective action. The behaviors that organizations want to change are social in nature, and that type of change requires modifying the psyche or culture of the group. One aim of OD, therefore, is to affect the organization's norms, beliefs, and values that, together, make up the organization's culture. The change process involves a reset of behaviors by reinforcing new assumptions about what the organization stands for, how employees are to conduct themselves, and what the organization is committed to achieving. It is not unlike someone who moves to a foreign country and must unlearn some habits and internalize new values that are more congruent with the expectations of the citizenry—cultural expectations that the country deems essential to its survival and success. Usually, one immigrant can learn to fit in to a new society rather easily, but the difficulty of cultural change mounts when the numbers of people involved increase. In organizations, large numbers of people who are accustomed to doing things one way suddenly are asked to behave differently. Box 1.4 describes just how difficult culture change can be using the natural laboratory and thirty-year history of East and West Germany as an example.[34]
- **Is a democratic process:** Democratic processes were a preoccupation of Lewin's. While democracy was culturally salient in the decade of Lewin's most important work as a counterbalance to fascism, the study that put democratic practices into the workplace was conducted by Lewin and associates (Lippitt and White) with fifth and sixth graders at the Child Welfare Research Station at the University of Iowa (then, the State University of Iowa). Lewin and colleagues examined the effects of leadership styles on aggression and productivity in children who worked under the auspices of different kinds of leaders. They found that democratic management styles in which the children could make their own decisions yielded groups that were more cohesive, productive, and

friendly than groups whose leaders used autocratic methods of management.[35] These findings were effectively applied by Lewin and his students at the Harwood Manufacturing Corporation, a manufacturer of pajamas. When Lewin and others began their work, the company was experiencing high rates of absenteeism and turnover and was losing money. Their choice interventions of employee involvement and group problem-solving seem humdrum today, but they were revolutionary (and successful) then, beating the popular arrival of quality circles by thirty years. Even today the idea of employee participation remains a modestly foreign concept because our thoughts remain dominated by programmed thinking; organizations are engineered or re-engineered for maximum efficiency and the big goals issued from the top prescribe the internal motions of the organization as if a fine timepiece. Lofty, top-down edicts, however, rarely result in substantive change as the "parts" all await their instructions.

BOX 1.4

Cultural Paralysis in Germany: Politically Unified and Culturally Worlds Apart

The effusive celebrations marking the fall of the Berlin Wall on November 9, 1989, were premature and misleading manifestations of what really was to come. The promise of "flourishing landscapes" of German unification has not transpired after more than twenty-five years of trying. The cultural, social, and economic differences between two peoples are no longer abetted by a wall but by a "mauer im kopf," or a "wall in the head." The transformation of a culture based on egalitarian principles, hardily enforced through rabid government oversight, into one based on libertarian principles and free expression has been elusive. In many ways, the unification process provides a vivid case study on how not to conduct a merger. One party, the West, controlled the process, and many East Germans who had dutifully waited in line for advancement felt cheated when high ranking positions in government and business were taken by the West. But still, it has been more than twenty-five years and the cultural cleavages between the former GDR (East) and FRG (West) by most accounts remain glowingly large. There is Ossis and Wessis.

The successful record of democratic values in the workplace led later researchers to explore other, more-nuanced leadership styles that had thematic consistency with the energy-enhancing properties of participatory management and employee involvement. Douglas McGregor, for example, probed the cosmology of managers and the effects of managers' worldviews on employees' attitudes and work habits and found that managers who operate under the assumptions of theory Y versus theory X achieved superior results. Managers who oversee employees under the assumptions of theory Y optimistically see employees as seekers of challenge, responsibility, and accomplishment. Accordingly, these managers invite these creative, industrious types to actively participate in the decision-making process of the group and give them the room they need to work to their potential. In contrast, managers who hold a pessimistic theory X view of human nature regard people as inherently lazy, incapable of making genuine contributions, duplicitous and untrustworthy, and avoidant of real work.[36] Consequently, managers believe that these employees need to be carefully watched and coerced into working. It should not be surprising that managers who expect little from people, get little in return.

Robert Blake and Jane Mouton also demonstrated that employee participation was an active ingredient to organizational success. Their well-known managerial grid is formed by the intersection of two core management dimensions: one is concern for production and the other is concern for people.[37] Like other theorists working within the OD space, Blake and Mouton do not regard concern for people and concern for production to be an either-or choice. In fact, there is no contradiction at all in managers who are high on both (called 9,9 leaders to reflect the high-end anchors of the rating scales used) and have been found to achieve superior results by creating trusting, collaborative environments.

A recurring theme in both the leadership and family relations literatures is that a leader's (parent's) behavior can be summarized along two dimensions. Parallel to Blake and Mouton's grid, the leadership literature often refers to these dimensions as "initiation of structure" and "consideration."[38] The family relations literature refers to the dimensions as "demandingness" and "responsiveness."[39] The respective interpretations are the same. Initiating structure means to have firm expectations and standards, to insist on mature ethical conduct, and to press for progressive achievements and independence. The consideration dimension is associated with warmth, noncoerciveness, bidirectional communication, and flexibility and responsiveness to the needs and interests of others; it is the emotional part of leadership that steps in to give support, guidance, and encouragement when the situation recommends it, while preserving an affective climate that is respectful of others' intelligence and abilities. Thus, a management style that judiciously combines concern with limits elicits the greatest productivity.[40] These managers collaboratively set goals, support communication flows up and down the hierarchy and across the organization, encourage teamwork, and promote employee empowerment and personal responsibility.

THE STRUCTURE OF THE BOOK

We will be introducing many more principles and methods associated with OD throughout this book. Our approach, however, is atypical. Whereas most explanations of OD typically concentrate on the subject matter by type of intervention, we organize the discipline by what organizations need to do well to succeed. Thus, rather than discretely examine each of the major buckets of traditional OD interventions, we discuss their use in the broader context of what organizations need to do well to be profitably healthy organizations.

This approach fills a notable gap in the OD literature that has deterred the broader acceptance and greater utility of the practice. Specifically, one missing element of OD is that it never expressly states where practitioners should focus their efforts. Thus, our book is organized according to ten principles for healthy organizational growth based on the strongest, fundamental, evidence-based concepts from social and organizational psychology that are the most relevant and applicable to organization change and development. The order of the principles, too, is deliberate. Specifically, the principles move from the general to the particular, covering the spectrum of levels of organizational life—organizational and interorganizational, group and intergroup, interpersonal and individual. Furthermore, we view the ordered set of principles as building blocks based on the likely scale of effects on the organization's success or demise. The first collection of principles include the establishment of a cooperative enterprise that can anticipate the future and change as necessary: a company will not achieve greatness in their absence (chapters 2–4). The next few principles that include flexibility, diversity, and the work environment are conceived as preventatives: their presence buffers organizations from catastrophic failures or systematic breakdowns (chapters 5–7). And, finally, the last cluster of principles are associated with increasing the capabilities of the organization mainly achieved through individual actors and their interactions (chapters 8–11).

CHAPTER TWO

Organize for Change

HERACLITUS'S APHORISM THAT the only constant is change rings true for organizations. With the increasingly quick introductions of new technologies and radical changes in markets, the shelf lives of both CEOs and their companies have become increasingly short. Although living forever is too much to ask of any institution, dying before one's time is senselessly tragic. Given the ubiquitous need for organizational change in today's turbulent business climate, mastery of the change management process is a significant contributor to competitive advantage and a necessity for survival.

Many companies reach a point in their histories in which their growth stalls.[1] Some are able to reinvigorate themselves and some of these companies succumb. The specific reasons for a company's premature death may be as plentiful as the number of companies afflicted. It seems, however, that some companies carry within their DNA the requisite ability to revitalize themselves and to produce and implement solutions in response to environmental conditions.[2] This chapter is about that transformation: about how some companies are able to regroup and profitably carry on in the face of market challenges, and how other companies flail and flame out.

A great number of organizational theories metaphorically conceive of companies as organic entities that grow and, over time, lose function and fitness, and then die.[3] The life spans of organizations can vary by company; however, many follow a similar arc of birth, growth, maturity, and death.[4] The number and sequences of passages theoretically proposed may differ slightly, but like all living systems, organizations grow and they die. Hambrick and associates, for example, traced the death spiral of bankrupt companies from initial impairment to death struggle to end—a process enacted over ten years interspersed with false hopes of recovery.[5]

The precise onset and course of organizational decline is difficult to decipher. Decline that appears to be abrupt may have been festering unnoticed for years. Take Mayan culture as an example. The Mayans experienced many periodic droughts to their agrarian lifestyle. The 175-year drought from 760 to 930, however, gradually thinned the population through emigration until those remaining met a precipitous end. As the drought persisted, "the food and water ran out—and they died."[6] Death came swiftly, but the Mayan demise was many decades in the making.

Given that the specific trajectories of organizational aging can vary, we can say that all change is precipitated by alterations in the external environment and that the effects can vary in nature, size, and rate.[7] Change can involve different goals and purposes, scopes, intensities, durations, and issues, with the latter ranging from singular, isolated concerns to multifaceted matters. It may suffice, and be more accurate, to think of change as having ebbs and flows, but as always in motion. Indeed, even the seemingly discontinuous pattern of change described as punctuated equilibrium may look that way only on the surface. Punctuated equilibrium is defined as a process with periods of quiescence interrupted by periods of extreme volatility. The staircase depiction of this effect (sometimes called the Devil's Staircase), however, can be replicated by continuous change with the frequencies of disruptions differentially aggregated in time: low-frequency events within a given period form the plateaus and high-frequency events form the inclines.[8] Something always is happening.

Although organizational devolution may be fast or slow, once the environment is no longer able to sustain all competitors and companies' states have weakened, the end usually comes quickly for the incurably feeble. As death unknowingly approaches, decline catastrophically accelerates and survival becomes untenable. This abrupt end was famously described by Malcolm Gladwell as the tipping point in which change is nonlinear—moving slowly and gradually until reaching a juncture at which the slightest nudge will throw an organization off balance.[9] As companies' hardships mount and organizations lose their ability to mobilize an effective response, even tiny disturbances (butterfly effect) can push them over the edge.

In general, people speak nonchalantly about change in organizations. But think about the scale of many organizational changes, and you will get a sense of some of the obstacles faced by managers. First, the transaction costs associated with change can be substantial. Systemic changes intended to strategically reorient a company can be very costly in terms of time and expense. Second, one person will not know everything that has to be done. All possible problems and solutions cannot be neatly lined up and methodically addressed. Still, that one person, through others, must get corporate behemoths to move in a new direction. Third, the issue of timing calls for the delicacy of Goldilocks—not too fast, not too slow, but just right.[10] Indeed, change agents have to find a rhythm that works and have to sequence and pace change in a way that is palatable to others.

The best solution for institutional survival is to forestall decline before it becomes too severe to rectify, and little problems become big, intransigent ones. That is not easy, as a recent study of twenty-two thousand companies showed that only a handful of the hardiest were able to withstand the gravitational pull of mediocrity over time.[11] Once decline commences, it is difficult to stop. Even if managers fully knew their true strategic direction, a crippled organization has several obstacles with which to contend as they struggle to recover. First, managers are forced to improve performance with dwindling resources, increased internal stakeholder strife, and, frequently, less managerial discretion because of the overriding wishes of debt holders, equity investors, and such.[12] Second, companies with dire liquidity needs often must take culturally damaging actions, such as layoffs. Unless handled prudently, these actions may hasten the subsequent exits of the best performers and impair productivity among the surviving workforce. P. C. Nutt has referred to this degenerative process as *de-developing* in which, through shrinkage, companies progressively lose the capabilities that could have made a rebound possible.[13]

During periods of decline, poorly managed workforces often see their best performers flee, leaving the least qualified to dictate the future. Arthur Bedeain and Achilles Armenakis liken this process to a dysfunctional cesspool in which the dreck rises to the top and fills with sludge below.[14] Joel Brockner and colleagues at Columbia University also showed in a series of studies that unfairly treated victims of layoffs impaired the productivity of *survivors*. These studies showed that the better departing employees were treated, the more productivity levels within the organization were sustained.[15] Treating others fairly satisfies survivors' sense of justice and reduces lingering feelings of survivor guilt. Therefore, if "cutback management" or "rightsizing" is pursued haphazardly and without empathy, the company in all likelihood will make themselves worse off and lower their chances of a comeback.

When we contemplate organizations' aptitude for change, we think of the change process as under the decisional control of the actors. That is, companies do not randomly walk into or out of messes. Although change is prompted by external factors, such as new competitive products that largely are outside the control of companies, responses are guided by sociopolitical factors that influence decisions made and actions taken.[16] People make choices that make a difference on the future performance of the firm, and these decisions determine whether or not a company can sustain its desirable activities and meet its goals.

We also think of change as developmental. After all, this is a book on organization *development*. Change and development are not the same things. For example, when we say we want our children to develop, we are hoping they will do more than simply change.[17] Therefore, we like to think that organizations undergoing material changes are making themselves stronger and more resistant to future shocks by the choices they make. In the parlance of Nassim Taleb, the institution becomes increasingly antifragile by recurrently fending off challenges and successfully handling critical environmental threats.[18] Therefore, we think of meaningful change as lasting rather than as partial or temporary patches to cosmetically brighten balance sheets and income statements. Through development, the company becomes a wiser, more durable organization. (Although we use the word "change," whenever used in the context of organizational improvement, we are assuming change that is volitional and developmental.)

An intelligent organization is one that is adaptive. To appropriate a definition from the psychological literature on intelligence, adaptation is the ability to remain successful in one's environment.[19] Adaptation refers to an organization's ability to gather, filter, and organize information; to store, study, and learn from it; and to disseminate and use the information in the decision-making process.[20] In essence, intelligent companies are able to coalesce the brain power of the entire organization and keep themselves moving and changing to fend off decay that afflicts all systems.[21] Intelligence involves an integrative capacity that we often associate with expertise: awareness of the key issues and knowledge of the facts as well as the ability to renew and update information, to understand the relevance of incoming information and its potential application, and to ask penetrating questions to elucidate complex problems. Conversely, functionally stupid companies make poor decisions.[22] These companies are noteworthy for their lack of reflexivity, justification, and substantive reasoning, which, respectively, involves an unwillingness or inability to question claims and practices, excessive laxity in requiring evidence and reasons for decisions, and a myopic and parochial view of business issues and problems.

The various ways companies use the information at their disposal are diagnostic of their intelligence. First, companies can change themselves to accommodate what is occurring in their environments. This is the customary way people think about change: as organizations that must modify their product and service offerings to meet emerging needs. Second, organizations can direct the markets to comply with their offerings. For example, Henry Ford had cars, but he needed roads. Therefore, he lobbied for the expansion of highways. Advertising also is a strategy whose purpose is to alter consumer behavior and to direct consumers to the products the company wants them to purchase or use. Third, companies that feel they can no longer compete in a particular environment may decide to leave the field. This was the strategy General Electric took during the Jack Welch years. If a line of business could not be first or second in their respective markets, they were divested. In other words, if a business could not succeed, as defined, the adaptative decision was to exit that business. Finally, companies can adaptively do nothing and take a wait-and-see approach. Rather than rushing headlong into a potential technological arena, for example, a company may choose to wait out the technology's evolution before taking more active steps. For example, before there was Facebook, there was Geocities, SixDegrees, Blogger, Friendster, and MySpace.

By most accounts, organizations are not adept at change. Many researchers have reported the rampant failures of change efforts, reporting failure rates as high as 70 percent.[23] This frequently cited figure may be overstated. First, the percentage likely pertains only to changes that are planned and ignores the host of unplanned changes that occur in organizations. Second, the figure does not account for the myriad types of changes, and it is doubtful they all would have the same success and failure rates. Third, some change efforts truly are stymied by influences outside the company's control. For example, Western Union gamely tried to convert from a telegraph company to a data information hub, but their efforts were impeded by worn regulatory rules and by companies that prodded regulators to keep the rules in place to keep Western Union out. By the time regulatory constraints were loosened, the competition already had a firm foothold on the market.[24] Despite these caveats, however, most practitioners would agree that the failure rate of change efforts is woefully high and, managed poorly, has negative financial consequences.[25]

When it comes to change, employees often are portrayed as the villains for poor outcomes.[26] A company's inability to change often is attributed to the unreadiness or resistance of employees under the presumption that change is hostile to them. Contrary to people's survival instincts and pliancy in other areas of their lives, change agents frequently self-servingly attribute lackluster results to those "others" who rejected the seemingly sensible rationales for the changes.[27] People certainly vary in their appetite for change. Look around at friends and associates, and you will see those who always seem to seek out something new and different as well as those who enjoy the status quo. Nonetheless, although personality traits may play a role in change outcomes, we need to look for more uniform reasons as to why change initiatives succeed or fail.

For one, people have to believe in the necessity and appropriateness of change, and that requires leaders who can build a consensus of meaning and action.[28] Leaders must translate what is happening into reasons and direction. As always, leaders are responsible for building the case for change, for creating a positive mindset for change, and for convincing others of the value and legitimacy of the change efforts.[29] Change readiness, then, may be conceived as a set of preconditions that includes attitudes pertaining to whether the change is needed, the degree of agreement with the suggested changes, the extent to which the planned changes can be successfully made, and the degree of institutional support for the changes.[30] Taken together, readiness, or intentions to act, can be summarized as depending on three general factors: attitudes, norms, and perceived control.[31]

Attitudes are the beliefs that people hold and the positive or negative consequences of those beliefs; thus, attitudes are emotionally valanced beliefs. For example, an attitude about the desirability of change will hinge on both the perceived factual necessity of the change as well as well as on how individuals view the effects of those changes on themselves and on those within their affinity group. Change processes, such as appreciative inquiry, may ease attitudinal acceptance for change by directing the institution's attention to what it does well and using that as the platform for transformation—versus recounting the many ways the company has screwed up. Thus, the "discovery" phase of change using appreciative inquiry partly involves identifying positive facets of the organization that may be beneficially employed during the change process. This starting attitudinal position is one that is more accepting of the organization's abilities and of its aptitude to change.[32] Indeed, of the many functions assigned to management, being the chief facilitator of generative dialog may be most central to identifying organizational needs, building a case, and producing ideas for change.[33]

Norms concern the standards of a group and the general expectations that members of a group have for one another.[34] Norms are consensual beliefs about group behavior regarding what to do and what not to do. Consequently, part of the change effort necessarily involves the shaping of norms or of a culture that is conducive to change. Studies have specified the requisite cultural conditions for change. These include maintaining a positive attitude toward the value of change, emphasizing an action orientation that espouses openness to change, fostering a belief in the organization's ability to change, and encouraging employee empowerment.[35]

Perceived control refers to the actions required for change and the ability of the group to execute them. This belief in the power of the group to perform well and effect change is called collective efficacy. People within groups hold beliefs about the group's capabilities to fulfill assigned tasks. Meta-analyses have found that collective, or team, efficacy consistently relates to performance: the greater the group's confidence in its abilities to be successful, the greater the performance.[36] Regardless of the perceived personal utility of change (benefits minus costs), therefore, change will not be pursued unless the goal state is expected to be attained. This anticipated success is the crux of the well-founded expectancy-value theory.[37] The potential value of an initiative piques interest and coaxes people to take a few steps forward. Enduring behavior, however, requires the reasonable probability that actors ultimately will be successful.

A second set of systemic explanations for the success or failure of change initiatives pertains to structural barriers. One barrier that companies may inadvertently erect concerns "innovation fatigue" or "burnout syndrome." Employees become too worn out to take aggressive actions when faced with too frequent and too intense change efforts.[38] They are physically and emotionally too depleted to undertake round after round of change. A truism in organization development is that the only good forms of change are those that do not reduce an organization's future capacity to change. Endless calls for change can subvert the long-term interests of the company. Indeed, conditions for burnout are ripe when change is constant and uncontrolled, for example, repeated reorganizations that are autocratically directed.[39]

A second structural impediment concerns the futility of change. This situation may occur when urgent requests are preempted by other disasters in-waiting. Essentially, every change initiative is aborted so that the efforts expended have no consequence. The company lacks what Deming has referred to as the "constancy of purpose".[40] Actions that could be effective are not executed because they are believed to be useless endeavors. Therefore, inaction is not about perceived inability, but rather about pointlessness. For example, we have encountered many instances in which employees do not take corporate course changes seriously because management is unable to stay centered and persist. Management announces many new starts but seldom finishes. Employees, being astute forecasters of behavioral payoffs, realize that repeated efforts in worthless pursuits are unwise and unfulfilling. Consequently, employees' best efforts are applied to acting, feigning zealous support to the executives' grand causes, while waiting for the ship to run aground or the clock to run out.

THE CHANGE PROCESS

What becomes clear with the aid of hindsight is that organizations with clear needs for some form of change frequently do not make the changes needed in a timely fashion. One of the foundational elements of organization development is an emphasis on context in understanding change and human behavior more generally. Indeed, one of the most celebrated articles in organization development was written in 1948 by Lester Coch and John French titled, "Overcoming Resistance to Change."[41] Their article partly was based on their experiences at Harwood Manufacturing under the oversight of Kurt Lewin and at the request of Alfred Marrow, a descendent of the company's founders. Lewin's basic thesis for change was grounded on field theory in physics and Gestalt psychology that maintained that behavior was regulated by surrounding contextual forces and that the route for change was (a) to discover these regulatory mechanisms, (b) to decrease the restraining power of these forces, and (c) to free up the opportunity for change. The mechanisms for change relied heavily on democratic principles and participatory management, a conjecture since found to affect the success of change efforts.[42] Thus, change was a matter of describing the complex web of regulatory factors that prohibits or enables behaviors and of finding ways to free people to take appropriate action.

Lewin's tripart process of unfreezing behavior, exhorting appropriate movement, and refreezing behavior to capture gains is typically the schema used for change within organization development circles, although Lewin viewed the process as more dynamic, complex, and nonlinear than commonly portrayed in textbooks.[43] Other theories of change offer similar steps. For example, evolutionary approaches to change entail variation, natural selection, and retention.[44] Human creativity and diversity produce the variety; iterated learning, tinkering, and trial and error reduce the choice set; and the selected option is reinforced by habits, routines, schema, and cognitive frames to establish new behavioral repertoires. Theories of this ilk emphasize an important point. It is the fittest that survive, not necessarily the best. Thus, companies often overburden themselves by an endless search for perfection when "just good enough" or "satisficing" will do. ("Satisficing" means accepting a solution that meets minimum standards or criteria; e.g., if you are looking for a piece of jewelry in a tourist town while on vacation, you can visit every store and then circle back and buy the best one you saw—if it is still there—or satisfice by purchasing the first piece you like that has the color, shape, and size of what you are looking for.) The theory of dynamic capabilities similarly views change as involving sensing, seizing, and reconfiguring, respectively, recognizing the need for change, mustering the requisite resources and taking action, and harnessing gains by introducing new operating procedures.[45] Many other formal change models exist, several of which are named in table 2.1.[46]

As it happens, the seemingly simple matter of noticing a need to change is not so simple. Many of us fail to notice events that require our attention and necessitate corrective or evasive action. Foremost, then, the inauguration of positive change encompasses a firm's sense-making abilities: a firm's ability to scan the environment, take in and interpret relevant information, and determine what actions might be required. This practice requires hypervigilance and sensitivity to potential competitive threats (recall Andy Grove's [former CEO of Intel] credo that only the paranoid survive as explained in his book with that credo's title). That said, companies frequently do not recognize the need to change when subsequent events clearly indicate they should have. This occurs when novel events are obscured by complex technologies or the company is ill-equipped to notice because it lacks

TABLE 2.1
Formal change methodologies

Method	Associated Name
Planning	Lippett
"What" and "How"	Connor
PAR (Participatory Action Research)	French; Schein; Tichy
Integrative Change Model	Beckhard & Harris; Bullock & Batten
Six Step Change Management	Beer
Change Wheel	Galpin
Lean thinking	Womack & Jones
ERA (Evaluation, Re-evaluation, Action)	Chen
Total quality management (TQM)	Juran; Deming
Six Sigma	Motorola
Process Reengineering	Davenport

Source: Adapted from Al-Haddad S, Kotnour T. Integrating the organizational change literature: A model for successful change. *Journal of Organizational Change Management* 2015; **28**(2): 234–62.

awareness or has a worldview that cannot make sense of impending threats.[47] Much of what we observe are social constructions based on our storehouse of knowledge and the way in which we have organized it. Therefore, people act upon and shape incoming information in ways that often certify the status quo. As Kuhn has argued, if your conception of the world is that it is flat, you will see things one way; if your conception is that it is round, you will see things in quite other ways. But you cannot see the implications of roundness until you suspend belief in flatness.[48]

The worldviews held by two one-time premier retailers may have obstructed them from seeing other market possibilities. Some ideas are simply incompatible with existing worldviews and it may be difficult to see the possibilities of an electronic marketplace when surrounded by brick and mortar. Both Borders, once the number-two bookseller in the United States, and Blockbuster, once the number-one video retailer, had opportunities to ride the wave of new technology but foreclosed on the alternatives. Netflix had approached Blockbuster about a partnership, which Blockbuster rejected.[49] Borders was spun off from Kmart in an initial public offering (IPO) in 1995 when Amazon was still in its infancy. At first, Borders sold books and music online through its own web, but found it was too expensive to keep up and too costly to the bottom line and ended up outsourcing their web services to Amazon from 2001 to 2008. During this period, Borders opened new stores and redesigned others. By the time they recognized the momentous changes occurring in consumer purchasing habits, it was far too late. It took Borders two years to rebuild their online presence; in the meantime, they lost eight years of learning about the new online marketplace. Borders declared bankruptcy in 2011.[50]

Therefore, the ability to notice is highly regulated by our perceptual and interpretative apparatuses that either point us in the right direction or lead us astray. The mechanisms can be psychological (e.g., too disturbing to think about), judgmental (e.g., not viewed as important), or conceptual (e.g., cannot fathom it). Thus, we can choose to ignore important signals that should alert us to danger; we can queue or delay certain interruptions in favor of others; we can filter information, selectively attending to less important aspects over more important ones; we can be dismissive of details and overgeneralize, thereby missing the core of a problem; or we can avoid information that contradicts our preconceptions by screening out inconsistent data. Indeed,

BOX 2.1
Confirmation Bias

You are presented with the following four cards:

A   B   2   3

There is a letter on one side of each card and a number on the other side. I make the following claim: If a card has a letter A on one side, then it has the number 2 on the other side. Which cards do you need to turn over to decide the truth or falsity of my claim? Most people say the "A" and the "2" or just the "A." In these cases, they are searching for confirming information, and not for information that would falsify the claim. This is the idea behind the confirmation bias: looking for information that only proves a thesis, or is consistent with expectations, ignoring information that would disprove. In this task, you would need to turn over the "3." This task also demonstrates a second logical fallacy of affirming the consequent. By turning over the "2," people infer that if an "A" is on the other side, they will have their truth. But that is wrong. If we said, "If the object is round, it is red," we could not conclude that anything red is round.

Sources: Wason PC. On the failure to eliminate hypotheses in a conceptual task. *Quarterly Journal of Experimental Psychology* 1960; **12**(3): 129–40; Johnson-Laird PN, Legrenzi P, Legrenzi MS. Reasoning and a sense of reality. *British Journal of Psychology* 1972; **63**(3): 395–400.

the latter bias involves a common prejudice of seeking out and seeing only evidence that supports our position and ignoring that which can disconfirm our beliefs (see box 2.1). More formally, the confirmation bias refers to people's inclination to seek out and interpret information that is consonant with preexisting beliefs or expectations.[51]

GETTING STUCK

Organizations can become operationally locked into certain trajectories, or path dependencies, that make change extremely difficult (see box 2.2 for an example).[52] Even though companies may be on the

---

BOX 2.2
The Case of Hoover Vacuum Cleaner

Companies become stuck in different ways. The case of Hoover vacuum cleaners illustrates a trap in which the company's institutionalized capabilities, along with myriad internal systems that anchored the design of a product geared toward dirt removal, prevented the company from changing when confronted with competitive pressures. All "innovations" during a period of ten years were "sustaining innovations" that simply added features to the company's current offering.

Hoover was formed in 1907 and like most durables at the time was sold door to door. With increased electrification of households and labor-saving scientific household management, the vacuum cleaner, washing machine, and refrigerator found an increasingly eager and prosperous consumer. Hoover adopted a robust selling culture, implementing many of the practices pioneered by National Cash Register (NCR): quotas, clubs, training, motivational conventions, publications, and plenty of material and symbolic rewards. From inception, it lured potential salespeople with a hard-driving masculine sales culture to partly counter its identity (when compared with car sales) as feminine.

Systemic periodic troubles aside, Hoover was a top seller and remained one of the four major vacuum companies into the 1930s. This is when Electrolux introduced the cannister vacuum cleaner which was lighter, more powerful, and more versatile than upright vacuums, of which Hoover was one. Despite the success of the Electrolux, Hoover clung to its "dirt agitation" system and high-priced selling expense, a benefit that was of lesser interest to consumers and an expense that cut into margins. They continued to make and market the upright vacuum and mollified declining sales by hiring more salespeople, thus augmenting their cost problem. Sales and profits continued to slide. The company whose name remains associated with vacuum cleaners continues to sell the appliance, but long ago lost its privileged place among the elite producers.

---

wrong road, they keep going. In general, path dependence occurs when choices made at critical junctures or formative moments affect subsequent decisions and actions that maintain current trajectories. A self-reinforcing, self-perpetuating pattern emerges. These processes replicate solutions that are no longer effective.[53] Lock-in can occur in different ways, and we next explore a few of those ways in the ensuing sections.

Herd Behavior

The essence of herd behavior is acting on limited information, primarily on the opinions expressed by others without due regard to personal beliefs. In the absence of complete information and uncertain solutions, people often adopt the perspectives of referent others versus investing in a search for answers on their own. A glance into the sky to see the v-shaped formation of geese flying overhead shows the herd instinct in the animal kingdom at work. The formation of the flock is created by each member following the behavior of its nearest neighbor. It is no secret that we humans, too, follow the pack, buying what others buy, doing what others do, and thinking what others think. Rather than following lead birds, however, we look to authorities and experts, trendsetters, and social influencers.[54] In systems, herd behavior is the prime explanation for bubbles and crashes in which people who are following the actions of others drive up stock prices until those bubble-highs no longer can be supported by the fiction that produced them. Indeed, with such extreme interdependencies among actors, little shocks can produce large shifts, or consequences, in systems. Think of the formation fliers where the tiniest miscalculation of the lead jet can have awful consequences for everyone as occurred with the Thunderbirds in 1982.

Many forms of conformity exist in the psychological and economic literatures and many explanations have been posited for its existence. Regardless, our proclivity to embrace the beliefs of others produces a virulent form of singlemindedness in organizations called groupthink.[55] The observation that people form a consensus of opinion that may diverge from the beliefs that individuals may personally hold stretches back at least a century to the ideas of "social somnambulism" and "mental unity."[56] All refer to the inclination of groups to form a unified, collective mind consistent with the prevailing norms of the group. Therefore, if the cultural norms underscore risk, the group's decisions will migrate in a risky direction, adopting a riskier position than many individual members would have adopted alone. The prototypical example of groupthink is the ill-fated Bay of Pigs invasion of

Cuba, an outcome attributed to the excessive hubris of groupthink. If, however, the norms underscore caution, group opinion will move in a conservative direction. In any case, the upshot of groupthink is to coalesce opinion without a complete vetting of alternatives. Instead, we rely on a heuristic akin to following the lead bird of a flock similar to the way in which purchase decisions are driven by five-star ratings on internet products.[57]

As coming-of-age movies convincingly show, people will go to great lengths to be included in groups that are important to them, and groups will exert tremendous pressure to ensure that their members adhere to group norms. Solomon Asch in the 1950s illustrated the power of group influence in a series of classic experiments.[58] In the most acclaimed experiment, the experimenter asked groups of six to eight people to compare the lengths of three lines to a target line of a given length. The task of the group was to say which of the three lines was closest in length to the target. In most instances, there was no question about the correct answer. All the people in the group were confederates of the experimenter except for one lone subject, who after hearing the answers of the confederates had to publicly state which answer he thought was correct. Each session involved eighteen matching trials with confederates giving the correct answers in only six trials. In the control condition, when answering alone, subjects said the incorrect answer less than 1 percent of the time— a small deviation from perfection that might be attributable to a mistaken report-out or other human error. When responding as part of a group, however, subjects gave an incorrect answer an average of 37 percent of the time. This experiment reveals the fine line between belonging and compliance. We often yield to the opinions of the group. We yield because we want to be liked, to be accepted, to fit in, to not be left out. The results of conformity experiments apply not only to physical stimuli, such as line lengths, but also moral questions. People will modify their opinions to follow group consensus on issues such as free speech, the use of torture, and other moral dilemmas.[59]

Conformity is most likely to occur when decisions are public, the group is desirable, the group consists of more than three people, and the group is unanimous in its opinion.[60] However, there are ways to guard against blind conformity. One way to protect against counterfeit consensus is to implement formal procedures designed to question decisions. In the 1500s, the papacy decided that the canonization process was getting out of hand when Guinefort achieved sainthood. Saint Guinefort was a dog who had saved a baby. In 1587, Sixtus V set up the office of Promoter of the Faith. The role of the office was to raise logical and analytical objections to proposed saints so that only the truly worthy would be granted sainthood. Because the duty of the office's occupant was to oppose sainthood, he was said to be taking the side of the devil or was the Devil's Advocate. This position proved to be very effective. Pope John Paul II eliminated the office in 1983 and more people were canonized during his tenure than in the previous five centuries combined. The formal adversarial system was instrumental in sustaining the strict definition of sainthood.[61] In a similar vein, executives we have spoken with at SAS reserve a portion of each meeting for dissenting points of view or, as placed on the agenda, "diverse opinion time" as a formal means to critically counterargue points of view.

A second way to combat conformity is to build an irreverent, transparent culture. The Motley Fool, the investment advisory company, is named after Shakespeare's professional jester, Touchstone, in *As You Like It*. Motley was a form of dress, typically a woolen fabric of mixed colors. That mode of dress lay outside the sumptuary laws of Elizabethan England, which restricted the wearing of certain luxury goods and essentially mandated that a person look the role he or she was assigned to in society. The licensed fool, however, was an individual of great wit who lived outside of society and who, because of that, could speak truthfully about society, even to royalty. We have thought that every CEO should have such a licensed fool by his or her side. Practically speaking, the founding brothers of The Motley Fool, Tom and David Gardner, dispensed with the fool and instead infused their corporate creation with Foolishness. The Motley Fool, which has no dress code other than "to not wear anything that would embarrass your parents," has internalized the honesty of its investment insights in its workforce by enshrining honesty as one of its core values: always tell the truth—especially to "royalty," which is an expectation for every Fool. In the absence of culture or an official jester, we have found that spouses are good foils to executive chutzpah.

Imprinting

If you have acquired baby ducks as pets that follow you everywhere, or have seen the old video footage of ducks marching behind ethologist Konrad Lorenz, you have a sense of what it means to imprint.[62] Founding traits and procedures established at the inception of the organization become hardwired. The idea behind imprinting is that during a brief impressionistic period, the original blueprint for an organization is laid by the founders based on personal beliefs and values with due awareness of industry practices. These characteristics are subsequently reinforced and persist far into the future, if not indefinitely.[63] For example, a detailed case study of the Paris Opera House describes how it has maintained its hybrid character (part public institution, part academic institution) and attendant procedures for hundreds of years.[64] This is fine if circumstances have not dramatically changed and what worked in the past, still works.

An unchanging state of affairs, however, is highly unusual. And, often, the need for change is most dire in the industry occupied by the Paris Opera House: services. The Opera House is partially protected from market economics through state ownership, however, as Baumol and Bowen have argued, many services such as education, healthcare, performing arts, repair services, and restaurants, to name a few, are not.[65] These services are labor intensive and involve handicraft (a personal touch). They are susceptible to decline because of what the authors refer to as the *cost disease*. In contrast to manufacturing where increases in costs are offset by increases in productivity through improved processes and technologies (so, even though workers are paid more year after year, for example, the unit costs per worker remains relatively flat), this tends to be untrue in services where after hundreds of years of playing Beethoven's String Quartet in C Minor the performance still takes nine minutes and four musicians. Symphony halls have to get really big, or the orchestra has to perform many more concerts to keep unit costs down. In essence, unless services find ways to increase productivity without compromising quality (e.g., unduly increasing faculty-student ratios; overreliance on inexpensive, adjunct faculty), the costs of operations and the prices people ultimately have to pay become too extreme to sustain. Indeed, without gracious donors or government sponsorship, the performing arts would collapse. We suspect that without handsome endowments many colleges will follow suit: unless they find a more efficient, consumer-acceptable method of delivering their product of education.

Structural Inertia

Structural inertia (or institutionalization) is like imprinting, varying mostly by the time when organizations ossify. They both share the same feature of having entrenched institutional arrangements that make it hard to reverse choices already made. These entrenched practices are especially self-reinforcing and durable when feedback systems are flawed. For example, companies may measure things that are not indicative of their faltering status opting, say, to look at profit margins buffeted by cost cutting versus declining market share.

As opposed to imprinting that occurs with the inception of business creation, inertia occurs whenever companies find strategic and operational recipes that work.[66] As companies grow, they seek greater efficiency in operations. These efficiencies entail the introduction of tighter standards of control and more explicit systems, policies, procedures, and everyday routines. These standards and associated processes, in turn, become more deeply ingrained with the company's burgeoning success. Unfortunately, these structures solidify as history provides cumulative proof regarding what works, and people become increasingly familiar with the methods and technologies used. A lineage of success also may make companies increasingly susceptible to gain frame effects. According to Kahneman and Tversky's prospect theory, people with accumulated wins become progressively risk averse, preferring to stay on a course that is producing predictable, incremental gains rather than chancing side adventures that risk losing what they have accumulated.[67] The harbingers of success become the preludes to failure.[68]

Escalation of Commitment

Escalation of commitment refers to maintaining a course of action when that course should be abandoned or redirected. Rather than climb out of the hole one is digging, people dig deeper.[69] Concerns about self-presentation often are implicated in this disastrous pattern. Rather than admit a mistake and confess to being on a losing course of action that would make a leader appear foolish, managers harden their commitment to their chosen decision.[70] To dispel the belief that one is the sort of person who makes bad decisions, the decision is rationalized as right and the self as uncanny. Although a mistake may have been made, the decision-maker persists at a course of action that piously magnifies the error.[71] These self-presentational effects may be intensified by the ownership, or responsibility, a leader has assumed for a particular action. This sense of ownership over and the degree of effort expended on a course of action may also heighten the perceived value of the action, thus making it appear to be more personally desirable. (The relationships between perceived value and sense of ownership and amount of effort are called the *endowment effect* and *the effort paradox*[72].)

Conversely, people may simply believe that everything will work out for the best. People who are confident in their abilities frequently have an abundance of it. In a word, people tend to be overconfident. In fact, it is a common bias that we humans generally seem to have. Many people have watched enough courtroom dramas to be familiar with one form of overconfidence illustrated by the notoriously flawed testimonies of eyewitnesses.[73] Eyewitnesses can be off by a long shot, mistaking the race of a suspect and the color and make of the getaway car. Nevertheless, they are supremely confident in their testimony, which they decisively deliver as fact. This form of overconfidence is an over-precision bias in which the accuracy of people's observations or judgments are off target. People also overestimate their performance expectations and abilities compared with a standard (overestimation bias) or to others (over-placement bias). Overall, people tend to think they are better than they really are, better than others when they are not, and surer of the truth than justified. Overconfidence in general is associated with exaggerated capabilities, greater imagined control over events, and underestimates of risk.[74] Thus, the majority of people believe they would survive a zombie apocalypse.[75] Business is a spectacular place to exercise overconfidence. We start businesses that we should not, roll out new products with tenuous markets, and engage in value-destroying mergers. Indeed, one study found that overconfident CEOs were more apt to merge their companies with other companies, falsely believing they could make serial mergers work. Overconfidence also has been implicated in miscalculations of research and development performance, misguided diversification strategies, overambitious international strategies, overreliance on growth through acquisition, and excessive debt financing.[76]

Despite the ominous drawbacks of overconfidence, humanity has not survived by rationality alone. In fact, we would not have Hershey's chocolate, Disneyland, or Ford cars had the founders given up after repeated failures and ceased investing in ambiguous futures. Plenty of evidence demonstrates that we are not rational *homo economicus* but irrational *hominem brutis*. Overconfidence is an asset that provides benefits for individuals and groups.[77] Thus, it may be a bias that has been naturally selected. In game play, overconfident players win at a disproportionate rate; overconfidence also may help underdogs win battles.[78] In a world of uncertainty (e.g., not knowing the exact capabilities of a competitor), overconfidence keeps people from walking away from contests or opportunities in which they might prevail and allows them to claim prizes they otherwise would not win. Confident bluffers also may keep competitors who might be superior players at bay. In one research study, participants were asked if they would be willing to compete against another participant on an intelligence test. The winner would get a cash payout and the loser would get nothing. Alternatively, participants could opt out and receive a nominal guaranteed payment. Before participants made their choice, they exchanged self-estimates of their percentile rank on intelligence. Decisions on whether to engage in the competition were primarily driven by a participant's relative ranking of intelligence compared with the other participant. The relatively high estimates of players discouraged others from competing. Whether from audacity or an actual rendering of perceived intellect, self-confident players give others pause.[79]

We are all better off because of people who confidently believe that they can achieve the improbable, or that they are right and everyone else is wrong—in short, people who never give up.

INNOVATION

We recently visited several companies that regularly appear on one of a number of "best companies" lists. Most of the companies we toured were still in their youth, less than fifteen years in existence, but had grown to be midsize companies (i.e., between $250 million and $1 billion in revenues). We asked if they worried about losing their mojo, and they were not. The reason for their aplomb lies in the culture they created. They avoided what Michael Beer has referred to as the fallacy of programmatic change.[80] Beer specifically is referring to change initiatives that must be authorized by management before they are undertaken. This slow, top-down change process that centralizes thinking is bound to fail.[81] Innovation is not driven by flipping on a creativity switch. If companies solely depend on announced changes, they are in trouble. Making change something a company does every now and then is tantamount to the atrophying of a muscle. Companies lose their creative strength without enough exercise.

Companies that are unafraid of the future embrace open innovation. Chesbrough proposed the idea of open innovation in which there is continuous circulation of new ideas internally and from the outside, inward. Not only does open innovation contribute to incidental organizational improvements but also may lead to transformations to an organization's business model: in the way the company defines its value proposition to customers, defines its formula for profit, its organizational structure and processes, and key resources.[82] Studies underscore the importance of open innovation to organizational performance. Research of 141 small to midsize manufacturers showed that firm performance was higher in firms that practiced open innovation.[83]

Some forms of change are large-scale and resource rich. These are big bets placed on the future, and companies need to make these. Nevertheless, the continuous need for innovation is essential and includes a host of constraint-based innovations that go by a number of names: frugal innovation, grassroots innovation, and bottom of the pyramid innovation, to name only a few (see box 2.3 for a more complete list).[84] The distinguishing characteristics are that innovations emerge from the cumulative efforts of many, with some inventions remaining small in scale, whereas others may snowball in size as they gather internal support, resources, and markets.[85]

These small-scale, ongoing interventions are akin to what French anthropologist Claude Levi-Strauss called bricolage.[86] He used the word to describe the resourcefulness of indigenous populations. Informed by keen knowledge and intimacy of the environment, he noticed people's ability to leverage everyday objects, combining and repurposing them for useful ends. Bricoleurs' societies specifically have several attributes. First, they have an inherent drive for action and problem solving. Thus, groups that are adept bricoleurs are embedded

---

BOX 2.3
Types of Constraint-based Change Methods

- BOP Innovation
- Bricolage
- Catalytic Innovation
- Disruptive Innovation
- Frugal Engineering
- Frugal Innovation
- Gandhian Innovation
- Grassroots Innovation
- Indigenous Innovation
- Jugaad
- Reverse Innovation
- Resource-constrained Innovation
- Trickle-up Innovation

Source: Adapted from Agarwal N, Grottke M, Mishra S, Brem A. A systematic literature review of constraint-based innovations: State of the art and future perspectives. *IEEE Transactions on Engineering Management* 2017; **64**(1): 3–15.

---

in cultures of doing. Second, they do not fret over what they do not have; rather, they see the possibilities in what they do have. Therefore, they refrain from using a lack of resources as an excuse for inaction. They are discerning scroungers who use their networks to secure the resources they need on the cheap. Third, they are inventive. They are able to assemble and apply materials in new and interesting ways. Think of a bunch of MacGyvers (a television bricoleur). Indeed, in business settings, this inventiveness applies not only to tangible products but also to financial instruments and services.[87]

The idea of bricolage is to fill observed needs by putting idle resources to productive use. Levi-Strauss juxtaposed the spontaneity and resourcefulness of bricolage from large-scale, planned, and resource-rich undertakings of engineers and the like. He was not dismissing this big form of innovation, only pointing out that a lot of creativity is built into the manipulation and application of everyday objects. We submit that these cultural undercurrents are critical for reinvention as long as proposed solutions are connected back to the organization for further development and implementation. That is, the innovations must be practical. Once adopted, innovations have to be "refrozen" by routines and operating procedures to become new parts of everyday practice.[88] Again, this appears to be a simple thing that follows the hard part: enact new procedures. Yet, many companies suffer from initiative decay by which the gains from change are lost because new practices are abandoned.[89] Indeed, retaining the hard-won advantages are so slippery that one organization gave this phenomenon a name: the improvement evaporation effect.[90] All of the things that go into making the change have to be sustained after the change. The persistence of the plans must be championed by leaders, new methods must be adopted and reinforced, people must be trained and retrained on new technologies and procedures, and so on. In essence, there is no mysterious red line of organizational change that, once crossed, suggests no further effort is required.

An extreme example of open innovation takes place at the Valve Corporation.[91] If you have ever used the digital platform, Steam, to download games, you have been introduced to Valve. The company was formed by two former Microsoft employees with a discrete emphasis on employee self-determination. The company gives employees the latitude to self-initiate projects, products, and platform, and to recruit their own teams for development. Encouraged to think about what they could do to produce the greatest value and what they can work on where they would derive the greatest sense of fulfillment, people ultimately vote with their feet, moving to projects that are the most satisfying and that are perceived to have the greatest potential. Steam was born in precisely this way when enterprising employees noticed that the video software they were working on could have broader applicability. Valve calls this process, "social proofs." In realty, it is an iterative decision process akin to quorum sensing in the animal world and the Delphi technique among us humans. Altogether, it is a fluid groundswell that relies on expertise to sense opportunities and to give shape and substance to airy nothing.

MORE CHANGE TO COME

In 1626, William Harvey described the circular flow of blood through our systems, noting how blood nourished our systems while replenishing itself. We renew and reuse what we have and, thankfully, only need to refill our nine pints on rare occasions. Soon after Harvey and colleagues' publications, economists began to write about the circular flows of money through households. Thus, in its rawest form, the circular economy is one in which money circulates but leaves the house one lives in unscathed.[92] Like Harvey's discovery of blood flows, the economy would be circular if in the process of creating value, the system was restorative and regenerative: that value would be created without destroying the land or using up the resources on which we depend.

Increasingly, companies will have to rethink their money-making logic and change in environmentally preservative ways. The reasons are becoming increasingly obvious, and we need not review them here except to say that we have our work cut out for us—and we do not have much time. Currently, more than 60 percent of the materials used in the production process are nonrenewable and the products that are produced have life spans of less than a year. These end up in oceans, waterways, scrap yards, and landfills.[93] Therefore, organizations are becoming more attentive to the four R's throughout the production cycle: reduce, reuse, recycle/remanufacture, and recover/replenish. Some changes may be relatively straightforward from a manufacturing perspective. For example, cell phones could be more readily reused if they were easier to dissemble and incentives were offered to consumers to turn in their phones. Other changes may be more difficult because of upstream or downstream dependencies.

Systems in the interconnected world are getting larger and larger and, with supply chains the way they are, organizations now are embedded in planet-wide endeavors. It is difficult to contemplate a company acting in isolation of global economic, social, and environmental concerns. Business clearly is aware of the size and urgency of the extant needs. Additionally, new reporting requirements, third-party ratings and performance indices, and a growing tranche of conscientious investors have inched businesses toward a more secure future. But the problems are immense, and much more will be needed as we convert our economy from a carbon- to non-carbon-based one.

For example, the needs for metals and minerals used in the production of new green technologies, such as solar cells, eclectic vehicle motors, wind turbines, fuel cells, batteries, wires and circuits, magnets, and much more, will grow exponentially. These elements nonexclusively include aluminum, cadmium, cobalt, copper, lithium, nickel, and silver, plus seventeen rare-earth elements, such as cerium and neodymium (these are not "rare" in the sense of "not enough," but rather in the sense that they are scattered, mixed in with other elements, and hard to secure). The mining, processing, and production processes involving these elements leave a large carbon footprint and quite a lot of the extraction and processing occurs at the expense of the environment (e.g., contaminated groundwater, tailings pollution, destruction of ecosystems) and workers (exposure to hazardous chemicals and toxic metals, exploitative labor practices). For example, the Democratic Republic of the Congo supplies most of the world's cobalt and now is one of the ten most polluted places on Earth. Much of the world's copper comes from Chile, where meadows have been transformed into salt flats and water sources in some areas have become depleted or contaminated.[94]

These problems are by no means confined to the mining industry. Energy, textiles, consumer products, and other industries have their unique issues regarding the sourcing, processing, and production of goods and services. The issues confronted belie easy solution, however, organization development can play a critical part by helping to shape organizational activities that incorporate all actors within an organization's sphere of operations into the calculous of profitability, and reward financial returns in the context of social and environmental progress: that is, evaluate companies on a triple bottom line. True practitioners of organization development cannot count year over year gains in corporate profitability a "win" without due appreciation of the quality of life of all those who contributed. If the purpose of business is to improve lives through the marketplace, then it would seem perverted to promote that objective while degrading the lives and lifestyles of those involved in the process.

Companies are moving in the right directions, and some like Patagonia have been there for some time. For example, Patagonia recently introduced a new beer, Long Root Ale. This is the first beer made with Kernza wheat. Kernza's deep roots need half the water of standard varieties of wheat, and because it is a perennial, it reduces erosion and captures more carbon from the atmosphere. Similarly, Patagonia recently introduced a new wetsuit made from the *Havea* plant. Patagonia extracts natural rubber from the plant using certified sustainable practices that are a cleaner alternative to the fabrication of the conventional neoprene wetsuit—a product made using petrochemicals and energy-intensive manufacturing processes.

A true circular economy will require social and technological invention and change. Foremost, we may need to think of change in the broadest terms: as a means to preserve and nourish life within a unifying fabric of economic, ecological, and human systems. Indeed, we endorse the criteria laid out by the International Systems Institute for effective, beneficent systems: operationally viable, economically sustainable, technologically feasible, culturally appropriate, psychologically nurturing, socially acceptable, environmentally friendly, and generationally sensitive.[95]

CHAPTER THREE

Anticipate the Future

THE CORPORATE BURIAL grounds are filled with tombstones that read, "We should have acted sooner." Once-great companies have found their final resting places in this expansive graveyard of slow-movers and has-beens. These companies failed because they were unable to adapt to changing conditions and yielded to capitalism's unapologetic survival of the fittest. The statistics are startling. As of 2017, only sixty of the companies on the Fortune 500 list in 1955 survive. A comprehensive study of twenty-five thousand publicly traded companies over a span from 1950 to 2009 shows that the half-life of companies is approximately ten years—meaning half of all companies disappear within ten years of their birth.[1]

The warning signs of faltering institutional health are clear. Empty desks, budget cuts, secretive closed-door meetings, accelerating departures of star employees and layoffs, reductions in perks, declining revenues, eroding margins, increasing receivables, and negative cash flows. Short-term manipulations of earnings (legal but uncharacteristic maneuvers that stretch accounting standards to the breaking point), ill-advised acquisitions, voided investments in product development and brand-building, or expedient cost-cutting may artificially prolong life, but these are perfunctory fixes that hide deeper financial scars. Like a decaying property, these superficialities keep the place livable in the short run but fail to make it stylish and more valuable over time. Indeed, a comprehensive survey of CEOs and CFOs revealed that over three-fourths of respondents admitted to foregoing some investments in long-term value creation to massage short-term earnings.[2]

Companies are not so much built to last as they are bound to fail— sooner or later. Even those companies that we think of as immune to adversity, such as Amazon, will someday face off against other carnivorous retailers. Even the world's oldest continuous organization, Japanese temple maker Kongo Kumi, recently came to an end after a 1,428-year run when their assets were sold to Takamatsu Corporation.[3] Apparently, the need for temples is not what it used to be, and the company was hobbled by a natural attrition in demand.

Not every organizational death is avoidable. In fact, it is unrealistic to think that a company will live forever without the need to undergo periodic regenerations in which a company becomes something different from what it once was. For example, Nokia moved from paper producer on the banks of the Nokianvirta River to technology company, and Abercrombie and Fitch morphed from a high-end gun store for the social elite to the apparel retailer we know today. These second lives, however, may not be what some companies want and, consequently, they might prefer death to an alien transformation.

Nevertheless, corporations do not have to linger indefinitely on the edge of life or die prematurely. Corporations can be constructed so that they are more durable and able to resist early decline. The preservation of life depends on having the navigational judgment and skill of leaders who prepare their companies for what lies ahead by peering into the future and charting a course accordingly. As it happens, however, when the future arrives, many companies cannot meet the demands that new markets and consumer tastes require. Why didn't these companies do more sooner? Why, despite what seems so clear in hindsight, did these organizations stick to a course that led to their eventual demise?

A significant portion of the answer lies in factors that divert corporate attention away from considerations about the future to a focus on short-term interests. According to McKinsey's Corporate Horizon Index, short-termism is growing more severe. The Index, based on more than five hundred mid- to large-cap companies, shows companies increasingly adopting short-term perspectives.[4] This trend is counterproductive. McKinsey finds that companies with long- versus short-term outlooks perform better on financial metrics such as revenues and earnings growth. One key to these companies' success is their greater expenditures on research and development (R&D). Companies with longer-term perspectives spend more than twice as much on R&D than companies with short-term perspectives, and they maintain, or even increase, these budgets during economic downturns. A recent study showed that this investment matters. Compared with companies that reduced R&D spending to produce favorable short-term earnings reports, companies that sustained their investments showed a 3–4 percent increase in patents and patent citations and a 36 percent increase in innovation efficiency (patents per R&D expenditure) over a three-year period.[5]

When we were kids, you could order a mirrored contraption of cardboard that allowed you to stealthily peak around corners to see what otherwise might go undetected. Who knows who or what was awaiting around the corner: a little sister perhaps? The clever tool allowed its users to act on what was in front of them as well as to anticipate things unseen with the naked eye. The spy lived in two worlds; the here and now and the one around the corner—a combination that ensured present and future safety and offered peace of mind.

Companies that are able to efficiently execute in the present while simultaneously preparing themselves for possible futures are called ambidextrous organizations.[6] The here-and-now executional or exploitative aspect of ambidexterity concerns the use of current knowledge and capabilities to refine and improve on operations, products, and services. The goals of exploitation are to increase efficiencies by wringing out excess costs and creating incremental value from existing organizational offerings. The future-oriented exploratory aspect of ambidexterity concerns the search, discovery, and development of new products and services. The goals are to satisfy emerging markets through select advancements in new technologies, designs, and processes. Like our yesteryear sleuthing, organizations must continue to extract profits from continuing operations while foreseeing and reacting to what lies around the corner. To be an adept [Wall] street performer, a company must be able to juggle more than one ball.

By way of analogy, consider the honeybee (*Apis mellifera*) colony. When honeybees locate a fruitful nectar-filled patch of flowers, they could maximize their current returns by directing their entire foraging workforce to that spot for harvesting. But they don't. Evolution has favored a different behavioral solution with one hundred million years of success speaking for itself. A portion of the foragers exploit the current, generous field of flowers while another group of foragers explore other fields, near and far, for the next new thing. Thus, when the current patch begins to run dry, other luscious patches will have been found and advertised as ready for the taking.

The evolutionary engine of the hive is designed to produce consistent, uninterrupted income flows of nectar. The bees could bring in more nectar at any given time, but then they would risk not knowing where to harvest next when prevailing revenues decline and, therefore, having to make do without a critical resource for a while. And, honeybees do not have much time to do without. Three to five days is the long term for them. Insufficient inflows for any longer than that would put the hive at risk.

In business, short term and long term vary by industry and culture. Time spans are culturally and situationally dependent. A technology company in the throes of persistent change and upheaval will have a different long-term outlook than a commodity manufacturer. Similarly, Eastern cultures tend to have longer-term outlooks than Western cultures and eschew publicizing short-term results in public forums that would give a false narrative of their true long-term intentions. Instead, Eastern-based companies prefer to describe their earnings as "sustainable results" to characterize their orientation toward consistency and durability.[7]

Consistent, continuous growth promoted by a combination of exploitation and exploration is a more desirable organizational outcome than widely oscillating income streams brought about by boom-and-bust cycles in which companies opportunistically succumb to the near term at the expense of the long term. We saw these unfortunate results when consulting to banks and mortgage companies immediately before the implosion of financial services during the 2008 recession in the United States. The housing bubble combined with low interest rates seduced banks into making interest-only subprime loans either for their own portfolios or to sell to hedge funds and others who, in turn, packaged and sold derivative bundles of problematic mortgages to investment companies and individuals. The abundance in this financial chain was predicated on the ability of homeowners to make their payments. When the housing bubble burst and interest rates rose, many mortgage holders were unable to repay their loans. Making risky loans was never a stated goal of most banks. Rather, banks yielded to the tempting diversion to make fast cash by offering interest-only loans secured against the seemingly ever-increasing rise in home prices. Consequently, bank failures ballooned during the recession and its aftermath with too many companies focused on the short term, an oft-cited root cause. If not for government largesse, the U.S. financial system may have collapsed. The mortgage crisis represents a high-profile case of excessive profit-taking but many other less obvious examples exist. For example, the U.S. auto industry's late foray into the manufacture of small fuel-efficient vehicles likely was due to a prolonged enchantment with the sale of higher margin trucks and sport utility vehicles. The industry delayed the inevitable and a favorable future market position in preference of short-term earnings.[8]

Companies experience economic troubles when the mix between exploitation and exploration is awry. Typically, the fault lies in too much corporate exploitation and not enough exploration, although in counter instances, companies may experience farsightedness or hyperopia (versus myopia), as well. The Apple Newton, for example, was a futuristic flop: a tool ahead of its time.[9] It was a personal digital assistant of the approximate dimensions of today's iPad mini. The Newton operated with a writing stylus; however, handwriting recognition programs of that period were imperfect. Additionally, processors at the time could not accommodate the graphical displays that were desired. We now know that the idea was good except for the fact that the technologies of the period could not adequately support Steve Jobs's vision. Changing World Technologies, a biofuel company, had a similar experience. The avant-garde company converted waste to short-chain hydrocarbons that it sold to electric utilities for power. Initial production costs were too high to compete commercially, however, and they declared bankruptcy after four years of operations. Today, many companies occupy that same space because the production methods have become increasingly accommodating to price sensitivities.[10]

Block chains, cryptocurrencies, big data, artificial intelligence, and machine learning can make one starry-eyed about the future. The surreal possibilities of a wandering imagination, however, can tip an organization's lean too far forward. Thus, companies can be swept up by the siren call of fortune, and neglect life-sustaining nourishment: an error as large as hedonistically living in the moment. Therefore, the unenviable task of business is to care for short- *and* long-term needs while also tending to countless other temporal cycles, such as inventory turns, product life spans, and infrastructure upgrades.

Unfortunately, a priori guidance is not available on the correct mix between exploitation and exploration, although institutional investors have made it abundantly clear that myopic companies that focus on short-term profits to the exclusion of other stakeholders and the longer-term interests of the company are not desirable investment targets. Overall, the appropriate blend is driven by leadership and is highly dependent on leaders' sensitivities to the environment and personal insights. The relative importance of near- or far-term elements may vacillate like a ship tacking into the wind based on several factors. For example, the importance of each element partially depends on the industry and speed of innovation within it, as well as the phase of the company within its life cycle. For example, start-ups naturally will be exploration-centric and mature companies will be exploitation-centric.

Practical considerations also play a part in what a company can, or should, devote to exploitation and exploration, and what it cannot or should not. The banks that dramatically increased the volumes of their mortgages before the crisis in 2008 were not able to underwrite loans with the same rigor as before because of volume increases and staffing shortages. In other words, the junk mortgages that required greater review, received less. If the objective was robust exploitation, banks should have correspondingly augmented their staffs and training. Similarly, we were working with a non-profit broadcaster that decided to order and purchase an impressive array of new programming—outsourced exploration, if you will. They did not have the marketing power or distribution channels, however, to fully take advantage of their purchase. That is, they could not exploit the opportunity to the extent that another, better endowed company might have. Regardless of whether companies wish to escalate exploitation or exploration, they have to analyze their current capabilities to ensure alignment with their strategies (see box 3.1).[11]

BOX 3.1
How Ability Informs the Strategy

Admiral Horatio Nelson's historic victory at Trafalgar against the combined French and Spanish fleets of Napoleon is largely attributed to his unorthodox strategy based on the select advantages of his outnumbered navy. With dedicated career officers and better trained crews, more navigable ships, and canons that could repeat fire every thirty seconds (versus the larger but less facile canons of the French and Spanish that took five minutes to reload), Nelson concluded that he could win the battle through close engagement and the boarding of enemy ships. Rather than engage Napoleon's fleet as navel protocol recommended—parallel lines of combatants firing cannons at one another broadside—he approached the French and Spanish ships in two columns, perpendicular to their position. (Navy manuals cautioned against this approach since oncoming ships are vulnerable to enemy canons with limited ability to return fire). Nelson split the enemy fleet into thirds before turning his ships to engage the lower two-thirds of Napoleon's fleet. Before the upper third of Napoleon's navy could turn and return to the battle, Nelson had already won.

Despite the evident need to plan ahead, a warning that children learn from reading *The Three Little Pigs*, we often do not. In fact, 67 percent of the three pigs did not. Preparing for the future is effortful and costly. The future also is uncertain. Because of the very good chance that a wolf never will come along and huff and puff, the temptation to make do with expedient solutions is high. Making difficult changes of uncertain necessity can seem painful and of dubious importance.

As companies become more complex and efficient, the rewards of repetition and the costs of change become more pronounced. The easy influx of current revenues drives out exploration. When the costs and benefits of new developments are assessed against the same standards used for existing products and services, commercialization of new ideas never measures up. Consequently, new initiatives do not receive the internal support needed for development. Exploration and new product developments will be perceived as intrusions when evaluated against efficiently generated results from well-rehearsed operations.

The rational conclusion will be to keep doing what the company is best at doing: leveraging its core competencies to the hilt.

Geoffrey Moore attributes the failings at AT&T, DEC, Kodak, Polaroid, Silicon Graphics, Sun, Wang, Xerox, and others to their reluctance to enthusiastically act on ideas for new products. Great ideas languished on the drawing board or as underfunded high-tech hobbies.[12] These companies subsequently were unable to compete with organizations with less history and greater entrepreneurial conviction. As Tushman and O'Reilly state in their seminal article on ambidexterity, these short- and long-term trade-offs often are forcefully debated inside companies.[13] The changing world does not entirely pass by these companies unnoticed. As the authors note, RCA was actively involved in transistor technologies that they understood could supplant their leading position as manufacturer of vacuum tubes and replace the innards of many of the electronic devices of the period. RCA's aspirations, however, were foiled by competitors such as Robert Noyce and Gordon Moore's newly formed Intel, which established research facilities that were more attuned to the commercial needs of their customers and that set up operations with a greater applied focus than, say, RCA.

Companies that are locked into the status quo and fail to deviate too far afield from precedent—whether products or procedures—repeat activities because they have been rewarded for engaging in them in the past. As a result, many companies continue what is profitable and refrain from actions that divert time, attention, and resources away from the sacred cows that generate the cash. Newer companies that are unhitched from historical baggage and significant changeover costs do not face these considerations. Thus, they can move more swiftly into lush emerging markets and displace reigning incumbents.

Executives must contend with plenty of pushes toward the short term. The short term is clear and salient. The short term is undertaken with greater certainty of outcomes. The short-term can be very rewarding. The short term provides executives with the continuing authority to lead by demonstrating their effectiveness in producing results. Furthermore corporate stasis is aided by distortions, or biases, in thinking such as the failure to see and understand the significance of new facts. For example, Smith Corona, the one-time typewriter manufacturer (see box 3.2), discounted the rise of personal computers, citing their expense and excess of features beyond their primary use as word processors.[14] A few insiders recognized the threat; however, leadership autocratically directed the company toward a word processing future in which the beloved typewriter would continue to play a central role. We can imagine that a person who has devoted their life to a company and cohesive suite of products would be reluctant to change from the familiar to the unfamiliar in which they had little expertise.

If the profitability associated with the tried and true enjoined the short term, then we might formally describe the plight of Smith Corona as victim to a competency trap. Competency traps are illustrated through the following simplified parable.[15,] Helen must choose between fulfilling an important task in one of two ways. The task is recurring, and she has routinely used Method 1 to attain results. Helen is a highly proficient whiz kid at the method and has always gotten good outcomes using it. She is not nearly as familiar with Method 2, but articles on its application and the accounts of others suggest it is by far the superior method. She tries it out a couple of times the best she can and after a couple of time-consuming tries that produce mediocre results, reverts to the method she is really good at: Method 1. Helen stays with this method even though a superior alternative exists. Had Helen been willing to absorb short-term costs while she learned how to use the new system, her longer-term outcomes would be vastly improved today. In the meantime, Helen can live comfortably with her choice because she never will realize the potential of Method 2, having abandoned it early during a trial period. She concluded that the efficiency of Method 1 was too great to give up and the results too alluring to sacrifice for the unrealized promise of Method 2. Note, however, that Helen's dilemma only exists because she is competent with Method 1. A person who is equally unfamiliar with both methods would select Method 2, where the learning curve is comparable to Method 1 but the outcomes are greater. Like the little boy in the *Emperor's New Clothes*, it is the inexperienced who only are able to see the truth.[16]

Sunk costs, too, may have contributed to Smith Corona's reluctance to change. Sunk costs are the tendency of people to continue an endeavor following an investment of time, energy, and money: past investments compel a future course.[17] Variously described as throwing good money after bad or as having too much invested to quit, economists note that rational decision makers should consider past

BOX 3.2
The Downfall of Smith Corona

The first "writing machine" was invented in 1868 by a journalist, Christopher Latham Scholes, and produced and distributed under the Remington name. The Smith Brothers were participants in the early history of the typewriter and in 1903 formed a company singly devoted to manufacturing typewriters. This company later (in 1926) merged with the Corona Typewriter Company to become LC Smith & Corona. The first typewriters were mechanical and required a heavy press of letters to fling individual keys onto a ribbon strip to imprint its unique letter onto a sheet of paper. Because adjacent keys often stuck together with fast typists, common combinations of letters were separated to prevent that from occurring (thus, the birth of the QWERTY keyboard versus a keyboard that, say, is alphabetized).

Smith Corona was an inventive "ink on paper" company throughout their storied history. They were first to offer a portable typewriter, electric-powered carriage return, removable ribbon cartridge, and electronic dictionary. The company's mainstays were light, user-friendly typewriters for personal (versus office) use and, as late as 1980, Smith Corona sold half of all typewriters in the world. Their typewriters were mainly distributed by the small office supply stores found on Main Streets of America and elsewhere. The company successfully morphed with consumer trends moving from mechanical, to electric (use of an electric motor to push keys forward), to electronic typewriters (incorporation of computer components for storage, formatting, editing and the like). To produce the electronic typewriter, Smith Corona established a research arm and hired a cadre of electrical engineers to complement the many mechanical engineers already employed at the company. The company spent about 12 percent of its revenues on building its research capabilities to compete in this new arena. Smith Corona subsequently extended the electronic typewriter to create a Personal Word Processor (PWP) that was essentially a computer with purely word processing capabilities. However, its software was proprietary and hard-coded. Some integration with computer components outside the Smith Corona family of products was introduced, but businesses outside of typing/word-processing gear never contributed significantly to the company's overall revenues.

Smith Corona powered into the 1970s and 1980s as a major conglomerate having purchased Glidden Company (paints and chemicals), Durkee Foods, Proctor Silex (appliances), and Allied Paper. These were later sold as Smith Corona's fortunes declined. For the most, Smith Corona waved off threats from the personal computer, considering it an expensive substitute to the product features that their typewriters and word processors provided. They believed that consumers would view the personal computer as an unnecessarily costly purchase. Smith Corona had an abbreviated co-branded partnership in 1991 with ACER, the Taiwanese computer startup, that wished to gain access to the American market through Smith Corona. However, neither party gained much from the relationship. Smith Corona's traditional distribution network was being gutted by big box office stores (there were nineteen super-stores in 1988 and eight hundred by 1993) and were of limited value to ACER. And, Smith Corona never participated in the manufacture of computers and, therefore, did not learn anything new that might have been helpful to them. Instead, Smith Corona reconfirmed their belief in the power of type and offered a suite of collateral materials built around their core offerings, such as dot matrix printers, laminators, and fax machines (much of this production was outsourced). With its strategy fixed, Smith Corona closed its R&D function in the early 1980s and integrated what remained of R&D with manufacturing.

Meanwhile, revenues began their precipitous decline in the early 1990s and went into freefall as Windows was introduced to make word processing and other applications on the computer easier, hardware costs declined, the availability of software blossomed, and internet connectivity became a staple in American households. Smith Corona filed for Chapter 11 bankruptcy in 1995. It emerged with renewed energy toward its historical core markets and was liquidated in 2000–2001.

expenditures as bygones and make new assessments based on current, alternative options.

Sunk costs occur when an initial allotment of resources entraps companies into losing courses of action. For example, a banker may make a commercial loan to a faltering, speculative real estate development, only to loan more money in an attempt to salvage the original investment. We surmise that Smith Corona's heavy investment in a word processing future by hiring leading electrical engineers and starting an R&D facility that was focused on integrating computer technologies into a bundle of personal word processing products hardened their position and made a switchover into personal computing less probable. In fact, it was not until 1991–1992 that Smith Corona attempted any foray into personal computing, but it was a lackluster assault and far too little, much too late.

In any case, sunk costs by which prior investment choices influence subsequent decisions may get a robust assist by the way we mentally bucket information. Nobel prize–winning economist Richard Thaler attributes the logical failings in sunk cost scenarios to faulty mental accounting.[18] Costs become losses when we are unable to get the return expected from our investment. For example, the purchase of a ticket to a sporting event (a cost) becomes a loss if you try, but for some unforeseen reason, fail to make it to the event. As soon as you close the mental book on a cost without due compensation, you lose. Therefore, people either keep the books open by investing more in the enterprise or dissociate with what they have done before (i.e., open a new set of books). For example, imagine you are going to attend a theatrical performance with general (no reserved) seating. The ticket costs $20. At the theater, you realize that you lost your ticket. Do you buy another? In contrast, suppose you intend to purchase your ticket on the theater's premises but when retrieving cash from your pocket you realize that you somehow lost $20. Do you buy the theater ticket? "No" is the frequent answer to the first question and "yes" is the answer frequently given to the second. In the first instance, a mental connection is made between what was spent and the prospect of having to spend more. The perceived cost of a $20 seat is $40. In the second instance, the purchase of a ticket and the loss of the money are conceived as separate events. Now consider buying an expensive ticket to a football game and, on the day of the game, there is a blizzard. Do you go? Most people say "yes" because driving in a blizzard doesn't nullify the expense of the ticket: they are put in separate mental accounts. Or, equivalently, you spend good money to go to a Broadway musical that turns out to be dreadful. Do you leave at intermission? Probably not because you would lose your investment. You go, or stay, because you want to get a return on your investment, even if it means doing something you would prefer not to do. But, these decisions should not matter because the money already has been spent regardless of what you do.[19] At the organizational level, the results are akin to the Abilene paradox in which a group ends up doing what no individual prefers often because the origins of agreement and plausible alternatives have not been appropriately vetted.[20]

Interestingly, because many animals are susceptible to sunk costs, some theorists have speculated that there must be some natural advantage.[21] One general explanation is that we assess future rewards by the amount of effort and expense already expended. Because it is difficult to predict actual future payoffs, past investments are used as proxies.[22] The larger the investment, the larger the expected reward. A second explanation concerns the minimization of waste (waste not want not). Because the minimization of waste is crucial to survival, sunk costs may involve an inclination to use up everything one has expended before doing anything else.[23] A third explanation for the survival advantage of sunk costs, which only applies to humans, is that sunk costs help us to honor future obligations. You pay for tickets to attend events in advance to assure your future self will follow through.[24]

One proven way to combat sunk costs is to present decision makers with alternatives so the choice space changes from "go" or "no go" to "continue this" or "change to that." This is a dissociative strategy. The choice between options forces people to consider allocations of resources anew based on the prospects of each option from that moment in time forward.[25]

In general, however, we have a propensity to choose current (or near-term) options over longer-term options even when the more immediate choice delivers a smaller reward. Sunk costs are nursed along by other biases, such as the status quo, existence, and omission biases. These implicit cognitive biases nudge people into believing that doing nothing is better than doing something. Collectively, these biases instill in people an inflated preference for the current state because present actions are viewed as more attractive and desirable, and less costly and effortful to execute (principle of conservation of energy). Doing nothing also moderates culpability should something go wrong. For example, studies have shown that people associate greater wrongdoing with acts of commission versus omission. Mock panels of jurors award higher damages to plaintiffs if the harms result from acts of commission versus omission—even though the actual harms are the same.[26]

Many of the decisions executives face explicitly involve temporal trade-offs, of the kind we encounter every day when, for example, deciding whether we should spend the money we have or put it aside to compound into a bigger stash of cash at a future date. This type of dilemma belongs to a class of decisions involving delay discounting in which smaller immediate rewards are preferable to larger delayed rewards.

Again, however, the deck is stacked in favor of exploit, or the short term. Think of it as figure and ground. When looking at buildings, the one in front of you is really big and the one in the distance is small (although, in actuality, it may be larger).[27] The issue, then, is knowing how to make the building in front of you look smaller and the one in the distance look bigger. Given our inclination to take the proverbial bird in the hand even when twice as many birds are in the bush, what are some ways we might intercede to give the future a fighting chance?

When considering alternatives in discounting dilemmas, the chief decision parameters are as follows:

- The relative size of the outcomes (and discount rate)
- The time delay between outcomes
- The probabilities of obtaining the outcomes

For future initiatives to have a chance of being preferred over present ones, the future alternatives must have certain properties. Relatively speaking, they must be big, temporally close, and probable. If an option is between accepting $10 today versus a guaranteed $50 payment tomorrow, most people would wait the day for the larger payment. As a future benefit grows, the discount rate becomes less steep meaning that future options progressively hold onto more of their value as their size increases. (This is called the *magnitude effect*; this effect holds for rewards that are likely versus unlikely.[28])

Frequently, organizations default to present activities and serendipitous opportunities because they have not expressed longer-term aspirations or envisioned a meaningful future. As in life, without a persuasive long-term goal, life becomes a series of short-term events. The long term simply is a series of transactions strung together. Therefore, one way to make future options larger and more appealing is through vivid, imaginative constructions of future states. In the vernacular of business, the future can become more captivating through an alluring vision. This vision is a periodically refreshed articulation of the essential, broad-brush features of a future state and not of particulars writ large, for example, to become a billion dollar company.[29] Vivid depictions of future states reliably orient people to desirable ends. These abstract, brief, credible, challenging, and clear statements provide aspirational, growth-related images of the future based on a process that Jonathan Swift described as the art of seeing things (in the visible world) that are invisible. Appropriately conveyed, these images have the power to orient and motivate employees, and to fuel venture growth.[30]

Prospection (i.e., envisioning a future state), or mental time travel, is a common technique that helps people to achieve longer-term goals and, conversely, reduces the inclination to act on impulse.[31] In addition to making the future more salient and seductive, realistic mental imagery of the future also speeds up time. As you know from personal experiences, time has a malleable quality. It goes faster when you are older than when you are younger and when you return from a first trip to an unfamiliar location than when you went. Therefore, having time move faster brings a desirable result temporally nearer: as does affixing a certain date and having intermediate milestones that let people know that they are getting closer to the goal. For example, people are more likely to persist toward a specific date of, say, July 1, 2116, versus an equivalent timespan for goal completion of four score and seven years from now without being side-tracked by temptations.[32] This is because the latter expresses a goal by how long you will have to wait (and time will drag); the former expresses expected goal attainment according to when an outcome will occur and the value it will have at that time. The same information is communicated in different ways to different effect.

Another reason that goals with distant, unspecified end dates are unlikely to get enacted is because, in addition to being too far away, they may seem improbable to fulfill. Embarking on an initiative with an indefinite terminal date, for example, may not seem doable. It would require an enormous amount of self-control and strategic discipline to go on without apparent end. Even with the special appeal of an ideal, time-bound goal, companies have to provide people with periodic markers or reminders that the future is achievable and worth striving for.[33] Leaders connote do-ability by being steadfast—as opposed to rigid and unyielding—in their pursuit. Leaders who repeatedly make and unmake goals or who otherwise appear uninterested in a goal's fulfillment convey a lack of personal conviction that sabotages the belief that any expressed aspiration will be met.

Similarly, leaders must plant signposts to maintain a workforce's healthy focus on the future or risk losing their attention to more immediate and satisfying endeavors. People who choose a future outcome still must find a way to get there without being hijacked by more immediate and appealing rewards. For example, many of the children in Mischel et al.'s famous delay-of-gratification tests (i.e., the "marshmallow" experiments) who selected the larger delayed option of goodies—as opposed to smaller immediate ones—ultimately gave in to the immediate reward during a waiting period.[34] The children chose the larger delayed option but ended up, mid-way, settling for the smaller reward. Much of the children's internal anguish concerned their inability to keep their eye on the longer-term prize and away from proximal enticements. The same misdirected attention occurs in organizations when an espoused long-term plan is derailed by, say, a bag of goodies in the form of exercisable stock options. For example, researchers have found that executives make smaller investments in future initiatives when attractive near-term incentives preempt long-term interests in favor of results that will heighten and deliver immediate rewards.[35] We can imagine that as Smith Corona's worldview seemingly was confirmed by consumers in the late 1980s, all internal signs pointed to fervent exploitation; in fact, Smith Corona never again ventured outside its primary product categories and markets until its failed attempt to partner with ACER. By then, however, Smith Corona stood on the precipice requiring only a gentle push from the budding computer industry to send it headlong over the edge into permanent decline.[36]

Although some studies have shown that joint decision-making moderates impulsivity and orients decision makers toward longer-term interests, research is scant on the roles and responsibilities of those who make exploit-explore decisions.[37] For example, it is interesting who regulates exploitation and exploration within the honeybee hive. Briefly, when forager bees return to the hive, they off-load their nectar to bees that are waiting near the hive entrance. These bees-in-waiting are called receiver bees. They take the nectar from the foragers and store it in the comb as honey. If it takes a forager a long time to locate a receiver, the forager realizes that the colony is taking in more nectar than it can currently accommodate. The forager, then, performs a dance (tremble dance) to recruit more receiver bees. They enlist the help of other bees doing other chores, thereby increasing exploitation. Conversely, if a forager upon returning to the hive immediately finds a receiver bee, she (all foragers are female) knows that the colony is bringing in too little nectar and that a greater foraging force is required. In this instance, the forager performs the famous waggle dance to call idle foragers into the field. The colony increases exploration.

The foragers, and not the receiver bees, regulate hive operations through their communications. The bees that give the orders are the ones who have the best perspective on what is occurring in the outside world, the quality of the nectar, specific dangers that await in the field, such as predators, and what the needs of the hive-organization are. The hive is adhering to the monastic (Benedictine) principle of the subsidiarity that states those closest to a problem should make the decision on how to solve it.[38] Hypothetically, if the staffing decisions were left to receivers, they might be reluctant to upregulate the use of foragers for exploration because the added costs entailed by the expanded exploratory force would blow the budget. We can envision a company not wishing to invest in a costly pursuit that may not yield substantive returns—particularly when everything seems to be going fine the way they are. That, of course, assumes what the bees do not: that a regular supply of nectar will continue to flow and that an efficient match between receivers and foragers will persist.

The goal of foragers is to (1) keep nectar flows consistent, (2) keep operations efficient by keeping the time foragers are not in the field (i.e., because they have to wait for receivers) as short as possible, and (3) to make sure supplies of nectar continue. The bees achieve these ends for three notable reasons. First, they have an immutable, collective understanding of their evolutionary goal of survival.

Second, honeybees have an uncanny ability to acquire, transfer, and use new information. We would say that honeybee colonies have high absorptive capacity. Overall, absorptive capacity refers to an organization's ability to acquire new information from the environment and to meld that information with current understandings—and either change its outlook on the marketplace altogether or modify its thinking on what and how it produces its goods or delivers its services.[39] These learnings may launch new exploratory actions or be used to refine current methods or merchandise. In either case, absorptive capacity implies an ability to monetize what has been learned by altering approaches to the market based on information gleaned. Knowing how to reconfigure resources to address environmental changes substantially depends on how well the organization is able to sense and seize opportunities that are available by identifying, filtering, sharing, and evaluating information about trends, customers, and competitors, and intelligently using that information to protect the corporation's assets.

Interestingly, although the idea of learning seems like a starkly intuitive precondition for adaptation, companies often choose other ways to protect their franchises: ways that dim the long-term prospects for success. Take Dunlop for example.[40] Dunlop was once the premier tire producer in Great Britain and one of the largest companies in the world. Dunlop started as a maker of bicycle tires in 1889 and moved into the manufacture of automobile tires for the burgeoning motor car industry in 1900. While the brand name lives on, its European operations were purchased by Sumitomo in 1983.

As the principal tire maker in Great Britain, Dunlop thwarted foreign competition by urging the British government to impose high tariffs on tires (33.5 percent), leading a coalition to standardize prices, and arranging an exclusive arrangement with British carmaker British Leyland. When tariffs eventually were lifted, common pricing was judged to be anticompetitive, and Dunlop's exclusive relationship with British Leyland dissolved following a worker strike at a major Dunlop facility, the company found itself vulnerable to the new world order.

Dunlop discovered that they were late to adopt radial tire technology—which they had dismissed as a gimmick—and to update aging plants. Although radials had many advantages for durability, fuel economy, and safety, the first steel radials pioneered by Michelin were expensive and had breakaway problems. Those problems, however, were resolved through new suspension designs on cars and the advent of fabric radials. Once radial design had been improved, Michelin was quick to seize 20 percent of the British market. Dunlop's factories also were well behind international manufacturing best practices. Indeed, after Sumitomo purchased Dunlop and modernized the factories, output increased 40 percent with 30 percent fewer people. Creating barriers certainly is one way to defend against competition, but these defenses come and go and poorly prepare organizations for the harsh eventualities of global business when that strategy eventually fails. Protectionism is a loser's game.

Third, the ambidextrous hive is made possible by the colony's ability to rapidly transform itself through slack resources. For the colony, these slack resources take the form of cross-trained bees that can switch between job roles and a pool of inactive foragers that can be called into service when needed. The most basic and fungible form

BOX 3.3
An Estonian Folktale and Tulving's Spoon Test

A young girl dreams about going to a birthday party in which her favorite dessert, chocolate pudding, will be served. Except, the rules of the party state that only children with spoons can have the dessert and the girl doesn't have one. Therefore, she must watch as others consume the delicious pudding. The next night, determined not to be disappointed again should she experience a similar episode, she brings a spoon to bed with her and puts it under her pillow. The girl has just passed the spoon test. The "spoon test" refers to a cognitive ability to project oneself into the future and to be duly prepared, even though the need for the spoon at the current time or in the current place is not evident: the child does not need and will not use the spoon in her bed.

Would you pass the spoon test? Maybe. But a lot of our preparations for the future are based on our current needs and that, as we have seen, may produce poor or delayed choices (like shopping when you are hungry). To pass what is analogous to the spoon test, a person has to dissociate with current needs, and project oneself to a future time and place based on a past experience.

Source: Wilkins C, Clayton N. Reflections on the spoon test. *Neuropsychologia* 2019; **134**: 107221.

of slack in organizations is financial in the form of credit and cash.[41] The more money that is available for exploratory investments, the less often the company will have to interrupt existing operations by taking resources from it to underwrite exploration. This creates a paradox. The best time for a company to increase exploration is while financial results remain strong and before it has an evident need. (See box 3.3 for an Estonian folktale on preparing for the future.[42]) If the company waits until its revenues are declining and the changes it must make become glaringly obvious, the window of opportunity for change may have already passed. As the window begins to close, so does the organization's ability to make investments in the future without cannibalizing income streams and assuming greater risks. Companies that wait too long to act will have limited chips to place on a limited number of bets, whereas companies with more financial slack will be better able to diversify exploratory trials in the hope that a few gambits will pay off.

Studies of Smith Corona indicate that the company had available financial resources in the 1980s for exploratory efforts but used their spare cash during that period to exploit their ink-on-paper capabilities. The first half of the 1980s were financially difficult as Smith Corona awaited the return on their investment in the electronic typewriter. Their new products indeed caught on, and Smith Corona witnessed significant gains during the late 1980s, culminating in an all-time high in revenues in 1989. They would declare bankruptcy six years later.

Managing the exploitation/exploration trade-off is difficult. Each set of abilities requires different and opposing operating structures. Exploration and exploitation are uncomfortable companions because the activities and capabilities required are dissimilar for the two. Exploitation involves implementation of overlearned practices that are mechanistic and routine. The creative press of exploration requires open, fluid, and flexible structures that allow people to play with new ideas and to formulate new offerings for different or emerging markets. Exploitation relies on stability and control to optimize profits. Exploration relies on autonomy, variation, and risk to optimize innovations. The two are imperfect cohabitants. The goal of the company is to reconcile an uncomfortable unity between competing forces.[43]

To moderate the inherent tensions between exploitation and exploration, the two functions often are housed in separate units.[44] The dual structures are typified by exploratory workforces in R&D departments, and everyone else doing the work—the exploitative force. The advantage of this division of labor is that the exploratory force is removed from a daily regimen that might constrain creativity by imposing unnecessary requirements in the development process. The result of corporate intrusions into the exploratory process is the emergence of some of the worst products ever developed. The Pontiac Aztek, frequently cited as one of ugliest cars ever built, was a product of far-reaching input and assemblage by committees. As one pundit at the time put it, the car looks the way Montezuma's revenge feels.[45]

In contrast, by isolating the R&D staff from the operating units, a danger exists that the group may lose sight of the true needs of consumers and will deliver products of marginal utility: strikingly brilliant ideas, yet with no market or immediate use, like a remarkably inventive Robinson Crusoe who has little relevance when he returns to society.

To ensure that new products and services are responsive to customer needs and can be folded back into the organization for implementation, companies insert integration devices into the development process. At the micro-level, this function usually is fulfilled by a single individual who serves as a boundary spanner between developers and users, for example, a function fulfilled by business analysts in information technology departments. These intermediaries tie customers' needs and requirements to new developments and technologies.

Integration is more complicated at the corporate level, but the idea is the same. For example, companies may establish cross-company oversight panels that monitor progress and add resources to initiatives with commercial promise but stay removed from daily decisions within the design process. In this way, the company can anticipate how new developments will be executed and what the associated costs will be as products and services unfold. A partial list of integrating devices is given in box 3.4.[46]

Large innovative advances often require structurally separate units. Drug development in pharmaceuticals, for example, necessitate an R&D function. The development process is long and expensive, and it must be handled through formal, intact structures. Not all exploratory actions, however, are large and lengthy. In these circumstances, companies may deploy more modest and less formal methods of exploration. Typically, these methods involve using the same people to do the exploiting and exploring. The effectiveness of these methods assumes that companies hire the right people who are curious, flexible, and

---

BOX 3.4
Sample Methods of Integration across Units

1. Common central manager or governance committee
2. Staff with ambidextrous abilities
3. Common vision and values
4. Spatially co-locate departments
5. Cross-departmental assignments and liberal people-sharing practices
6. Independent integrator function
7. Common platforms, systems, and tools
8. Common goals and rewards

interested explorers. One way to engage in exploitation and exploration with the same people is to carve out time for designated groups of employees to work, say, half-time on a particular problem. The advantage of this approach is that people with rich domain knowledge are asked to think about the next generation of products and services. SAS, for example, takes this approach when adding functionalities to its statistical and visualization software.

Some companies encourage innovations to percolate naturally. They produce the right culture and environment that permits independent thinking and grassroot ideas to arise from the ground up and diffuse throughout the organization.[47] For example, engineering contractor Intuitive Research and Technology Corporation (INTUITIVE) instituted a Creative Incentive Program for new concepts. If the company likes an idea, they will dedicate funds to its development and split the proceeds with the inventors 50–50. Similarly, the investment advisory service The Motley Fool gives employees who have become proficient at their jobs the chance to start "passion projects." These projects start small at the employee's initiative and expand if interests, converts to the cause, and resources allow. Similarly, many companies have mechanisms for employees to submit ideas for improvements or new products and services. These ideas, then, are vetted by internal committees and promising ideas are examined further for potential development. Still other companies such as 3M famously provide employees with time for side projects: to experiment, develop new products, and create new technology platforms. 3M gives employees 15 percent of their time to work on whatever they like. The company has quite a lot to show for this freedom to pursue pet projects: from masking tape and Post-it notes to, more recently, a purifier that facilitates protein-based drug discovery.[48] In total, company employees have developed more than fifty-five thousand products. Additionally, 3M awards peer-selected scientists and researchers six-figure grants to work on what "no sensible, conventional person in the company would give money."[49] They have another saying as well: "If you want to be comfortable with the future, you better be part of creating it."[50]

In truth, these carve-out programs do not generalize. Giving a plethora of highly motivated, inquisitive, and socially oriented (toward the greater good) scientists time to reflect on pet projects is one thing; however, giving less qualified and motivated people the same option is another.[51] This is the argument against the hope that one program can become the provider of all innovation. Rather, the cultural beacon should draw great ideas from anywhere and anyone, using a mixture of methods. A belief that the only people who can think creatively are the people in R&D is a tremendous waste of organizational talent, an unnecessary drain on morale, and a surefire way to diminish the organization's capacity for invention.

CHAPTER FOUR

Encourage Cooperation

WE RECENTLY HELD an offsite retreat for a technology company where one of the participants asked how they would know if their organization was working at full effectiveness. We replied, "If people were giving you their best ideas." In technology, employees have powerful incentives to withhold information and abscond with ideas that can launch lucrative new businesses. This technology company would have no definitive way of knowing if their people were sharing their best ideas, but it would know about the people who left and started businesses that could have benefited their own organization. We also know that the more individuals' interests depart from those of the organization, the greater the loss in efficiency. How could this division of motives and goals produce anything but heightened performative frictions? Groups of individuals all working on their own behalf is a poor prognosis for success.

Organizations present paradigmatic cases of social dilemmas in which personal and collective interests collide.[1] Societally, these dilemmas manifest as public goods or resource dilemmas. In public goods dilemmas, people are encouraged to contribute to a social good in which they will share regardless of what each person contributes. Thus, people can reap rewards while expending little effort and making negligible material sacrifices. These are free-riders, or shirkers, who accept the benefits produced by others but who give little back in return. If you have too many free-riders, the public good disappears (e.g., goodbye public radio). In an organizational setting, if too few people help one another, the collective welfare that arises from joint actions will decay.

In resource dilemmas, people must decide how to take from a common pool of resources with the proviso that overextraction will deplete the pool and become unavailable to everyone. This tragedy of the commons exists from the temptation of each person to take as much as he or she can and, therefore, eliminate the good the group collectively relies upon. The tragedy popularized by Hardin's classic paper describes a group of herders who have equal and open access to a plot of land for grazing their cattle.[2] Each herder has a personal incentive to place as many of his cattle on the land as possible. Yet, if all herders followed the same strategy of maximizing personal use of the plot, the grassland would become irreparably damaged and all would lose. In an organization, one can imagine the detrimental consequences of each employee using resources for their personal pleasures, comfort, and goals to the exclusion of the group's welfare.

Many of the environmental problems we face today are the result of resource dilemmas dominated by short-termism in which personally advantageous acts spoil or diminish the resources we all share. These situations illustrate *social traps* in which the pursuit of self-interest impairs the welfare of the group. Thus, the individual who seeks the ease, comfort, and convenience of driving to work, when combined with similar actions by others, contributes to congestion on the highways. The pursuit of private interests creates results that are in no one's interests. Or, consider a dilemma in which more than six billion players must each forego conveniences and invest time, effort, and money to prevent contamination of the planet and Earth's atmosphere, but they do not equally share the costs of failure in the near term. Thus, the obstinate solutions to climate change.[3]

Removing oneself from the entanglements of these dilemma-situations is difficult for two reasons. First, many self-serving rationales are available for taking too much or giving too little. Consider, for example,

Two members of a criminal gang are arrested and imprisoned. Each is placed in solitary confinement without a chance to communicate with one another. The prosecutors lack sufficient evidence to convict the pair on the primary charge but have enough to convict both on a lesser charge. The prosecutor offers each prisoner a deal. Each is given a chance to betray the other and receive a lighter sentence.

		Player A	
		C	D
Player B	C	R,**R**	S,**T**
	D	T,**S**	P,**P**

R = Reward outcome, T = Temptation outcome
P = Punishment outcome, S = Sucker outcome
C = Cooperate, D = Defect

		Player A	
		C	D
Player B	C	3,**3**	1,**4**
	D	4,**1**	2,**2**

The rational play for each player is to defect, but that will yield lower outcomes than if they both cooperated.

Figure 4.1 The prisoner's dilemma.

the following: "My contribution would be so incidental it won't make any difference" (the drop-in-the-bucket rationale); "I would give but that wouldn't assure me that I would receive the goods I want" (reciprocity justification); "If I didn't take as much as I could, someone else would and where would I be?" (sucker justification); or "Most people don't give anything, so why should I?" (crowd justification).[4] A wealth of perfectly reasonable justifications exists for taking the most egocentric path. These rationales seem innocent in isolation, but they are deadly in organizations: "The organization doesn't pay me enough to give my best ideas away." The ethical wiggle room is substantial.

These reasons are abetted by a second factor, the nature of dilemmas. Social dilemmas are hard to solve because the most rational decision in a prototypical dilemma is self-interest, a choice that may be amplified by emphases on rational decision making in business and a bottom-line mentality.[5] A focus on the bottom line diverts attention to profit maximization and away from other relevant intervening values.[6] The hallmark, then, of social dilemmas is that self-interested behavior is the dominant action regardless of what others do, even though cooperation would produce the best results over time.

Suppose you are asked to take $10 and either secretly insert the money into an envelope or pocket it. You then are asked to exchange envelopes with another person—given the same instructions—with the qualification that the money in the envelope that is handed over will be doubled. What do you do? Chances are you would keep the money. You would be no worse off if the other acted in kind, and should the other person pass along $10, you now are $20 better off— plus the $10 you kept makes it $30.[7] This dominant self-interested feature of dilemmas is illustrated in figure 4.1 in the context of the prisoner's dilemma game.[8] To succeed, companies must find a way to penetrate the tough exterior of self-interest that is deeply embedded in social dilemmas.

The cooperation problem raised by dilemmas such as the prisoner's dilemma is, "How do we mitigate the pull of rational self-interest to garner greater cooperation?" The problem is more dire in real life than in the laboratory as many exchanges in the lab settle into cooperative patterns if the play occurs with the same people over time. Players generally adopt a tit-for-tat retaliation-and-forgiveness strategy in which cooperation is repaid with cooperation and competition (self-interest) with competition. The eventual solution is détente produced by the mutually assured destruction that noncooperation would bring.

Our world is much bigger than those faux worlds established in labs. We deal with many different people for different lengths of time. The larger the pool of people and the more transient the relations, the riper the field for slippery operators to exploit others and then disappear into the crowd. In fact, if our relationships were totally random, defectors would thrive and drive cooperation into extinction. If no one was related and meetings were chance, natural selection would favor the defector—a person who pays no costs, distributes no benefits, and

---

BOX 4.1
Heider's Four Reputation Heuristics

- A friend of a friend is a friend
- An enemy of a friend is an enemy
- A friend of an enemy is an enemy
- An enemy of an enemy is a friend

---

reaps the greatest rewards. With many selfish neighbors, cooperators are at a disadvantage.

But relationships are not random. They are based on preferences, spatial relationships, and networks. And people will sort themselves to ease the stress of interpersonal wariness and vigilance. To defend against exploitation, people will emigrate to relational others who they know to be cooperative. That is, cooperative neighborhoods will form as refugees flee from contaminated environments.[9] But the splintering of organizations in which people seek out safe harbors does not meet our standard of a well-run organization. For example, we once consulted to an advisory firm where people would fudge the nature of projects in the firm's enterprise system to avoid contact with certain people that assignments of a certain type would involve—and, instead, they would pair up with people with whom they knew they would get along. We are going to need a more widespread, stable, and effective solution than the one that assortative behavior produces.

Strong organizations are built on the expectations of goodwill and cooperation. We prefer to work and relate to people we can count on: who have accumulated the rich currency of reputation based on hearsay and past actions that have evinced trust and consideration.[10] These perceptions have far-reaching implications in institutions because we make inferences about others we do not know based on their relationships to those we do (see box 4.1).[11] Without a foundation of trust and the positive expectations of others that assure employees their beneficial acts will not be exploited, everything else a company does to affect change amounts to tinkering around the edges.[12] Execution will tortuously grind like gears out of sync until people discover that relational abuses are not worth the physical and psychological trauma inflicted, and leave. Conflict is inevitable in organizations, and no better interpersonal elixir can manage it constructively than trust.[13]

As an essential source of social capital, trust in others' right motives is key to facilitating exchange and social interaction, and enlivening employees' civic engagement in the enterprise.[14] The value of trust to organizations is unequivocal. Trust fosters greater satisfaction, social solidarity, optimism, charity, cooperation, well-being, and team performance.[15] Overall, trust acts as a purification system that filters out ambiguous statements and unintended slights so that people assume the good intentions of others and, as a result, give them the benefit of the doubt. Conversely, in cases of extant distrust, every errant comment or boorish act imperils relationships that may take days—or even years—to patch up.[16]

Self-maximizing behavior only is rewarding over time when not everyone is playing by the same self-interested rule, but that changes quickly with experience. People will get even and, if made to look foolish by a betrayal of their trust, will get more than even.[17] Furthermore, people will not help those who they believe will not help others, or who are seen as "unhelpful" and, consequently, less likely to "pay it forward." People selectively channel aid to others who they perceive as being helpful. In one study set in a grocery store, experimenters wanted to see when customers with various loads of groceries would allow a confederate with one item (a bottle of water or a bottle of beer) to move ahead of them in line. The more groceries in their baskets, the more likely they were to allow the confederate to move ahead. In this case, the perceived need and value of assistance was greater. However, this was less likely to occur for the confederate with the beer versus the water. Why? The shoppers attributed certain characteristics to a purchaser of a single bottle of beer as a person less likely to "pay it forward."[18]

Controlled experimental studies show that generosity spreads with at least three degrees of separation. This contagious aspect of cooperation is what has made cooperation evolutionarily adaptive and an essential part of organizational success.[19] (Incivility and egocentricism also spread if unleashed.) Figure 4.2 illustrates three ways cooperation generalizes (from direct reciprocity) under the presumptions that other people are generous in spirit and have the welfare of others in mind.[20] Pay-it-forward reciprocity is exemplified by a study situated at a drive-through fast food restaurant where a customer paid for

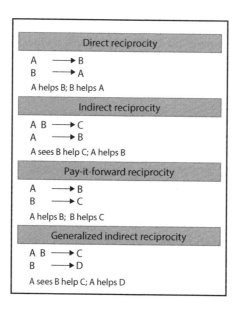

Figure 4.2 Varieties of reciprocity.

the order behind him. The researchers tracked how long the chain of goodwill would persist: for four hundred customers, as it happens. And other coffee and burger shops have observed pay-it-forward sequences twice as long.[21] In these instances, givers give with little hope they ever will benefit from their good deeds. The premise is that the totality of the system will prosper as a result of these simple acts of kindness. A naturalistic organizational study showed the same generalizability of goodwill. Select employees were asked to perform random acts of kindness toward a designated group of employees. The recipients of the kindnesses not only were happier than control subjects (employees who were not targeted for benefit), but they acted kindlier toward others. Their incidence of kind acts increased by almost three times beyond the giving of controls.[22] The nonspecific, unscored give-and-take among members of groups enhances trust and is part of the binding power of friendships.

Achieving a stable, cooperative order is the central problem in organization development. It is hard to think of an instance in which collective benefits are achievable without cooperation.[23] We are not alone in making this assessment. Talcott Parsons considered the attainment of social order (attaining cooperation among large numbers of people) *the* sociological challenge, and Nobel Prize winner Elinor Ostrom viewed it as *the* central problem in political science. The objective of organizations, then, and the focal quest of this chapter, is how to mold enterprises into productive, cooperative wholes.[24]

A parsimonious way to think about the task ahead of us is to conceptualize how we might alter the costs and benefits of the matrix in figure 4.1 into one that is conducive to cooperative decision making and actions. We want to *transform the matrix*.[25] One way this might be achieved is by hiring people who are cooperative. People differ in their other-regarding tendencies. Some people have a greater concern for others, assume that others are basically trustworthy, tend to place greater emphases on group goals and norms, and are more attuned to the well-being and fitness of the group's members.[26] Therefore, many companies select new hires on culture fit or values to ensure a more agreeable workplace. Several companies we have visited have dual selection committees that operate independently: one committee evaluates talent; another evaluates fit with the values of the organization. Prospects must successfully pass through both committees to receive an offer.

The most obvious means to "transform the matrix" is to change the payouts, which is achieved through rewards and punishments. Therefore, a company might, for example, reward employees' displays of cooperation or provide public accolades for teamwork. Organizations could integrate rewards for team play into a balanced scorecard for bonus payouts or build cooperation into the performance management program as a line-item assessment. Conversely, a company could sanction or punish those whose behaviors are uncooperative. Although research varies on the relative impact of rewards and punishments on behavior change, in general, both methods are effective but provide incomplete and unstable solutions.

One drawback to rewards and punishments is that reliable administration requires monitoring or some form of behavioral observation that is not always possible or desirable. The costs of tight oversight are high and the psychological strains of surveillance interfere with the independence and trust of the workforce.[27] Second, once a culture is overrun by self-interest, those who are self-interested are reluctant to penalize others for the very behaviors they perform. The figurative blind eye becomes a more pervasive means of dealing with deviance.[28] Third, punishment often antagonizes people and interferes with the harmonious social relations that a company wants to instill. Overly severe punishment creates vendettas and may induce retaliatory acts.[29] Fourth, the use of rewards and punishments are weak forms of behavior regulation because they make cooperation conditional. The positive expectations we have toward others thins when behaviors clearly are regulated through contingencies. Indeed, studies show that people trust others less if they see that behavioral compliance is secured by rewards and punishments.[30] Furthermore, large contingent rewards and punishments often fail to produce desired changes in attitudes. The reason for this failure has a long history associated with cognitive dissonance. The concept of dissonance is much researched, and many competing explanations for results have been offered. However, repeated experimental demonstrations reveal that people are uncomfortable with inconsistencies in their thoughts or between their thoughts and behaviors. In turn, they seek to remove the disparities.

The classic demonstration of dissonance effects comes from Festinger and Carlsmith, who gave subjects $1 or $20 (in 1959 dollars) to lie about the enjoyability of an objectively boring task.[31] Those who were offered less money reported liking the task more because it presumably is harder to justify their lie with a puny incentive. Aronson and Carlsmith observed much the same a few years later using the well-known forbidden toy paradigm.[32] In this paradigm, children either are given a lenient or stern warning to not play with an attractive toy and, following a free play period, are assessed on their liking for the forbidden toy. Children given a mild warning reported liking the toy less—why else not play with it? Thus, the perceived autonomy with which a person acts influences the degree to which their attitudes will change and values will be internalized. In furthering attitude change, then, it behooves companies to keep rewards and punishments at reasonable levels; many lasting changes in behavior only need nudges such as mild sanctioning.[33] For example, people who merely anticipate approval or disapproval increase giving in the dictator game (an economic game that gives the dictator-subject the unqualified right to divide a sum of money between her or himself and another player).[34]

Behaviors can be changed in other, less intrusive ways than by modifying payout matrices. Companies can change the nature of relationships. The dilemma in the prisoner's dilemma assumes that people are self-interested actors and that the goal of the game is to maximize one's own outcomes whenever opportunity permits. People, however, have other relational motives and different perspectives on one another's interests.[35] For example, a person can try to maximize others' outcomes (benevolence) or their joint outcomes (cooperation). The type of relationship we have with others influences how we approach our encounters. A one-time meeting between strangers is different than the daily rendezvous of, say, husband and wife. Strangers and friends do not play the prisoner's dilemma in the same ways. For example, friends cooperate more in the prisoner's dilemma as opposed to strangers.[36] Additionally, friends are more likely to risk playing for more lucrative, uncertain options in coordination games than strangers, who opt for safer, more certain, low-paying alternatives.[37] Therefore, an ideal way to solve a social dilemma is to change the character of the relationships so that the interests and goals of the parties involved are mutual.

In the following sections, we consider three *related* ways to change relationships: social affinity, positive interdependence, and social identity.

SOCIAL AFFINITY

Those of us who have spent time in organizations know that building a sense of camaraderie can feel forced, as an afterthought or wishful quick repair to broken relationships and severed lines of communication. The panacea of the corporate retreat or one-off "funishment" designed to promote fellow feeling and bring people harmoniously together is hopelessly flawed. Or worse, many employees discover through these sporadic and ill-conceived assemblies how far apart they really are and that cursory attempts to glue people back together simply showcases widespread divisions. People find out that they are not alike, do not fit in, and wonder why they are there.

Good companies expend a great deal of time and energy creating strong social bonds among employees. Indeed, a primary aim of leadership is to facilitate the creation of social bonds among employees and encourage system-wide cooperation.[38] In well-conceived enterprises, affiliation is inconspicuously woven into the institutional fabric starting with the onboarding process. These processes begin before newcomers arrive and proceed with a host of social experiences designed to build relationships and employees' sense of efficacy. Group activities may seem superfluous to the Type A ilk who do not think socializing constitutes real work; however, building strong relationships is real work with genuine payoffs. Just as the games that children play are not just games but safe encounters with the real world, the amusements in which companies engage are not just amusements. They are affective bridges to the institution where positive sentiments color relationships and influences performance.

We once were suspect of the multitude of celebrations some companies stage, but now we understand why. Real people recognize special occasions, life transitions, and rites of passage, and the importance of celebrating, mourning, comforting, laughing, and healing together. We celebrate birthdays, weddings, births, and anniversaries; we help others in need; we grieve others' losses. We do these things because this is what real people do for one another, sometimes because they care for the other, and sometimes because the doing creates the caring.[39] The rituals and traditions of everyday life transform the ordinary into momentous occasions that promote interpersonal warmth and reaffirm communal values. Durkheim saw rituals as a primary way for groups to confirm their intimacy and continuity.[40] These bonding rituals are like booster shots, continuously bringing people together to participate in the life of the community, to underscore the prevailing beliefs of the community, and to pay tribute to exemplar community members at appropriate times. Indeed, social norms of reciprocity and fairness, politeness rituals, and etiquette are the raw materials that make social engagements predictable and pleasurable. They are essential to preserving the amicable and harmonious relations on which organizations depend.

Prescribing the way people are expected to interact is a crucial way to encourage thoughtfulness and restraint when one is tempted by the mood of the moment, by reactionary impulses, and by self-interest. The all-American pastime of standing in line (the British are quite good at this, too) illustrates the value of etiquette.[41] Suppose we are in a queue for our morning coffee. Although some people in line most likely will need their caffeine fixes more urgently than others, the operative rule is "first come, first served." This rule ensures that the person at the back of the line, who may want coffee the most, cannot walk to the front of the line to request service first.

Etiquette requires people to exercise self-control and to refrain from acting on impulse according to their personal wants and desires. These sorts of politeness rituals combined with the requisite self-control, graciousness (e.g., restraint from muttering annoyingly in line), and sense of fair play prevent chaotic grabs for whatever is in reach. Line aficionados understand that they all have similar needs that will be satisfied in time equitably.

Most anything that people do together that involves collective effort can produce positive interpersonal results. We recently were asked by a prestigious medical school to name the one thing we suggest they do to improve the well-being of residents. We recommended that each department select a charity in which to donate time each month, as many companies do. As it happens, volunteering not only helps the recipients of aid but also positively affects the volunteers as well.[42] Volunteering fosters greater psychological well-being and life and job satisfaction in the volunteers. Charitable acts also build social capital among groups. They create tighter networks and closer social ties, more intense feelings of connectedness and social well-being, and greater interpersonal trust and cooperation. Furthermore, people who engage in prosocial behaviors become less focused on themselves and more focused on others.

POSITIVE INTERDEPENDENCE

Relationships matter. So do the tasks. A series of experiments conducted by the husband–wife research team, the Sheriffs, showed that previous fractious groups could cooperate with the introduction of superordinate goals (see box 4.2). The well-known Robbers Cave experiments illustrated how formerly competitive individuals could be brought together to work in harmony.[43]

Laced with political overtones, postwar researchers explained that unity and cooperation were possible under the right conditions. Those conditions found eloquent explication in Morton Deutsch's concept of interdependence structures.[44] Cooperation is more necessary and more likely when there is a high degree of interdependence on tasks, outcomes, and goals. Often these are aligned, but they are not the same. Interdependence on tasks means that dependencies exist between the execution of one job and another. For me to do my job, you must do yours.

BOX 4.2
Robbers Cave Experiments

Between 1949 and 1954, the husband–wife research team, the Sheriffs (in repeated attempts), manipulated conditions at a boy's summer camp at Robbers Cave State Park in Oklahoma, first, to provoke animosities between two competing groups—the Eagles and the Rattlers—and second, to see if and how hostilities could be ameliorated. They found that having the groups work jointly toward a shared goal could repair relations among members of the groups. The extremely competitive and tense social climate that the researchers induced abruptly ended when the campers came together to restore the water supply to the camp that ostensibly had been vandalized. Voluntarily coming together to restore a good that would be available to all was enough to improve campers' attitudes toward former competitors and the quality of relations.

Interdependence of outcomes means that team success, such as winning a game or losing a game, relies on undivided results. Certain aspects of performance may be carved out and attributed to certain individuals, but important end results are indivisible. Some researchers have considered common fate (the interdependence of outcomes) to be the quintessential property for cooperative groups, providing the necessary psychological connectedness of group members and serving as a strong predictor of performance.[45] Indeed, it is difficult to think of a body as a *team* when each member experiences different outcomes.

Interdependence of goals means that everyone is striving for the same ends. In the Robbers Cave experiments, the goal was to restore the water supply to the camp that purportedly had been vandalized. Shared goals are important not just because they signify a common pursuit but because they help to predict what people are supposed to be doing. The common knowledge of a shared pursuit provides a firm footing that everyone will act in a certain way. Indeed, a fundamental tenant to team efficacy is that people will participate in concert only if everyone is similarly committed to the same goals. Certain experimental games simulate hunts (stag hunts); you can catch small animals alone or go after the big stuff in groups. If everyone participates and positions themselves in the proper places, you will be able to capture the stag. If, however, confidence is low that people will abide the work that must be done, then people will opt for the default position—just go after the little critters by themselves—since without unanimity of effort, big initiatives will fail and render all work useless.

The ability to influentially convey a common purpose is one of the most basic and essential leadership skills.[46] Articulating a compelling common purpose is heralded as a linchpin of leadership excellence and team performance, and as a critical tool in shifting focus from individual to group interests. The grand purposes of organizations are specified in their vision statements that are intended to compellingly portray future states—without descending into pious platitudes or empty verbiage (e.g., "to achieve ever higher profits").[47] The best visions generate vivid verbal portraits that appeal to observers' experiential systems so that they can feel and touch the future.[48] For example, a measured amount of sugar verses a calorie count is more persuasive and influential on the food choices people make.[49] Someone in a weight-loss program we once attended used to carry around a twenty-pound barbell, providing a more profound depiction of his goal by showing what walking around with the extra weight really means.

One common misconception of generating a common purpose is that it automatically produces common action. We tend to believe that if our goals are well aligned, our actions will be too. A common purpose, however, does not ensure *coordination*. For example, a basketball team of five ball-hogs may have a common purpose but the players will not work together well.

The need for coordination underscores a truism. The greatest ally to cooperation is communication: communication about what is important, how an initiative will be approached, what people will be involved and when, and so on.[50] Communications enable people to make explicit commitments to courses of action, to debate the ethics of decisions, to elucidate norms, to appeal to rules, and to forge closer relations and social ties.[51] Overall, the ability to communicate (directly or through reference to the same script) allows people to reach consensus more rapidly and work together more effectively. So, in the United States, when two cars reach an intersection simultaneously, to avoid collision, the car on the right knows it has the right of way.

In addition to explicit instructions and communications in their various formats, an invaluable coordinating mechanism in organizations is culture. The culture provides the requisite understandings for coordinated action. Say, for example, you are a New Yorker with plans to meet a friend tomorrow. Furthermore, assume that you are living in the pre-smartphone age and are unable to contact your friend in advance. Where and when do you meet? Most New Yorkers say they would go to the clock in Grand Central Station at noon. It is commonly understood that Grand Central is a place where people meet in New York. These meetups are possible because New Yorkers have acquired a shared understanding of where these take place.

Many of the everyday coordination problems we face are easily handled by the shared expectations for behavior we acquire through norms, conventions, and other social constructions that together account for a sizeable part of what we think of as culture.[52] Consequently, we know how to dress for different occasions, how to have pleasurable two-way conversations, and which side of the road to drive on, without embarrassment, discomfort, or catastrophe. One of the rules we taught our children as they were learning to drive was to not be nice (within reason). That sounds harsh, however, being nice introduces deviations from conventions that other drivers may not recognize—thus stopping on a highway to let another driver out into the flow of traffic is nice but may not be appreciated by the driver immediately behind who has other ideas about traffic flows.

Culture makes behavior more predictable, facilitates coordination and lowers transaction costs, and enables people to self-regulate their actions without persistent prompts from third parties. Strong cultures usher efficiencies because they remove the waste of deciphering behaviors and expedite routine interactions by eliminating the continuous need for rediscovery and invention.[53] These immense benefits cued Peter Drucker's popular saw, "Culture eats strategy for lunch." Companies that realize the importance of culture take the time to mold a rich assortment of artefacts (e.g., symbols, rituals, language), norms, practices, and beliefs into consistent, coherent messages that telegraph expected behaviors and establish distinct group identities.

SOCIAL IDENTITY

Part of the coalescing power of culture is that we are emotionally connected to people who share our ideas, interests, humor, and world views. The values and attitudes we share through culture are partly what unites and gives us our distinct social identities as members of countries, organizations, and groups.[54] This categorization as a member of a group is significant since the greater people's affiliation with a group, the more important the group and the more motivated members are to fulfill its goals.[55] Indeed, had the United States heeded one of the recommendations of an interdisciplinary task force on Covid-19, early responses to Covid-19 may have been more compelling. The task force urged the nation to underscore the common good through appeals to a sense of identity, unity, and purpose to elicit healthy, preventative behaviors.[56]

Interestingly, making a group does not require much. A host of studies use what is referred to as the minimal group technique.[57] Simply, surreptitious connections between people create special affinities. For example, people who were led to believe that they had shared tastes in artists, shared dot estimation abilities, shared musical preferences, or shared perceptual judgments formed stronger social ties and were more cooperative within than between groups. We know that these manipulations are effective because people report feeling a greater connection to those with whom they have been randomly bound and act more favorably toward them versus others (this result has been called *the mere membership effect*).[58] It is as if we, as humans, are primed to belong whereby a sharing of perceptions, interpretations, and experiences are enough to induce the feeling of being a part of the in-group.

A recent meta-analysis showed the importance of social identity to organizations. The authors examined the relative effects of general interest variables (e.g., job involvement and job satisfaction) and organizational identification on in-role (job) and extra-role (e.g., helping) performance, and they found that identification was the best predictor of performance. Both variables are important, but as the authors note, organizations have a tendency to spend a disproportionate amount of time, money, and energy making sure people are satisfied with their work and too little attention on identity-enhancement programs.[59]

Creative organizations build a strong sense of inclusion, solidarity, and identity in many ways. Do the following thought experiment: Take a moment to reflect on your college or university experiences and the methods they used to create high identity institutions; so high, at times, that people feel grateful many years after graduation and continue to donate money even after they already paid a great deal for their educations. What did those institutions do to foster such a tight connection? We suggest they did many of the strategies discussed next. A good social entrepreneur could take these criteria and easily forge group solidarity in their own organizations.

Categorization

The employees at Patagonia call themselves Patagoniacs. Instructure has a panda bear mascot that shows up at corporate events in full body suit. The first thing you get when you join Insomniac Games is a mountain of swag emblazoned with the corporate logo. That sweatshirt with the corporate logo has a function to keep you warm, but you have to decide to put it on, be willing to publicize your affiliation, and want to appear the same as others in the organization who have chosen to wear the exact same sweatshirt. Therefore, these symbols— like the mascots of sports teams and flags and anthems of nations— enhance physical similarity and perceptions of unity.[60] They also make groups seem more real as logos and other organizational paraphernalia serve as stand-ins for real group characteristics. That panda mascot has come to symbolize a "rare breed" of employee that always is willing to test the limits of the possible.

Common Experiences

Sometimes common experiences take the form of doing things in unison such as marching in a band. Here, groups develop what William McNeil has called "muscular bonding."[61] The simple act of mutually doing activities in some choreographed form helps to solidify group identity. Activities in companies typically are more loosely structured; nevertheless, they are laid out in patterned sequences that employees follow at particular times together. Think of it as a pilgrimage: a time when a cohort of employees travels off-site to a mystical place (e.g., an all-expense paid trip to the Home Office) where they will find the answers they have been looking for and the previously unknown will be revealed. Or, these can be simple journeys such as an annual lunch with the CEO or more intensive and time-consuming affairs such as multiweek trainings that all employees attend during certain junctures in their careers.

Competition

A recurring theme in sci-fi movies is the alien invasion and a world that must come together to defeat a common foe. The common threat to the welfare of the world shines a light on our shared humanity and distinctiveness as creatures with wants and needs. Companies have enemies, too, that are out to rob employees of their way of life. War metaphors abound to help employees recognize the good guys from the bad (e.g., price wars, warrior leaders, takeover battles, raiders, scorched earth policies, war rooms, target companies, and proxy fights). These wars between competitors (e.g., PepsiCo versus Coca-Cola; Amazon versus Walmart) are pronouncements of differences by which the in-group sneers at the out-group, rehearses its own virtuousness, and solidifies the place of employees among the righteous and chosen.

Distinctiveness

If membership criteria are broad and ambiguous and the borders of a group are extremely porous, then the task of building a sense of community will be much harder. The familiar Marx Brothers quip that I wouldn't want to belong to a group that would take me, applies. The implication is that a group that takes anyone is not special. Therefore, groups that are more selective and careful

---

BOX. 4.3
Widening the Circle

Rats, like people, can feel empathy and go to the aid of others in need. In fact, rats will forego a nice chunk of food to save another rat from drowning. But that all depends on who rats allow into their circle of friends. White rats raised with white rats only will save other white rats. However, white rats raised only with black rats will only save black rats. White or black rats raised with both white and black rats will save any rat. Once you get to know someone, you realize they are worth saving.

to hire based on certain attributes will cultivate a workplace of peers who value their place more highly among a cadre of others who are equally unique. Importantly, the distinctiveness of an ingroup does not necessarily imply a lack of diversity. For example, racially diverse groups are as cooperative as homogenous groups. Superficial similarities and differences are trumped by the range of experiences and factors that bring people together and give them a sense of one. For an intriguing set of experiments that illustrates how rats develop an inclusionary sheath and widen the circle of belonging, see box 4.3.[62]

Equal Status

An employee once told us how she would see the CEO of Instructure, Josh Coates, sitting with employees early in the morning over coffee discussing the organization, their careers, and a miscellany of other concerns. At all-employee meetings at QBP (Quality Bicycle Products), executives, founder included, sit among the employees and do not sit in a cluster by themselves. Employees notice these things. These subtleties convey that while people have different responsibilities and relative importance to the business, no one is better than another as a person. Everyone is afforded equal respect. Therefore, the minimization of status (e.g., titles) and power differences (e.g., refer to employees as members or associates and managers as developers; executive open-door policies) is a way to emphasize inclusivity and belonging—that there are not many small groups, but one big one.

Language

We live in an acronym-filled world. One of the things that distinguishes one group from another is the language they speak. When we go into companies for the first time, some of what we hear is not intelligible without translation. Only insiders, those who are members of the group and in the know, could possibly understand what their unique acronyms, such as GQC or LFR, mean. Language and codes are the operators of in-groups; if you want in, you need to learn the secret handshake and local dialect.

Representation Acts

People often are asked to do things on behalf of a group that heightens their identity with the group. For example, giving tours, giving a talk under the aegis of the organization, or representing the company at a trade show all require employees to publicly endorse the awesomeness of their organizations. It is well known that attitudes affect behaviors, but it works the other way around, too. Employees' perceptions of the organization and their connections to it may positively change because of acting out behaviors that demonstrate their fidelity to their institutions. As William James once pointed out, when encountering a bear, we may run because we are afraid, but we also are afraid because we run.

Symbolism

Symbols abound. Specifically, we are thinking of those that denote "members only." These can be subtle, such as special entranceways, special employee discounts, or even the color of badges that are reserved for "employees only." Collectively, these enhance the salience and benefits of belonging to a group. Relationships often begin with artifacts, activities, and symbols that designate union; for example, weddings, with special attire, vows, the ceremonial exchange of rings, and kiss to seal the deal. WD-40 does something akin to vows when it asks new employees to take the "maniac pledge."[63] These vows include taking responsibility for getting answers to questions in which employees do not know the answers, making decisions, and admitting to mistakes, called learning moments. The vows request that people promise to acquit themselves in particular ways as members of the team. And, then, consider the multitude of ways that companies metaphorically assimilate employees into the fold. For example, many years ago we were introduced to tool manufacturer American Saw & Mfg. who had new employees inscribe their names into blocks of wood that were then displayed on a *Wall of Quality*. Everyone's names are displayed together on the Wall and the person gets his or her etched block when they retire. Similarly, the first thing you see when entering the offices of QBP is a series of serpentine bicycle chains mounted on the walls with 750 wallet-size portraits attached. The faces and names of every employee are neatly displayed in chronological order from their date of hire. With orderly spacing and artful consistency and precision, every employee is inextricably linked.

BILLY CUNNINGHAM DIDN'T BAT

Many years ago, we had by far the best baseball team of ten- to twelve-year-olds and won a decisive game three in the title match. We did not, however, win the game. The rules clearly state that every player must play at least two innings and bat. And, Billy Cunningham did not bat. We lost the game and the championship by forfeit. It was a sad day, indeed, but not an unfair one. A bit of commotion ensued but once the clamor subsided the verdict was clear: we had lost the game. We lost because we all understood that we would compete by a set of rules that everyone had agreed to. The tacit agreement is this: if you are going to win, you will have to win in a certain way. Constructive competition involves the implicit recognition of an honor code among participants and observers. Specifically, mature play entails a catalogue of attitudes and attributes associated with sportspersonship: a commitment to one's vocation; respect for rules, conventions, peers, and opponents; and a sense of fair play, grace in victory or defeat, and élan. The ability to remain calm and maintain focus under pressure, to tolerate petty injustices and bad calls, and to bounce back after stumbles, are part of a larger complex of extra-role and prosocial behaviors that give organizations a competitive edge. To see the opposite of sportspersonship on display, go to a little league baseball game in today's era in which the behaviors of players and fans have become so abusive that leagues are finding it increasingly difficult to find umpires.[64]

Results of competitions can be disappointing; however, competition is important. Healthy competition is inextricably bound to learning, development, and achievement. It encourages engagement, mastery of a task, desire to achieve one's best, teamwork, and critical thinking.[65] Therefore, for all our talk about cooperation, our intent never has been to dismiss the importance of competition. A company needs cooperation to succeed, yet it requires people to have exceptional personal goals to excel. The success of companies necessitates personal striving in conjunction with cooperation. That is, companies need people to cooperate and compete at the same time: they need coopetition.[66]

The charge for organizations is to create an environment that makes constructive competition possible without losing sight of corporate aims. For example, mutual fund managers have large remunerative incentives to outperform other fund managers and receive the accolades of investors, analysts, and the press. Corporate practices, such as compensation plans that motivate competitive individual performance, produce greater variability in profits among families of funds, generate more volatile cash flows, and result in a lower overall reputation of the advisory group than advisory groups that promote higher levels of cooperation among fund family managers. These latter families have fund managers who are more likely to engage in cooperative behaviors—sometimes at personal expense. For example, affiliated funds may invest in other funds within the same family when redemptions from those funds are abnormally high. In contrast to the tournament-style play of competitive managers, which produces a repository of hit-or-miss funds and uneven returns, high-performing managers who are willing to cooperate yield more reliable cashflows and maximize the value of the entire fund family.[67]

One ally of healthy competition in organizations is creating a sense of abundance versus scarcity. In general, conditions of scarcity produce unfriendly competition and vice versa.[68] When executives, refer to scarcity and abundance mindsets, they are alluding to features of the environment that elicit greater or lesser harmful infighting among employees and greater or lesser cooperation. We have seen the concepts of scarcity and abundance most readily applied to the availability of jobs in companies and the ability of employees to advance in their careers. Through robust and flexible development, pay, and career programs, employers are able to accommodate employees' interests and ambitions in plentiful ways, for example, through growth in disciplinary depth and provisions for special assignments, cross-training, and interdepartmental or functional career moves—and employees see that they have nothing to lose in another person's success. A sense of abundance allows people to be generous with their time and expertise. The company offers an intricate lattice of possibilities versus placing people on narrow and straight career tracks. Consequently, competition induced by scarcity is tamed.

When few job opportunities are available, people who want the position must intensely compete for it. These circumstances usually encourage a glut of self-promotion, superficial cooperation, wasteful ingratiating activities, such as "face time" (worthless time spent in viewing range of a supervisor), and political drama: time killing diversions typically compensated for by grabbing hours out of one's personal life. Even worse, studies have shown that rivalries within companies promote odious acts, such as unsporting behaviors, deception, and unethical tactics to win competitions.[69] In fact, the desire to win and the associated preservation of self-worth and status supplant the tangible reward as the motive for performance, with deleterious results. First, losers in these career contests are over two times more likely than the average employee to quit the organization in the ensuing year. Second, scarcity and competition redirect individuals' attention to differences between themselves and others, thereby pushing people apart; conversely, abundance and cooperation direct individuals' attention to similarities among themselves and toward a regard for others' needs and welfare.

In organizations of plenty that remain keenly aware of employees' talents, interests, and aspirations, employees understand that others' successes will not spoil their own ambitions. Trust in the system allows people to unselfishly promote the interests of others without having to feel deprived.

CHAPTER FIVE

Remain Flexible

WHEN OUR CHILDREN were younger, they participated in an annual Maypole ceremony. It was a well-choreographed tradition. It would be fair to say, however, that despite its ritualistic elements, no contemporary Maypole ceremony was identical to the year before. The individual players brought an element of eclecticisms to the proceedings, and intruder wasps, children's missteps and stumbles, or snagged ribbons were cause for stylish maneuvers that could disrupt perfection as drawn on paper. Nevertheless, the event never departed from what could be identified as a Maypole dance, and observers never were disappointed with the spectacle as their maturing offspring marched to a tethered rule of order.

These annual variations on a theme worked *because* the dancers could deviate from scriptures, not *despite the fact*. These improvisations enabled the dancers to smoothly twist along and wind their way to the dance's inevitable end. Indeed, the least adaptive and most error-prone dance would be one that merrily proceeded without regard to what was occurring in the surrounding area. The performance would be compromised if adjustments were not made for, say, a fallen comrade.

Thus, we expect sensible departures from routine when the occasion calls for it.[1]

Most organizations thrive on the rhythms of routines. The orderliness of organization is the way companies make business plans, set budgets, and review performance. Routines define what must happen, by who, and when. These recurring cadences are like heartbeats that give institutions life. Routines reduce confusion and conflict and increase the speed of execution through plug-and-play orchestration. These patterns, however, invite a paradox. Efficiency necessitates rules and repetition, but shifting circumstances necessitate adaptation and change. Therefore, organizations must be at once disciplined and flexible. Organizations that can do both have the wherewithal to morph with circumstances and to regain their shape once the need for transformation has passed.

Companies must be pliant without becoming scattered and chaotic. They must prudently react to the unexpected during turbulent times and flexibly bend when rushes of demand are placed on them by internal and external customers. The aim of flexibility is to be profitably responsive to environmental conditions by adjusting to the variability in the volume of customers, the number of products and services customers desire, the speed with which goods or services are needed, or the magnitude of custom requests to standard offerings.[2] "Profitable" is the operative word. Therefore, throwing money and people at a process problem would not be considered solutions because of the huge penalty in cost that flexibility would impose. Specifically, flexibility refers to an organizational ability to change and react to circumstances without incurring negative costs in time, quality, expense, or performance. Indeed, we will go one step further and say that employee flexibility should have a positive effect on corporate performance in terms of both mitigating risks because of exogenous shocks as well as improving stock returns. Indeed, a recent longitudinal study of firms coded as more or less flexible showed that flexible firms were more resilient in times of uncertainty and more profitable over the period of the study.[3]

Not every process requires flexibility, but those situations are increasingly rare. As long as people accepted one Model T, the process for its assembly was straightforward. The assembly of automobiles became more complex when consumers began to demand new models of different colors. The greater product differentiation that followed from more expansive consumer tastes, the seasonality of new models, consumer purchasing habits, and such required more flexible forms of organizing. Burns and Stalker,[4] and like-minded authors who followed them,[5] pointed out that organizational processes needed to conform to the requirements of the environment. Burns and Stalker specifically contrasted mechanistic and organic forms of organizing, maintaining that the former was more conducive to stable, predictable environments and the latter was more conducive to dynamic environments (see table 5.1).[6] And, indeed, this generally has been true. For example, a recent study of 167 manufacturing plants indicated that more flexible (flat, decentralized, multiskilled employees) organizational structures were more efficient in producing mass customized outputs than mechanistic structures. The more uncertain and variable the demands of the environment, the more organic and flexible a system needs to be.[7]

In this chapter, we discuss what it means for an organizational process to be flexible. We proceed with the following caveat: although the term "flexible" can pertain to a spectrum of process elements, our focus as organization development (OD) practitioners is on people's skillsets and the methods by which staff counts are determined and employees are deployed. Specifically, we are concerned with a company's ability to reconfigure its human resources in response to environmental demands to preserve service and production levels.[8] Therefore, we note in passing that different forms of flexibility exist, but these will

TABLE 5.1
Mechanistic and organic organizations

Mechanistic	Organic
Centralized control	Decentralized authority
High task specialization	Multifunctional employees
High standardization	Some flexibility/adjustments
Vertical communications/ Reporting paths	Network/lateral communications
Tight supervision	Participative management
Rigid rules and procedures	Personal discretion
High formality	Informal exchanges

Source: Adapted from Burns T, Stalker GM. *The management of innovation.* New York: Oxford University Press (rev. ed.), 1994.

not be central to our discussion. Technologies and machines, structures, people, and processes all can be more or less flexible.[9] For example, a Philips screwdriver has one intended purpose, whereas a Swiss Army knife has several that can be variously deployed. With that advisory, our commentary primarily will be directed to people and ways to enhance organizational flexibility by expanding the skills and abilities of the workforce or by increasing (or decreasing) their numbers.

Efficient processes involve the adept merger of several elements. Every process has a logically related set of tasks to perform, and technologies, people, communications, and frameworks that enable the execution of these tasks. These elements are stuck together by culture and mechanisms that promote coordination. Several models of culture exist, but one we have seen explicitly applied in the operations literature was developed by Westrum.[10] His descriptions of culture were designed to showcase the differences between generative and pathological cultures that spur or curtail process efficiencies in information technology environments. These divergent cultures are summarized in table 5.2 and, as can be seen, are illustrative of destructive or beneficial milieus that may pertain to any process found in any company. The generative, performance-oriented culture reflects workplaces in which new ideas flourish, cooperation is rewarded, and people feel jointly liable for the outcomes they achieve. Therefore, errors are public, nonincriminating affairs and are cause for collective problem solving, correction, and learning. Such cultures are evidenced by the nonthreatening way some organizations handle mistakes. For example, BambooHR asks employees to circulate their errors without fear of recrimination through an Oops email inox. The aims are to announce

TABLE 5.2
Pathological and generative cultures

Pathological	Generative
Low cooperation	High cooperation
Messenger shot	Messengers trained
Responsibilities shirked	Risks are shared
Bridging discouraged	Bridging encouraged
Failure leads to Scapegoating	Failure leads to inquiry
Novelty crushed	Novelty implemented

mistakes made, to make others aware of them, and to broadcast the steps that were taken to correct them. Therefore, the company communicates that mistakes are an inevitable part of the human condition, happen, and are fixable.

In contrast, pathological cultures crush initiative and produce alienated environments in which people keep their heads down and remain silent, still, and invisible. This self-imposed exile is a way to avoid detection and arouse the critical glowers of others. The less one interacts with others, the safer one is from extended hostilities. These repressive regimes propagate insular employee perspectives and encourage behaviors in which employees do their small, circumscribed parts and little more.

One issue that undoubtedly is familiar to anyone who has ever been a participant in a cross-functional process pertains to silos, or the issue of coordination among independently functioning units. Silos appear when people are comfortably sequestered in their specialized departments and are removed from happenings outside their secure environs. The mechanisms for managing their interdependencies are absent. Clearly, if people are not communicating and information flows are unconnected, a process will not be efficient regardless of anything else a company might do. In fact, what little semblance of structure exists when (internal) processes fail is further undone by workarounds—by individuals who circumvent processes to get what they need. When processes are broken, it is tempting to think that things could not get worse, but they can. Formal procedures can dissolve into free-for-alls. Companies sometimes euphemistically refer to this chaos as "relationship cultures."

Therefore, organizations can help their cause by creating ways for information and materials to successfully travel across functional lines and tie the group's activities together. In most ways, cross-functional teams succeed using the same facets of teamwork as any other team: through goal identification, strategy formulation, and system monitoring. Additionally, the work of cross-functional teams is further enabled by making the entire process visible to the people involved.[11] This visibility ensures that processors are working from the same mental model with the same understandings of the bigger picture. The display of the complete process also highlights everyone's instrumentality toward, and accountability for, the end results. A comprehensive view of the entire process allows all parties—upstream and downstream—to see how they are performing as a unit. Too frequently participants are sheltered from the results of their work, for example, they never get to hear a customer complain about the atrocious service and, consequently, never have the same impetus to change as those who are directly exposed to customers' dissatisfaction. In fact, one of the factors that makes systems reliable is the ready acknowledgment of situational failure and preparedness for learning and improvement, qualities that regular team briefings can help sharpen.

Relatedly, the connectedness of a system is furthered by sound knowledge management—by wrapping the requisite operational and technical knowledge around the entire process. In that way, those who have a role in the process are kept well informed and, consequently, can make intelligent, nuanced decisions and advance changes accordingly. Studies show that adept knowledge management, or the ability to acquire, convert, transfer, apply, and protect knowledge, is critical to the dynamic capabilities of organizations.[12] Sound knowledge management promotes cross functional understandings, enhances sensitivities to changing conditions, and stimulates reengineering priorities, plans, and actions. An organization's capability to process knowledge effectively reduces the impact of environmental uncertainty and increases effective responses. Therefore, companies that are able to generate new and relevant knowledge and diffuse, share, and apply it are more versatile and responsive to external conditions.[13]

Every process has inputs, throughputs, and outputs. The nature and issues concerning these processes, however, depend on the ingenuity of those involved. For example, bottlenecks are familiar in many U.S. airports (and organizations) because too many people converge on too few checkpoints at certain times of the year, week, and day. That is not a problem you will find at Singapore's Changi's International Airport because people go directly to their gates and are checked there.[14] The customer's burden of waiting is shifted to the responsiveness of security who must allocate labor to the right gates in a timely manner. In the case of Singapore's airport, authorities make prudent use of floaters, or agents who serve in a generalist capacity and are assigned dynamically to go where the needs are greatest. In many companies, managers serve in the role of floaters, stepping in to aid their teams when and where the situation demands.

The counternormative approach of how to check passengers at airports demonstrates an important, often overlooked, fact. Process development is a creative endeavor that often turns on a simple challenge to assumptions, like solving a riddle. For example, hotels were spared expensive repairs in just this manner. Tired of customer complaints of waiting for elevators, hotels once thought they needed more and faster elevators. A psychologist, however, suggested that perhaps what hotels needed were more patient customers. In response, hotels enabled customers' persistence by putting in windows with views by the elevator banks, hanging artwork and mirrors, creating seating areas with reading materials, and such—things to make the time, not the elevators, go faster. The same sort of mental gymnastics transformed Honda's assembly process at its most advanced plant in Thailand. The plant contains the world's first moving cell assembly line called the Assembly Revolution Cell Line. Rather than standing at an assembly line performing a singular task, four workers step onto a moving platform that tracks with Honda Civic shells and, with carts of parts by their sides (only the parts they will need), install ten to twenty parts. The people walk less, become more versatile in assembly through the execution of multiple related tasks, and are more cognizant of the entire assembly process—passing on their observations to developers. Production efficiency has increased by 10 percent.[15] This process would not have been possible if someone had not challenged the assumption that people are supposed to be stationary in assembly— that only the line could move.

Breakthroughs in process come when existing assumptions that frequently go unspoken are identified and questioned. It involves a mode of thinking, called divergent thinking, in which the uses of objects are reimagined or assumptions that have entrapped thinking are challenged and new ideas are set free (for an example, see box 5.1).[16] Thus, novel design thinking is a prelude to enhanced processes. The same sort of originality is valuable to other aspects of process as well, as when designers consider how to balance the demands on a system with the system's capacity to respond.

In New Haven, Connecticut, a line forms daily outside of Pepe's Pizza, a landmark eatery in the city. Patrons stand outside and wait their turns to be seated and served, frequently indifferent to the weather. Pepe's could move to another, larger location with greater seating capacity, but their current location has historical significance. Although the proprietors built a small spillover space nearby for those patrons who do not want to wait and are willing to pay for a lesser

---

BOX 5.1
Duncker Candle Task

Fix a lit candle on a wall without wax dripping on the floor using only a candle, a box of matches, and a few tacks.

Once people abandon the assumption that it is the candle itself that has to be attached to the wall and that the matchbox only as a receptacle for matches, the problem-solver gains new perspective. The box can be attached to the wall with tacks with the candle placed in it.

---

experience than offered at the original site of the restaurant, they have decided to marry demand with capacity in a different way than creating a larger space. Pepe's knows that their lines are chic but that people will not stand in line forever. Therefore, they have more wait staff per table than typical, and service is based on variations of a single product so that tables turn rapidly. Those waiting outside know that their turn will soon come.

Emergency rooms take a different approach, although the goals are similar. Emergency departments must provide the right number and mix of personnel in a way that balances utilization and revenues against the acuity of the case load and wait times. Emergency rooms are notorious for their crowded waiting rooms and lines (although, interestingly, those waiting never really know where they are in the line and feel more like lottery winners when their names are called). In fact, many people who visit emergency rooms leave without ever having been seen. Emergency rooms manage demand by conducting triage to channel traffic based on the severity of patients' conditions and attempt to siphon nonemergency cases out of the system by promoting patients' use of telehealth phonelines, colocating (with the emergency department) general practice walk-in clinics, or encouraging the use of in-home care.[17] Thus, effective processes are those that regulate input and output rates in a way that productively meets the needs of customers (or patients). These regulatory methods are enlisted with the aims of increasing demand, decreasing demand, rechanneling demand to other resources, or altering the timing of demand. For example, reservation systems are demand-influencing methods that inventory people so that they are aligned with the organization's ability to serve them. In any case, the objective of the organization is to fulfill demand in the most cost-beneficial manner possible through prudent mutations in capacity.

Many real-life allocation decisions mirror one that has been of substantial analytical interest since first proposed in 1888, called the newsboy problem (now called the newsvendor problem). The newsvendor problem is a classic problem of decision making under uncertainty that directly relates to the capacity decisions that businesses must make, including—per our interest in people—the investment in various flexible staffing arrangements. Despite rigorous forecasting methods, the decisions companies make will never be perfectly efficient in the absence of perfect clairvoyance.

As opposed to staff, the newsvendor problem pertains to the capacity concerns of inventory. In the standard problem, the vendor must decide on the optimal number of newspapers to order from the publisher. The newsvendor has only one chance to make a purchase of a perishable good in advance of the upcoming selling period. The number is not predictably discernable because of random fluctuations in demand. The problem consists of how the vendor will use his or her single opportunity for orders. An overage in capacity will produce waste and excess costs. Too little investment in capacity will result in lost orders and underage costs.

The seeming simplicity of the problem has led to myriad complex analysis and possible solutions. Although theoretically optimal solutions exist to these problems, the problems do not necessarily reflect the realities of continuing operations, multiple opportunities to place orders, or incomplete information. Even so, people do not make mathematically optimal decisions and, therefore, the problem has provided a decades-long window into the thought processes of decision makers who make capacity decisions as experimenters manipulate different aspects of the problem. For example, when product profit margins are high, people tend to under-order, and when product profits are low, people tend to over-order. It may be that when profit margins are high, decision makers may see little to be gained (and a lot to lose) with incrementally more purchases and tend to be risk averse. Conversely, when profit margins are low, decision makers may see a lot to gain (and little to lose) with incrementally more purchases and tend to be risk seeking.[18] Although people have a theoretical basis for the

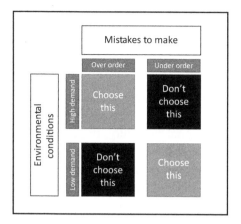

Figure 5.1 Make the right mistakes.

decisions they make, our general suggestion in determining capacity is more prosaic, yet, sound. Organizations frequently will not know what a correct decision is until it is too late and, given that mistakes are bound to happen, our advice is to choose the right mistake to make. The grid in figure 5.1 shows the types of capacity mistakes that can ensue from high- and low-demand situations, including the mistakes you might prefer to make.

A general rule for ensuring a capable response to fluctuating demand is to have as much variety in the organization as the environment in which its sits (this is known as Ashby's rule).[19] The more variety in demand in the form of volume, products, and services, the more variety in response capabilities the system should have. In general, a system should have a response repertoire that is consistent with the variety of forces acting upon it.

The business goal of flexible labor is to retain the company's ability to align human capital with the temporal requirements of the organization, including customer demand, machine running times, and the like. It costs money to be flexible, however. Therefore, flexibility must be introduced in a way that creates value for the organization while preserving employees' enthusiasm for their work. This is easier said than done since flexibility and employee satisfaction often are at odds with the anesthetizing monotony of repetition and efficiency. A dedicated OD practitioner, however, will insert employee satisfaction into the staffing calculus and balance the interests of employees with management and other stakeholders in the design of work.

Organizations add labor flexibility in two broad ways: in numbers or by functional enhancements, appropriately labeled numeric and functional flexibility, respectively.[20] Some typologies make finer discriminations (e.g., differentiate between casual and permanent employees), but these are easily handled by our basic dichotomy. In both instances of numeric and functional flexibility, the goal is to align talent with the business need in a cost-beneficial way to avoid understaffing and impairing performance or overstaffing and adding to costs. Given that goal, sometimes wage–reward flexibility is included in the labor–flexibility bailiwick. Wage flexibility becomes most prominent during recessionary periods when organizations must rapidly adjust to dwindling fortunes. Without making permanent reductions in staff, firms can decrease employees' salaries or furlough employees. We prefer the latter approach. Planned and phased furloughs can be made in a way that maintains sufficient employee counts without visiting undue hardship on employees. In this case, pay is reduced but so are work hours. In contrast, lowering wages may be better than the alternative, but it requires people to do the same work for less. If the change is temporary, we see no likely ill effects. If the practice persists, however, employees will begin to view the practice as exploitative, particularly if executive pay plans keep executives whole.

Regarding numeric flexibility, the numbers of people (full-time equivalent, FTE) can be adjusted by adding time using the existing workforce or by adding people. Adding time frequently involves working hours past the normal thirty-five to forty hours per week. For many employers around the world, this can be an expensive option because eligible employees are entitled to extra pay over their hourly rate for working beyond a set number of hours. In the United States, overtime is defined as hours worked in excess of forty hours during seven consecutive twenty-four-hour periods. Those who meet the legal standards for overtime pay are entitled to a minimum of 50 percent above their computed hourly wage. Companies can pay overtime to anyone, but they must pay overtime to workers who are not exempt from the labor regulations. Thus, overtime is an easy but potentially costly means of introducing flexibility into the workplace.

Overtime has additional costs other than direct monetary ones. The dangers of persistent overtime among workers—whether paid or

BOX 5.2
Death by Overwork

Kenichi Uchino dropped dead at 4:00 am while at work. He was a quality control manager who worked on the production line but also spent many extra hours attending to various duties, routinely working eighty-hour weeks. Mr. Uchino was thirty years old when he died.

Those who support change in the number of hours people work in Japan place the annual death rate due to *Karoshi* (death by overwork) at ten thousand per year. This figure does not count fatalities due to *Karojisatsu* (suicide due to overwork).

unpaid—are well known. Excessively long hours have negative consequences on health, family, well-being, and leisure. These hours do not have to be as onerous as those worked in Japan (see box 5.2) to be physically and psychologically debilitating.[21] Although no magical number of hours exists that delineates the line between "too many" and "just right," our bodies know the difference. Those who work lengthy hours without respite are susceptible to burnout. Burnout is a condition typified by exhaustion and physical distress. Common symptoms include tension, fatigue, depression, confusion, and anger.[22] Additionally, people who experience burnout become more negative toward the organization and find it increasingly difficult to perform effectively, with every objective a tiring, uphill climb.

Although the literature shows that prolonged workdays in succession lead to exhaustion and health risks, the relationship does not always obtain. Specifically, if people like their work, are appropriately rewarded, and have some control over their schedules, the effects of burnout are attenuated. In contrast, when the job demands are strenuous—for example, people are working under severe deadlines, concentration is intense and unrelenting, the work is laborious, and the overtime is unexpectedly mandated—the added hours can take a severe toll on individuals' longer-term ability to perform. The problems of mandatory overtime, for example, are well known in nursing with well-established relationships between overtime and nurse fatigue, practice errors, injuries, adverse patient outcomes, and increased absenteeism and turnover.[23] Although several states are taking actions to restrict mandatory overtime in health care, these results illustrate the general point that poorly planned overtime may complicate the problem the organization is attempting to solve by increasing absenteeism and turnover. As the work time becomes more burdensome and absences and turnover increase, the need for more time ensues until the vicious cycle is broken. This downward spiral highlights the fact that flexibility becomes increasingly difficult to achieve if the workforce is unstable. Therefore, one productive way for a company to become more responsive to environmental instability and uncertainty is to keep absenteeism and turnover at low levels.

An extension of the workday also can be achieved through on-call work. One way to think about on-call work is as conditional overtime: work that is conditional on the need for the employee's services arising after regular hours. Substitute teachers are the prototype of on-call workers, but physicians, IT specialists, midwives, utility workers, and marine and airline pilots also are commonly on-call. People on-call may receive extra compensation, often in the form of a stipend or flat amount. It may look like companies are potentially paying something for nothing, but the human costs of on-call duties are substantial, including sleep disturbances, interference with personal lives, mental health problems, and cardiovascular and gastrointestinal dysfunction.[24] Indeed, many retailers have discontinued the practice altogether, admittedly in response to legal probes that have accused businesses of abusing the practice.[25] These probes followed studies that showed the stranglehold of on-call work on people's lives when the on-call time is lengthy and calls into service are last minute.[26] The law, however, may have saved retailers from an awful business practice as a massive study recently found that last-minute calls reduce productivity in restaurants by more than 4 percent.[27]

Unless an urgent need can be handled remotely, on-call work confines the location of off-duty workers to where they must remain available if called upon. These employees also must restrict their activities to those that will not disrupt their ability to work. Airline pilots on-call, for example, should not drink. The restrictions placed on employees' personal lives coupled with the low-grade anxiety of never knowing when one will be called into work are stressful conditions. Therefore, we advocate the use of on-call time be limited to "sporadic" or "occasional" (e.g., place employees on a rotational on-call roster).

If work routinely extends past normal working hours, one alternative to overtime is the use of part-time employees. In contrast to what is popularly believed, most people work part-time voluntarily.[28] A small percentage of people work part time who are available for *and* want full-time work. Basically, most people who work part time have other obligations they must meet, which makes working a full-time schedule unfeasible—such as tending to an aging parent. At least for those whose part-time work fits their lifestyle, the work is seen as satisfying while, at the same time, adding allocative efficiencies to the workplace. Recent studies with pharmacies and retailers showed that a mix of part-time and full-time employees increases profits—up to a point.[29] That is, profits rise with increased blends of part-time to full-time work until an optimal level is reached before profits plateau and then decline. One explanation for the fall-off in efficiency, productivity, and profits as proportions of part-time employees to full-time employees increase concerns a net decline in the workforce's experience and skill—and in the case of temporary part-time help, such as employees hired during holidays, a potential lack of cumulative commitment to the organization. The lower hourly pay of part-time workers partially reflects this lesser experienced and trained faction (this pay gap between full- and part-time employees is called the "productivity penalty"). These ostensive deficits in the capabilities of part-timers partially can be fixed (part-timers still will not have the same range of on-the-job experiences) by including part-time employees in the full suite of developmental programs that companies offer. Any cost savings derived by excluding part-timers from these programs is offset by declines in employees' productivity and devotion to their work—a feeling that can be further eroded by the common omission of these employees from companies' lucrative benefits programs.

One possible alternative to part-time work is the use of flextime work schedules. Like part-time work, flexible scheduling is a way to fit more hours into a nonstandard workday and, with well-coordinated timing, affords corporations more coverage during periods of heightened demand. Flextime sets the boundaries of the starts and stops of typical days and allows employees to select blocks of time within that framework to work. The day can be scheduled continuously or discontinuously—for example, a person could work early mornings, skip midday, and return to work late afternoons. With appropriate planning, the day can be lengthened through the aggregate time selections of employees and overlaps in personnel can be scheduled during periods when the work needs are greatest. In this regard, flextime is one way to control overtime costs because everyone is working standard, yet overlapping, hours.

Longitudinal studies find that the implementation of flextime increases productivity, particularly when implemented with a focus on aiding employee conflicts with work and home versus for purely instrumental reasons to the company—that is, when there is a mutual benefit to employers and employees.[30] Nonetheless, the positive effects of flextime can be thwarted by cavalier schedule changes that are at cross-purposes with the aims of the program. To be effective, these programs require some give and take among management and staff. For flextime to obtain its almost-too-good-to-be-true benefits, there must be an ample supply of group civility, communication, openness, and trust so that people can work out schedules in ways in which they feel that the benefits and burdens of the arrangement are being distributed fairly over time.

In general, employees like flexible labor arrangements because of their ability to arrange times that fit their work and personal lives. Indeed, an econometric study indicated the flexibility of working from home is worth about 8 percent of a person's salary.[31] The flexibility of tele-work and the kindred concept of ROWE (Results Only Work Environment) allows employees to work when and where (if possible) they want as long as they meet individual and team objectives. Given the exploding use of telecommuting in the Covid-era, however, the practice has become controversial with both ardent detractors as well as enthusiasts. As with many differences of opinion, the benefits of tele-work appear to be realized when there is a modicum of use, rather than at the extremes. The data clearly show that in the right doses, telework is effective. Employees with greater latitude to attend to work and family duties have greater job satisfaction, lower stress, better well-being, and higher morale.[32] Employers also benefit from installing flexible work practices through greater employee engagement and lower absenteeism and turnover.

The right amount of time of working from home appears to be 15–20 hours per week.[33] Too little flexibility and the benefits are lost. Too much time at home creates too much social and professional isolation, derails careers, and contaminates the boundaries between work and home, increasing work-life conflict.[34] Thus, exclusively working from home does not work. Indeed, studies show that employees who work exclusively from home work longer hours (by, in part, repurposing former commuting times), but that extra time does not produce gains in productivity. Rather, that added time is expended on meetings and after-hour texting and emailing.[35] This expanded day may attest to the human inclination to use all the time available: if you have the time, take it, and when you don't, work smarter and waste less time. Thus, a five-year study of 3,000 employees in Iceland revealed that a reduction of 4 to 5 hours per week had no effect on productivity.[36] Wherever and whenever one works, then, one can appreciate the *Economist's* long-time admonition in Bartleby's Law that 80 percent of meetings are a waste of time for 80 percent of the people in attendance.[37] These ravenous gatherings may be a hard habit to break, however, especially for managers who do not know what to do when they cannot see their direct reports who are working from home. Their insecurities and lack of felt purpose and control might be enough to fill the calendars of Zoom-weary remote attendees. Therefore, the quality of management is one of a number of factors (along with other factors such as the state of technology) that can facilitate or undermine the benefit of working from home.

When the workload becomes too great to handle through modest reconfigurations of a workday or prudent increases in time or part-time help, companies often have to add numbers by adding shifts of employees. In our global order, sometimes these shifts can occur in various places in the world so that everyone is working a daytime shift regardless of the time of day for the customers. For service providers that operate customer service centers, this worldwide staffing and *geographic flexibility* offers 24-7 coverage. If additional crew are needed to augment shift workers, companies have two options. They can add facilities and run several day-shifts, or use the same facilities for two or more shifts. The hardy corporate vote goes to the latter alternative.

The extra pay associated with shift work is marginal to the company and readily embedded in the price of the product. A shift differential generally increases employee pay by 7.5 percent to 10 percent per hour (government provisions set these rates for qualifying employees in the United States, but most employers adhere to these rates regardless of eligibility). Nevertheless, companies may incur additional costs in other ways. Shift work results in employee health problems, disruption to their personal lives, and higher risks of on-the-job accidents. For the roughly 20 percent of the people who work outside of standard daytime hours, shifts aggravate sleep, and are associated with weight gain and higher incidences of type 2 diabetes, coronary heart disease, stroke, and cancer.[38]

Studies on shift workers have found that some of the negative effects can be reduced. For example, providing longer breaks, introducing robust wellness programs, and maintaining accommodating ambient conditions, such as good ventilation and proper lighting, can be helpful to overall employee wellness. If the employee is on a rotational schedule, a two-day break before the changeover is made can ease employees' transition into new bodily rhythms.[39] Additionally, because the newest and least skilled employees often are assigned the worst shifts, organizations should provide a training bridge to ease their deployment and make sure that more experienced employees are available for assistance in the early stages of their employment to reduce the frequency of accidents.

Companies also can expand their numbers through external sources, such as temporary agencies, independent contractors, or outsourcers. The use of outsiders to supplement staff often is attended by an implicit or explicit assumption about the workforce: that "core" employees have valuable firm-specific skills and are central to the organization's success, and "peripheral" employees supplement the work of the core through the use of more generic and fungible skillsets.[40]

Temporary help originally served as a shock absorber function with, most often, office workers supplementing the regular permanent staff during upticks in work (see box 5.3).[41] Temporary workers form a cadre of workers known as contingent staff because their work is contingent on the completion of a project or the expiration of a contract. Temporary workers are employed by other host organizations who rent out their employees' time to organizations on an as-needed basis. Nevertheless, if contractually permitted, these temporary jobs may become permanent internal positions when an organizational need for a full-time slot arises and money is available to fund it. In these cases, organizations will have had the chance to observe the performances of temporary workers and to select the best.

An organization also may lop off entire pieces of work, such as payroll, janitorial services, food services, benefits administration, call centers, and even parts of the research and development process, and give the associated responsibilities to others to perform in so-called outsourcing arrangements. Outsourcing broadly applies to the attainment of goods and services from outside parties that could be provided internally. When outsourcing work is given to third parties, companies

BOX 5.3
The Rise of Temporary Agencies: Manpower

Manpower was the first temporary agency. Employment agencies at the time (1948) only supplied permanent workers. When Elmer Winter, a lawyer in private practice who could not type, needed a long brief for the Supreme Court, he and his partner Aaron Schein-feld called on a former secretary who resigned when she had her first baby. The temporary agency Manpower was born. It struggled to expand services trying to convince the model obtained to any discipline in which there were spikes of activities or seasonality, such as retail at Christmas, florists at Easter, or accounting during tax season. Employers at the time were largely wedded to the idea that employees should be permanent, as a moral matter. That changed when paper-based systems needed to be digitized. Northwestern Mutual insurance Company had its documents transferred onto IBM punch cards and stored, requiring a borrowed crew of key punch operators. The industry for temporary help—which expanded to wider use of consultants—was changed.

typically discriminate between activities that are central to its money-making capability and those that are peripheral to it, ceding the peripheral to others and keeping the corporate nucleus of work to themselves.

At times, companies require work from independent contractors that is central to the organization's mission but that constitute skills that companies do not need in the long term or that they will acquire through the transfer of knowledge from the contractors. This arrangement can get a little complicated in two ways, especially for longer-term projects. First, many countries have strict legal definitions for independent contractors. These laws prohibit employers from treating independent contractors like employees. Independent contractors are expected to have multiple client relationships, have their own tools of trade, have other customers, and regulate their own time with the project aims and deadlines in mind. This type of agreement offers advantages and disadvantages. The advantage is that the laws protect independent contractors from abusive practices of organizations that confine and direct workers like employees but that do not pay them benefits. Conversely, well-intentioned employers have run afoul of the rules by trying to incorporate independent contractors too completely into the company's operations and treating people the way one would imagine people would like to be treated—as appreciated allies of the employer's mission. Good intentions aside, to avoid the long arm of the law, the relationship between the company and the contractors must remain at arm's length. The temporal impermanence of the work and the interpersonal distance in its performance mean that organizations can be convivial and accommodating to contractors, but not to the extent and favor that they treat everyone else.

This leads to a second matter. Although independent contractors must be accorded a certain degree of independence, this does mean that they cannot be managed. They were hired for a purpose and, consequently, to receive the full benefits of contractors (at the lower hiring, training, and replacement costs than full-time staff), the relationship with vendors must be competently supervised. The company needs to assign a person to manage the vendor relationship who is at a comparable skill level as the contractors, understands the outcomes to be achieved, and can push the contractors to accomplish things they otherwise might have thought impossible. Furthermore, the project overseer needs to be adept at team-building, be business savvy with the keen ability to understand and enforce contracts, and possess good interpersonal, communication, influence, and problem-solving skills.[42]

The main way to add functionality to a given workforce is to cross-train, or add skills to current members of the workforce. The training frequently is focused on technical know-how, procedural improvements, and different aspects of the operations. Often, too, training is concentrated on equipment used and complementary tasks like computer skills, set-up skills, minor repairs, or basic troubleshooting. These latter skills are critical because they can lower switchover costs: the time and effort it takes for one person to step into a job vacated by another. For example, when you are at the supermarket and you are in line when a cashier change is scheduled, you want the new cashier to plug into the system quickly to get the line moving again. For that to occur, the cashier not only must know how to operate a cash register but also how to establish themselves as a new primary user; efficiency will be further heightened if that same cashier can conduct basic fixes like replacing an uncooperative roll of tape.

Cross-training is closely aligned with process redundancy but it is not quite the same. Redundancy is a way to ensure the robustness, or resilience, of a system: to maintain the functionality of the process despite changes in the environment.[43] Thus, running duplicate systems when converting enterprise technologies or having available backup (e.g., when Elyse is out, William can do it) are ways to ensure that processes remain immune from operational disturbances. Thus, redundancy usually concerns some form of replication across people or systems. Cross-training pertains to the multifunctionality of an individual or to the number of tasks a given worker can perform. The more a person can do, the more flexible they are, and the more options an organization has for deployments. A recent study on utility players in baseball illustrate the point.[44] A capable starting player who is skilled at two or more positions allows managers of those teams to make more flexible lineup selections and provide more options if a player, say, is injured and players need to be moved around. Researchers calculate that this flexibility adds a couple of wins to a team's record per season.

The illustrations in figure 5.2 show different degrees of cross-training.[45] The illustration in figure 5.2(a) is the least flexible arrangement, all else being equal. A certain task must be performed by a given

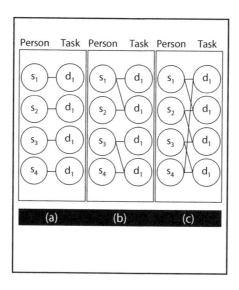

Figure 5.2 Cross-training to meet demand.

individual. Still, even in these restrictive circumstances, organizations have flexible options. First, the burgeoning, often frustrating, use of automation can be used to scale back demand or redirect traffic to more suitable providers. This same automation permits routing flexibility so that if Person A is unavailable for a given task, the activity can get moved to Person X who is trained to perform the same task. If, however, certain tasks can be performed only by certain people (e.g., provide a signature), then it helps if the tasks in figure 5.2(a) can be batched (several forms needed for signature are assembled and presented at the same time to the signatory every week), or if the order of operations as depicted in figure 5.2(b) can be changed (e.g., currently, Person A waits until accounting approves a position for hire before Person B posts the position; however, the logical sequence does not imply that the same operational sequence must be followed—Person A can create the requisition and have it go live once formal approval is given). Processes are structured the way they are for many reasons, but processes in which the order of operations can be changed will be more flexible. And so, too, will processes such as those rudimentarily exhibited in figure 5.2(b). This shows that a given person can accommodate more than one throughput. If Person A can help the caller with say, auto as well as homeowner's insurance, the more flexible the process.

The illustration in figure 5.2(b) shows blocks of people who can respond to different demands. This is a realistic depiction of cross-training in which a person can perform two discrete tasks. However, as the number of learned increases, productivity declines. These diminishing returns are because of increased training times, deficits due to a lack of practice, and forgetting tasks. Thus, productivity erodes as people take on too much.[46] In many instances, organizations use a variation of what is shown in figure 5.2(b) that builds career progression into the process formulation. Thus, figure 5.3(c) depicts a step system of nested skill sets. People are progressively given greater responsibility and move into higher ranking positions as they acquire higher order skills after a certain number of contact hours and training.

Job rotation often is used in conjunction with cross-training. Technically, job rotations have been defined as lateral transfers that do not affect a person's place in the organizational hierarchy or their salary grade.[47] Although job rotations mostly are lateral moves, they do not have to be. They can be up, down, or sideways. Job rotation is implemented for different reasons.[48] The most straightforward and customary reason is to foster employee development. At the same time, it gives organizations a chance to see how employees perform in new, challenging situations. The ease and effectiveness of job rotation depends on the nature of the tasks and the learning or overlap and transferability of skills. Job rotation is a favorite practice of lean manufacturing because operators or technicians acquire a better overview of the production process, which facilitates problem solving and increases flexibility in response to labor shortages and fluctuations in demand.

Another reason to rotate people through jobs is to provide musculoskeletal relief in physically demanding occupations. For example, the cheery-looking strawberry is a low-lying fruit, so pickers hunch when working. It is backbreaking work for about $10.00 per hour, or less. Swanton Berry Farm produces great strawberries. A guiding precept of the farm is the dignity of farm labor. It provides farm workers the best pay scale in the industry with an hourly wage versus piece rate, a medical plan, a retirement plan, vacation pay, and holiday pay. Importantly, they switch workers among crops to keep the work more interesting and to prevent overuse of specific body parts to reduce strain and injury. All of this increases the cost of strawberries; however, studies by agricultural economists conclude, not by much.

Despite the best of plans, people have scheduling conflicts and external events can unpredictably impose pressures on organizations. Organizations must respond in ways that the best of plans cannot accommodate. In these instances, staff improvisation, or schedule patching, comes in handy.[49] Given that the management of schedules often leaves little window between planning and the execution of changes, solutions depend on actions outside of the formal plans. In these instances, researchers have found that the best solutions may be for employees to make up solutions as they go along by plugging scheduling holes opened by personal or work-related needs.[50] Thus, for irregular occurrences in home- or work-life, the voluntary changes made by the employees themselves in instituting impromptu adjustments is frequently the best, and only, course of action.

The issues in this chapter are significant because the labor costs within some industries consume between 50 percent and 80 percent of operating costs. Because of this, staff-planning should be a central concern and activity of OD practitioners. OD spends a great deal of time on organizational design, but forecasting staff needs has not become a stable quill in the OD arrow. Given the primacy of human resource planning to organizational success, determining an ideal number of workers (internal and external) who have the proper compositions of skills and are correctly assigned to jobs should be within the OD arena.

Large-scale workforce planning can be a mathematically intensive affair that may account for some reluctance of practitioners to wade too far into this area. Some planning models require advanced calculus and linear goal programming, The precision these optimization models afford, however, are rarely necessary for estimating staff requirements. Indeed, pure mathematical models often oversimplify real-life conditions and rarely acknowledge the many uncertainties that can infringe on desired organizational outcomes.[51] In this regard, OD shines as practitioners are familiar with the many variables in addition to worker costs that can affect results, such as the timeliness and quality of care or service. These variables include the current organizational structure, the skills and experiences of employees, the availability of the labor pool, turnover, absenteeism, and retirement rates, anticipated leaves of absence, availability and quality of training, regulatory and task-related changes, and more.

These analyses will not answer some questions, such as how much, if any, slack to maintain within a system. That is, should companies maintain a surplus of human resources? Like having excess financial resources, having slack in personnel has been associated with an ability to exploit competitive opportunities, build new capabilities, and innovate, as well as to buffer companies against unexpected threats and disruptions to operations.[52] Our experience on this matter corresponds to the results of a recent study.[53] As might be expected, when organizations are small or in the start-up phase, slack is a luxury ill-afforded. The strategy is set and there is no incentive to experiment. As organizations grow and the numbers of companies' offerings and potential competitors multiply, having slack is advantageous to those companies that have clear, sound long-term objectives and understand the best ways to use their surplus capital. Unfortunately, no definite line exists that demarks where the value of slack ends. Although some slack seems beneficial to organizational development and innovation, there comes a point when too much slack seems to produce idle hands.

CHAPTER SIX

Create Distinctive Spaces

JEREMY BENTHAM DOES not get much coverage in these modern times. Those who have heard of him today know him for one of two reasons. First, his final wishes were to be taxidermized and put on permanent display at the University College London and be wheeled out for parties should his friends miss him. He has sat at the college for the past two hundred years. Second, the idea of an "all-seeing" panopticon occupied his attention for three decades.[1] Bentham imagined a circular, donut-shaped prison with a glass encased guard station in the middle. The outer circular building contained the prison cells that were the thickness of the structure. Windows on the outside of the ring allowed natural light to enter. The inner windows were designed so that guards could see into the cells, but the prisoners could not see out. Therefore, the prisoners would never know if they were being watched. If you think about Apple's new-ish headquarters as a prison with an observation tower in the middle, you would have an idea of the design concept Bentham contemplated (see figure 6.1 for Bentham's conception). As oppressive-sounding as this construction seems, Bentham's idea was far superior to the alternatives at the time.[2] It was never built.

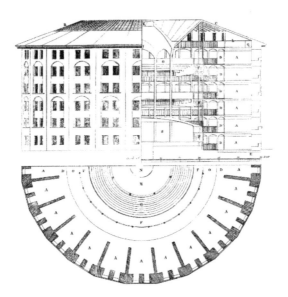

Figure 6.1 The original panopticon design by Jeremy Bentham.

Source: From The Works of Jeremy Bentham, vol. IV, 172–173; public domain, https://commons.wikimedia.org/w/index.php?curid=3130497.

Bentham believed that the concept of the panopticon could be applied in any theater in which surveillance was necessary *to positively affect behavior.* Because people did not know whether they were being watched, they would self-monitor and behave in normative ways. Thus, institutional design could be used to enforce the internalization of values and positively affect behavior change. As it happens, Bentham co-opted the idea for the panopticon from his younger brother, Samuel, who was commissioned by a Russian prince to build a factory. Samuel designed the factory in a circular configuration so that owners could keep an eye on the serfs. In turn, the brother had stolen this idea from a Parisian Military School where the design enabled the masters of the school to surveille the bedchambers of students.[3]

The idea of building supervision into factory design was a prologue to scientific management as the Industrial Revolution advanced. As industry became more mechanized and inputs and outputs more easily quantified, management's desire for precision grew—a desire, we might add, that has not entirely vanished from the 21st century business landscape as evidenced by the intensity of measurement in

Amazon's distribution centers.[4] The workplace became increasingly quota and count focused, and compliance with standards and fulfillment of productivity goals required more intense observations of employees. Furthermore, business owners and management consultants, such as Josiah Wedgewood and Frederick Taylor, recommended austere work environments in which effort was economically focused on the tasks at hand.[5]

Although companies incrementally added productivity enhancements to the workplace, such as job specialization, interchangeable parts, and assembly lines, by the 1920s and 1930s, businesses began to think more expansively about productivity, including the ambient conditions in which work was performed. Thus, the Committee of Industrial Lighting sponsored a series of studies at the Hawthorne plant of the Western Electric Company in Cicero, Illinois. The sensible thesis of the studies was that the physical working condition of illumination would affect worker productivity. Despite the questionable quality of the experiments, the dominant conclusion at the time was that observed productivity gains were attributable to supervisory attention and concern, and not to lighting.[6] In hindsight, it is difficult to disentangle the provision of adequate lighting from a concern for workers. We once consulted to the distribution centers of a major supermarket chain where lighting intensities were reduced to save on costs: Employees interpreted their low-light conditions as a disregard for their welfare. A recent study confirms these employee sentiments: A survey of healthcare professionals across ten hospitals showed that the relationship between the quality of the physical environment and job satisfaction and organizational commitment was mediated by feelings of support—those who believed they worked in better working environments felt more valued by management.[7]

Nevertheless, at the time of Hawthorne, the study results invigorated the burgeoning human relations movement despite what some believe was greater experimenter allegiance to a social cause than empirical fact—allegations that were not just confined to Hawthorne but to other seminal findings of yore when a priori principles seemed to trump observations.[8] The results, however, were sharply inconsistent with intuitions and roundly contradict present-day findings that show that the quality of the work environment affects employee health, well-being, and performance. In fact, estimates of lost productivity because of poor environmental working conditions are as high as $160 billion annually in the United States.[9]

Indeed, it is hard to find studies that do not support the commonsense linkage between the quality of the work environment and employee satisfaction and performance. Even so, organization development (OD) has not, as a discipline, been overly concerned with the physical environment.[10] Although OD practitioners have periodically echoed calls for the physical environment to be included within its content domain aside such mainstays as job characteristics, organizational features, and other entrenched socioemotional factors in the workplace, environmental conditions have remained mostly neglected within OD quarters despite having comparable significance to employee health and satisfaction.[11] The yeoman's work of workplace design has been done by architects, facilities managers, and real estate agents despite the evident implications of the physical environment to motivation and basic human needs—not only for comfort but also psychological needs for autonomy, privacy, aesthetic experiences, and such, making workplace design an imperative for managerial attention.[12] Indeed, companies that can complement their products or places beyond the pedestrian and merely useful through profound experiences will find more loyal followings.[13] Given the factual relations between physical design factors and workplace satisfaction, decision-making, behavior, and health, the remainder of this chapter explores the myriad ways these influences occur.[14]

The basic dimensions of environmental indoor quality include thermal comfort, air quality, lighting, acoustic quality, ergonomic features of furnishings, and the general cleanliness and maintenance of the office/shop floor. The U.S. Leadership in Energy and Environment Design (LEED) system specifically rates indoor environments on several of these dimensions. Studies show that corporate adherence to indoor environmental standards substantially improves labor productivity. One study found that employees in green-certified buildings scored 26.4 percent higher on tests that assessed cognitive functioning across nine domains, including strategic thinking.[15] Although this and other studies on environmentally friendly workplaces have found enormous effects on cognition and labor productivity,[16] we are reluctant to tie all influences to environmental factors. Companies that transform their workplaces into becoming more environmentally hospitable tend to be adept at planning, monitoring, and assessing. Therefore, some of the observed results may be due to the general competencies of the organizations that undertake and succeed at change.

If you reflect on your personal ability to optimally function when features of environmental quality are suboptimal, you will realize what the research results consistently find. Discomfort is heightened and employee satisfaction and performance decline. A prevailing explanation regarding the effects of poor environmental quality on performance is that aversive environments are stressors that tax our bodily systems and redirect attention and cognitive resources away from work tasks.[17] The connection between environmental comfort and stress is more than theory because air, thermal, lighting, crowding, and noise quality have been associated with lower levels of both self-reported and physiological measures of stress.[18] And stress is expensive. By one estimate, workplace stress accounts for a $190 million annual price tag in access costs and 120,000 deaths.[19]

Anything that disturbs working memory and cognitive resources has the potential to disrupt employee performance. Our ability to perform largely concerns our ability to process and retain critical information in working memory. The reservoir of information that we can hold, store, encode, and retrieve for later usage is finite. Therefore, performance will be impaired to the degree that the work environment diverts mental processes away from core tasks. It has been shown that even simple cognitive and perceptual motor tasks are performed more accurately when simple partitions that permit greater focus are erected between workers.[20] Environmental conditions also may reduce people's ability to inhibit their emotions. For example, the temperature-aggression hypothesis has long-standing support in the social sciences that shows that aggression and crime increase with the temperature in both laboratory and in vivo settings.[21] Researchers have offered several different explanations for these effects, but it is plausible that the heat depletes people's reservoirs for self-control and yield the findings observed.

Therefore, the built environment can be thought of as a potential competitor for scarce mental and emotional resources that can either enable or undermine learning and task performance. These environments can be supportive of coping behaviors, personal replenishment, and performance, or they can be nonsupportive.[22] These influences do not have to be conspicuously large and consciously noticeable. Thus, background noise and speech can impair performance even though an employee may not be objectively aware of the sounds. For example, the "irrelevant speech effect" refers to a phenomenon in which memory and meaning making are adversely affected by incoherent or amorphous background sounds.[23] The same results have been found with visible posters and drawings that may imperceptively take up mental space and crowd out more task-relevant matters from working memory.[24] In this regard, studies show that memory retrieval improves when people avert their gaze from their surroundings. Of particular note, even the presence of others in one's immediate work area has been found to redirect attentional focus and impair performance.[25]

The effects of poor working conditions are evidenced by a collection of resulting symptoms known as sick building syndrome. Symptoms include difficulties in concentration, fatigue, irritability, and headaches.[26] Thus, employees prefer window exposures and natural lighting, well-ventilated spaces and fresh air, temperature controls to accommodate personal preferences, and acoustical comfort in which noises, such as voices, echoes, and the clock-clack of office gadgets, are tempered through soundproof paneling, soft furnishings, and satisfying layouts. The fashionable architectural maneuver of removing ceilings to expose piping and concrete slabs amplifies sounds. Therefore, design decisions can have profound effects on performance. A study by Lamb and Kwok found that one environmental stressor reduces performance by 2.4 percent. The addition of a second stressor reduces performance by 5.4 percent and the addition of a third stressor reduces performance by almost 15 percent. Therefore, poor environmental conditions syphon personal resources and employee energy away from work activities and disrupt performance.[27]

In view of these consistent and long-standing findings on the effects of environmental quality on employee performance, it is a little surprising that the open office gained as much traction as it did with some devotees still touting its efficacy. Indeed, even today, with evidence mounting against the functionality of open offices, about two-thirds of the workforce continues to work in areas best described as "open." Surveys routinely reveal that employees do not like open offices and physically and emotionally respond poorly to them. They find them to be visually, socially, and acoustically disruptive.[28] In so many words, a good number of employees also see the open office as a modern-age panopticon where staff sit like wounded animals in an open field subject to the predatory gazes of bosses. Although, as it happens, bosses do not like the situation either, preferring quieter, private spaces to think and reflect.[29]

The basic idea behind open offices seemed good. Work was becoming increasingly interdisciplinary and partitions presented barriers to cross-functional dialogue and collaboration among employees. Therefore, the open office was partly viewed as a remedy to what was ailing organizational quality and efficiency, namely, operational isolation. Furthermore, companies noticed that these benefits could be achieved at lower facility costs. Open versus "closed" (cellular) offices can accommodate the same number of employees at a lower cost per square foot. Thus, the trend in open offices is reflected in the declines in space per employee, from 400 square feet in 1985 to 150 square feet in 2020.[30] This would not be the first time in the history of design that cost savings won out over people's preferences. Following the Second World War, self-anointed visionaries such as Howard Roark, Ayn Rand's hero in the *Fountainhead,* delivered what the British people decidedly did not want: cheap concrete flats versus small homes with gardens.[31] Nonetheless, studies show that architectural cost savings in the workplace may be short-lived, as they are offset over time by deterioration in job satisfaction and employee well-being.[32]

The respectable thesis behind the rise of open offices was prompted by the notion that people who are closer to one another are more likely to talk. This relationship is illustrated by the Allen curve (see figure 6.2), which illustrates that as the distance between workspaces

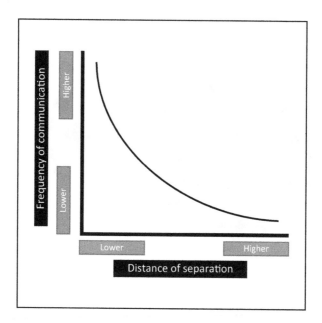

Figure 6.2 Allen curve.

decrease, communications increase.[33] Although this relationship is generally true, this is not the case in the workplace. One study found that open spaces led to a decline in face-to-face interactions by 70 percent as people retreated to private areas for thought-invigorating places of solitude.[34] Indeed, the fear of disturbing others undermines the sociality and communications the open design was supposed to facilitate.

A famous perception psychologist, James Gibson, argued that our environments are as much social constructions as they are physical constructions, and designers must understand both to understand what a place affords or what it will be used for.[35] According to Gibson, we do not perceive qualities per se, but what the situation, or an object, affords. Our observations are contextualized and, like the visual illusion depicted in figure 6.3, what we "see" is influenced by the circumstances in which objects appear. Thus, the proverbial water cooler is a place that affords fresh water to people, but situated in the right space, it also affords a place to convene and talk. Thus, while it is true that proximity breeds communication (and conversely, distance and physical terrain, such as steps, discourage interaction), it does not do

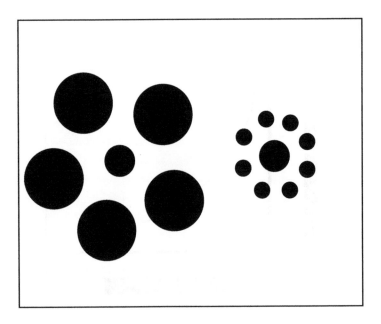

Figure 6.3 Ebbinghaus illusion.

so in a theater, in the library, or in the workplace—because the social meanings in those places forbid it.

Sometimes we do not see what a place might afford. We are sure when people put in water fountains, they were not initially thinking that they would become places like the Okavango Delta where an abundance of African wildlife converge. Once you do know what a space can be used for, it is possible to design for it. Let's say we are executives and we have an open-door policy. An office on the top floor of a forty-four-story building will not afford many impromptu encounters, if that is what we really want. Offices on the ground floor will. The layout and surroundings are communication devices that partially dictate the uses to which a place can be put.[36] And, these uses can be positive or negative. We can understand the precept of broken windows in this way.[37] The broken windows designate which actions are permissible and which are not. The social disorder and lack of oversight and care convey the permissibility of rule-breaking or afford an opportunity for crime. For example, a series of six controlled field experiments showed that graffiti and littering increased the incidents of other counternormative behaviors, such as theft, because the legitimacy of rules in the environment was tenuous.[38] Similarly, messy common rooms increase the incidence of littering by approximately 40 percent compared with neat common rooms. Norms are broken where they already have been broken.[39]

Thus, the implied uses of open spaces for work have not resoundingly facilitated the kinds of conversations organizations had hoped for. Yet, as with most things, there are exceptions. People communicate about many things and one thing that people in proximity share in the workplace is know-how and expertise. Indeed, seating employees next to star performers pulls up those employees' performances, and newcomers who are situated near teammates are quick to assume the work habits of the group, such as meeting deadlines.[40] Employees help each other to evaluate options and solve problems when they arise.

Nevertheless, by and large, not only have open spaces largely failed to achieve their intended objectives but also have interfered with personal well-being and productivity. Open offices are attended by feelings of crowdedness, excessive noise, lack of temperature controls, and, for women, the distracting, omnipresent gaze of men. Many of these negative effects are accentuated when areas for retreat into privacy and quiet are insufficient.[41]

Still, it would be a mistake to dispense with the open office alto-gether. Not every study shows that they impair performance. This is because not every office is a pure example of open or closed. Rather, organizations increasingly use hybrid forms of open and closed spaces. Some of these designs opt for open offices with private retreats, such as meeting rooms and quiet areas scattered throughout the premises for social and business gatherings. Thus, when American Airlines opened their new headquarters, it included more than one thousand private meeting spaces. Additionally, designers continue to sketch in quiet areas such as libraries to provide the solace employees need for deep thought and performance.[42]

Conversely, offices can be designed with personal office areas and various common and specialty spaces. In general, there is an increasing desire for multiuse, multispace environments. Organizational environ-ments now expressly contain different features and layouts for different purposes. For example, the design for Johnson and Johnson's new offices in Bogotá, Colombia, divided space into functional areas, including "open collaborative," "open focus," "privacy areas," and "team dens."[43] After all, we have many different reasons to communicate and some ven-ues are more or less relevant for each. We explain, ask questions, evalu-ate, make proposals, collaborate, and demonstrate, and the physicality of spaces will vary in how well they fulfill communicative aims. Lilly's redesign of their 475,000-square-foot headquarters is another case in point of the transitions occurring in the physical work environment (see box 6.1).[44]

Despite the growth of open, designer workplaces, a strong argu-ment still can be made for the inclusion of personal offices. Indeed, employees' self-reports clearly associate personal space with satisfaction with their environments and frequently select open-space seating as their least preferred option. The reasons behind this satisfaction with personal office space are manifold. First, employees like to personalize their spaces. Surveys reveal that 70 percent to 90 percent of employ-ees want to decorate their spaces with sundry photos, memorabilia, and tchotchkes and this, in turn, fosters a homey feel of psychological comfort and security.[45] Like furnishing our homes, we use our spaces to tell others, and ourselves, who we are and aspire to be. Indeed, some companies encourage this homey feel further by having throw rugs on the floor and hiring retiree couples to make the coffee, bake in the kitchen, and tend to employees' children should they need to be at

BOX 6.1
Lilly Transforms Its Workspace

Lilly had a typical farm cube for its 3,300-member workforce. Surveys showed rampant dissatisfaction with the design because of impediments in informational exchanges, decision making, myriad distractions, and lost productivity. The company reconfigured the space, increasing the amount of shared and temporary space and decreasing the per worker footprint. The new spaces were task specific with quiet rooms for work that requires concentration, cafes and team rooms for collaboration, and small havens for private conversations. The changes resulted in roughly two times the employee satisfaction at half the cost per employee. Better yet, the estimated hours lost because of noise, drop-by visitors, and waiting for feedback and approvals substantially declined.

the workplace.[46] Understandably, then, one controlled study of offices showed that people who were empowered to decorate their offices exhibited higher levels of well-being and commitment to the organization, and were more productive (i.e., time to complete assigned task and number of errors) compared with controls.[47]

Second, an office provides a powerful cue that work is to be done. In contrast to unassigned work areas (e.g., hotel lobby, booth in corporate cafeteria, couch in the game room), a reserved area for work is a powerful signal that work should be done there. For example, one study using virtual reality technology investigated people's attention and concentration on a cognitive performance task when working in a characteristic office environment versus a Tuscan garden.[48] The results showed that those who were engaged in a typical workplace demonstrated greater attentional focus and better concentration. We infer that people who can accomplish more during a day will feel more fulfilled and satisfied with their jobs as well.

Third, people become attached to places to which they have an emotional connection. These connections to place have a name: topophilia—in reference to a situated space, these are places that have personal meaning and social and material significance.[49] Recall Sheldon's ineffable attachment to his favorite spot on the couch in the television series *The Big Bang Theory*. As many theorists have noted, a space becomes a place when it is endowed with value and takes on meaning, and these meanings are produced through a sense of identity and psychological ownership, need fulfillment, social bonds, and feelings of attachment. These are the things that make leaving a place so hard and throwing out the familiar so difficult. A place rests on a framework that we belong, provides the features we need to flourish, and offers safety and security.[50] The more people feel at home—feel that they are in the right place—the more content they will be and the less likely they are to switch brands whether hotel, retailer, restaurant, or place of work. "Atmosphere-dominant" companies realize this. For people to feel rooted, companies have to provide the proper ground.

Companies remain reluctant to invest in private offices, however. Cost is one reason, as we have noted. But this reluctance also stems from other pervasive trends in the workplace such as the increased use of telecommuting—a trend that likely will persist given organizations' increased experiences with remote work during the Covid-19 pandemic. This trend was well underway before the Covid-19 pandemic as the number of telecommuters doubled in the United Kingdom over a ten-year period, according to the U.K. Office for National Statistics, 2018; a survey by the International Workplace Group, 2018, indicated that 70 percent of professionals telecommuted at least one day per week in the United States.[51] The pandemic will permanently enlarge these percentages.

Psychologically, employers' judicious use of telecommuting has been a godsend for employees who have greater flexibility to contend with responsibilities at home and work.[52] Still, as people retreated to their homes during the swell of Covid-19, telecommuting will continue to be a lively topic of discussion. Some major employers such as IBM, Yahoo!, Goldman Sachs, and Bank of America already have voiced their opposition to telecommuting, whereas companies like music-streamer Spotify, financial processor Square, text-messager Twitter, and software tools developer GitLab are 100 percent remote.[53] Indeed, the experiences of many start-ups have been mostly positive with a pure telecommunications existence that relies on collaboration platforms, such as Teams and Zoom; internal communications through Slack or Skype for Business; and workplace apps, such as Notion and Gather.[54] These trends undoubtedly pair with many readers' experiences whose nomadic grown children work for a company, say, headquartered in

London but who are embarked on journeys from Berlin to Hong Kong to Sydney.

The solution for telecommunicating in most establishments will be somewhere between all or none. What we can say with surety is that what makes teams work well online are the same things that make them work well offline: team leadership, quality communications regarding roles and tasks, group cohesion, and interpersonal trust. In that regard, while face-to-face encounters can augment social bonds through common experiences, the technology can reproduce many interpersonal experiences that can promote successful teamwork. For many, the times ahead will be a step back in pre-Industrial history when artists and artisans could craft their goods independently and later would join with others to finish and distribute their merchandise.

Looking ahead, the future likely will be a hybrid that integrates a smaller corporate physical presence with more intensive online interactions. The big question will repeat itself: "To what degree does this hybrid model elevate or blunt performance?" The question is deceptively complex and lacks an easy answer. The literature on the effects of telecommuting on performance finds evidence both for and against the practice. Like most research, the answer is, "It all depends." The answer hinges on the context and frequency of the practice (e.g., current locations of employees), the amount of trust and goodwill among management and employees, and the quality of the telecommuting software. For example, the more communications seem nonmediated by technology and emulate face-to-face encounters, the more effective they are in facilitating discussion, generating ideas, and fostering performance.[55]

The architectural implications of the out-of-office trend is that even when people need a dedicated work space, they need it less than half the time. In fact, about two-thirds of people say they work remotely at least a portion of the time.[56] Therefore, much of corporate seating either has become nonterritorial or buffet style along a table. Some companies have open seating; people are free to sit where they want within a given area and, accordingly, are provided with lockers to store personal possessions. In this "hot seating," we may have come full circle from the cringeworthy, soul-deadening corporate landscape portrayed in the now-classic *Office Space* to the complete dehumanization of the workplace through anonymous seating arrangements. At least, that is the way employees see it. *The Economist* has likened unassigned seating to the cult British TV show, *The Prisoner*, where the protagonist is referenced by number only. In the same article, the writer mentions a study that found that it takes people an average of eighteen minutes to find a seat in the morning.[57] Consequently, people have inched their way to the office at earlier and earlier times to be sure they get their preferred place. Thus, companies that deploy these practices may think these arrangements will lead to more comingling among employees, but in reality, it heightens anxieties, consumes time without producing any greater collegiality, and produces more negative attitudes toward work and the workplace.[58] People like familiarity and routines and will find a spot that best suits them. Your own experiences surely will verify this. When repeat meetings are held, where do people sit? In the same seats they sat in last time, and the time before that. Thus, even in the absence of assigned seating, people will gravitate to those spots that have become "theirs." In an attempt to alleviate the uncertainties and confusion pertaining to hot seats, many companies have begun to regionalize seating arrangements into neighborhoods or teams, at least at specified times of the day. This somewhat reduces the decision space and allows those who need to work together to do so.

In general, whereas the workplace of the past tended to be conceptualized in purely functional ways, it has become increasingly clear that building out spaces with due regard for broader human concerns will produce superior results. These human concerns, or needs, are hierarchically stacked with physical comfort and health at the foundation. Higher-order needs include functional supports that enable jobs to be performed well, followed by psychosocial needs, such as privacy, growth, and creativity, inclusion, and such. A helpful way to think about contemporary workplace design is to conceive of it as part of a complex along with organizational structure, job design, and information flows/technology that, together, attempts to support the needs of people as they execute their duties. That is, the work environment is a fundamental part of a sociotechnical system in which goals are pursued in humane ways. The affective and aesthetic quality of the workplace is as important as the work being done. As such, issues such as time for thinking, innovation, teamwork, collaboration, job rotation, job challenges, and such cannot be divorced from where the work is performed. The "where" is as vital as the "what," "how," and "why."

By most accounts, the physical environment could use some work. Only about one in four employees say they work in an optimal environment. Nevertheless, companies have become more attuned to the potential incapacitating effects of the some-150 musculoskeletal disorders that can afflict people and have responded with specialty shoes, chairs, computer stations, and desks to counteract the debilitating effects of longer-term nerve and muscular injuries resulting from repetitive motions, positioning, lifting, and such through ergonomic interventions and judicious job design.[59] Additionally, health-related interventions have extended well past the ergonomically sensible apparatuses and work designs to include a bevy of health-promotion options. These changes include standing, sit-stand, and walking desks; healthy food choices; health clinics; recreational and workout facilities; health-related instruction; and walking and bicycle paths. They also have infused environments with more "green" options, such as potted plants and living walls, garden cafes, and hydration stations to let the outdoors in. Additionally, companies have become more thoughtful about the build-out of specialized spaces for, say, creative endeavors. Like Edison's Invention Factory, creative spaces such as fab-labs, makerspaces, and living labs are collaborative areas with shared resources and clear and open lines of communication where innovative ideas can flourish.[60] Researchers have compiled a lengthy list of environmental attributes that may contribute to creativity.[61] These typically include spaces for idea generation; whimsical displays and experimentation; interesting patterns, textures, and shapes; a limited stable of soothing colors; ample work space; projections of thoughts through technologies; and favorable environmental factors, such as natural light and materials, fresh air, and clean, cold water.[62] Stimulating environmental features inspire innovative thinking. Indeed, cue-rich, aesthetically pleasing environments have been shown to be sources of inspiration and imaginative thinking. Simply working in a pleasant versus ugly room affects people's energy levels and sense of well-being.[63]

One corporate trend that is refreshingly catching on is the inclusion of nature into architectural design. Renowned biologist E. O. Wilson coined the term biophilia to denote the relationship between people and nature, which he believes to be a natural one.[64] Nature can include the real thing or analogs. Analogs of nature include artworks of landscapes, nature photographs, nature sounds, and nature-themed wallpapers and murals. They also can include simulated environments that denote nature, such as textured floors of natural stone and wooden building materials, biodynamic lighting that mirrors natural light or, as at Google, organically patterned carpet. The real things include plants, water features, gardens, fish tanks, fireplaces/fire pits, courtyards, adjacent parks, and office window views/natural lighting. Expedia built its new-ish Seattle headquarters with the idea of biophilia firmly in mind. For example, sliding glass doors can be opened to create indoor breezeways and the company's forty-acre park-like grounds contain trails that are WiFi-wired for outdoor meetings and training sessions; in fact, employees can work even as the weather cools by nearby fire pits.[65] At Samsung's new headquarters in San Jose, California, every third floor of the ten-floor office building has outdoor spaces. Some terraces are designed for quiet reflection and thought, and some have built-in activities such as putting greens. Similarly, Amazon's main campus has living walls with more than two hundred plant species and its East coast headquarters in the greater Washington DC area will have a neighboring park with local fauna, flowers, and waterfalls.[66]

The value of nature in the workplace was first recognized in the 1950s as part of the German *Bürolandshaft* (office landscaping) movement. In concert with those times, the provision of plants in the workplace primarily was a humanizing force to combat alienating industrial wastelands. Research has proven, however, that exposure to nature has substantial physiological and health-affirming benefits.[67] For example, studies in hospitals showed that patients with window views of nature recover faster and have shorter postoperative stays, and patients in rooms furnished with plants and flowers need fewer postoperative pain killers and have lower physiological markers of stress than those in more starkly furnished rooms.[68] Employees with window exposures to nature experience corresponding positive effects of reduced stress, greater feelings of well-being, and higher productivity.[69]

A two-year longitudinal diary study in Britain found that people who spent two hours or more per week engaged in outdoor activities reported better health and sense of well-being than those who did not.[70] The same results are found with much shorter timelines (e.g., eight weeks).[71] This conforms to other research that indicates that people who take forty-five to fifty-minute walks through nature perform better on creativity and working memory tasks than controls.[72] Thus, companies like bicycle producer and distributor, QBP, have the right idea. They encourage lunchtime walks and walking meetings through the adjacent nature preserve and bicycle meetings on the quiet surrounding streets. Hartig has called these nourishing naturalistic getaways "booster breaks" that lift a person's spirit and vigor.[73] Furthermore, walking together also seems to mitigate interpersonal conflict and to promote interpersonal warmth and rapport, as if conveying through movement the conviction of "moving on" together.[74]

The health advantages of nature have been well-documented to the point that a national hospital system in Scotland now allows doctors to write scripts for outdoor activities as part of a healing regimen. Pediatricians at the University of California, San Francisco, have begun to do the same. Concerned about people's lack of access to nature as a stress reliever and mood enhancer, doctors have begun to prescribe nature walks.[75] Indeed, entire countries are taking up the cause. The South Korean government is establishing meditative healing forests for its highly stressed citizens, and Sweden provides citizens tax incentives for adopting a lifestyle attuned to nature, such as commuting by bike (that lifestyle of living close to nature is called *friluftsliv*). Overall, research consistently finds that employees who have greater contact with nature also experience less stress and stress-related health complaints and have better problem-solving skills, more energy, better attention, enhanced coping skills, greater socioemotional health, and improved productivity,[76] a nexus between nature and design that dates back millennia to the principles of feng shui, literally, *wind* and *water* (see box 6.2)[77] Exposure to nature also elicits greater prosociality in people. For example, people who stood among massively tall Tasmanian blue gem eucalyptus trees versus next to a concrete building were more likely to help an experimentally planted passerby who dropped belongings.[78] In fact, any transcendental or spiritually tinged exposure has similar effects.[79] Imaging studies show that contacts that stimulate experiences of awe have physiological concomitants associated with activity in the parietal cortex. The parietal cortex is the part of the brain that is associated with attention, impulse control, planned and spatial reasoning, sensory processing, and more.[80] This part of the brain also has been associated with greater connectedness between oneself and someone or something outside oneself. That is, it is the part of the brain that tells us we are not alone and that there are matters of greater concern than our immediate personal needs. Nature and spirituality give us an outward focus toward others and on matters of broader concern to a community.

BOX 6.2
Feng Shui

The value of nature to psychic health is more like a rediscovery than newfound awareness. The ancient Chinese concept of feng shui (literally, wind and water) of living in harmony with nature and the invisible vital forces of ch'i has been around for millennia and remains visible on the Hong Kong skyline with buildings with distinctive exteriors designed with feng shui in mind. The practices have a practical origin. Villages were built on south-facing slopes above rivers for increased exposure to sunlight, decreased exposure to wind, increased access to water, and better defenses against invaders. More generally, the practice today underscores the importance of an aesthetically appealing environment that includes prescriptive design elements, such as a balance of colors, natural light, avoidance of sharp corners and long narrow corridors, and uncluttered space.

In that regard, perhaps we should expect companies to elevate our spirits a bit more. On a recent visit to the Music Center in Los Angeles (the home of Los Angeles' performing arts), we sat on the newly designed plaza with pulsating fountains, large interactive screens, and an enthusiastic public—flanked by imposing arts pavilions. The plaza beamed with vitality, and we could not help envying the people who worked there. Despite the drudgery of work that we all must endure from time to time, how could employees not feel uplifted by the place? But that is the point of arts institutions. They want people to be transformed when they enter—that is, to cross over into a new reflective environment. They use the aesthetic to distinguish the interior world from the world outside and invite people in to experience something more intense and enlivening than the everyday.[81] Salesforce has the right idea. Employees pass through a 108-foot high-definition video of rivers, forests, and cascading water as they enter Salesforce's main offices in San Francisco.[82] Through rich visual and metaphorical experiences, organizations hope to disrupt individuals' routine ways of thinking, to energize, to separate from the humdrum, and to urge them to question the customary. We realize this is a lot to ask, but we suggest companies reflect on what it might mean for employees to cross over their thresholds and to step inside, and specifically to find whether their souls are alit or have come to die.

CHAPTER SEVEN

Diversify and Inclusify
the Workforce

THE ISSUE OF diversity frequently is relegated to a small corporate department. Its minute size and unassuming place is disproportionate to diversity's importance and potential impact on a firm. Justly applied, diversity is associated with the improved psychological and physical welfare of members of underrepresented groups and greater job satisfaction for everyone throughout the workforce. Organization-wide, diversity is associated with improved problem-solving ability and creativity, greater cultural sensitivity to products and markets, a larger pool of qualified candidates, and a more flexible and environmentally responsive workforce.[1] In addition to the many business benefits, the pursuit of diversity underscores a corporation's commitment to social justice and principles of equal opportunity. Indeed, we believe that the business-case advantages should not overshadow the moral arguments for more equitable workplaces.

Owing to demographic trends in the United States, organizations awakened to the changing complexion of the workforce and to the emergence of diversity as employment fact several decades ago. The iconic Workforce 2000 report by the Hudson Institute in 1987 was central to a surge of interest in a diverse workplace, mainly because some of the results were falsely interpreted in cataclysmic terms.[2] Many readers erroneously believed that the majority white male work population would be surpassed by minorities and women (or, more generally, *minoritized groups*) by 2000 and that wholesale organizational changes would be required to accommodate the size and rapidity of the change. Although some results were poorly portrayed, in actuality, the study maintained that minorities and women would incrementally constitute a greater proportion of new hires in the future because of baby boomer retirements, globalization and immigration patterns, college graduation rates, and an increasing number of historically underrepresented ethnic groups and women who were opting into the workforce. Women and minorities would constitute an incrementally growing share of the workforce; however, it would be 2045 before they eclipsed white males in absolute numbers.

In many ways, we always have taken diversity as a given in the workplace. We assume diversity's importance whenever a task requires a combination of functional abilities for completion. For example, it takes a village of designers, computer scientists, engineers, and manufacturers to build a car. It takes a team of surgeons, radiologists, anesthesiologists, nurses, and allied professionals to restore people to health.[3] Therefore, we do not question the wisdom of needing different kinds of people who must pool their physical and intellectual assets to solve problems. We may wonder, however, how the hiring of underrepresented groups fulfills those needs.

People of different races, cultures, and genders have different life trajectories and experiences and, as a result, unique worldviews, thoughts, and feelings. Additionally, because of different socialization experiences and different abilities in managing relationships, heterogenous groups have different interaction dynamics in which more questions are asked, more ideas are elicited, and communications are more open. Indeed, one study of boards showed that women influence the oversight effectiveness of boards by improving group processes.[4] These inherited and acquired differences among people with dissimilar backgrounds offer myriad points of view and aptitudes that companies need to be productive. For example, it is hard to fathom how Procter & Gamble could effectively cater to its myriad customers without diverse product teams who have a firsthand understanding of the unique needs of their customers. Indeed, creative enterprise depends on the generation of multiple ideas and novel, nonredundant inputs of diverse populations to promote new pathways of thought. Specifically, the creativity of a team depends on the group's ability to generate new ideas, elaborate on information, build on one another's thoughts, and constructively piece together data into well-formulated solutions.[5] Consequently, companies that embrace diversity are more likely to enhance firm value through, for example, innovations such as the number of patents per research and development (R&D) dollar spent.[6] If the Darwinian principle of divergence is correct, diverse systems also are more likely to develop an ecological division of labor by which enterprising agents adapt to find and fill niches to exploit. Thus, we can imagine the agents of a diverse enterprise recognizing the untapped voids in markets.[7]

Many studies demonstrate the efficacy of diversity to organizational governance, risk management, innovation, and growth. For example, boards of directors have been shown to operate more effectively when they have a greater representation of women. A long-term study by Credit Suisse of companies with market capitalizations over $10 billion found that boards with at least one female director outperformed companies without female representation by 26 percent (in stock returns) and averaged higher-net-income growth and smaller debt-to-equity ratios.[8] Several other studies show similar results with more diverse boards associated with higher quality earnings, less volatile stock returns, and greater market values.[9] For example, a 2016 survey by researchers at the Peterson Institute found that increasing female representation on boards and in senior management from none to 30 percent was associated with increases in profits by 15 percent.[10] Furthermore, evidence suggests that the reported effects are causal. A longitudinal study of the French CAC40 found that companies with greater gender diversity on their boards had directionally higher returns on equity.[11] Research further supports the fundamental idea of diversity as the contributory mechanism for heightened organizational value by demonstrating that women add a unique skillset to boards. Kim and Starks examined the breadth of knowledge of board members on such factors as financial acumen, international experience, and operational and technological knowledge. They found that the more heterogenous the board, the wider the distribution of knowledge.[12] In turn, these more expansive views contribute to a richer understanding of stakeholders and offer a keener perspective on business areas that might otherwise be overlooked.[13]

Greater representation of women on boards also yields important side benefits. Companies with more women on boards have more women officers in senior management positions, line positions, and among the higher paid; have a more positive outlook on corporate social responsibility and community affairs; activate more CEO resignations following extended periods of poor performance and organizational decline; moderate risk-taking as evidenced by lower variability in total stock returns; improve customer satisfaction; and temper executive compensation.[14] The effects of diverse boards ripple throughout organizations. Companies with more diverse boards implement more unique employee-friendly work-life programs that increase employee satisfaction.[15]

The same pattern of results for boards applies to diverse management teams. (The results of a typical study are shown in box 7.1.)[16] More heterogenous management teams repeatedly have been shown to relate to better firm performance. For example, one study found that management teams with greater heterogeneity in educational, functional, industry, and organizational backgrounds were more sensitive to changing consumer needs and more adept at producing beneficial suites of market-responsive goods.[17] The same study indicated that organizations with more diverse top management teams had

---

BOX 7.1
Illustrative Study and Results

A sample of 318 organizations was selected based on company size, region, and age, and racial and gender compositions were determined for each using the national organizations survey. The following table shows the relationship between racial and gender diversity and sales revenues.

Racial/ Gender Mixes	Racial Diversity			Gender Diversity		
	Low	Med	High	Low	Med	High
Sales (in Millions)	52	324	809	45	303	640

A similar pattern of results was obtained for number of customers, market share and profitability.

higher firm performance as measured through a simplified formulation of Tobin's Q (the ratio of the market value of the firm to total assets).[18] Similar effects are seen in teams more generally.[19] Mixed, heterogenous gender teams in business simulations generated higher sales and profits than male dominated teams and performed better over a three-year period.[20] Analyses of R&D teams found that teams with more diverse blends of tenures were more productive; specifically, they had higher proportions of sales that came from products and services that were new to the market and new to the company. Research on venture capital firms found that 10 percent increases in women in firms resulted in 1.5 percent increases in fund returns and more than 10 percent increases in profitable investment exits.[21] And, more diverse teams of traders make more precise valuations of commodities.[22]

Diversity, then, has significant consequences for organizational effectiveness. Indeed, diversity is the great stabilizer in dynamic systems, which include organizations, as well as ecosystems, the brain, and cities—any system from microbes on up.[23] To use an example supplied by Page, imagine that in a world of no diversity everyone has found an optimal solution to a problem: metaphorically, everyone is standing on a mountain peak. Next, suppose the plates of the earth move and the peak now is a smaller crest on the side of a higher mountain. The world has passed by the once-best solution and stranded the nondiverse population in a suboptimal place. In a diverse world, not everyone would have been standing on the peak so that after the tectonic movement some people would now be standing on the higher ground. Therefore, diversity allows the system to adapt—to resiliently counter abrupt changes in the environment—as well as to retain equilibrium by not creating all-or-none scenarios.[24] A more illustrative metaphor of the calamitous effects of homogeneity involves a boat tilting to waves at sea. To correct the tilt, a homogenous crew simultaneously run from one side of the boat to the other, overcorrecting the boat's pitch in the opposite direction. This oscillating pattern grows more extreme until the boat capsizes. A heterogenous crew would have prevented disaster by recurrently sending only a few members back and forth across the deck to achieve a more steady state.

These examples illustrate one of the key advantages of diversity: it enables more reliable systems by delivering more consistent levels of performance over time through manifold functional capabilities. A large

portfolio of functional abilities and strategies buffers organizations—
and organisms—against sudden disruptive environmental changes,
providing groups with a natural form of insurance. This ability is what
makes organizations resilient.[25] Diverse systems are more resistant to
disturbances—rocked less by environmental shocks—and more rapidly return to an equilibrium following upheaval.[26] With more severe
disturbances, communities may completely reorganize in response,
creating in the vernacular of ecology, a regime shift in which the organization significantly departs from its baseline condition.[27] Several
years ago when malware attacked the Symbian operating system on
cell phones, the damage was negligible because each phone manufacturer installed slightly different versions of the operating system—
creating a diverse repellant to widespread infection.[28] The same principle applies to internal systems in which diversity mitigates losses from
attacks. The loss-dampening effects of diversity are well-known and
ubiquitously applied in industries such as avionics, nuclear power, and
telecommunications.

Companies, like environmental ecosystems, require large numbers of
different agents to enhance system reliability (defined as the ability of
a system to maintain a consistent level of performance over time) and
resilience (defined as an ability to absorb change and disturbance while
maintaining operational normality).[29] Actions speak for themselves in
recognition of these principles. We diversify our investment portfolios
to even out returns, eat a variety of foods for balanced nutrition, and
encourage a range of economic investments within geographic regions
to produce more stable and recessionary-proof industrial infrastruc-
tures.[30] Survival counts on diversity. Pastoral societies in East Africa
rely on the judicious use of mobility and herd diversity as the means
to combat fluctuations in environmental conditions. Livestock are
moved according to temporal and spatial weather patterns of rainfall
and forage. Herders also travel with a wide variety of livestock that
includes camels, cattle, goats, and sheep. These functionally diverse
herbivores are productive under different environmental circumstance.
For example, if drought impairs cattle fecundity, camels may continue to produce milk.[31] Similarly, the recent documentary film, *The
Biggest Little Farm*, describes how two hundred acres of dead land
are revitalized into a thriving farm through the agricultural ethos of
biodiversity. For example, the farm went from a dilapidated mono-
crop operation to a thriving farm with ten thousand orchard trees

encompassing seventy-five different kinds of stone fruit, lemons, and avocados. According to the farm's owner, problems persist, but the system they created responds faster to infestations and epidemics and is more resilient in the face of climate change, with less soil erosion, an ability to store more groundwater, and higher levels of carbon in the soil than a typical farm.

Nevertheless, even with the increased emphases on, and benefits of, affirmative action and its conceptually less affecting sequel, diversity, progress in diversifying the workplace has been halting.[32] In fact, many companies have made little progress despite bold assurances for change. For example, Silicon Valley's attempt at change was mostly unsuccessful.[33] Without having first embraced a culture of tolerance for individual differences, and achieved a respectable critical mass from underrepresented groups, these companies run afoul of the Red Queen Effect: running faster and faster to just remain where they are. In the absence of progressive talent acquisition strategies with targeted outreach to women and other underrepresented groups, the potential pool of candidates may never reach a quorum that can sustain multiple minoritized hires. In fact, without Herculean efforts, organizations are unlikely to make any headway in diversifying (i.e., it will not happen organically).[34] At the very least, customary methods of hiring must be supplemented by what one study on federal contractors called "screening capital" that consists of harnessing referral networks; building strong relationships with intermediary organizations, such as schools, associations, and employment agencies; developing fair, unbiased testing methods; and implementing formal selection methods.[35]

As a matter of course, companies should periodically assess the diversity of their recruitment and applicant pools and remain attuned to any insidious biases that may intrude on the hiring processes. For example, the wording of job postings or descriptions of companies may subtlety discourage, or encourage, certain applicants over others. An advertisement for a sale's position that highlights a highly competitive, aggressive work environment where the fittest survive will be sure to turn off some applicants, and others on. Many companies also make wide use of employee referral programs because they are cost-effective recruitment devices that yield high-caliber employees who are better qualified, more satisfied, and less likely to quit than applicants from other sources.[36] However, employees are most likely to recommend people they know and like for employment. People tend to like others who are just like them. Indeed, one of the most robust findings in the social sciences is that we like people who have similar physical attributes, interests, values, attitudes, personalities, and hobbies. Thus begins a vicious circle of sameness in which companies hire then attract then hire certain kinds of people. For the underrepresented, getting ahead often means tapping into white male networks. One study conducted over a fifteen-year period showed that women who access the so-called boy's network exponentially increase their chance of serving on a board. For example, a women's probability of serving on a board increases by 116 percent in large companies if she plays golf.[37]

This propensity to lure like-minded and relatively similar people has conformist downsides that easily are avoided by selecting people on the right cultural dimensions. Broadly, these include a shared appreciation of the company's mission; common values on how people are to work together and individually; and, a mutual understanding of how risks are assessed and decisions get made.[38] Nevertheless, the power of similarity is strong and the inclination to like and be attracted to others who are similar to us is one of the most robust relationships within the psychological literature.[39] Research has shown this relationship is fortified in stressful or uncertain circumstances, which is an outcome that may hasten companies' self-destruction by increasing homogeneity when under duress. When people are faced with seemingly intransigent problems and high stress levels, they prefer to surround themselves with others who are similar for comfort and confirmation.[40] Specifically, the desire to be with like others intensifies when people are uncertain about themselves, their place within the social strata, or the right thing to do. As one study in banking showed, troubled companies tended to reduce the diversity of their boards and recruit for domain expertise. The result was to accelerate their demise by circumscribing their assessments of the environment and the array of options they entertained.[41] Related research demonstrates a similar penchant for troubled organizations to narrow information flows. Troubled organizations more heavily filter information through increased centralization, thereby depriving themselves of more wide-ranging perspectives on the environment. Discourse becomes increasingly constricted and behavior increasingly lemming-like. Additional evidence in cognition suggests that greater homogeneity within groups promotes cognitive laziness or, conversely, people in heterogeneous groups think harder than people in homogeneous groups. In contrast to similarly composed groups, members of heterogenous groups expect differences of opinion and, consequently, are more engaged and effortful participants. For example, more diverse six-person juries more accurately recall case-relevant information and more astutely apply case facts in deliberations.[42]

If diversity is to become reality in organizations, one thing for certain must occur: we must end discriminatory practices. That is, to increase organizational roles of underrepresented populations, companies have to inaugurate fair hiring, selection, and promotion practices and eliminate discriminatory barriers that keep capable people out of the organization or confined to areas in the workplace where advancement opportunities are limited. In an era in which we are acutely aware of the problems of discrimination and seemingly enlightened, it is tempting to believe that these problems have been largely solved. Far from it. The news furnishes a regular supply of companies that have been tagged by accusations for sexism, harassment, and bro cultures; the game developer, Blizzard, being one of the most recent.[43]

The literature on bias in hiring and promotions is voluminous and continues to demonstrate discrimination with eye-popping clarity with significant adverse physical and psychological effects on those victimized.[44]

Despite the many thousands of articles in this area, we can highlight a few key, recurring findings aided by the wonderful synopses provided by Katherine Phillips at the Columbia Business School and a recent review by Hebl and colleagues.[45] While we focus our comments on gender and race, much of what we say in these areas equally apply to sexual orientation, religion, age, disability, and weight.

Men and whites are selected over women and minorities despite having identical backgrounds and qualifications. A typical study involves showing decision makers two identical resumes, save for the names that imply the gender or race of the applicants. Racial and gender stereotypes intervene, and people infer attributes not contained on the piece of paper. If a member from an underrepresented class is invited for an interview, they are less likely to get a call-back because they are wearing a hijab; assumed to have a contrary sexual orientation; or are unattractive, an ethnic minority, or of an age of a "maybe baby" that is viewed as a potential inconvenience to the employer. Two recent studies highlight the size of the problem. The first example comes from a working paper in which the authors mailed out 83,000 job applications to 108 companies.[46] Pairs of applications were matched on background and credentials; only the names were changed to denote race. The corporate response rate for blacks was approximately 10 percent to 20 percent lower than for whites. Another study of recruitment platforms found similar results. Controlling for jobseeker characteristics, call back rates were 4 percent to 19 percent lower for candidates with immigrant and minority ethnic groups. Women received 7 percent fewer responses but only for positions/professions dominated by men.[47]

The same stereotypes that type-cast entire classes of people according to overgeneralized beliefs about the group's personality, preferences, or abilities are used to block the entry of women and minorities into higher level positions because of a presumed absence of position-specific attributes. Thus, women, for example, are overlooked for leadership jobs because they ostensibly lack the agentic qualities such as emotional toughness that is required.[48] These affronts are easily justified by the lower performance reviews women receive than men, mostly owing to the ascription of unnerving personality traits, such as being too judgmental. Should women ascend the organizational heights, they often are assigned fewer flattering roles on teams. Women, for example, often are nominated to be the team clerk and scribe because of their superior organizational skills.[49]

Also, men are given greater credit for successful outcomes than women, and women are given greater blame for unsuccessful outcomes than men.[50] Thus, women and minorities have to be more qualified than men to be considered for select positions and promotions. The latter, well-documented *double standard* states that more evidence is required to establish the competence of people within underrepresented groups and to establish the incompetence of white males. A substantial body of research shows the persistence of these effects: the standards that women and members of minoritized or underrepresented groups must meet are higher than those of white men.[51] Therefore, even as more and more minorities and women have entered the workplace, career progress has been limited. These closures to advancement have been allegorically depicted as glass ceilings, glass cliffs, concrete walls, glass slippers, and sticky floors. (Box 7.2 summarizes these; for research on the falsity of the Queen Bee Effect.[52]) These metaphors symbolize real barriers that regard women and minorities as less capable and less deserving or as foils to others' personal ambitions.

BOX 7.2
Ceilings, Walls, and Floors

Glass Cliff: A phenomenon in which women versus men are placed in precarious, high-risk situations where the likelihood of failure is high

Glass Ceiling: Describes the barriers that underrepresented groups face as they try to climb the organizational hierarchy, and the limits to career ascendency

Bamboo Ceiling: While Asian Americans are perceived as excellent workers, they are less likely to be promoted into management roles

Glass Slipper: A job has to fit the perceived social identity of the aspirant—a princess has to be selfless, kind-hearted, and beautiful

Glass Chains: Women (typically) are subdued by religious prescription or strong cultural/ familial norms

Sticky Floor: Typically, low-wage, low-mobility work that is believed to be well-suited for certain kinds of people

Snow-Woman Effect: Accumulation of snubs, passed over opportunities, and family obligations that marginalize contributions and curtail career progress

Queen Bee: The idea that powerful women present the greatest barriers to other women's advancement (a theory that appears to have been debunked by studies that show women are tremendously supportive of other women)

Source: Hyun J. Leadership principles for capitalizing on culturally diverse teams: The bamboo ceiling revisited. *Leader to Leader* 2012; 2012(64): 14–9; Arvate PR, Galilea GW, Todescat I. The queen bee: A myth? The effect of top-level female leadership on subordinate females. *Leadership Quarterly* 2018; 29(5): 533–48.

And, then, many women and minorities must experience indignities in the workplace that most males and whites do not in the form of harassment and everyday microaggressions.[53] The latter are insulting and invalidating putdowns that take many forms from impolitic gestures to outright dismissiveness. These microaggressions often have innocent intent and sometimes are disguised as compliments ("For a minority, you are really smart"; "What's a pretty thing like you doing working in a place like this?"), but they all communicate hostile, derogatory, or negative slights and insults, and have the large reverberating impact of conveying secondary status to others.[54] The *New York Times* in a jarring expose recently discussed the plight of Black doctors who patients often assumed entered their rooms to empty the trash.[55] Similarly, a black, female physician who went to the aid of a distressed passenger on an airline was asked to show her credentials.[56] Regardless of the speaker's motives, the cutting meanings of microaggressions are not lost on those to whom the comments are directed. Invariably, the comments isolate people and foster distrust among groups. Unless pardoned, they have a corrosive effect on organizations and teams. We were in a team meeting that included one Black woman when, as a one-off remark, a voice over the conference speaker maintained that minorities have an easier time getting hired into the organization because of lower hurdles. What was pronounced as "fact," was interpreted as "dismissiveness" and "disrespect."

Research has afforded some insights into how discriminatory decisions can be curtailed. For one, underscoring the importance of selection decisions and a person's accountability for making the best decisions can reduce bias. Instituting accountability practices, such as affirmative action plans, diversity committees, diversity metrics in performance reviews and incentive plans, and visible diversity-related staff positions, get results.[57] These practices translate into companies that have, for example, more diverse management teams. More generally, accountability for diversity initiatives increases diverse representation by 10 percent.

Mentorship programs have proven particularly effective in bolstering diversity. In combination with other diversity-enhancing approaches, assigning influential mentors facilitates retention and upward mobility among underrepresented groups.[58] In contrast, not having a mentor interferes with career progress and professional notoriety. First-time women and minority board members are provided with less mentoring from incumbent members regarding normative practices and, as a result, receive fewer invitations to participate on other boards. This may account for the fact that although women and minority representation on boards has been rising, women and minorities seldom are asked to participate on more than one board: only 8 percent of women and 5 percent of minorities do. Consequently, these underrepresented members will not enter the pantheon of the corporate elite, which requires participation on more than one board.[59]

Additionally, better processes and better trained reviewers contribute to less prejudicial selection choices. One well-supported means to combat bias is through highly structured recruitment and selection procedures.[60] These entail careful articulation of job content and selection criteria, and the establishment of valid and reliable methods for reducing the applicant pool to a chosen one. The more impressionistic the procedures, the more bias that intrudes on the decisions made. In that regard, the more noise that can be removed from the hiring processes, the better. For example, filtering out irrelevant sociodemographic information from resumes, and blinding reviews and tryouts to specific identities improves selection accuracy.[61] The classic case of blind reviews occurred when the Boston Symphony Orchestra decided to hold blind auditions for musicians to eliminate, mostly, gender discrimination. Biased judgments continued until the floor leading to performance pit was carpeted and reviewers could no longer hear gendered footsteps.[62]

In general, the more accountable people feel for the correctness of the results, the more difficult the task, and the more they are aware of how mistaken attributions can subvert the process, the more deliberate and proactive people become and less likely they are to be thrown off by distractors. Specifically, people learn to think slow versus fast. Slow thinking is under cognitive control: it is effortful, deliberate, and selective. Fast thinking is involuntarily, automatic, inflexible, and subject to biases.[63] You may be familiar with the Stroop task in which subjects are shown words of colors printed in different colors. They are asked to recite the color of the word. Difficulties arise when, for example, "brown" is printed in red. In these instances, people will make errors particularly early in the task. If, however, they know about the possible incongruencies in advance, they can instantiate more active controls to minimize the interference and the errors. In essence, people are able to redirect their attention toward goal-relevant information and away from irrelevant information.[64] The anticipation of possible irrelevant information allows people to gain greater supervisory control over information intake, selectively guiding their focus to the most pertinent task-related data.

Business alone cannot remedy all of society's deepest ills nor do they erect all the barriers. Some are thrust upon workers by society, upbringing, and nature.[65] For example, women do the lion's share of work of childcare, medical appointments, shopping, cleaning, and cooking—and are financially penalized for it.[66] As the population ages, no relief appears in sight as women now assume a greater role in the care of their aging parents. The Covid-19 pandemic has introduced even more house-bound duties that women again disproportionately assume. The uneven responsibilities between men and women take a cumulative toll in costly layers of career derailers: the spiraling collection of career stoppers has been referred to as the "Snow-Woman Effect" (see box 7.2).[67]

"Personal choice" is a flip answer to the unequal allocation of duties within households as these choices come with significant economic and personal costs. One major survey showed that not only do women have to be more qualified than men to get a directorship, for example, the additional responsibility is associated with higher divorce rates.[68] Policies in the United States provide no relief. Stated bluntly, family-related policies are pathetically antediluvian. Universal childcare is expensive. The United States devotes the smallest percentage of its gross domestic product (GDP) to childcare of any industrial nation. Overall, the United States expends just 1.6 percent of GDP on family benefits, which places it well below the mean of all member countries of the Organization for Economic Co-operation and Development. Additionally, of 15 industrial economies studied, the United States is the only country that does not require paid maternity leave and is but one of only two without paid paternity leave. Some leaves in the industrial world are six months or longer and are paid at a rate of 70–100 percent of current salary for an average range of fourteen to twenty weeks. The Family and Medical Leave Act in the United States requires that employers provide twelve weeks of unpaid parental leave and reserve the individual's position until the parent returns to work, but the act applies only to businesses with more than fifty employees, and employees must have worked 1,250 hours during the prior year (about twenty-five hours per week) to be eligible. Consequently, only about 50 percent of workers qualify, and getting those meager provisions through the U.S. Congress took many years of partisan tussles. Apart from the law, a recent exposé in the *New York Times* discusses the surreal obstacles pregnant women face in the workplace and their treatment as "lepers" versus people giving life.

Overall, the evidence amply shows that complicit cultures, implicit biases, a lack of powerful role models and mentors, inadequate access to training opportunities and resources, and select menial assignments play significant obstructionist roles to the progress of women and minorities in organizations.

Generating more diversity in the workplace is one obstacle to overcome. Trying to fully leverage the value of diversity is quite another. For each of the positive outcomes of diversity we discussed previously, there is an opposing finding. Many studies on diversity have produced null to negative effects. Surveys reveal that although many companies value diversity, men and women continue to have different experiences. Many women continue to feel marginalized in high-profile positions: as not credible and a lesser equal among peers. Indeed, in general, the contributions of women and minorities are devalued on teams on which the supposition is made that the placement was due to diversity versus merit. People of color and women, in these circumstances, are undervalued: they are viewed as less competent and their contributions to the group are minimized.

Specifically, the benefits that can be derived from diversity depend on several factors. First, the benefits of diversity only are realized in certain circumstances. Diversity does its best work in cases in which problems and tasks are complex, and a wider berth of knowledge and viewpoints are instrumental to task fulfillment. When a task is straightforward, a variety of input is unnecessary. In fact, lively discourse on a simple problem may slow down the process and encumber it with frustrating useless details. Therefore, the additive effects of complementary skills and abilities are greatest where, in fact, they would do the most good: when tasks are complicated and require frequent interactions and exchanges over prolonged periods.[69]

Second, although diversity is a concept whose meaning we broadly understand, the definition of diversity is murky. That makes it hard to say when an organization has it (diversity), or not. Diversity applies to a wide range of characteristics that may not be of equivalent organizational value to the tasks at hand. Additionally, groups may differ on the range of attributes possessed by group members and the amount of overlap or separation among members on relevant attributes.[70] Thus, you can introduce diversity without improving your chances for success if you have not mixed the right ingredients of capabilities in the right proportions. In addition, many of the conventional measures of diversity insufficiently capture the nuances of the construct and changes over time.[71] (See box 7.3 for one of the most common measures of diversity, the Blau Index.[72]) Does adding one woman to a

---

BOX 7.3
Blau Index

The Blau index is one of the most frequently used measures of diversity.
$B = 1 - \Sigma P_g^2 \times 100$, where g is the number of groups and P is the proportion of members within each group; for example, two of ten board members are women: $(1 - (.2^2 + .8^2) \times 100 = 32$.

Diversity can change through addition, substitution, or subtraction.
Addition: Adding a woman, B becomes 40
Substitution: Replacing a man with woman, B becomes 42
Subtraction: Removing a woman, B becomes 20

---

board make the board diverse? How many additions of disparate types of people make a group diverse? The answers are complicated as they seem to be, "It depends." Indeed, given the differential statuses and perspectives of "majority" and "minority" groups, each has different ideas about where the line between diverse and nondiverse lies.[73]

The answer to what makes an organization diverse has practical implications. Too little representation presents concerns of tokenism or of representation-based concerns that women and minorities will be evaluated through the lens of their ethnicity or gender.[74] Consequently, members of minoritized groups often feel scrutinized by others and unduly pressure themselves to prove their mettle. Whereas increasing numbers may be a necessary part of the solution, this alone is not sufficient.[75] Sufficiency requires that the addition of people who are unalike in many respects are able to work productively together.

This raises a third barrier to attaining the advantages of diversity. Although diversity introduces desirable variability, it also can introduce undesirable conflict among people that impairs team performance. Such differences can lead to distrust among members that disrupts constructive communications and teamwork. Therefore, the very thing that presents opportunities also can interfere with group cohesion and decision making.[76] As a consequence, a group may become locked into dysfunctional conflict and never realize its inherent potential.

Thus, diversity in groups may create factions and interpersonal frictions called "faultlines," those impenetrable boundaries that people are forbidden to cross. Said succinctly, diversity does not do much good if people, say, of different races do not get along and are unaccepting of one another's advice or assistance. It is fair say that in instances in which the inclusion part of diversity is absent, as in "diversity and inclusion," the introduction of diversity does much more harm than good because the group is negatively affected by higher levels of interpersonal warfare. Unfortunately, the idea of inclusion often is treated as the proverbial stepchild that comes along with something more important. Yet, without it, trust is impaired and relationships falter.[77] Whereas diversity expresses a value system that prizes differences, inclusifying (to use the word originated by Stefanie Johnson in her 2020 book, *Inclusify: The Power of Uniqueness and Belonging to Build Innovative Teams*) provides the vital lubricants of mutual acceptance and feelings of worth that make diversity work. For example, a study of 224 R&D teams from twenty-nine companies found that the diversity within these groups yielded productivity gains only when the internal networks were dense—that is, when the groups had formed strong working relationships.[78]

As neatly illustrated by the Romans (box 7.4), inclusionary practices are not new and may contribute to the preservation or dissolution of

---

BOX 7.4
Inclusion in the Roman and Persian Empires

Observers of history have argued that the continuity of the Roman Empire and the relatively short duration of the Persian Empire owe to differences regarding the inclusiveness of the two cultures. For Rome, inclusion was largely achieved through military service where it was natural to inculcate Roman values and learn a common language. The life-or-death service also necessitated high levels of interdependence among the soldiers, which engendered trust among diverse parties. Most importantly, military service provided a path to citizenship for non-Romans with the rights and privileges it entailed. States-persons, including emperors, could come from anywhere within the Empire: emperors came not only from Rome but also from Spain, Africa, and the Balkans. In contrast, the peoples the Persians conquered were never admitted entry as participants into Persian society; their allegiance was secured in exchange for economic and political stability afforded as a protectorate of the Empire.

empires.[79] In the industrial business era, the need for inclusion stretches back to the early twentieth century. Cummings Engines, founded in a garage in 1919 in Columbus, Indiana, adopted the financial founder's sense of community and social responsibility. Despite not making a profit for nineteen years, the company decided to remain open and keep people employed. In the 1940s, a grandnephew of the family founders remained true to the family's vison of social justice when choosing to hire Black Americans and women and desegregate the factory lines. Cummins was a company ahead of its time in promoting racial integration well before the civil rights movement and a national consensus had been reached on the issue. Since they first desegregated factory lines in the 1940s, the company has consistently appealed to its organizational history and identity to reinforce its values and support a culture of diversity.[80]

During the turbulent 1960s in the United States, major employers such as Polaroid, Connecticut General Life Insurance, Exxon, and AT&T looked for ways to reduce conflict caused by new hiring mandates and the rising diversification of the workplace. And it was not just corporations that saw the need to forge closer team ties. Communities, schools, and government agencies all saw the need to stich new seams in a fabric that was rapidly changing and coming apart. They reached out to the organization development (OD) community for help with team integration. For OD, it was a homecoming of sorts. The need to build group solidarity resuscitated practitioners' longstanding interest in interpersonal trust, tolerance, and social justice.[81] Often overlooked in OD texts is that many of the seminal OD practitioners of this period were women, such as Billie Alban and Edith Seashore.[82]

These OD practitioners quickly discovered what seems to have been oft forgotten today. Building trust in groups in which members are suspicious about one another's character and abilities takes time. The goals of integrating groups, reducing biases and discriminatory behaviors, valuing differences, creating mutual perspective and understanding, and promoting a diversity climate focused on fairness and equality are long-term holistic initiatives that require the weight of the entire organization for success. It became clear that the occasional intervention designed to bring people together will fail miserably without cultural preparation and postintervention persistence.[83] In this regard, we all can be humbled by expedient, but superficial, attempts to bring people together that have been unsuccessful. Unfortunately, much of the meaningful change efforts of the past has disadvantageously morphed into a ravenous $8 billion diversity training industry with a focus on consciousness raising, legalisms, and compliance that produce short-term changes in beliefs but little to no longer-term changes in behavior.[84] Producing a greater appreciation of the legal and organizational issues at stake has its place, however, changing behaviors requires more intensive and abiding interventions. Indeed, analyses indicate that sporadic, fact-based training has little to no effect on key outcome measures of reducing prejudice and discrimination, facilitating constructive intergroup relations, and enabling better utilization of team skills and abilities. In general, traditional trainings in organizations tend to be short-lived, ineffective, or counterproductive (e.g., elicit backlash effects). To be effective, trainings must be ongoing and coupled with other organizational initiatives, such as mentoring.[85] A recent article in *Nature* also shows that changing attitudes about diversity may evoke more inclusive behaviors. In conditions in which prodiversity attitudes were viewed as normative, members of marginalized groups had an increased sense of belonging, reported more inclusive treatment by others, and performed better.[86] Although most measures of inclusivity follow the example in this paper and depend on subjective reports, inclusivity may be tracked and measured through network analyses. Through email exchanges and other tangible interactions, it is possible to graphically depict members who are central within networks and to identify who lies on the periphery.

In many respects, we do not need to invoke the ideas of diversity and inclusion to recognize the value of acceptance for our mental health and ability to perform. Belonging is one of our most basic human needs regardless of the mix of people. Wherever we are and whoever we are with, we want to feel essential, influential, and welcomed into the life of the community. Diversity simply makes those possibilities more difficult by presenting a more challenging starting point from which to bring people closer together. As a beginning, however, we can make it easier on ourselves by considering the different ways in which groups can be diverse. For example, faultlines are more severe when within-group attributes are strong and between-group attributes are weak. In the parlance of statistics, community building is easier if

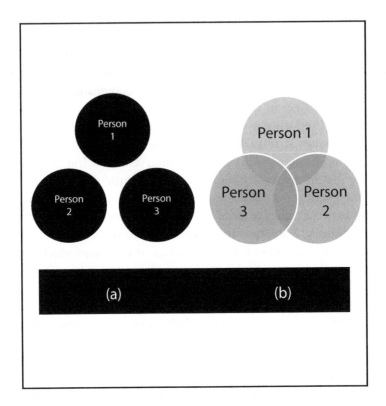

Figure 7.1 Two forms of diversity.

not all the variance is unique—that is, if groups have some variance in common. The diagrams in figure 7.1 show two groups of three people each. Both groups are equally diverse. In figure 7.1(a), however, the groups are more dissimilar than they are alike, and in Figure 7.1(b), they are about as dissimilar as they are alike. In the latter case, perhaps members of the disparate groups went to the same schools, have similar interests and hobbies, hold similar organizational positions, or at one time worked for the same CEO. They are different but connected. The connections blur the faultlines that can be more or less salient, or activated.[87] The less salient the delineation among people, the easier it will be to promote teamwork.

Diversity is a group attribute, not an individual attribute. As such, consciously or not, group differences become organizationally meaningful when they hold the potential to divide the group according to those perceived differences. For example, boards that were highly differentiated among factors such as age, gender, years on the board, number of boards, and so forth, were associated with lower firm performance: the separation among subgroups was too great to bridge.[88]

From its earliest days, OD has concentrated efforts on building the capabilities of groups to elicit the full participation of members and collective use of their skills. These tactics include the creation of shared goals, emphases on common outcomes, frequent interactions, and group reflection on their processes and effectiveness; these are the traditional OD methods that date to the 1940s, if not earlier. As guardians of social justice in organizations, it seems fitting that much of OD practitioners' efforts have been to bring those who are different together.

CHAPTER EIGHT

Promote Personal Growth

MOST COMPANIES SURELY would agree that having employees who are more capable is preferable to having employees who are less capable. Overall, better people produce better results. Beyond that self-evident fact, companies must make a range of decisions regarding the specific capabilities they wish to engender in their workforces, and the best ways to engender them.

But let's take a step back before discussing the ways in which organizations promote employee growth. Many companies are not as concerned with developing their people as finding them. Conditions in several industrial countries converge to make the pool of eligible candidates slim. First, during periods of economic expansion, labor markets become extremely tight. Indeed, it was during the booming internet economy of the late 1990s that McKinsey declared the war for talent.[1] In these giddy days, there were too few people to go around. Competitive advantage could be won by those companies that were able to produce generous pipelines of job candidates and pools of choice talent. Second, education systems in some nations have not been graduating enough people with the prerequisite foundational skills for employment (i.e., reading, writing, listening, oral communications, and math skills) nor are they producing sufficient numbers of people who have degrees in the STEM (i.e., science, technology, engineering, mathematics) disciplines for which the emerging needs are great and are accelerating. Third, people of working age are declining in many industrial countries. Figure 8.1 shows the expected near-term attrition of employees from the workforce as they reach retirement age.[2] Fourth, people have been dropping out of the labor force at an alarming rate: at least in the United States. The labor participation rate of working-age men and women is the lowest it has been in over four decades, with technological innovations and trade responsible for a portion of the decline.[3] Given the falling birth rates within the industrialized world, the prospects are dim that the numbers of people entering the workforce will replenish those who are departing.[4] These influences, taken together, will continue to produce unsettling sociocultural consequences in some countries. The countries' options will be to bring more people into the labor market who formally have

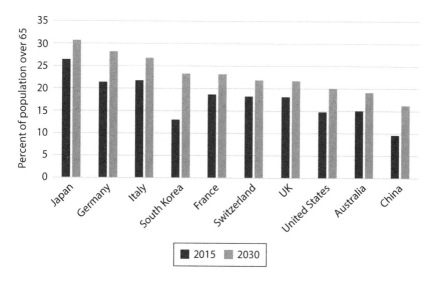

Figure 8.1 The developed world will, on average, get 5.5 years older over the next 15 years.

Source: Data from O'Connor S. World will have 13 'super-aged' nations by 2020. *Financial Times*. August 6, 2014.

been excluded (e.g., women); loosen immigration requirements, visa quotas, and guest-worker policies; or shift more work oversees and imperil a nation's capacity to make and build.

Some companies will find it much easier than others to secure the talent they need because they will have created cultures and programs that fit the needs of the people they target for employment. These employers will have fashioned a robust brand to attract qualified candidates and will have backed their promises by delivering on the experiences that employees expect. Companies that clearly publicize who they are through the business press and other public statements and documents, such as annual reports, recruitment materials, and companies' jobs websites, and allow candidates to peer inside their walls through career fairs, internships, company tours, and such, minimize the risk employees take when choosing employers by revealing things about themselves that otherwise would be hard to detect. Thus, unambiguous messages about the company's espoused values, products and services, and financial status and outlook provide the facts on which employees can base their decisions.

As it happens, one area of special concern to employees in making job choices is their anticipated career prospects and the learning and training opportunities that are available.[5] In this regard, the news is pretty good. The training and development dollars invested by companies has nearly doubled from 2012 to 2017, evolving into a $100 billion industry.[6] The average training expenditure per corporate learner was approximately $1,000 in 2017. Many studies document the effectiveness of these training dollars on specific outcomes (e.g., safety, individual performance).[7] Studies also have found that increased spending on employee development increases productivity, product innovations, and other aggregate measures of corporate performance.[8] Although some research is numerically precise in showing the influences of training on company productivity, this research is complicated and the size of the effects will vary from company to company and industry to industry.[9] The evidence, however, demonstrably reveals the benefits to training, which, as expected, reinforces the commonsense thesis that knowledge and information are central factors to competitive advantage. Thus, despite the difficulties in conducting research of this type and wagering conclusive quantitative statements, the research routinely finds that enhancements to organizations' human capital (and its parent concept, intellectual capital) have positive effects on operating performance.[10] Indeed, what is true for companies is equally true for nations. Human capital variously defined as the quality of schooling, learning, and health accounts for approximately 20 to 50 percent of the income dispersions among countries.

With the emerging Information Age and waning years of the Industrial Revolution, intangible assets are replacing physical assets as choice sources of organizational performance and value. Chief among these nonphysical assets is intellectual capital. The measure of intellectual capital is contentious, but the consensus is that intellectual capital is a composite of human, relational, and structural capital, where—

- Human Capital = knowledge, skills, experience, capabilities, education, and attitudes
- Relational Capital = social relations among employees and the extensive connections between various stakeholder groups (management and the board; management and customers) that make up collaboration networks
- Structural Capital = the informational and procedural infrastructure composed of knowledge management systems, corporate culture, policies and processes, and the physical work environment

Unfortunately, no critique-free, agreed-upon measure has emerged, although a couple of measures account for a large body of the research studies. The most common measures have been Tobin's Q and value-added intellectual capital, although literally a hundred measures have been proposed.[11] Because it is hard to assess the net benefits of everything a company does to foster the growth of its people, human resources frequently defines its contributions to intellectual capital through the outcomes achieved by the compendium of programs it installs to promote employee growth from recruitment to retirement. Therefore, effectiveness is gleaned by the programmatic results obtained from the talent acquisition through talent development phases, such as time to start (time to fill a position), offer acceptance rates, training participation rates, referral program success (jobs filled through referral), and absenteeism (average days absent per employee). If the company is able to function effectively and each program evaluated on its own merits appears to be doing what it is supposed to do, then it is assumed that the company must be doing many of the right things with respect to the workforce.

A viable talent management program is one in which a company has a well-identified pool of external job candidates, enough competent coverage of existing positions should the company experience unexpected losses in personnel, and short- and long-term succession plans throughout the organization. These staffing initiatives are accompanied by vigorous career counseling and development (discourse on an employees' longer range goals and an attendant action plan), career planning workshops and vocational assessments, mentoring and coaching programs, and the availability of in-house training and financial assistance (e.g., tuition reimbursement) to support employees' career objectives.[12] A catalogue of some of the common training and development options is provided in box 8.1.[13] Many of these approaches are enhanced by new delivery methods, such as distance learning, blended learning, and social media (e.g., discussion forums, virtual/augmented reality).

Having a thoughtful intersection of human resource programs is important to ensure that organizations have adequate pipelines and reservoirs of capable people who are ready to step into new roles or jobs when the time is right, but talent management also involves the

---

BOX 8.1
Types and Methods of Training

- Assessment Center
- Case Study
- Games-Based Training
- Internship
- Job Rotation
- Job Shadowing
- Lecture
- Mentoring/Apprenticeship
- Programmed Instruction
- Role-Modeling
- Role-Play
- Simulation
- Stimulus-Based Training (e.g., work of art)
- Team Training

panoply of decisions that have to be made about jobs and people. Because programs can be copied, the decisions that companies make within the talent space can set them apart from others. That is, while people-related programs can be emulated, the decisions surrounding the means and quality with which people are developed and deployed cannot.

Broadly speaking, the decisions organizations make about development cluster in four areas. First, should programs and practices be differentially applied to particular jobs or people? For example, Instructure—a leading developer of learning platforms—is primarily a software engineering company. All job candidates at Instructure go through the same rigorous hiring process except the selection criteria for engineers is exceptionally high. A much smaller percentage of engineering applicants ultimately gets selected compared with the rest of the employee population. Because the talent management philosophy has identified these positions as mission critical, the organization uses more stringent standards when selecting people into these positions. Or, assume that certain people in the organization display a high level of precociousness. Do you expedite their growth or enforce a standard developmental sequence that admits people into programs or advances them into certain positions only after a specified amount of time has passed? No prepackaged solutions exist to these questions. Companies distinguish themselves partly on the basis of the answers they provide to these and related matters.

A second cluster of issues concerns the definition of a career and how it is organizationally assembled. Do you conceive of a career as narrow or broad and, if broad, how might you modify your programs to accommodate this more expansive view than heretofore has been the case in corporations? Careers once were almost exclusively narrowly defined along clear pathways. Employee advancement involved plodding along that path with periodic exposures to developmental opportunities that would allow employees to take their next steps. In the extreme case, this progression was the laborious lifelong climb of the Organization Man.[14] Although this avenue certainly remains prevalent, even here employers have enlarged employee options by creating dual career ladders: one ladder that accommodates upward movement in supervisory duties and breadth of responsibilities, and the other that accommodates greater depth of knowledge and intensification of duties within a specialized role. Overall, employers and employees recognize the inherent career limitations of restricted opportunities and the advantages of a more far-reaching view on careers. Most notably, a wider career berth gives employees more numerous and challenging work opportunities and relieves them of the breathtaking finality of a lost opportunity. Instead, should employees lose out on one job, they are aware that alternatives exist and will come along in due time. As such, corporate career paths, indeed, have become less linear, more abundant, and more lattice shaped, allowing employees to cross career bridges that once were viewed as prohibitively dubious job moves.

The changing nature of work foretold the coming of multidimensional careers. Careers increasingly have become more transdisciplinary because work has become more cerebral and the competencies required for success have become more transferable across jobs. For many jobs, the decisive factors for proficient execution involve general qualities, such as analytical abilities, problem-solving skills, and interpersonal acumen. Therefore, employees can readily move around the organization in situations in which the acquisition of domain knowledge is not a major limiting factor.

These changes in the way careers are defined and managed have necessitated new human resource practices. For example, to aid atypical redeployments, Edmunds started an experimental internal internship program. When positions temporarily open through leaves of absences, say, employees with the requisite baseline aptitudes and interests may apply for these positions. This is like the use of internal job postings for internal candidates, but with more provisional consequences from the perspective of both employers and employees: a failsafe of temporariness should things not work out as planned. The internship program at Edmunds is part of a larger suite of programs that work in concert to continuously upgrade the abilities of the workforce and to ensure that the work people do is consistent with their passions. This network of programs begins with biannual conversations in which employees reflect on their accomplishments and look ahead toward those activities they would like to do more of if they could do anything in the company.

Other companies encourage intercompany moves by allowing job shadowing (observing the work of others in a natural setting) and holding internal job fairs and seminars to promote the work and projects taking place in different parts of the organization. Even in circumstances in which movement up or across areas is unachievable, however, organizations have "in-job" promotions that recognize targeted enhancements to employees' skills and abilities. Promotions are based on fulfillment of personalized development plans that are grounded on achieving certain skill levels and successfully carrying out specific tasks and activities.

The third set of decisions that talent managers make concerns replacements when positions become vacant. Posed as a question, "Who is the best fit for the open position and most likely to succeed in the job?" The answer may not be a person from inside the company because the essential skills are not resident, or the organization is looking for a new perspective on a facet of operations. For example, when Big Ass Fans decided they wanted new insight on testing and quality assurance, they imported talent from the automotive industry.

Even though 65 percent of organizations believe that leadership development and succession planning are their highest human capital priorities, the problem with succession management is that few companies say they have a formal program (about 33 percent). Of those, only about a quarter extend the program below the first one or two layers of management and into nonmanagerial positions. If these percentages are close to correct, it would be safe to say that most companies give scant forethought to succession. Instead, the organizational focus tends to be on replacement planning (finding bodies) versus identifying the right internal (or external) job candidates and expending the necessary effort to develop them.

Succession planning is, by definition, a developmental program. The purpose of these programs is to identify the best people for more advanced positions, nurture their progress, and then provide the support they need to succeed in their new roles. In making these momentous decisions, a lot can go wrong. An errant placement can have significant negative effects on the organizational climate and performance. Incompetent, uncivil, or absentee management will undermine the best organizational ideals and goals. Conversely, if done well, the benefits of succession are significant. Succession ensures smooth business continuity, demonstrates good governance practices to third parties, cultivates improved organizational capabilities, and promotes interorganizational cooperation.

The preparatory work needed for employee advancement in management roles varies from company to company, but the general aim typically is to deepen technical skills, broaden operational exposure, refine leadership abilities, and provide new guided challenges. This process frequently is accompanied by pedagogical instruction in the following: analytical skills; strategic thinking; decision-making; critical/creative thinking; collaboration and teamwork; social skills; and special instruction on dealing with the media, government agencies and regulatory bodies, analysts, customers, and employees. Box 8.2 summarizes developmental options for leaders and future leaders.

BOX 8.2
Grooming Successors

Special Assignments

Stretch Assignments
Exposure to Different Organizational Roles, Jobs, and Assignments
Opportunity to Start, Grow, or Transform a Business
International Assignments

Opportunities for Real-Time Feedback

On-the-Job Coaching
Participation in High-Level Meetings
Job Shadowing

Leadership Roles

Service on Nonprofit Boards
Task-Force Leadership
Involvement in Industry and Professional Groups
Volunteer Community Service

Instruction

Formal Leadership Programs
Self-Study
Coursework and Workshops
Specialized Training or Educational Programs

The fourth set of development-related questions pertains to the significant task of deciding what to train people on. Given scarce dollars, in what areas are training expenses most productively applied? In addition to applied job skills, development generally involves the following: communication skills, such as listening and giving feedback; group effectiveness skills, such as negotiation and teamwork; personal management skills, such as goal-setting; adaptation skills, such as problem solving and creative thinking; and influence and planning skills, such as leadership and project management.[15] For the most part, the training that is conducted is initiated based on requests from the workforce, formal needs analyses, legal or regulatory mandates, or obvious necessity. Most training has the clear rationale of being job-focused or is designed to maintain a safe and secure work environment that is free of accidents, federal violations, hackers, and managerial miscreants. Additionally, if development pertains to advancing employees' ability to perform to their potential, then the intersection between what happens inside and outside of work cannot be ignored.

The domains of home and work intersect and mutually affect one another. Indeed, life satisfaction (the combined effects of work and home life) is associated with greater career satisfaction, job performance, and organizational commitment. Therefore, one atypical, yet important, area that merits trainers' attention is the vast arena that makes life, overall, more satisfying.[16] It would be hard to argue that one had a successful career if half a life was diminished in that pursuit. Thus, researchers in the area prefer to speak about "whole careers" that encompass engagement with nonwork areas of life and attainment of personal goals.[17] This more well-rounded and wholesome career outlook that encapsulates all areas of life makes life more satisfying and work more engaging.[18]

Caring for the whole person matters, first, because good organizations prefer their employees to live authentic, holistic lives rather than compartmentalizing behaviors according to whether they are at work or at home. Indeed, it is what employees tell us they want for themselves. Life is more satisfying when people feel at home with who they are.[19] Therefore, good companies look for ways to incorporate the distinct aptitudes of employee skills into the fabric of the company. For example, one company we have worked with holds an annual developmental soiree. Unlike other developmental events throughout the year that are heavily focused on work-related skills, this one gives employees the opportunity to instruct on a range of subjects (e.g., learning to sail, cheese tasting, smoothie making, hip hop). Employees told us how much they appreciate the chance to share aspects of themselves with colleagues through this instruction, claiming "This is a place where I can be myself."

Second, a holistic perspective on development makes sense because people who have richer work lives fare better at home, and those with richer home lives fare better at work—with both domains working in unison to produce more gratifying lives.[20] Most people cannot escape the inevitability that work and nonwork time are interwoven. Studies routinely find that overall satisfaction with life is a good predictor of engagement in the workplace. Furthermore, life satisfaction seems to be the antecedent to positive work behaviors and not the other way around. Although these effects clearly are bidirectional, evidence suggests that in a chicken-and-egg scenario, it is life satisfaction that comes first.[21] Developmental interventions, therefore, that increase life satisfaction, increase job satisfaction (which increases life satisfaction, and so on). That is, life satisfaction leads to more positive work attitudes and behaviors, with the reverse true to a lesser extent. Because of these results, we are proponents of measuring employees' life satisfaction to glean insight into what companies might do differently or better— rather than concentrating attitude surveys solely on work programs.

Third, asking people to view themselves as whole people may prevent insular bottom-line thinking. Despite a modernist expansion of the institutional framework of industry from stockholder to stakeholder, the primary purpose of business is to make money. This fact would be easily confirmed if we sent a team of anthropologists into our minisocieties of for-profit organizations with the task to dissemble the values of these cultures. Would you be surprised to learn that money makes these places tick? The researchers would emerge with a neat list of the number of meetings, email exchanges, reports, presentations, and conversations whose central themes were financial results. Other topics inevitably would arise, but they would pale in frequency and intensity to discussions of profitability.

So? It seems perfectly sensible that humankind devised institutions to facilitate the manufacture and trade of goods for societal benefit and that people inside companies should have sensibilities to the profit motives of those institutions and of the business role employees are asked to adopt. We might applaud a person who is adept at making money as a fine businessperson, but the institutional value system of which they are a part may be hazardously narrow. Indeed, the corporate ontology of profit and loss is a precursor to bottom-line thinking. This mode of thinking creates tunnel vision in which financial performance overwhelms other concerns that a rounder role and self-conception may deter. The one-dimensional thinking of profit maximization has been associated with myriad ills, including social undermining, decreases in interpersonal helping, and outright deceits. In general, activating thoughts of money heightens self-interest and reduces feeling of interpersonal trust, empathy, and cooperation.[22] It is like a game of whack a mole during which attention is concentrated before your eyes and you lose sight of what is happening all around you. Just hit as many moles in the head as you can and you will be rewarded. Thus, the mantra at Wells Fargo that "eight [accounts] is great" may have been attention grabbing, but it had consequences such as those found in research studies. People cheat to make their numbers, willingly piling on products to unsuspecting customers.[23]

Therefore, some of the growth opportunities that companies sponsor enable employees to live healthier, richer, complete lives. The most direct and common means to happily reconcile employees' home and work lives is to help them to manage the host of obligations they have at home and work through an assortment of programs. These include support programs, such as flexible work arrangements and part-time work, child- and elder-care assistance, parenting resources, employee health and wellness programs, favorable family leave policies, and other family-oriented supports, such as on-site dry-cleaning and postal services.[24] Research shows that these programs are effective in easing employee stress and enhancing organizational commitment when the company encourages the use of the programs without penalizing employees for that use—for example, allowing employees to actually take a full vacation totally disconnected from work.[25]

A less apparent though equally important means by which companies support growth of the whole person is by devoting portions of their training budgets to offerings related to general life skills. For example, BambooHR offers a nine-week course in financial acumen, called Financial Peace University, that includes budgeting, building up emergency funds, and dealing with debt. FONA International sponsors programs in estate and financial planning, mental health (First Aid USA), and personal guidance through a spiritual lens (Corporate

Chaplains of America). N2 Publishing conducts regular lunch and learns structured around three themes: financial security, relational and physical health, and professional development. On the sprawling SAS campus, employees can access grief, eldercare, depression, financial, and divorce counseling through a Work-Life Center staffed with social workers. In general, skills that generalize across different spheres of life improve overall well-being and life satisfaction. For example, teaching employees coping and problem-solving skills at work leads to higher life satisfaction, presumably because these are skills that are useful in any domain, not just at work. Employers have told us over the years how instruction at work saved their marriages, made them better parents, and made them more fiscally responsible.

Among the several different theories about how work and nonwork interact, most note that the two domains are inseparable—although some people may resort to mental gymnastics as a mechanism for coping with an imperfect situation. For example, unable to find satisfaction in one domain, a person may elevate the importance and significance of another.[26] Perhaps an individual who feels confined to a job that is just a job will look to hobbies and interests outside of work to find happiness: life begins when they spin through the corporate turnstiles and out of the building. Few people, however, would find this an ideal outcome when the alternative could be satisfaction at work and at home. In general, positive events in one sphere uplift the other. Material, affective, and instrumental resources are usable across domains, with those acquired in one domain nourishing the other. Thus, money, skills, friendships and close relations, and psychological support transcend boundaries and lead to more fully functioning people wherever they may be.[27]

That said, the most notable way organizations expect people to improve is in job-related ways by honing expertise. For organizations to increase their capacity to perform and stay at the forefront of the market, they must keep people moving from novices to experts on those elements of the job that are critical to performance excellence. Expertise pertains to the acquisition of specialized skills through training and experience in a domain. It is evidenced by increased sophistication in a discipline, complex problem-solving, and improved task performance—attended by high situational alacrity and refined sensibilities to standards and approaches that guide decisions about what has to be done and the best way to proceed.[28] Like Sherlock Holmes, the expert sees things and makes connections that an untrained eye does not notice and has the breadth of knowledge to understand the implications of the evidence before them.[29] Succinctly, experts know more, recognize meaningful patterns and connections, and are quick to distill complicated problems to workable solutions. The work of the expert as opposed to a nonexpert is efficient, precise, and fast, occurring with fluidity as if the task was under unconscious control. Like experts in other domains, experts in business fields are more facile in structuring or organizing their knowledge than nonexperts as well as more adept at noticing what is most important within the business landscape and linking that information to other data of relevance.

The means by which this metamorphosis from novice to expert occurs lays on a theoretical continuum anchored by two extremes, one that entails a natural evolution and one that entails effort. One anchor is symbolized by Sir Francis Galton and the other anchor by John Watson. Galton studied the family trees of eminent artists and professionals, such as scientists, and found that achievements ran in families and, thus, attributed excellence to natural abilities. John Watson, one of the fathers of Behaviorism, claimed that under the right controlled environmental conditions, he could make an expert of anyone regardless of their native talents. With the proper contingencies and level of practice, a person could become a star performer. The theory—nature or nurture—we implicitly embrace makes a difference since one, the Watson approach, assumes that anything is achievable through conscientious practice and diligence, whereas the Galton approach assumes that people are naturally endowed and that one's gifts will blossom in due time with experience.[30]

The way people think about the development of talent or its more specific offspring, expertise, has practical implications for organizations.[31] People who see personal growth as something that they and others can affect through their efforts have so-called growth mindsets. The assumption is that people can make significant strides in their performance through training and deliberate practice: practice that is goal-directed, effortful, and concentrated on specific facets of performance.[32] In contrast, if most of performance can be explained by genetic proclivities, what people can do is largely fixed. Accordingly, people with this worldview on development have fixed mindsets. With this perspective, the job of the talent manager is one of keen selection, functioning more as a talent scout than as a developer.

The difference between growth and fixed mindsets is nicely high-lighted in an intriguing set of studies. Heslin and associates have shown that managers with fixed versus growth mindsets hold more unshake-able views of employees' performances.[33] For example, in one study, the research team first assessed managers' beliefs about people's abili-ties (fixed or growth tendencies). They then asked these managers to watch a video of a poor employee performance and to rate the perfor-mance. In a later video, they watched the same hypothetical employee perform well, and asked managers once again to evaluate the per-formance. The performance ratings of managers with fixed mindsets did not significantly change from their first assessments. Conversely, the ratings of managers with growth mindsets evaluatively tracked the actual performances depicted.

Managers with fixed mindsets form opinions regarding the abilities of employees and they ascribe fluctuations in employees' performances to influences that are external to the person, such as luck—because the person is presumed incapable of changing through personal will and tenacity. Within an attributional framework, people with fixed mindsets see variations in performance as fleeting chance occurrences that temporarily depart from their preconceptions.[34] In the vernacular of attribution theory, people with fixed mindsets may be hardened, error-prone attributionists who see the actions of others as due to internal factors, such as dispositions and abilities (*fundamental attri-tion error*), but excuse themselves when things go awry by viewing their own behaviors in the context of external factors, such as insuf-ficient resources (*actor-observer differences*).[35] Performance improve-ments, therefore, do not create cause for celebration because the results are believed to be aberrational departures from a set point. The result is that we quickly give up on poor performers who ostensibly are beyond help. Conversely, people with a growth mindset believe that their capabilities, including creativity, are malleable and can be improved given the right environment and the right opportunities and challenges. Additionally, those who embrace a growth (versus fixed) mindset are more able to learn from their mistakes, are more accept-ing of feedback, and tenaciously persevere toward goals.[36] Fortunately, studies—mainly conducted in schools—have found that mindsets can be altered. Students who believe their poor performances are due to uncorrectable defects can have their belief systems retuned. Brief interventions that reduce the negative effort beliefs of students (the belief that having to work hard implies lack of ability) and fixed trait attributions (that one does not have what it takes) that inhibit students capacity to perform result in increased academic achievement.[37]

Since the publication of Malcolm Gladwell's book *Outliers*, we have encountered more and more people who falsely think they can master anything with ten thousand hours of practice (or in ten years).[38] In truth, as encouraging and optimistic as this viewpoint is, people have limits. Even if we overlooked the fact that expertise applies to a wide range of tasks and activities that take different amounts of time to perfect, some people will become experts more quickly than others—the prodigies—and some will never become experts—the very experienced average.[39] For example, more intelligent people (a largely acquired attribute) benefit more from the same amount of practice than less intelligent people on certain tasks, such as chess play.[40] Companies often conflate experience with expertise when in fact the former is a necessary but insufficient condition for the latter—that is, some people, despite lengthy experiences in a field, never develop past mediocrity. In fact, studies show that deliberate practice (i.e., really good practice) accounts for only about one-third of performance and, for some tasks, accounts for almost nothing.[41] Obviously, then, becoming an expert and proficient in a field requires more than practice. What else is involved in the development of talent, then?

One obvious factor is anatomy. Physical features and body composition are important for many physical endeavors and motor-perceptual activities. These are inherited qualities and constitute a large part of the reason that artists, sports figures, and entertainers run in families. People are not going to be basketball stars at five-feet tall or great pianists with short stubby fingers. Second, expertise (and job performance) is highly correlated with cognitive abilities and personality that, again, are largely formed in the womb and are diagnostic of individuals' vocational interests and the disciplines in which they choose to become experts. That is, native attributes are starter kits for what people tend to enjoy and eventually will be good at doing if they are fortunate enough to locate exactly what that is—their calling, so to speak. For example, people who score highly on verbal abilities on standardized tests tend to dominate the arts and humanities and those who score highly on mathematical abilities tend to dominate the physical sciences.[42]

Getting the match between employees' interests and work is critical, then, as people will perform better in fields that are more consistent with their inherent aptitudes and passions.[43] The entire idea
behind vocational and career testing is to help people find a line of
work in which they will excel because of their interests and the related
capacities they most enjoy developing and using (see box 8.3).[44]
Companies help employees channel their energies to where they will
be most effective by clarifying and guiding employees in considering
their future career selves, asking, for example, "What were you doing
when you felt most engaged and alive?" "If you could do anything at
all, what would it be?" "What types of activities or jobs do you foresee
yourself doing that would allow you to use what you enjoy most?"[45]

BOX 8.3
John Holland's Career Types

Relating employee interests to occupations has a lengthy history in
industry, particularly as it relates to career counseling and job placement. Inventories designed to identify employees' (or students')
preferences for certain types of work date to the early twentieth century. One common measurement that many companies as well as
segments of the U.S. military rely on is Holland's six-factor scale to
assess the type of work people enjoy performing. This scale, abbreviated RIASEC, contains the domains of interest listed below. Read
the summaries to see whether what you enjoy most is consistent with
the activities of your current job.

Realistic: Activities that include practical, hands-on problems, and
    solutions
Investigative: Scholarly, intellectual activities involving the search for
    facts
Artistic: Unconventional, creative activities that involve working
    with forms, designs, and patterns, often requiring self-expression
Social: Activities that involve working closely with others, generally
    as teacher, helper, service-provider, caregiver
Enterprising: Starting up and carrying out projects that involve
    leading others, persuasive communications, and decision making
Conventional: Performance of activities that follow established pro-
    cedures and routines

The best companies, then, always are trying to calibrate the interests and abilities of their people to the work, backed by the conspicuous rationale that employees who are absorbed and energized by their work are more committed to the organization, perform better, and stay longer than those whose jobs are misaligned with their true interests and abilities. Because the things that people are extraordinary in performing seem easy to them, employees' superpowers are not always obvious to them. Therefore, it makes sense to quiz employees on, and comment about, those things they do best. With a better understanding of employees' signature strengths (i.e., the four to seven attributes that are especially appealing and deployed most frequently when the chances arise), it is possible for companies to find ways to play to those strengths.[46]

The theory behind strengths-use is straightforward. People feel most satisfied and fulfilled when they are growing, engaged in those things in which they take the greatest pleasure, and making generous use of their capabilities. The benefits are enumerable. People who regularly use their strengths are higher on engagement, self-esteem, efficacy, job satisfaction, well-being, meaning in life, positive affect, and quality of life. They also display greater resistance to stress and are more socially skilled in dealing with setbacks.[47]

A few years ago, we attended a wedding in rural upstate Vermont, where we learned of a development process that is reiterated every generation. An old army transport vehicle carried guests down a dirt road to a lovely remote piece of land with stream and pond—a onetime meditative retreat for the bride. This hidden place was in Richmond, Vermont, which to most readers will be an unfamiliar speck in a vast and relatively unpopulated domain. The world's ski community, however, knows the place well as home to the skiing Cochran family who have produced three generations of collegiate and Olympic champions. When we were there, another Cochran family disciple, Robby Kelley, was the reigning national giant slalom champion. Upstart Ryan Cochran-Siegle had just won gold in downhill and combined at the Alpine Junior World Ski Championships in Roccasoro, Italy, and more recently was part of the U.S. ski team at the 2018 Olympics in South Korea. We tell this story of family excellence because these world-class skiers all learned their craft on a small hill in their backyard—a gentle sloping mound of earth that stretches no longer than a couple hundred feet. The action is enabled by a self-installed towline and makeshift lighting strung from trees. It would be facile to attribute the family's successes to the privilege of genes, for the real explanation is more basic. They owe their success to practice, habit, and astute and sensitive guidance.

First, an expert who truly understands excellence oversees skier development. This person knows what to watch for and attend to. These overseers know the skills that learners must master as prerequisites for success, and they focus on process versus outcomes. The Cochran's have always understood that the fastest down a course at any given time is not necessarily the best equipped to compete on the international stage, where a nanosecond flaw in style and form can be costly. Said differently, the focus of training is on mastering a skill, not on achieving a certain performance outcome. Mastery goals repeatedly have been shown to foster greater interest and persistence in activities. Second, practice involves isolating skills and correcting performances in gradual increments. The best way for a neophyte Cochran to learn to ski is on a small hill. Skiers will not learn faster by starting on a mountaintop. There would be too much that is wildly wrong to fix, and too little enjoyment derived by the skier from the scary descent to persist in the activity. A mentor must be able to isolate features of performance for the learner to work on, so throwing a person into the proverbial fire would not allow for the necessary discriminations to be made. Thus, the best way to learn from practice is in small and steady improvements where the success rate is high, but not perfect. People are happiest when they are learning well and growing despite the occasional fall. Third, effort and practice need to be applied toward those aspects of performance that are most important, that will make the biggest difference, and that people are best at doing (and therefore are activities that are self-rewarding). It does not make sense to spend undue time mitigating weaknesses and closing gaps that may be superfluous to long-term aims and performance. Yes, fix what has to get fixed, but keep in mind that the goal is greatness versus proficiency. Skiers gravitate to events that use their strengths and where they can truly excel. Artists do the same thing. They work in mediums or with themes that they enjoy and are best at executing. They expand on their expertise by straying from proven abilities and experimenting with new ideas and techniques in adjacent areas. Some strengths naturally bleed into weaknesses, so improvements may be observed in once-troublesome areas. Nevertheless, rather than fixing what is broken in employees, managers should find ways to use and improve the most skilled dimensions of their talents.

Strengths-use has, with good reason, become fashionable in business. However, the idea has been around in mental health circles for decades. Therapists feared that the diagnoses for patients would be debilitating, in themselves, because they defined people by what they were not able to do, or by their deficits. The fear was that the stigmatizing labels would produce self-defeating behaviors in patients who would be inclined to see themselves as handicapped. Thus, the unintended consequence of therapeutic help was to fuel the persistence of the disorder by defining people by what was wrong with them. Consequently, professionals urged a new focus on what people can do well to foster positive change while keeping the deleterious diagnoses to themselves. Thus, as counterweight to shortcomings, many practitioners believed that people could more readily grow and meet personal goals if they recognized those features in themselves in which they excelled and applied their rich array of assets to build on and deploy as circumstances required.

Business subsequently adopted the same ideas. Rather than ask people to fix what is broken, which may have little impact on performance and be entirely inconsistent with employees' interests (in fact, many things that people are poor at are those things they do not wish to do), many training and development departments concluded that improvements in performance could be obtained by relying more on employees' array of assets. This does not imply that all shortcomings can be ignored; some can get in the way of performance and a person's success. For example, we have found that some people's aptitudes for leading are so sorely absent that they have little to no hope of ever successfully leading a group unless their flaws were somehow remediated. The current trend, however, has been to move away from the historical focus on gaps or deficits and place greater attention on helping people to identify what they are good at and enjoy doing.

One straightforward way to achieve these ends is through a deliberate career planning process and to buttress these efforts with the requisite psychological and material support. The one-on-one relationships between employees and mentors or coaches have been found to be one of the most effective ways to produce change and develop skills in proteges. Although the purposes of coaches and mentors are slightly different, the guided instruction and advice giving of each delivers timely psycho-social support and, over time, increases career satisfaction, skill acquisition, and individual and team performance.[48] Another way to take advantage of employees' full capabilities is to mold an existing job to the preferences, interests, and abilities of the jobholder through job crafting. Because jobs are essentially human-made constructs, every job can be modified or fine-tuned to cohere to the capabilities of the position's incumbent by adjusting the nature and scope of tasks.[49] And, sometimes the repetitiveness of our days causes us to lose sight of the importance of our work. Our work feels like the Sisyphean toil of rolling rocks uphill and never getting to the top. But we occasionally do make it to the top and we sometimes simply forget that meaningful work is not easy work. Meaningful events may be recurrently satisfying and uplifting, but often some of the most penetrating and declarative episodes in life are arduous, terrifying, calamitous, and sad; not happy occasions at all but gut-wrenching affairs that give us a newfound awareness and reignite our energies. We simply need periodic reminders from friends that what we are doing is valuable and worth the effort.

Although it is tempting to construe learning and development as passive consumptive activities, much of this growth depends on a person's regulatory abilities to set standards, exert the necessary effort for improvement, and monitor gains against goals while fending off temptations to work on simpler, more easily achievable objectives. Overcoming the lure of appetizing diversions involves self-discipline, self-control, and grit. People who lose weight, eat more healthily, exercise more, and perform better are those who are well-equipped to regulate their attention, emotions, and behaviors. Indeed, the elite in the sciences, arts, and sports have one thing in common: they have developed good habits that allow them to do things even when the probability of a reward is quite low and elements of the task are painful (e.g., skiers who train in freezing temperatures and suffer aggravating falls). Therefore, although practice per se is important for development, the instrumentality of factors that make good practice possible cannot be underestimated.

We marvel at people's raw abilities but lose sight of the competencies that lie beneath the surface—their capacity to challenge themselves when tired as well as their resilience to come back after discouraging blows, to listen to and accept difficult feedback, to keep a positive outlook and invasive impulses and emotions in check, to develop supportive and encouraging relationships with others, to remain focused on long-term goals, and to sustain conviction in their capabilities. They have the personal and social competencies that surround their skills and efforts, which enable them to grow. They have the self-regulatory capacity to form good habits.

Habits are amazing and critical to development. To illustrate how habits work, let's put mice in a maze that looks like a cross.[50] We teach the mice to turn right at the junction to find cheese. One mouse is trained just a little bit, and the other a whole lot so that it develops a habit. Habits are defined as learned patterns of behavior that automatically (with little conscious deliberation) occur in response to cues from the environment (when you get to the intersection of the cross, turn right). Habits are well-ingrained chunks of behavior that our brain has decided should be automated. Because we are doing the same thing over and over, our brains put those sequences on automatic pilot so we can attend to more serious concerns that could use greater reflection and our undivided attention. Certain things just would not get done regularly without habits. You can brush your teeth only so many times at bedtime for the self-reinforcing value of clean teeth; environmental cues and associated routines have to take over the chore.

Researchers know that a habit is formed when a mouse will run for the cheese even if it makes it sick, or the cheese has declined in value, or has been removed from the maze (diminutions in value are often manipulated in labs by allowing mice to gorge themselves before presenting a reward, or by injecting mice with a substance that will make them sick when they ingest the reward). With habits, behaviors are under stimulus-response (action) control internalized as a "get cheese" sequence, abbreviated as S > R. When I get to the crossroads (S), I take a right and run to the end (R). Under diminished rewards, the mice who have not yet developed a habit will stop running because the sickening cheese, for example, has lost its value. The behavior will extinguish.

In contrast to habits, many goal-directed behaviors are under instrumental control: people take actions based on the expected outcomes. These behaviors are sensitive to changes in the value of outcomes and to the contingencies between actions and outcomes. This relationship is represented by an action-outcome formula (A > O). When a lump of cheese diminishes in value, an experienced mouse will change course to find a more satisfying outcome. Assume that we have been dropping the mice into the maze from the south side and then decide to switch things up and begin putting the mice into the maze from the opposite, north side, so that everything is reversed from the mice's point of view. The instrumental mice head down the corridor, pause at the intersection, inspect the area for potentially rewarding moves using their senses, and turn left toward the cheese (which is where it always has been). On the other hand, the mice under S > R control turn right, and right again—again and again. Using more advanced techniques than mazes, researchers have found the same results with people. The very thing that is supposed to help us navigate through life successfully has become our nemesis. The fact that the "cheese" is not there or makes us sick does not matter. Habits thus persist even when the outcome is no longer the preferred response.

Mice that continue to operate under strongly established behavioral protocols can look pathetically stupid and resistant from the perspective of more successful mice who may regard them as loathsome, antiquated creatures for their ineffectual action when a hardy brick of cheese is within sniffing distance. In contrast, perhaps we are not very good change agents. If you do not want your mice nibbling on bad cheese or curiously repeating behaviors that objective observers would regard as ineffective, you will have to change processes, restructure the environment, entrain action to new cues, and spend a lot of time retraining people so they overlearn new behaviors. But sounding warnings, arming employees with facts, and making urgent calls to action will not be enough to instigate change. You have to reengage the attentive thinking parts of their brains that recognize new realities and behavioral consequences. For that, you will have to reward new behaviors.

Habits are important because they get us to do things that we ordinarily do not want to do but would keep us safer or make us better if we did them. Thus, we underscore the importance of hiring people with self-control, self-discipline, and sound coping skills who can establish their own contingencies for prescribed behaviors. For example, musical virtuosos or world-class athletes practice every day at the same time for a set period, at first under the nourishment of self-administered rewards and then out of habit—or selective cues. Many of the qualities that allow people to take control of their affairs and grow falls under the rubric of emotional intelligence, or the ability to identify, monitor, control, and use emotions and emotional content effectively in interactions.[51] We variously describe people with high emotional intelligence quotients as empathic, self-aware, and self-controlled: as having the host of characteristics that permit awareness of internal states of mind and understanding how to respond to, or moderate, the real issues at hand in emotionally charged situations.

People who are superior at perceiving and using emotional cues are more effective, personally and interpersonally, than those without those capabilities. Many studies have revealed the advantages of emotional intelligence on work performance, leadership effectiveness, customer satisfaction, academic achievement, problem-solving, well-being, and life satisfaction.[52] Teaching people to be more self-aware and to modulate their emotions, therefore, is a prescription for more enjoyable social interactions and more effective job performance. In social settings, emotional intelligence is mandatory. Awareness of the emotional strata of group interaction is essential in responding to group members' true needs and in building a hardy base of interpersonal goodwill that provides a safe and trusting work environment. Groups with higher emotional intelligence unequivocally perform better and more effectively grow their abilities as a team. For example, when organizational needs arise, teams with higher emotional intelligence pursue a more genteel and incisive process to determine who would benefit most from an assignment as one key consideration in the long-term success of the group. People receive more opportunities and are more visible within emotionally intelligent groups.

Given the importance of emotional intelligence as a key element to interpersonal and organizational effectiveness, progressive companies such as PURE Insurance now make emotional intelligence a fundamental part of their development programs. At PURE, all employees, new and old, undergo instruction in emotional intelligence. Several controlled studies show that the instruction works. One eighteen-hour training program made up of understanding emotions, identifying one's own emotions, identifying others' emotions, regulating one's own and others' emotions, and effectively using positive emotions improved attendees' well-being, life satisfaction, mental health, and social relationships.[53]

Despite the fact that companies dedicate substantial resources to formal training, most personal growth in organizations (80 percent) occurs through informal, or incidental, means.[54] Therefore, companies can achieve the best developmental results by creating a stimulating, cooperative learning environment in which people help themselves and one another to grow. Informal learning occurs when employees make sense of the experiences they have in their day-to-day jobs through interactions with others, mentoring and coaching, and self-directed learning and personal exploration.[55] The learning that takes place can be subtle. For example, Big Ass Fans outsources its cafeteria lunches to local providers and introduces different cuisines from around the world daily to expand employees' experiences and tastes. Or, the learning can be less subtle as when engineers at Big Ass Fans have experiments running atop their desks for passersby to muse at. The intent is to arouse curiosity and a desire to learn. These largely unscripted measures can be used in tandem with more deliberate prescriptions to nourish employees' inspiration. For example, PURE Insurance gives employees $1,500 per year to explore whatever interest they choose from yoga instruction to Jiu-Jitsu to Formula One racing. The program is part of a wider company effort to instill the habit of learning so that questioning, seeking, and creating are as natural as eating and sleeping: essential sustenance for a satisfying life. Similarly, sabbaticals can satisfy the same purpose of liberating employees from the humdrum and reigniting their zeal to achieve personally alluring goals and to passionately chase after growth-fulfilling aspirations. Employees who have been at Patagonia for one year qualify for a fully paid two-month environmental internship, typically as volunteers. Applications are reviewed by an employee review committee. Patagonia grants most reasonable requests, as funding allows, with 125–150 of two thousand employees taking internships per year. The Motley Fool allows paid sabbaticals of eight weeks after an employee has completed ten years of service. Although sabbaticals occur infrequently in organizations that have them, they have outsize effects on employee attitudes.[56] Sabbaticals are highly visible signs that organizations value employee growth and, therefore, are seductive attractors of job candidates as well as a proven means to heighten career satisfaction and organizational commitment.

In summary, premier companies use the compendium of corporate developmental practices not only to educate but also to continuously engage people's curiosities and appreciation for novelty and impact. Consider the precocious Marie Curie who defied the odds of her gender and times to become a two-time Nobel Laureate and one of the key figures in the history of science.[57] She had a learned home life with inquisitive supportive parents and teachers; she found prominent mentors and advisers at the University of Paris who provided quality instruction; and she found a scientific soulmate and devotee in husband, Pierre. She had conducive learning environments and knowledgeable curious peers to direct her passions. No high achiever can say they did it all on their own. Excellence requires a nurturing environment, a learning climate, and the incessant push toward excellence. And, of course, raw abilities. Creating this sort of framework in which employees thrive and grow to their potential is up to companies to offer in myriad ways and forms and, thereby, to convey through these practices that learning and development are integral features of the work environment and are expected.

CHAPTER NINE

Empower People

THE IDEAL FOR many organizations would be to have cohorts of self-confident employees making decisions and taking actions on the frontlines. Surrendering authority to those who are closest to the action and are most prepared to respond to the needs of customers seems like a sensible way to conduct business. When organizations push decision making out to the rank and file and employees feel secure and emboldened to act with impact on their own initiative, we think of the workforce as empowered.

Roughly 70 percent of organizations say they use employee empowerment practices, but it is likely that claim grossly overstates the rate at which empowerment actually is enabled and succeeds.[1] Like a wonder drug that promises to restore youth, repair hair loss, and reset body weight, empowerment in organizations often promises too much that too easily can be obtained. It is promoted as a catchall cure whose magical powers offer organizations speed, quality, creativity, and profits with little operational exertion.

Studies show that empowerment works when properly implemented. Companies experience fewer errors, faster turnaround times, and better customer service, as well as higher job satisfaction, organizational commitment, and team performance.[2] However, many companies do what amounts to a parent handing the keys of a high-performance car to their teenager and hoping, day after day, that the car will return intact. Simply handing over power to another gives little assurance that something positive will come of it. And yet, that is precisely what some companies do. A transition from centralized controls and a host of checks and balances to greater distributed authority, however, is a significant shift in culture and operations that involves increased information sharing, technological enhancements, participative decision making, extensive training, quality leadership, and sociopolitical support, collaborative problem solving, and team trust. Said succinctly, empowerment entails wholesale changes to the way things are done and a bevy of organizational supports. Often the necessary preparations have not been made and empowerment strategies subsequently flounder.

Additionally, empowerment initiatives also may collapse because managers are reluctant to give up control, employees are reluctant to accept responsibility, or both. A study within a hotel chain headquartered in Europe (with brands in Eastern and Western Europe, the Middle East, Asia, and Africa) shows how personal iniative may be differentially expressed depending on conditions. Frontline service providers assessed their general efficacy using a standard questionnaire. Supervisors were matched to these respondents and asked to evaluate employees on a seven-item, agree/disagree service performance measure. A sample item was, "Takes ownership by following through with the customer interaction and ensures a smooth transition to other service employees." Service providers who rated themselves higher in general efficacy also were rated higher by their supervisors in the quality of service they delivered. This was true, however, only if the attitudinal climate at the hotel was perceived as one in which employees were expected to act on their own initiative—that is, where employees had the organization's explicit permission to satisfy customers' needs as they thought best. Therefore, employees can *feel* empowered and be ready to act, but an organization can negate the advantages of empowerment by withholding consent from employees to act outside set protocols and obtaining the necessary approvals.[3] Sans the authority to act, the ability and motivation of employees to contribute are lost. The aim of this chapter is to bring together the elements that make the investment in employee empowerment feasible and worthwhile.

The advantages of empowerment are illustrated in a simulation that compares a directive management style with one in which managers allow their people to execute more freely and deliberately as their capabilities permit. Multiple teams of five, including the leader, participated in the Leadership Development Simulator (which originally was developed for the Squadron Officer School at Maxwell Air Force Base). The simulation is complex and is carved up into ten rounds corresponding to ten discrete decision-making periods. The teams must manage many assets to discover targets on a shared task screen. If our reading is correct, the simulation seems to be like a multi-player game of Battleship on steroids, in which beneficial outcomes are highly dependent on collaboration, information sharing, and information integration. Two types of leaders were selected to run the team: leaders who scored highly on having a directive leadership style (taking charge of a group, giving team members instructions), and leaders who scored highly on having an empowering leadership style (encouraging team members to assume responsibilities on their own, advising team members to exchange information). The respective styles were reinforced through videos of either a directive or an empowering leader that were shown to the team leads. The results showed that directed teams perform better than empowered teams in the early rounds of play. The directed teams' performance plateaus, however, whereas the empowered teams show consistent improvement over time until they surpass the directive teams' performance in the later rounds of play. In the early rounds, the empowered teams get acclimated to the simulation environment, but as they test and explore, their emergent cognitions and increased information gathering, learning, and coordination pay off.[4]

Similarly, a field study showed the beneficial effects of people who feel psychologically empowered. Assessments of 441 nurses within five hospitals taken over three time periods showed that greater empowerment directly related to a higher composite performance score (consisting of general competencies, integrity, and specific measures of clinical practice such as coordination of care). The results also revealed a bidirectional pattern by which higher levels of empowerment increased performance, which in turn increased empowerment at a subsequent time period. This is precisely the finding we would expect: confidence in one's ability to execute increases performance which increases confidence.[5]

This finding is consistent with many others showing that empowered employees feel more efficacious, are more satisfied with their jobs, are more committed to the organization, perform better, and report better health and well-being.[6] At the company level, cultivating empowerment through a suite of institutional practices that emphasize personal responsibility, tolerance for risk, and open informational exchanges yields fewer organizational errors, faster turnaround times, and better customer service. At the supervisory level, supportive managers who encourage honest dialogue and independent action despite the fact that these, at times, may involve discussions about uncomfortable truths and failures are likely to engender an energized and empowered staff.[7]

The idea of empowerment is as old as the Industrial Revolution. In the United States, the term gained currency in the years running up to the Second World War and during the ensuing decade.[8] The period was marked by considerable employer–employee strife and, with the advent of the Great War, people such as future Supreme Court Justice Louis Brandeis wondered how a country could ask people to die for principles that they were denied at home in the workplace, noting the chasm between political liberty and industrial absolutism. The swelling belief among thought leaders was that democratic ideals should apply equally to employees of companies as to citizens of nations.[9]

The seeds of modern organization development may be traced to this period and to those writers who, like John Dewey, were asserting the rights of workers to self-determination, creative expression, and personal fulfillment. These writers included John Commons, Ordway Tead, Henry Metcalf, and Mary Parker Follett.[10] All similarly argued that employees should have a voice in the terms and conditions of employment and be able to protect themselves against harmful, capricious acts of management—that employers were morally obligated to include employees in the decision-making apparatus of the firm.

Several progressive organizations at the time did just that through voluntary employer–employee associations. These associations were variously called work councils, shop committees, cooperative associations, and, later, employee representation plans. Wm Filene & Sons, the Boston retailer, was an example of such an employer. Approximately two dozen elected employee representatives reviewed store policies and procedures in tandem with management and mediated issues regarding employee relations, including grievances. Importantly,

Filene's readily recognized the union membership of employees who chose to belong.[11]

Unions initially embraced voluntary employer–employee representation plans, believing that in flagrant instances of corporate malfeasance these would convert into union plans with the associated powers of collective bargaining. As these plans expanded (many by government mandate during the war to forestall strikes that would slow industrial output), unions increasingly viewed these arrangements as a means to remove unions from companies—as was forcibly done at Ludlow—or to prevent companies from unionizing (see box 9.1).[12] New Deal legislation such as the Wagner Act concluded that the power differentials between employers and employees were too great to allow voluntary associations and, henceforth, outlawed them in favor of government oversight of formally constituted unions. (Legislators also believed that unions, along with the enactment of a minimum wage, would lead to higher wages and help rescue the United States from the Great Depression.)

BOX 9.1
The Ludlow Massacre

Colorado was home to one of the largest vertically integrated steel conglomerates in the world, Colorado Fuel & Iron (CF&I), a Rockefeller Family–controlled entity. When the United Mine Workers of America went out on strike for higher wages and better working conditions, they were evicted from company-owned housing and set up tent cities throughout the state. The largest of these cities was in Ludlow, home to 1,200 strikers and their families. The National Guard was called in to quash growing tensions between the strikers and the company-paid detective agency, Baldwin-Felts. The National Guard abetted the detective agency, and in April 1914 opened fire on the strikers (killing six men) and burned down their encampment, inadvertently killing two women and twelve children. An armed ten-day siege ensued along a forty-mile front between strikers and the National Guard that was halted when President Wilson intervened with U.S. troops. The incident provoked public outrage and aroused a gradual change in sentiment that became more antagonistic toward corporations and more favorable toward unions.

Although these new laws prevented systemically organized supervisory groups (sans unions), they did not eliminate management's ability to introduce participatory methods into the workplace as long as companies steered clear of rights specifically reserved for unions. In this sense, the democratization movement had lasting effects on the workplace: first, as a counterweight to the heavy-handedness and controls found in some organizations; second, as an effective means of improving workers' quality of life; and third, as a collaborative mechanism for lifting companies' bottom lines. Enlightened management was participatory management.[13] Managers could create a more satisfied and productive workforce by promoting egalitarian values of information sharing and candid two-way exchanges in which managers and employees could mutually influence one another.

In practice, participation can take many different forms, occur at different intensities of inclusiveness, and pertain to different levels in organizations—for example, two people, a team, or a business unit. Thus, open-door policies and open-book management in which critical financial information is shared with employees are forms of participatory management. Expressions of opinions through employee surveys and focus groups are forms of participation as are idea-generation methods, such as suggestion boxes, brainstorming sessions, committee meetings, and company-wide forums. The corporate mainstay of collaborative goal setting also is a form of participation and involvement. Of all of the work that has been conducted on goal setting, one persistent result concerns the energizing effects of employee input and choice on goal attainment.[14]

The ability of people to have a meaningful voice in organizational affairs, and to be heard, is an essential way to confirm a person's worth and to emphasize that their needs and interests are not to be trifled with. The importance of voice received lasting literary acclaim from Albert Hirschman's classic work on exit-voice-loyalty. Hirschman's original thesis was applied to dissatisfied customers who he conceived as having a choice between voting with their feet or voicing concern about an objectionable product or service, and how the provision for voice could create or intensify customers' loyalty to a product or commitment to a brand.[15] Subsequent theorists have applied exit and voice to employer–employee relations and envisioned voice within a larger participatory framework whereby employees, to various degrees, could be meaningfully and advantageously incorporated into the decision-making processes of the organization. Allowing people to earnestly express their thoughts and opinions validates their importance to the enterprise, elevates the perceived value of their contributions, and increases engagement.[16] In contrast, the deleterious results of a lack of voice and perverse neglect for others' well-being are stupendously on display in Henry Hudson's final voyage (see box 9.2).[17]

Participatory management, perhaps, received its most visible expression in the burgeoning use of quality circles during the 1980s in the United States. (A quality circle is made up of six to twelve employees who meet regularly to solve problems affecting their work area, usually with an eye toward enhancements in quality, reductions in cost, or

---

BOX 9.2
Henry Hudson's Bad Day

Hudson set sail in May 1610 down the Thames to find a northwest passage to Japan and China. The spices of that region were highly sought in England; however, the means to obtain them by sea travel around Africa or South America were long and treacherous. Funded by wealthy mercantilists, this was Hudson's fourth attempt to find a route through the Arctic to the other side of the world. He set out with twenty-two crew that included his son, John, and by November the ship, the *Discovery*, was locked in ice on the southern shore of what is now Hudson Bay. With six months of provisions, the crew had expected to be home by November; however, Hudson had prolonged the trip in search of a western passage until it was too late to return home. As the ice thawed and the ship broke free, the men—some with scurvy and many, at times, feeding on frogs and moss when game and foul could not be caught—were roiled by Hudson's hesitancy to expeditiously return home despite their pleas. As a result, the more scurrilous members of the crew staged a mutiny. They set Hudson, his son, and seven crew adrift in a lifeboat and returned home. Hudson was never seen again. Known as a competent navigator but poor leader, it would have been a wise moment for Hudson to have heeded his crew's desires and turn his ship toward home at the first chance. (Postscript. Several men, including those who avowedly incited the mutiny, died of wounds sustained from the native populations during their return voyage, and with pages from Hudson's journal missing and the men's evident starvation, the surviving crew were found not guilty of mutiny.)

increases in productivity.) Quality circles reportedly were launched in Japan in 1962 at Nippon Wireless and Telegraph Company and were based partly on Deming's work during the previous two decades.[18] In the 1960s, "made in Japan," was a euphemism for "cheap." By the 1980s, however, Japan was the standard-bearer for quality and the rest of the world was playing catch-up. Almost half of all listed companies on the New York Stock Exchange with more than five hundred employees had a quality circle in the 1980s; some estimates place usage as high as 90 percent of the Fortune 500.[19] These plans often were wedded with gainsharing plans that offered employees a portion of the business' proceeds on a quarterly basis if they could figure out ways to reduce costs or increase outputs beyond set standards.

Quality circles often are conceived as a subset of total quality management (TQM) that involve a quantitative piece related to member training in statistical methods (e.g., Six Sigma). Despite meta-analyses that reveal the effectiveness of quality circles in improving performance, "quality circles" have an old-time sound and feel to which people anecdotally associate with "failed fad."[20] True, quality circles were a fad, but only because many companies thought they had to implement them to remain competitive, whether they needed them or not. Indeed, quality circles are the forerunners to many of the avant-garde team-based organizational structures we have today, such as holocracies: nonhierarchical structures in which work is organized into fluidly changing groups that assemble, dissemble, and reassemble as conditions and objectives warrant—similar to the mutually adjusting expert teams (adhocracies) advocated by Mintzberg years ago.[21] Quality circles, therefore, are still around in many incarnations that emulate—and often replicate—the old quality circles. They range in name from project teams, TQM teams, autonomous teams, tiger teams, skunkworks, self-directed work groups, self-managed teams, and new venture units, to name a few. The groups vary in makeup depending on the size and nature of the initiative, sometimes having members only from specific disciplines, such as research, and sometimes including a cross section of the enterprise. All these groups share the ability to internally control work assignments and the way members apply their skills to realize a goal. Some groups, like quality circles, are well integrated with the operations of the company. Other groups with a greater dedication to innovation have looser connections to current organizational activities to avoid nonessentials that might be imposed by the mothership. These teams, nevertheless, are required to keep their focus on commercial ends and the inevitability of folding any discoveries or breakthroughs back into the organization for execution.

If companies once were disillusioned with worker participation in resolving problems, our experiences suggest that much of the disappointment concerned the nature of the work. Much of the work was standardized and routine; thus, groups could make modifications on the fringes but once a few fixes were made, there was little else they could do. Those aforementioned gainsharing plans abated in short order once the last drop of profit was distilled from assembly lines. This situation constrained what could be accomplished: structures were highly mechanistic, versus organic, and these situationally strong environments tended to hold behaviors tightly in place. The fault, therefore, did not lie so much in small group practices, but rather in what could reasonably be done and affected without heavy investments in new equipment and technologies.

The limitations presented by antiquated, mechanistic processes and bureaucratic structures on the stratagems of groups were duly noted by Rosabeth Kanter who prescribed more nimble and pliable designs as necessities for organizational survival.[22] If companies did not change and become more responsive to their environments, they would suffer the fate of the Woolly Mammoth. Indeed, slow and inflexible, once-stalwart companies more readily began to disappear or were swallowed whole by swifter competitors. The activation of empowered employees necessitated changes to the design of organizations that provided employees with greater latitude to act.[23]

The old top-heavy structures that were believed to causally relate to Earth's fifth great extinction were reconstituted to be more enterprising and adaptive. In practice, this meant removing highly stacked layers of management, widening spans of control, and loosening tightly controlled processes that afforded employees little wiggle room. In truth, companies never had to be as stodgy as some became. If mathematics is an able guide, four layers of management can accommodate an organization of fifteen thousand employees and eight layers of management can accommodate an organization of one hundred thousand employees (with average spans of control of four direct reports per layer).[24] Nevertheless, there is power in numbers. To obtain rank, status, and money, an ambitious manager needed to control assets and information, which typically meant people. The more people under one's supervisory umbrella, the better.

Recently, the general trend has been to delayer organizations and widen spans of control. For example, the number of direct reports to the CEO has more than doubled over the past forty years, from an average of five to ten. New direct reports primarily were added from functional areas, such as human resources and information technology, that formally were tucked under other disciplines. Increasingly, too, CEOs have dispensed with intermediaries such as the chief operating officer, with the CEO now serving in that capacity.[25] Changing organizational relationships, experimentation with new designs, and the situational freedom prompted by modern technologies are, perhaps, the reasons we have seen the long dormant concern for spans of control rebound with zeal. A topic that drifted into obscurity once again produces anxiety about costs and norms of correctness (see box 9.3).[26]

BOX 9.3
Spans of Control and Normative Standards

Spans of control have been of keen interest for millennia with many proposed formulaic recommendations. In Exodus, Moses was advised to divide up administrative burdens by having rulers of thousands, hundreds, fifties, and tens under their command. The Roman armed forces similarly divided up their legions into cohorts of ten that, in turn, were composed of six *centuria*, each with ten tent groups (with eight men per tent). More recent theorists have speculated that a span should be, in general, no less than four or no greater than fifteen. Clearly, spans this broad provide little guidance. Furthermore, a bounty of variables such as the complexity of the work, level of technological sophistication, and the amount of supervision required will influence the number of direct reports that can be feasibly and effectively managed. Consequently, we deploy a normative standard that looks at the relationship between levels of management and the widths of spans of control: a span should be no less than the number of levels of management under one's auspices, including one's own level. Thus, a person who oversees five levels of management should have no fewer than five direct reports. (There is substantial variation at the last supervisory level of management; however, the rule otherwise holds up in practice.) The precision of the rule may be incidental to the thought processes it elicits regarding the balance that has to be obtained between building an organization up and building it out.

Although these organizational changes were initiated by the desire to forge more flexible institutions, flatter organizations do little to enhance agility. A flatter structure is not the same as decentralizing authority.[27] For example, a manager within a highly compressed institution may exert *more* direct and deliberate influence on decision making deeper in the organization—the opposite of what might have been intended. Even in a flat organization, a manager can act as a centralizing authority and can undercut the feelings of empowerment of those underneath them. Therefore, the structure is a contributory force for empowerment, but it provides no guarantee that the organization will achieve the adeptness and spontaneity it seeks unless the actual work gives people the room to act and leaders create hospitable climates for them to do so.

FORMULATION OF JOB SATISFACTION

The changes that were occurring to organizational structures were coincident with changes in the nature of work more generally. As work evolved out of the machine age to, as Peter Drucker anticipated, the knowledge and information era, the leeway to act with consequence became greater.[28] Work was becoming increasingly complex, pliable, and varied; jobs, in turn, were becoming more open-ended. Jobs could be enlarged, enriched, or expanded. That is, most jobs could be modified to produce more intrinsically satisfying work that was richer in content and more august in responsibility. They could be imbued with more autonomy in decision making, meaning, and impact, yielding many of the desirable characteristics that enliven work.[29]

Many of the of the components that people seek from jobs were well captured in Hackman and Oldham's classic formulation of job satisfaction consisting of task identity, task significance, skill variety, autonomy support (discretion), and feedback about performance (technically, feedback is not a feature of the work per se, but a condition that is necessary for gauging progress).[30] These roughly correspond to the psychological ingredients of empowerment that includes meaning, sense of competence, self-determination, and impact.[31] Collectively, these offered what people have always wanted from a day's work. Work that provides people with a greater sense of purpose and directs activities toward ends that are perceived as important (including building relationships and helping others); have a social impact or make contributions that matter to someone; are consistent with one's skills, values, and identity; stimulate and draw on individuals' intellectual and creative powers; and allow people to develop to their full potential.

Task Identity

Task identity is the ability to take pride in the complete assembly or completion of work from start to finish, or to work closely within a group to complete a job in its entirety. A sense of craftsmanship and pride of accomplishment are preserved by maintaining a person's connection to his or her whole creation. Think of how a young Da Vinci must have felt when asked to paint half a painting, leaving the other half to another accomplished artist. (These paintings recently were on exhibit at the Yale Art Gallery in New Haven, Connecticut.) Da Vinci could not have been pleased despite the excellence of the other artist. Da Vinci clearly was just more excellent.

Task Significance

Task significance refers to the degree to which the job has an impact, positively affecting the beneficiaries of the work: The work has a sense of purpose and has meaning to someone. The mission of a company often provides enough rationale for the importance of one's efforts. People within a healthcare system understand why they are doing what they do. Still, it is possible to become absorbed in the details of one's job and be blind to the reasons the job is being performed in the first place. To that end, it helps to provide tangible reminders to employees about why their work matters. For example, a study by Grant showed that the call time and revenues of fundraisers increased by 142 percent and 171 percent, respectively, as a result of spending five minutes conversing with a scholarship recipient.[32] Similarly, radiologists wrote longer, more diagnostically comprehensive reports after they were shown a photo of their patients.[33] Ritz Carlton's legendary service largely hinges on employees' (called "ladies and gentlemen") daily reviews on how they positively affect the lives of guests (see box 9.4).[34] In general, engendering a sense of mattering increases employee satisfaction and the probability that they will remain with their companies.[35]

BOX 9.4
Impact and Empowerment at the Ritz Carlton

Known for their world-class service, Ritz Carlton serves as a train-ing ground for companies who wish to emulate the hotel's success. It begins with an intensive twenty-one-day orientation, thirty-day coach-accompanied on-the-job training, and a minimum of 125 hours of continuing education and cross-training (to instill collaboration and flexibility) per year. Lessons are reinforced through daily line-ups in which the dimensions of service are reviewed and people are able to share their "wow" stories: stories that depict how a Ritz Carlton lady or gentleman (as employees are known) responded to a guest's problem with an extraordinary, and responsible, act. For example, a child returned to the Ritz Carlton to search for her lost teddy bear (from a Ritz Carlton tea) that she had left behind. Unable to find the bear, the employee quickly purchased another bear and drove it up in a company limo for delivery to the girl (who was endearingly surprised to see that the bear had grown up since she last saw it). Every employee has $2,000 to spend on rectifying guest problems in the manner they see fit. Empowerment, or "responsible freedom," is key. Endowed with self-confidence through generous, ongoing training, each service provider has the authority to make decisions on the spot in behalf of the ladies and gentlemen who are their guests.

The significance of one's work also can be enhanced through chari-table or socially responsible actions. Coffee houses have fair trade policies to ensure that a cup of coffee benefits farmers thousands of miles away, hoteliers such as Concord Hospitality repurpose their used bathroom products to ensure hygienic goods are available in develop-ing countries, and companies such as Patagonia sell socially and envi-ronmentally responsible products, including their very first, reusable climbing pitons, to assure their customers that they can enjoy nature while sustaining it.

Skill Variety

Skill variety refers to the ability of an individual to use the full com-plement of their knowledge and skills versus repetitiously using nar-row competencies from their repertoire. This aspect of the job, when designed properly, requires employees to exercise an array of capabilities to test what they can do and accomplish, progressively developing their skills and abilities as responsibilities get broader in scope and the complexity of the work deepens. Each additional job element requires more knowledge and greater skill to obtain results.

Work Autonomy

Autonomy relates to what, how, and when work is to be performed. Fundamentally, work autonomy means having a say in what needs to be done and the best ways to achieve the ends for which one is responsible. Autonomy, then, concerns giving people the opportunity to decide what is best under the circumstances. One of the most vivid examples of autonomy, personal control, ownership, and accountability we have observed was at the statistical software, analytics, and data visualization company, SAS. SAS is located on sprawling wooded acreage in the Raleigh-Durham area of North Carolina. Its appearance is reminiscent of a college campus complete with fitness center and pool. The gardens and lawns that sit between buildings and among the collector-grade sculptures are impressive. These landscapes are the immaculate works of gardeners who each have their unique plots to tend in the manner they see fit. Executives repeatedly tell us that they want their employees to think and act like owners. The ability of employees to control aspects of their work, like that of the gardeners, is central to feelings of ownership. Having the capacity to rearrange, modify, and improve upon are attributes of possession—that is, people who can use the resources at their disposal are motivated to transform the organization for the better.

Feedback

When it comes to feedback, we have two suggestions. First, if managers and employees have established solid relations of trust and respect, then there is a wide berth for easy, honest, ongoing feedback, assuming managers give feedback in a nonthreatening, considerate manner. Feedback is much easier to give and take when it is mutually understood that the best interest of another is the goal. Few people are especially keen to be evaluated, and most are generally sensitive to feedback that can both refresh as well as devastate. No perfect recipe exists for giving feedback. In general, we deemphasize formulaic feedback, such as mixing good news with bad news. Rather, we endorse open dialogue and mutual goodwill, which together can temper negative reactions to words that may at times be clumsily misspoken.

Second, we advocate the cultivation of feedback cultures in which advice is readily invited and received. Information gleaned through solicited feedback is viewed by recipients as richer in content and more useful to performance than the same information uninvitedly given. When feedback is solicited, the motives of the advisor are seen as more benevolent.

Specifically, we encourage nurturing cultures of gratitude when people readily recognize one another's feats. For example, Edmunds created a program that allows fellow employees to recognize one another for behaviors that are instrumental to job success (and to allocate $1–$5 of cashable or exchangeable "Ed Bucks" per acknowledgment). These behaviors are appropriately called Top Drivers. Examples of Top Drivers include the "cool cucumber" (confident enough to hit the gas on projects, even when the road ahead is uncharted; learns from mistakes; always focuses on the solution) and the "curious cat" (always asks questions; seeks answers everywhere; is forever learning and applying lessons; works outside the comfort zone). At FONA, the flavors company, people have "Hero Cards" conspicuously displayed on their desks. The cards allow employees to spontaneously recognize one another for extraordinary accomplishments that support the core values of the organization, by attaching stickers of different colors to the cards—the color representing a beneficial action illustrative of various values.

The most, clear, direct, and reachable goals combined with sound job design provide the right nutrients for empowerment. Empowerment additionally presumes that accountability for results is duly transferred and a person can competently meet their work obligations: that they not only think they can obtain the desired results, but that they really can as well. This can-do mindset, backed by true ability, is called self-efficacy.

Self-efficacy refers to a person's conviction that they have the ability to effectively reach specific, desirable outcomes.[36] Efficacy, or its companion lay term, self-confidence, involves a set of beliefs that affirmatively influence the initiation of activities, the degree of effort spent, and the persistence needed to see a task through to completion. These beliefs include the conviction that an individual has the abilities to perform a given task, is optimistic about the success of the undertaking, and has the psychological wherewithal to resiliently beat back obstacles and other impediments that interfere with progress. The same principles regarding efficacy extend to groups, albeit groups provide additional cues about the team's ability to perform.[37] For example, the members of teams can observe the competence of their colleagues and determine whether the group has the requisite number of staff and mix of capabilities to execute well. Members also are sensitive to the assorted markers of function or dysfunction within the group: the level of trust within the group, the fondness of members for one another, the degree to which members identify with the group, the quality of interactions, communications, information sharing and decision making within the group, the effectiveness of the group in setting goals and planning, the group's collective understandings of roles and responsibilities, and the ability of the group to learn, change, and adapt. People form opinions about the team's ability to organize and execute at the unit level, which dictates the amount of effort a given member might expend toward the team's performance.

Because efficacy develops primarily through experience and mastery, leadership plays a crucial role—as usual. Managers' expectations matter a great deal as those can undermine, or uplift, employee confidence. The classic demonstrations of positive expectations on behaviors have been in schools. Students who have been fictitiously designated as high achievers to teachers outperform children in control group classrooms. The results of positive expectations on performance have been replicated many times and extended into the workplace.

Unquestionably, the beliefs we hold about our abilities affect whether or not our goals will be met. That is, the expectations we have of ourselves and others influence the results that we, and they, produce.

These self-fulfilling prophecies can move us forward or hold us back. The transformative power of positive expectations is known as the Pygmalion effect.[38] The mythical Greek Pygmalion is a sculptor who chisels the ideal woman, Galatea. Pygmalion longs for Galatea to be real, and the goddess of love, Aphrodite, obliges by transforming the statue into flesh and blood. George Bernard Shaw picked up on the idea of personal transformation in his play *Pygmalion*, suggesting that the best way to change the flower girl, Eliza Doolittle, into a lady is to believe that she can become someone other than who she is, and to treat her accordingly. Eliza's metamorphosis is partly contingent on the faith others have in her to change.

Negative expectations about others' abilities is called the golem effect. A golem is from Jewish legend. It is an anthropomorphic creature made of inanimate material such as mud or clay (like the clay people in *Flash Gordon* that terrified us as children). A golem often stands for an uncultivated oaf and therefore is used to describe a person from whom little is expected. In the workplace, the golem effect shows up when supervisors' low expectations of employees degrade their performance—a frequent finding.[39] High or low expectations alone, however, are not the reasons for performance increases or declines. Opinions do not directly produce the benefits or damages. People who have high (or low) expectations of others treat them in certain ways. For example, those with high expectations of others may display confidence in others' talents by giving them new challenges, increasing their responsibilities, reassuring them following setbacks, and freeing them to make the decisions for which they are capable. Conversely, when we have low expectations of others, we may give simpler assignments, overexplain on actions to take, are quick to step in and take over the work when problems arise, and are more critical when things do not turn out as planned.

Behavior change and continuous improvement in performance depend on the conviction that we have control over our affairs, can cope with disappointments, and are able to achieve goals that matter to us. We are not just helpless actors to whom good and bad things happen. If all goes well and we are appropriately encouraged and supported, our confidence to expertly execute actions in various social contexts grows.[40] We become increasingly self-assured that we have the ability to effectively reach specific outcomes. In contrast, consider an environment in which everything you do is wrong. You should have done this or that and are corrected or punished for having exercised judgment contrary to what your manager believed necessary or were expressly authorized to make. You quickly learn that deviating from tried-and-true behaviors, although woefully repetitive and boring, is preferable to the chancy actions that spur managerial ire. You, the employee, are incapacitated by indifference, unsure that any novel response you make will be adequate and rewarded. In these circumstances, people become the opposite of empowered. As people who come to believe that all good or bad that befall them is outside their control, they become helpless (see box 9.5).[41]

Empowering leaders place a premium on development, look for ways to integrate learning into everyday activities (e.g., lunch and learns, speaking engagements, special projects), and, most importantly, transfer power and accountability to employees through participatory

BOX 9.5
Learned Helplessness

Positive psychology was born in an animal lab at the University of Pennsylvania in the 1960s. At the time, researchers were investigating the effects of aversive conditioning on learning. Dogs first exposed to inescapable shocks were placed in a shuttle box (Solomon box) that contained a small barrier in the middle. The dogs could escape the shock delivered on one side by hopping the barrier. Dogs that never received the inescapable shocks prior to being placed in the box quickly learn to avoid the shocks. Those dogs previously exposed to shocks never learned to jump the barrier when placed in the shuttle box; if, by chance, the crossed the barrier, they never learned that their response was successful. Later, studies with humans found that those who believe that no response would be efficacious develop symptoms reminiscent of depression: sadness, loss of interest, fatigue, indecisiveness, and feelings of worthlessness. Thus began Seligman and others' decades-long foray into research dedicated to counteracting the troubling self-defeating effects of learned helplessness.

work practices and delegation.[42] For example, several companies we have consulted with mandate that managers delegate a significant project or assignment downward for execution as part of the annual planning process. The communication is straightforward. Every manager is responsible for developing the talents of their people by assigning progressively challenging projects commensurate with employee interests and abilities. A few companies we have visited have gone so far as to retire the term, "manager," in favor of "developer" to highlight the duty of development over control.

Like in baseball, the field of play in companies is set by values, norms, rules, goals, and budgets. Within these few boundaries, the manager empowers employees to play ball and, once the game begins, he or she steps onto the field only a limited number of times to advise, coach, or reposition and change personnel (see box 9.6). The manager defines the direction, establishes the contours for action, supports player development, provides the freedom to make choices, and provides adequate ongoing support and guidance to ensure success.[43]

BOX 9.6
Play Ball

Tom Caporaso, the CEO of Clarus Commerce, is fond of baseball—so fond he serves as a little league coach. Although baseball is not a metaphor that Tom pushed and is admittedly one that has limitations, we noticed the similarities between a championship baseball team and Clarus Commerce. Clarus has a lot of team speed, which they use to quickly respond to customer needs. In just the single day we were on the premises, we saw several customer requests quickly met by what to us sounded like sophisticated coding challenges. We may be wrong about the code, but not about the company's reaction times. Make an error? You correct the mistake and are expected to stay in the game. You also are expected to back up teammates, dedicate yourself to continuous improvement, and accept wins and losses as a team, neither taking undue credit nor passing blame. The idea of a team is that success depends on coordinated effort, but it does not remove the need to acknowledge personal achievements. In a lavish ceremony at the end of the year, Clarus recognizes employee distinctions, such as Rookie of the Year and Most Valuable Player, through handsome glass trophies with engravings of the company's logo. Perhaps most important, however, once play begins, the manager will step onto the field only a limited number of times. It is up to the players to play. The field of play is set by goals and budgets. Within these few boundaries, the company authorizes employees to play ball. This empowerment enables Clarus to move quickly according to conditions on the ground and to diligently meet changing customer needs.

Leadership that empowers requires a paradoxical transformation of relational power in which the person with more power and authority, the manager, helps others to enlarge their capabilities.[44] The types of leaders that embody this transformational power go by different names: transformational, empowering, and ethical leaders.[45] All of these varieties have elements that are well encapsulated by what it means to be a servant leader—that is, leaders who sublimate their interests to the welfare of others and the institution.[46] The effects are profound. These empowering servant leaders have been found to increase intergroup trust, goal focus, self-confidence, and the sharing of information, as well as increase creativity, job performance, customer service, and sales.[47] For example, the direct selling teams of a Korean cosmetics company led by servant leaders (as opposed to nonservant leaders) experienced greater quarter over quarter sales growth. Further analyses showed that the favorable outcomes were due to the greater sharing of expertise and specialized knowledge among team members.[48] A study of seventy-six restaurants with takeout services found that performance (a composite of carryout accuracy, delivery accuracy, customer satisfaction, facilities audit score, and sanitation audit score) was significantly higher in cases in which servant leaders created a service culture—developed people, gave back to the community, put the interests of others ahead of their own, freed employees to handle problems, and refused to compromise on ethical principles.[49]

Servant leadership is subtle. On one hand, groups require direction and need leaders who decisively serve as the final authority on matters of importance. On the other hand, evidence suggests that when influence is wielded as a blunt instrument, performance and satisfaction within groups are impaired. Again, it does not matter to which leadership theory you subscribe. Any credible theory would require the following of you:

- To provide psychological anchorage of safety and security
- To provide encouragement, guidance, and support (both material and emotional)
- To nurture the development of potential
- To create expectations, clarify roles and role boundaries, and set rules and limits for task performance
- To exhibit and pass on positive values: respect, trust, and service to others
- To engender the ability to change and adapt—and to deal effectively with stress and adversity
- To promote curiosity and self-development and to help employees locate their passions
- To maintain employees' positive outlook on their prospects for success, as individuals and as a part of teams

The virtues of power sharing and delegation of authority contribute to a favorable climate of openness, proactivity, self-determination, and responsible care for the organization. "*Freedom to . . .*" contributes a big part of the satisfaction we derive from work. Freedom to use our brains to decide the way work should be carried out is an elementary facet of job satisfaction. So, too, is having some control over the context of the work, such as the timing of the work, the place of work, and the order in which tasks need to be accomplished. Minimally, people want to have some control over the work they produce and be *free from* coercion and related autocratic tactics, such as threats (loss of promotion, loss of time off). Without suitable room for decision making and independent action, employees will never consider the work theirs and will never feel compelled to undertake the extraordinary.

Producing a culture in which people feel accepted, valued, safe, and vital is a critical aspect of organizational performance. Creating such a climate asks a lot of management, but the good ones can guide employees while also keeping employee passions alive and their sensibilities open to new ideas and experiences. Some people are more brittle than others and may need greater managerial care to sustain their sense of worth and efficacy. Conversely, organizations that are afflicted by unforgiving and unsupportive management miss out on all the things that a healthier outlook on employees' value and energies would bring. They miss out on the benefits of having people who feel liked and accepted; are more accepting of their shortcomings; take greater responsibility for the consequences of their actions; worry less about rejection and feel less emotionally disturbed by negative feedback; take more risks and engage in more experimentation; unwaveringly persist with projects; and can fail without feeling irrevocably defeated.

CHAPTER TEN

Reward High Performers

ORGANIZATIONS FIND MANY ways to be ordinary. Despite the incessant rhetoric of attracting and retaining the best, organizations often stuff their offices with mediocre performers. The reason is simple. The decisions of these organizations regarding hiring, pay, promotions, and retention are based on factors other than merit: factors that intrude on skill-based considerations, such as friendship ties, tenure, favoritism, politics, and discrimination. The people who would be best at doing the work are not the ones doing it. The consequences to organizations are obvious.

In this chapter, we explore the prerequisite of merit in creating high-performance organizations. Although the concept of merit is straightforward, we discuss the several ways that companies subvert its use and impair organizations' long-term health. Conversely, we discuss ways to ensure that merit-based decisions are appropriately made and applied.

Merit presumes that decisions regarding the way rewards are distributed are grounded on abilities and contributions. The idea that people who contribute more should get more in return relative to others is a principle that children as young as thirty-six months grasp. For example, preschoolers who observe two people baking cookies divide the spoils according to the amount of work each performs.[1] In fact, most social mammals have a keen sense of distributive fairness. Capuchin monkeys that feel cheated through an unfair distribution of rewards will refuse to continue with an experimental task or will throw their miserly reward at the experimenter in protest.[2] Humans behave similarly. In ultimatum games in which one player recommends a distribution of rewards that another player can accept or reject, players tend to reject unfair offers even though that player receives nothing as a result and is worse off for it (the distributing player also suffers a loss in ultimatum games; however, players will still reject offers even if the allocator is unaffected by the decision, albeit rejection occurs to a lesser degree).[3] Therefore, clearly fairness entails more than pure, rational economics.

Fairness is culturally ubiquitous, and theorists believe that it is evolutionarily rooted in social societies to promote cooperation. When something seems unfair, our brains send us emotional signals to inform us that something is amiss that must be rectified. Thus, feelings of injustice serve as warnings that the quality of our relationships are endangered and that some form of remedial action is required.

Justice can be restored in several ways, some of which mend relationships and some which irrevocably sours them. If a person feels slighted, the most straightforward repair is for the person to point out the iniquity in the hope of eliciting due compensation or an acceptable apology. If the injustice persists and an individual believes they are under-rewarded, they may take several actions—none of which is particularly good for organizations. First, they may lower the time and effort they devote to their job or reduce their collegiality and helpfulness toward others as a way to realign their contributions to the perceived rewards they receive. Second, if the organization through the actions of management is viewed as the begetter of injustice, then an employee may get even with the organization through theft, sabotage, reputational damage, or other retributive actions designed to lower the outcomes of the institution. For example, a disgruntled employee at Tesla in information technology recently altered the code used in the Tesla Manufacturing Operating System, causing extensive damage.[4] This employee is a modern-age variant of a long line of production saboteurs that include luddites (who broke knitting frames) and chartists (who pulled plugs on steam engines that fueled factories). And, third, the employee can terminate the relationship by exiting the organization with the associated cost of replacement estimated to be approximately the same as the departing employee's annual salary.

When executed well, merit-based pay for performance plans increase job satisfaction and motivate action.[5] Indeed, contingent pay is part of a complex of practices that together form high-performance work systems. These systems are made up of rigorous recruitment and selection procedures, liberal allowances for training and development, employee participation and decentralized decision-making, flexible work arrangements, performance management programs, and pay for performance and incentive compensation plans. High-performance work practices collectively affect organizational performance by enhancing the capabilities of the workforce, increasing commitment to the organization, empowering and motivating employees, and promoting cross-functional relationships and information sharing. These composite programs have been reliably associated with higher productivity, profitability, growth, innovation, and service.[6]

The effects of the incentivizing elements of rewards are well known and codified as The Law of Effect: people will enact behaviors for which they anticipate a valued reward and will continue to exhibit those behaviors for as long as the reward is expected. The figurative carrot, however, is not universally appealing or effective. In practice, the link between reward and performance is not straightforward. The association is complicated by the many different kinds of rewards, different kinds of performances, and different kinds of motivational states, and these interact in countless ways.

Given the volumes written on the topic of why people do what they do, this chapter will not settle the matter of motivation. Indeed, just about anything declarative about motivation will be controversial. Even the seminal, often-cited thesis of Frederick Hertzberg, which today seems tame, created a stir following the 1959 publication of *The Motivation to Work*. Hertzberg claimed that motivators fall into two classes that he referred to as hygiene factors and motivating factors. The latter roughly describes intrinsically appealing aspects of tasks, such as feelings of achievement. The former identifies external or extrinsic factors, such as money, that, if amply provided, eliminate dissatisfaction but do not substantively contribute to satisfaction. At the time of his thesis, the claim that extrinsic motivators are not as potent to satisfaction as intrinsic factors was viewed skeptically. Since then, however, we can say that Hertzberg's claims mostly have been supported.

This is not to say that money or other extrinsic factors are unimportant to our satisfaction and welfare. Money affords greater freedom from the mundane; more choices and options; resources that can be deployed to reduce stress or enhance convenience; a sense of security, autonomy, and control; and acquisition of goods that can be applied to meeting personal needs and goals. Given the advantages of income and wealth, it is not surprising that money positively relates to better mental and physical health, and negatively relates to mortality. As Abraham Maslow sagely asserted, money is one of those substances that accommodates basic needs and liberates people to pursue other more fulfilling concerns.[7]

Debate rages about exactly what those concerns are, but we believe that academic psychologist Carol Ryff has it about right in her articulation of universal needs.[8] Ryff originally developed her ideas of well-being—what people need to flourish—by synthesizing accounts of quality of life from philosophy, the humanities, and social sciences. The set of needs she proposes substantially overlaps with, or subsumes, those laid out in other need theories.[9] We are confident, therefore, that her list covers needs that generally are agreed on as essential for individuals' happiness and personal welfare. Additionally, we see no reason why the psychology of different age cohorts (i.e., generations) would differ on Ryff's proposed conceptualization of needs. People want the same basic things, which does not change with a person's date of birth. But the weighting of motivations may change with age and experience may inform how personal needs can best be fulfilled.[10] For example, millennials seem to think that starting one's own business may be the best route to autonomy and purpose.[11]

The results of Ryff's work yield six needs:

- *Positive relations/belonging*: Has warm, pleasurable, and trusting relationships with others; feels connected and accepted by others
- *Purpose in life/meaning*: Believes that one has important aims in life and a clear sense of direction

- *Autonomy:* Freely acts according to one's standards, values, and beliefs
- *Self-acceptance:* Holds a positive evaluation of oneself, accepting of who one is inclusive of strengths and imperfections
- *Environmental mastery/confidence:* Competently manages one's life, maintaining personal composure, control, and efficacy in problematic and emotion-infused situations
- *Personal growth:* Progressively develops expertise and continuously advances toward personal potential

This list highlights rewards that come from within, or that are intrinsic to the person and the activity in which they are engaged. Most people are well-versed on the distinction between external and internal rewards as reasons for action. With external rewards, the locus for behavior is external reward, such as pay. With internal rewards, the activity serves as its own reinforcer. The behavior is repeated because people enjoy engaging in the activity, thereby deriving their own pleasure in the doing. The challenge, purpose, novelty, and engagement of the work provide the rationale for doing the work. Thus, one of the easiest ways to motivate employees is to help them find their calling.

On one hand, people clearly do things because of the extrinsic, or external, rewards they will receive as a result. On the other hand, people also derive pleasure from the actual work they do. These two forms of motivation—extrinsic and intrinsic—interact. For example, research shows that the promise of reward in exchange for performing behaviors that people enjoy diminishes the satisfaction a person takes in that behavior and the likelihood that the behavior will be repeated in the absence of the reward. The seminal studies in this area were conducted with children and replicated on adult populations. For example, Lepper and Greene showed that children who were told that they would be monitored and receive a reward following an activity showed less interest in the activity two weeks later.[12] Rewarding activities that people enjoy crowds out the pleasure they derive from the activity by controlling its performance and making the completion of the task the justification for doing it.[13] This *undermining effect* is particularly pronounced when the incentives to act are direct, proximal, and salient: when, in the vernacular of business, employees have a clear line of sight.

BOX 10.1
Pay for Performance in a German Steel Company

A German Steel company is a major producer of sheet metal for the auto and beverage industries that employs 2,500 people. The company's fortunes declined in the 1980s because of errant mergers, new foreign competition, and the privatization of former state-owned enterprises. It experienced its first loss in 1993. Through a secession of remedial actions, however, it was able to correct course and return to profitability. A few of these corrective measures were the establishment of semi-autonomous work teams; an increase in pay 15–20 percent above the market for the metals industry to attract workers to, and retain them within, a rural location; and introduction of a monthly team incentive plan (for twenty-five production teams) based on production unit output. Investigators examined the effects of the plan over a ten-year period in conjunction with the team structure. They found that the incentive increased production by 3.4 percent. These benefits, however, were erased by decreases in quality (scrap waste) and increases in machine down times (the latter occurred because people ran the machines for longer periods without stopping them for scheduled maintenance).

Box 10.1 describes a typical case in which an organization ties pay to performance, and it illustrates some of the complexities surrounding pay for performance plans.[14] The case shows that express contingencies between pay and performance increase quantitative outcomes, such as productivity. Thus, the company saw increases in tonnage output as a result of the financial incentives it had put in place. The case also shows that quality outcomes decreased, which is consistent with a recent meta-analyses that shows that the effects of financial incentives on task performance is weaker for quality than quantity.[15] Quality and creativity tend to be regulated by the inherent interest people have in the work—or by the work's intrinsic properties. The more pleasurable the work, the higher the quality and creativity of employees.[16]

Although it is uncertain if the steel company could improve quantity and quality at the same time, if possible, they could have offered incentives for quality improvements. Research indicates that quality and creativity can be enhanced when specifically set as goals.[17] In these instances, the reward directs people's attention to the intrinsically satisfying aspects of the work: to the challenge of coming up with new ideas or finding better ways of doing things. The financial reward becomes a secondary add-on benefit: the proverbial icing on the cake.

In addition to its direct influence on performance, contingent pay has another, less appreciated, effect on organizational performance through sorting effects. Sorting effects occur when appropriately rewarded high performers stay with organizations and lesser rewarded poor performers self-select out.[18] The changing complexion of the workforce induced by successful merit programs can be substantial, with notable results. For example, in one study, researchers looked at productivity gains in an automobile glass installation company before and after pay was more closely connected to productivity. About half of the gains were attributable to the incentive properties of the new pay system. Another half, however, were attributable to changes in the configuration of the workforce as less productive employees dropped out and were replaced by more productive employees.[19] Therefore, merit pay programs often serve as filters that strain low performers from the system. Although turnover is inversely related to organizational performance—the higher the turnover, the lower the organizational performance—this association depends not only on the magnitude of departures but also on who is coming and going as well.

Clearly, the complexion of the workforce affects organizational performance. We recently saw a question posted on LinkedIn in which the inquirer asked for ways to hire the best people. Had we responded, we would have said that to attract and hire the best talent, a company should already have the best and should actively promote that fact. There is truth to the old saw that the people make the place. It simply is easier to recruit people into groups that have reputations for excellence. High performers are more likely to want to join and remain with companies with other high performers who can make them better and more successful through the instrumental and social support they receive.[20]

Joining talent-rich organizations makes a difference. A study of sell-side security analysts in investment banks found that independent rankings of these analysts were higher when they were surrounded by similarly high-ranking analysts and better performing colleagues in related departments.[21] The same results occur in the arts and sports. For example, actors who are surrounded by a better cast and production crew are more likely to be recognized for their roles.[22] High-quality teams not only aid the best on the group. The analysts who benefited the most from high-performing coworkers were those who were recognized for their excellence but not at the top of the rankings. Indeed, it is common in teams that the top members will lift the performances of good, but less capable, members. In a simple example using motor persistence, Otto Kohler showed that collective performances can exceed the sum of what people can do individually (i.e., the Kohler effect). He asked individuals to hold a bar out in front of them for as long as possible. Those same people were then asked to repeat the task, but this time in a group and with their arms stretched out over a rope so that when the arm of any individual gave out and hit the rope, a timer was stopped and the performance for the group was recorded. (This is a conjunctive task in which the group's performance is as good as the worst performer.) The greatest increases in times occurred with individuals who had the lowest individual results.[23] The Kohler effect is readily seen in naturalistic settings. In relay races, for example, inferior swimmers record faster times than they do in individual contests.[24] The times of the slowest swimmers when measured individually increase in the group setting.

Extrapolating to working groups, we can see several possible reasons for this effect and the principles that leaders may want to keep in mind when managing teams. First, people are interdependent in that they share a common goal. Second, each member is indispensable to goal success. Third, every member has a vested interest in each other's success and they are depending on each other to do their best. Fourth, the observation of others performing well stimulates upward comparisons and healthy internal competition: the mere comparison with another who is performing well facilitates performance. This latter effect is longstanding in the scientific literature. In the late 1890s, Triplett showed that children wound a fishing reel faster when paired with another child than when alone. This everyday phenomenon of *social facilitation* can be experienced, say, at the gym when running alongside another on the treadmill. The mere presence of another runner may be enough to spur you on to exhausting, heart-palpitating speeds.[25]

REMAINING ORGANIZATIONALLY FIT

Remaining organizationally fit is like exercise. It unfortunately takes our bodies a long time to build strength and endurance, but no time at all to lose them. Thus, once the executional abilities of the workforce are weakened, building up capabilities again requires more effort than the managerial neglect it took to tear them down. The erosion of organizational abilities occurs in four easy steps:

Abandon Merit

Most organizations say they have merit programs in place. These programs, however, often are so horribly misshapen and riddled with bias that these may be described as false meritocracies. They are merit programs in theory but not in substance. The companies go through the laborious, time-consuming motions only to yield dubious, often counterproductive, outcomes. As the causal connection between performance and pay and promotions are severed, those who are most able to leave the organization for more hospitable places, do.[26] The futility in advancement and growth in compensation based on factors under one's direct control, in addition to the specter of undeserved accommodations for lackluster performers, are too much for superior performers to take.[27] Consequently, mediocre performers become cemented in place and crowd out high potential newcomers who rapidly see their futures curtailed by less ambitious and less talented employees.[28]

Employees are most satisfied with their compensation when certain conditions are met.[29]

- Equitable: The company has a pay-for-performance organizational charter and expressed desire to reward the most deserving.
- Accurate: Efforts are made to mitigate false assessments and suppress bias (see box 10.2 for common rating biases).
- Reflective of contributions: The nature and size of rewards are commensurate with the magnitude of the contributions.
- Consistent: The same standards are applied evenhandedly across the organization.
- Correctable: Each person has an opportunity to describe their accomplishments and to appeal decisions that seem wrong.
- Representative: Evaluations consider the totality of performance and are not isolated incidences or behavioral slices of a much larger performance domain.

Most of these conditions can be satisfied through internal reviews called calibration sessions and the use of a senior-level, cross-functional rewards oversight committee. This committee reviews evaluations and

---

BOX IO.2
Common Performance Biases

- **Centrality**: The Lake Wobegon effect—raters view everyone as average to slightly above average
- **Range Restriction**: Raters tend to make very small discriminations among people and, thus, use only a small portion of the rating scale in their evaluations
- **Leniency**: The inclination to rate people higher than actual performance would warrant
- **Severity**: The inclination to rate people lower than actual performance would warrant
- **Selective Recall**: In attempting to reconstruct a year of performance, the most recent events will be the most salient
- **Halo (Horns)**: The tendency for favorable (unfavorable) impressions and general likability (unlikability) to color judgments about performance
- **Attributional (The Fundamental Attribution Error)**: Actors view their behaviors as occurring in a situational context (as affected by external events such as luck) and observers see that same behavior as motivated by personal traits (e.g., ability): self-raters, then, tend to be more forgiving of performance problems than supervisory raters, and evaluate themselves more highly
- **Perspective**: High performers tend to rate themselves more harshly, and lower, than poor performers rate themselves

---

pay decisions throughout the organization and has the power to make adjustments if needed. This committee also generates reports of results that it disseminates to key managers so that they can see the decisions and supporting rationales that were made throughout the organization. The calibration sessions are meetings that occur at each level of management. Managers review employees: evaluations and recommended pay increases, abilities and aspirations, and developmental opportunities outside of employees' immediate areas. In general, the calibration process ensures that performance standards are uniformly applied and that people are in the right roles, are doing the work they enjoy, and are growing. Indeed, juxtaposing tangible standards with levels of performance is an effective means of improving the validity of performance estimates.[30]

Compromise Performance Standards

As organizations are overtaken by poor to middling performers, correcting a culture of mediocrity becomes increasingly difficult. For starters, poorer performers have mistaken perspectives of their true abilities. They evaluate their abilities as higher than the facts admit. Because they do not have the appropriate professional and vocational norms to hold up as standards of excellence, they falsely believe they are better than they are. (This is called the Dunning-Kruger effect.)[31] Indeed, research has shown that high versus low performers are better able to calibrate their performances to valid cues and standards because they have better metacognitions about what they know and do not know.[32]

The Dunning-Kruger effect has two negative consequences. For one, it breeds complacency. Employees' inflated sense of aptitude and accomplishment gives them little incentive to work at improving. Thus, they remain moribund in their self-satisfaction. Their performance is arrested with their delusional security that they have done everything within their power to make things better.[33] This has been called the "double curse of incompetence."[34]

Second, as good as they think they may be, they nevertheless are able to recognize people who are better. Moved by feelings of inferiority, hostility, envy, and resentment, and believing that they may lose their privileged access to power, status, and money to high performers, they make sure that high performers are never hired or are able to prove their mettle by undermining their work by withholding critical information and resources; spreading rumors, demeaning, excluding, criticizing, dismissing, and abusing; assigning superfluous work or work overloads; and using other subversive means to cut others down to size.

The victimization of high performers is a well-established finding in field and lab investigations. The research evidentially supports what we have popularly recognized for some time. The Japanese have a saying, "The nail that sticks up gets hammered down." Scandinavian countries have the concept of Jante law: a set of rules that maintain that people should not stand out above others.[35] Other Western cultures have the tall poppy syndrome that involves the idea of eliminating conspicuous rivals.[36] The idea of extinguishing worthy competitors may date back to Herodotus (see box 10.3).[37]

BOX 10.3
Tall Poppies

Periander, the Tyrant of Corinth, sends a messenger to Thrasybulus, the Tyrant of Myletus, for advice on how to rule. Without saying a word, Thrasybulus walks the messenger into a field of wheat and annihilates the tallest stocks, destroying the choice parts of the wheat. The messenger returns to Periander with this vivid description of Thrasybulus obliterating the most prominent wheat in a field. Periander got the message: cut down anything that rises above one's own stature. He decapitated the best people around him.

Source: Herodotus, *The Histories*, Book 5, 92e-g.

These negative effects are most acute in competitive environments that are conceived as zero-sum games in which one person's gain is perceived as another's loss. These conditions can be tempered by workgroup identification and abundance mindsets (e.g., manifold career opportunities).[38] The formation of a workgroup identity and a strong sense of team suggests that all individuals are working in behalf of the group. One individual's success is viewed in the context of the team: as elevating the entire group as opposed to raising one's personal status. Thus, people can excel if the superlatives attached to performers are traceable to the idea that the team made the exemplary performance possible. No one stands apart from, or above, the interests of the group.

Fail to Act on Personnel Issues

One of the most common regrets expressed to us by senior managers over the years is that they did not act on personnel issues swiftly enough—or at all. In general, executives need to address two types of personnel matters. One concerns cultural fit. A person may be a superb performer but imposes costs on the organization because their style does not mesh with the values of the organization. The paradigm cases are (1) the high-performing yet egocentric, self-aggrandizing, uncooperative person—the narcissist, for example—who only does what is in their own interest and gives nothing back to the institution; and (2) the micromanager who, for well- or poorly intentioned reasons, continuously inserts themself into projects and never allows others to grow and thrive. Like helicopter, or bulldozer, parents (in parts of Europe, they are called, "curling parents" who sweep the path clear for their little stones), they intervene at every hint of trouble, protecting their young wards from error, tribulation, and distress. Unredeemable versions of these managers must go.

The other problematic person is one who is not fully competent to perform the expected array of duties, including the people who have been "doing the job for years." They are not, however, working to the extent and quality desired. As difficult as dismissal may be, if success is the goal, it cannot be secured handily without the right people in place. Keeping them where they are or sequestering them in marginal roles are not the answers. Business has the reputation of interpersonal brutality by displacing people with or without cause. Because decisions to terminate are hard for most executives, many adopt a prolonged wait and see attitude that they later regret.

Separations do not have to be angst ridden; they can be handled empathically. Health Catalyst, a health analytics company, for example, considers separations a no-fault incident for reasons resulting from poor performance or cultural incompatibilities. Both parties were mistaken about the relationship and, consequently, the company allots a minimum of three months of severance pay to employees so that life may go on for the employee without putting him or her in financial peril. Additionally, companies such as PURE Insurance, a premium property and casualty company, offers employees a host of career transition options: PURE extends benefits coverages, assists with resume preparation, facilitates networking, provides coaching and advisory services, and covers relocation costs. These practices support honest communications between employees and their employers, ease tensions that may arise during separations, and promote a content league of alumni.

Loosen Hiring Practices

An executive once said to us, "If you don't want performance problems, don't hire them." He well understood how quickly an organization can be compromised by relaxing hiring standards. The counterpoint is clear. Have well-articulated selection criteria for each position, train hiring personnel on interviewing techniques, and rigidly stick to established hiring and selection protocols. Having well-thought-out hiring procedures minimizes the insidious ways that low-caliber applicants may infiltrate organizations. For example, roughly 70 percent of companies have employee referral plans. In general, these are cost-effective means of hiring people who tend to perform better and stay longer than those who enter through external avenues.[39] A prototypical program is one in which employees can recommend candidates for employment and, if the person is selected and remains with the company for 45 days to six months, the referring employee receives a cash bonus. People who are concerned about their careers, however, may have an incentive to refer less-qualified candidates into one's own area. Additionally, people who are not especially committed to the organization or who are self-interested actors may refer others simply for the money or to advance candidates who will be beholden loyal supporters.[40] These adverse results would be hard to obtain with thorough hiring procedures in place. Some companies take extra precautions by entertaining only those referrals that come from outside the referrer's immediate area and only after employees have been in the organization for a minimum amount of time and are confident of their place in the organization.

Most companies are not strictly meritocracies. This is a good thing. As Michael Young's satirical sociological novel, *The Rise of the Meritocracy*, suggests, merit can be overdone.[41] At the extreme, merit can have a *Hunger Games*–like quality in which some people acquire more than they need through their talents and others have barely enough to survive. The exaggerated meritocracies in which the most able parlay their reputations and capabilities into greater rewards such that the rich get richer and the poor get poorer is called the Mathew effect (see box 10.4).[42] Given the biblical overtones, it is unsurprising that talent and rewards have a moral nexus that finds expression in the Protestant ethic.[43] The Protestant ethic encompasses a composite set of beliefs that through dedication, hard work, and a degree of asceticism, one will find fulfillment and reward. Those who exercise God-given gifts will be blessed and rewarded and those who do not, the idle, condemned. Unfortunately, in real life, we often make the logical fallacy of affirming the consequence. If people get what they deserve, we also tend to believe they deserve what they get—an economic morality play of sorts that provides a hardy defense for the status quo.[44]

In organizations, merit, or the principle of equity, is not the only distributive rule that is used. The values organizations wish to inculcate

BOX 10.4
Parable of the Talents

In the parable of the talents, a magister entrusts eight talents to three servants while he travels: five talents for one servant, two for another, and one talent for the third. A talent originally was a unit of weight (25.86 kg) associated with the content of silver and gold in coins. A talent was a lot of money: at 0.46 per gram of silver in 2018, one talent today would be worth $11,896. Thus, a talent was exclusive to the wealthy and represented a unit of high inherent value. The two servants with more talents invest the money and produce a handsome return for the magister. The third servant safeguards his talent by burying it and is rebuked for not making more of his talent.

are inadequately supported through merit alone. The social ideal of semimeritocratic organizations is to balance equity with allocations based on equality and need.[45] On certain occasions, each distributive rule makes sense to implement in organizations. For example, a company may decide to pay people a living wage regardless of abilities or market circumstances. Patagonia, the socially responsible retailer for outdoor enthusiasts, pays a living wage using one of the several available calculators. The company believes that providing a minimum quality of life supersedes other considerations in the distribution of resources. Similarly, many benefits, such as health and welfare plans, serve the same function. These benefits provide minimum safeguards for employees' well-being that frees them from the insecurity that can intrude on performance and undermine personal welfare. Some companies also maintain significant reserves to assist employees when they have emergencies. Relieving employees from worry and providing greater surety that their basic needs will be met fosters higher levels of organizational commitment and performance.[46]

As with most allocation rules, there are appropriate and inappropriate applications. For example, during our lengthy time in consulting, we have heard of circumstances in which employees (mostly men) were given pay increases following the birth of a child to lend financial assistance to the growing family. As it happens, this practice is common enough that it has a name and a tangible consequence: the so-called fatherhood wage premium has been estimated to account for 3 percent to 10 percent in salary above singles and childless couples.[47] Therefore, in situations in which a baby blanket or gift card would do, these companies blemish a system that ostensibly was reserved for merit. Employees' needs could easily be handled through other mechanisms as opposed to using reward outlets that were never intended for these purposes.

Equality is simply a rule that recommends that people share in the bounty of one's efforts equally. It makes sense to treat people equally when either their individual contributions or the outcomes of their efforts cannot be carved up. For example, a win or loss in sports cannot be divided among members of the team. Similarly, system-wide profits or credits for a videogame product cannot easily be parsed and traced to the contributions of each person. Consequently, organizations often share a percentage of the profits equally among employees and include all contributors on the credit roll.

It is possible to recognize team and individual performance at once. A company may recognize a team as an entity while recognizing particular members for their specific achievements. For example, a company can celebrate team wins but also call out individuals for personal accomplishments, creativity, and exemplification of cultural values. Many corporate incentive plans have these mixed components in which a portion of a pot of funds are distributed among members equally and a portion is distributed to members based on individual performance.

The complementariness of equity and equality in organizations is critical. Good organizations try to maintain a balance between the two, and with good reason. Egalitarian distributions are designed to promote cooperation and healthy social relations. Equitable distributions recognize personal achievements that tend to foster competition.[48] Companies want the best of both worlds. They want people to strive on their own accord while also maintaining quality social relations to minimize the interpersonal conflicts necessary for smooth execution. They want personal excellence without cutthroat competition and want cooperation without social loafing or free riding. In this regard, the divisibility of performance may be essential. Indeed, without distinct responsibilities and ways of telling the contributions of one person apart from another, people are likely to exert less physical and mental effort. In 1913, a French agricultural engineer named Max Ringelmann asked individuals to pull on a rope, and then repeated the exercise with groups of people pulling. In measuring the force of the pull, he observed that group members put in less effort than each person pulling alone. He further noticed that as the group size grew, the loss of individual effort became more marked. Thus, when personal responsibility for results is diffused or when individual efforts are hard to discern or perceived as unimportant, people tend to ease up on the intensity to which they will exert themselves, or socially loaf.[49]

Some determination of a person's value has to be made at some time whether as measures of contribution to a team or annual achievements against goals. Yet measurement is a frustrating topic for several organizations that believe it has become a nuisance that is too unpleasant to continue.[50] Nevertheless, despite high-profile corporate defections from the end-of-year evaluation rite that include Adobe, Dell, IBM, REI, and Microsoft, the performance appraisal process remains a staple in most organizations.[51] Done properly and with conviction, the process can work. Recent studies have shown that evaluation scores are functionally informative and are associated with merit increases, promotions, and other organizational decisions.[52] The traditional process, however, has not accomplished its desired ends in all organizations and, therefore, a few companies have chosen to opt out.

The reasons for this abandonment of a formal performance appraisal procedure are threefold. First, the retrospective aspect of the review is superfluous to performance improvement; second, life inside organizations has become more unpredictable and transient, and annual cycles are poorly suited for faster paces and rapid pivots in direction; and, third, work increasingly is performed in teams versus by sole contributors. In general, attention has shifted away from measurement toward ongoing dialogue between managers and employees, continuous feedback, and personal development. Taken together, companies view the performance management process as a lot of work for which they see little return.

We have reservations about total abdication of performance evaluations. We applaud the emphasis on communications and personal growth; nevertheless, companies that have jettisoned formal ratings still must render evaluations about people for myriad reasons at various times. Our fear is that in the absence of a formal process, decision making will be ambiguous and of questionable accuracy—that the appraisal process will go underground and become hidden and prejudicial. We understand the connotations that negative evaluative labels can have. We also understand managers' fears of damaging employer–employee relations through direct, albeit diplomatic, nega-tive feedback. Furthermore, we recognize that a rigorous process can be highly time-consuming. Nothing says, however, that performance reviews must be conducted with the same intensity on every person every year.

Quite a bit could be said about performance measurement; thus, our comments below are not exhaustive. Instead, we highlight a few items that receive less attention in the business literature.

- *Performance may not be normally distributed.* In a comprehensive study of more than six hundred thousand researchers, entertain-ers, politicians, and athletes, the paper's authors found that per-formance is distributed according to an exponential power law as opposed to the more familiar normal distribution in many circum-stances (see figure 10.1).[53] The thicker positive tale indicates that there are more high performers than the typical normal distribu-tion credits. Therefore, if companies were to force people into a normal distribution, they would be underestimating the true num-ber of high performers. (The power distribution also suggests that most people are ordinary, at best, but the sample the researchers used would have included only people who met minimum quali-fications and, therefore, "average" in that context may be "above average" or "good enough" to be included on a list.)
- *Performance may be best measured on a ratio scale* (known as a general labeled magnitude scale[54]). A plethora of rating scales exist. We would be hard-pressed to qualify many of these as

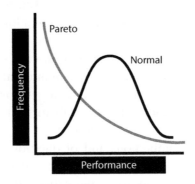

Figure 10.1 Normal and Pareto distributions.

psychometrically sound to be used in practice as they would not meet minimum standards for reliability and validity. There is much room for improvement. Apart from those problems, most of these measures of performance presume that the distances between ratings are equidistant. For example, the conventional four- or five-point scale that evaluates employees on the extent to which they meet expectations, or adhere to certain, specified behaviors, assumes that the distance between one and two is the same as between a four and a five. Our experiences, however, suggest that performance may be best assessed on ratio scales in which distances between "good" and "very good" and between "bad" and "very bad" are not the same. This corresponds to managers' frequent requests for more rating room at the top of the scale so they can make finer discriminations in performance. A sample magnitude scale is provided in figure 10.2. As deployed, sample behaviors would be scaled and overlaid onto an instrument such as the one depicted. Furthermore, as a means to square the the

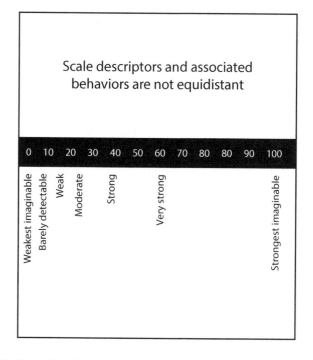

Figure 10.2 Generalized labeled magnitude scale.

232 Reward High Performers

lower and upper anchor amongs people, respondents are asked to reflect on the most extreme or intense experiences in any domain that pertain to the attribute being measured; in that way, the scales are similarly calibrated to individuals' range of experiences.

- *Managerial performance training helps.* Studies indicate that organizations that provide more performance management training have performance systems that deliver more valued outcomes, such as increases in individuals' performances and greater employee retention.[55] Frame of reference training is one aspect of training that is proven effective in producing more accurate evaluations. With this type of training, trainees learn to associate sample behaviors with specific conceptualizations of performance so that people who observe the same behaviors interpret them in the same ways.[56]

- *Assessments are more reliable when made of multiple items, on multiple occasions, by multiple people.* Taken together, these "multiples" afford a better sampling of behaviors and a more accurate rendering of performance. These principles are well-supported in the psychometric literature. None of these, however, are used regularly in organizations. The idea behind multiple items is that any concept of performance will be poorly captured, or summarized, through a single item. For example, there are many ways to describe "Provides excellent service." "Excellence" may be defined as "timeliness," "courteousness," and "competence."

Multiple situations necessitate ongoing communications and feedback. If managers are close enough to the work, they can suitably fill this role. Increasingly, however, organizations have been using recognition programs to gather ongoing feedback to capture and describe the feats of their personnel. Recognition plans come in all shapes and sizes. Discretionary continuous plans are ways for colleagues and customers to spontaneously thank one another for their special efforts through a kind word. Recognition plans also can involve formal criteria and ceremonies in which winners can be:

- Selected by individuals, committees, or all-company votes
- Selected by upward (employees vote on managers) or downward (managers vote on staff) votes: For example, Edmunds, the authoritative source for all things cars, in a highly visible leadership program called Pave the Road, selects the best managers for

recognition on standing criteria each year. These criteria include managers' ability to inspire, develop, and connect employees (e.g., to resources, people, committees), while preserving employees' welfare (e.g., not burning them out). The ratings are cross-validated by interviews and three winners are selected and announced at the annual all-employee meeting. The company produces videos of employees describing what they have enjoyed about their managers and how these managers changed their lives.

- Awarded to individuals or teams: For example, North Carolina publisher N2 reserves a portion of its monthly meeting to recognize exemplary contributions to the company. We were on premises the day the entire Editorial Department won. Amanda, the head of the department, is a wonderful visual artist. She drew likenesses of each of her staff members wearing Marvel-esque superhero outfits and described each of their super-human powers in a wonderful and moving tribute to the team.
- Recognized with cash or symbols: Sometimes the award can be big. For the super-exceptional performer of the year, Arkadium, a New York–based digital marketer, bestows the Infinite Possibilities Prize. Twenty-five thousand dollars is given to an employee to do anything he or she wants from going on an extended yoga retreat to working with an established novelist on a first work of fiction. Many times, however, the only symbolic show of appreciation that employees want is a thank you.
- Recognized for financial or nonfinancial results: N2 also holds an end-of-year ceremony in which they bestow Lunch Pail Awards. These whimsical, highly sought-after awards go to the outstanding performers or pure exemplars of institutional values. The award is a metal lunch pail from the 1930s with the person's name etched into the side with car keys.

One interesting facet of recognition plans is that, regardless of their formality and timing, they not only affect the beneficiaries of the awards but also other members of a group. In fact, research shows that team members are positively influenced more than the award recipients. In one study, groups of eight subjects were given a data entry task to perform in two sessions. After the first session, either none, one, three, or all were publicly provided with thank you cards for their performances (correct entries per minute) in session one of the task. On average, people who were thanked did significantly better during the second session. However, people who saw others receive the notes of thanks performed even better.[57] Either through want of betterment or greater appreciation, the performances of the unrecognized improve.[58]

To a large degree, recognition programs provide various perspectives on performance and, therefore, satisfy the condition of having multiple evaluators. Sometimes, however, a company will want to deploy more formal evaluative procedures particularly regarding the quality of management—and deploy 360-degree reviews. These are evaluations of individuals' performances that use anonymous input from multiple proximal parties as the sources of information. Because correlations between supervisory and employee ratings of performance are small to middling, the added information from coworkers at different organizational levels enhances the width and depth of performance data and increases the reliability and validity of the ratings.[59] Once again, the benefits of the 360-degree feedback extend beyond the individual to the system as a whole. For example, a study of 250 firms and ten thousand employees found that the use of multisource feedback was associated with higher sales per employee. These effects are attributed to improvements in employees' functional abilities and greater knowledge sharing promoted by the feedback.[60]

- *Performance is multidimensional.* Performance can be conceived in different ways. Broadly, performance can be conceived as what gets done and how it gets done. The former concerns outcomes— that is, the things produced or created. The latter pertain to personal qualities that enable people to effectively perform. These are typically thought of as competencies, defined as the knowledge, skills, and abilities that employees possess. Having critical competencies that allow people to succeed across functional areas typically is what we say when an employee has potential. They have capabilities that generalize across situations and, when properly utilized, are instrumental in producing results. Thus, doing well on the current job may or may not be predictive of performance in new roles, but having the requisite competencies should be. Organizations often will merge these two aspects of performance into a three-by-three matrix (a "nine-box") in which accomplishments (outcomes) form one axis and competencies (potential) form the other and then make pay and development determinations based on where employees fall in the matrix. The integration of information in this way conveys the right messages: that two of a manager's most important duties are to develop employees' potential and to help them to succeed.

A summary of many of the ideas used to enhance and reinforce performance discussed in this chapter are summarized in box 10.5. Although we relegate the need for feedback to a single item in the list, this should not understate its importance. Much has been written on the why's and how's of feedback, and we need not retrace that ground here. Nevertheless, we will say that the easiest and best way of giving and receiving feedback is naturally—in a manner that is built into the routines of the organization and that is as automatic and effortless as breathing. In this regard, some organizations are adept

---

BOX 10.5
Path to Performance

Hire and promote managers who have high standards and understand what great performance looks like.
Gather information about different kinds of performances throughout the year from multiple people at multiple times.
Provide continuous coaching and **feedback** that is immediate, specific, and actionable (do not mandate dialogue, but recognize managers who do this well).
Clarify what "performance" means and construct the proper scales accordingly.
Calibrate performance ratings and recommended pay increases across the organization to ensure equity; this process has been found to improve accuracy of evaluations.
Train managers on how to equate various performance standards to ratings on a scale (frame of reference training).
Make development a fundamental part of the program; set aside time and resources accordingly.
Make the program matter by paying financial and nonfinancial tribute to the best performers.

at creating feedback environments where individuals are comfortable constructively exchanging information of both positive and negative valence.[61] For example, at Arkadium, feedback is a continuous, positive, habitual experience. A modest sample of their feedback culture occurs every Monday at the staff meetings that are held without fail. A portion of every meeting is reserved for "Li'l Wins and Big Thank Yous" in which people are able to recognize individuals and teams for special efforts and results. It is a period patterned after a Quaker tradition in which Friends sit silently together and, when moved to share thoughts inspired by a spiritual connection, they stand and do so. The practice gives people a way to be mindful of the efforts of others and to publicly express gratitude for good work. If the research is correct, these feedback practices maintain open lines of communication, clarify task activities and goals, and generate more creative and innovative solutions to problems.[62]

Ultimately, when companies become ordinary it is because managers allow it. The decline begins innocently around the edges with a few poor hires and politically motivated pay and promotional decisions. The effects of these decisions slowly encroach on the whole organization. As degeneration accelerates, it becomes increasingly difficult to halt the decline as the oozing body spreads.

In dynamic settings in which the quality of the workforce is subject to change, it is critical to be unyielding on several fronts to keep the company vibrant—to assert positions that are immovable. Thus, we provide our admonitions, the *five nevers:*

- *Never compromise on hiring:* In addition, good organizations continuously monitor the hiring process and make refinements as needed. For example, they will collect and analyze information on who succeeds in the organization and modify hiring criteria to be most diagnostic of job performance.
- *Never keep people who are unable to perform the work:* Nor should you keep people whose actions dismantle operative institutional norms and values. We caution that performance depends on many factors and we have seen countless instances in which a person failed in one role but flourished in another. Therefore, we encourage companies to contemplate whether people who are failing in their current roles might have potential to excel elsewhere. We also recommend that companies not bifurcate the

workforce into stars and everyone else, and exclusively attend to the former and forget about the latter. All companies have the all-important, unheralded B-players whose solid performances and dependability constitute a stable core of the organization and further a more ambient enterprise.[63] These employees should have equal access to all the developmental and career advancement opportunities that are available to the stars.

- *Never allow expedience and politics to intrude upon merit-based decisions:* We qualify this statement by reiterating that not all decisions should be merit based and that good companies try to find the right balance of allocations based on different distributive goals. This includes the necessity of balancing merit with need and equality to alleviate anxieties and foster social cohesion.

- *Never detach the provision of benefits from the enactment of performance:* In organizations, everything given to employees is predicated on the organization's ability to pay; thus, it is necessary for organizations to maintain a strong sense of reciprocity between staff and themselves—to keep attitudes of excessive entitlement in check (that people have a right to benefits that they do not have to repay in kind).[64] Thus, we encourage companies to maintain a persistent, unwavering beat of performance as an organizational backdrop so that mutual expectations between employers and employees are clear.

- *Never accept an unqualified manager:* Like an orchestra, leadership is a mediated art form. The way leaders get their message across is through the virtuosity of management throughout the organization—poor management, poor musicians, poor music. Indeed, Gilley and colleagues list actions that qualify as managerial malpractice, which include trying to fix the incorrigible and hiring, promoting, and retaining managers who do not have the proficiencies and interpersonal acumen to work with others effectively.[65]

CHAPTER ELEVEN

Foster a Leadership Culture

LEADERSHIP IS AT the heart of everything discussed in this book and constitutes the explicit or implicit foundation of every organizational model for performance and success. All models have distinct features, but the preponderance of these models are conceived as systems with multiple parts that leaders must assemble into coherent wholes. We provide sample models and their components in table 11.1.[1]

All of the models describe how organizations transform incoming raw materials into consumable products and services by portraying the formal and informal, human and technological, organizational components that are responsible for this transformation. And, all of the models imply an internal consistency among organizational elements that leaders present to employees as a unified message through the din of practices, procedures, and activities. Fundamentally, then, leadership is an expressive art, or communicative practice, whose net effects are transmitted and felt through culture.[2]

We, admittedly, are partial to the Burke-Litwin organizational model, however, with good reason. The backbone of the model, which we have reproduced in figure 11.1, expressly tethers organizational success

TABLE II.I
Sample organizational models

Name	Components	
Leavitt	Technology	
	Tasks	
	People	
	Structure	
McKinsey 7S	Strategy	Style
	Structure	Shared values
	Systems	Skills
	Staff	
Burke and Litwin	Strategy/mission	Culture
	Structure	Systems
	Tasks	Individual needs
	Leadership	Management practices
Nadler and Tushman	Informal organization	
	Formal organization	
	People	
	Tasks	
	Strategy	

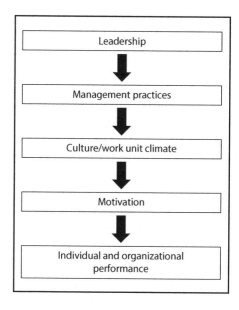

Figure 11.1 Burke-Litwin organizational model (portion).

to leadership and specifically claims that the leadership-performance connection is mediated by culture. Thus, leaders enhance performance by developing a climate that is conducive to high performance. This intuitive set of relationships between leadership, culture, and performance has been of keen interest to researchers for some time and will occupy most of our attention in this chapter.

The popular press consistently stresses the dependence of organizational success on culture. Bestselling business books routinely tout the imperative of culture to organizational performance, such as *Corporate Cultures* by Deal and Kennedy, *Theory Z* by Ouchi, *In Search of Excellence* by Peters and Waterman, *Built to Last* by Porras and Collins, and *Good to Great* by Collins.[3] *Fortune*'s annual roll call of the best companies to work for is based on anonymous employee reports of the culture under the implicit assumption that healthy cultures are associated with financial success.[4] Corporate executives certainly are believers in that claim. Some 92 percent of them believe that culture is directly related to firm value.[5]

As an invisible social force with profound effects on behavior, the importance of culture as an integral complement to strategy, control systems, authority structures, and such makes sense.[6] As we have made clear throughout the book, shared beliefs and values reduce the transaction costs associated with communal goals. In particular, companies with strong cultures—beliefs, norms, and values that are thoroughly and deeply engrained in the organization—delegate and communicate more, require less internal monitoring, coordinate activities more swiftly and effectively, rely less on influence tactics to get things done, and produce more satisfied and motivated employees.[7]

One of the most exhaustive studies of culture was performed by John Kotter and James Heskett who tracked the cultures and performance of comparable companies over four years.[8] The results showed that companies with healthy cultures had about five times the sales and ten times the stock returns over the period examined. Other studies with more modest timelines similarly demonstrate the tie between culture and financial performance.[9] For example, an ambitious study of thirty-two high-technology companies showed that the traits of CEOs are directly related to culture, which, in turn, was related to both financial (e.g., revenue growth, Tobin's Q) and nonfinancial (e.g., analyst recommendations, employee attitudes) outcomes.[10] Sufficient evidence has accumulated to suggest that culture, indeed, is a factor in organizational performance,[11] especially when companies have a clear mission, a penchant for teamwork, and homogeneous and strong cultures (i.e., commonly and robustly felt).[12] Furthermore, a summary of this research attributes strong cultures to healthy, effective leadership.[13] Indeed, research shows that the cultures companies develop are largely associated with the personality traits and actions of executives.[14] In fact, about a third of the variability of cultural attitudes and beliefs can be traced to management's personal proclivities and practices.[15] Thus, leaders distill and frame the complexities of the world into prototypical behaviors that characterize desired meanings that others experience as culture.[16]

The criticality of culture may be felt most acutely when organizations merge, and a mismatch in cultures results. Although the reasons and percentages for merger failures vary by industry and type of merger (e.g., focused versus diversification), it is conceivable that about 70 percent of all mergers fail to produce the financial results expected, and some are just plain ruinous.[17] For example, when Daimler acquired Chrysler, the deal was hailed as a merger of equals and blessed by the respective boards. At the time of the acquisition, both companies were profitable. By the time Daimler shed Chrysler, Chrysler's value had declined by roughly three-quarters over a nine-year span—a direct loss of $37 billion.[18] Both companies grossly underestimated the cultural divide that followed the purchase. First, Daimler assumed much more strategic and operational control than an association between equals would have resembled. The disillusioned employees at Chrysler watched as careers were derailed, promotions overruled, and expectations thwarted. Second, the formal and highly structured management styles at Daimler were at odds with the more free-flowing and relaxed styles at Chrysler. Every practice from administration of pay to the reimbursement of travel expenses became a new source of irritation to Chrysler employees. Thus, began widespread disaffection, critical employee departures, and a consistent unraveling of the venture until Daimler's only alternative was to salvage what they could of the remains.[19]

Everyone who has worked in an organization knows the affective power of leadership and culture, both good and bad. The clearest, most direct evidence for the effects of leaders on performance is from team-level analyses that examine how positive and negative supervisory behaviors influence groups. On one hand, several studies have

242 Foster a Leadership Culture

documented the adverse effects of abusive supervision and incivility on employees' mental and physical health, job satisfaction, and performance.[20] One grim illustration of the ill effects of incivility comes from a recent medical simulation. Twenty-four teams from neonatal units throughout Israel took part in a simulation in which a mannequin connected to medical instrumentation was depicted as suffering from a serious but common disorder called necrotizing enterocolitis, a condition in which bowel tissue disintegrates. The teams' task was to diagnose and treat the infant. Ostensibly, an expert was observing the teams' performance and could communicate with the teams. In the control condition, the expert made no extraordinary comments. In the rude condition, however, the expert exclaimed that the quality of medicine in Israel was poor and that the team would not last a week in his department. The results: composite diagnostic and procedural performance scores were significantly lower for members of teams exposed to rudeness than the scores of members of the control teams, thereby showing how modest doses of incivility can impair medical care.[21] Uncivil oversight fractures psychological safety within teams and disrupts healthy exchanges among team members.[22] In the simulation, teams in the rude condition were less likely to share information and seek help.

On the other hand, supportive, inclusive management practices that provide assurances of safety allow people to take reasonable risks, make mistakes, speak up and challenge the status quo, ask for help and request resources, and contribute in ways one thinks best without fear of reprisals or being undermined.[23] These senses of security are conveyed by egalitarian workplaces that downplay power differentials, enforce norms of respect, encourage the approachability and accessibility of executives, and invite give-and-take feedback in considerate, constructive ways. The evidence overwhelmingly shows that groups that are able to produce safe environments have members who more openly and beneficially interact, learn and grow, display greater creativity, and conceive of themselves as potent and efficacious actors.[24] This translates into better individual and organizational performance and lower turnover.[25] Companies have good reasons to make people feel safe.

Unfortunately, once incivility and uglier forms of misconduct are released into the workplace, the plague spreads.[26] Coworkers and other observers who witness the mistreatment of colleagues are affected.

These third parties experience increased stress and lower morale, mental health, productivity, and commitment to the company, and they perform more poorly on problem-solving and creativity tasks.[27] Furthermore, team performance is impaired as the effects of abusive supervision of some members of the team spread to adversely affect other members.[28] Incivility has expansive, destructive consequences. It is fair to say that incivility is contagious, ominously spreading its dark culture throughout organizations and into family life.[29] We describe a particularly pernicious form of leadership in table 11.2 called the dark triad.[30] This composite of traits, when exhibited by CEOs, has been found to disrupt the smooth workings of top management teams and to have cascading negative effects on attitudes throughout the organization.[31]

In contrast, positive supervisory behaviors that are, for example, encouraging, open, supportive, expectant, and kind, enhance the psychological capital (self-efficacy, hope, optimism, and resilience) of employees and have positive consequences on their general welfare and

TABLE II.2
The dark triad

Narcissism: Arrogant, with a highly inflated sense of self-importance and desert; over-evaluates skills, appearance, intelligence, etc.; doesn't admit to mistakes or take advice, although may feign to do so; infatuated with themselves.

Psychopathy: Does not conform to rules or norms; impulsively engages in risky or dangerous behaviors; cunning and self-interested with disregard for the truth.

Machiavellianism: Self-centered, pragmatic schemers who, through deceit, manipulate others into getting what they want; exploit situations and others for personal gain indifferent to others' plight.

Some of the Things They Do	Some of the Effects They Have
Reject ideas and initiatives, undermine, coerce, scapegoat, invade privacy, behave vindictively, intimidate, humiliate, control/micromanage, reward/ help themselves	Low job satisfaction, low productivity, distress and anxiety, exhaustion, absenteeism, turnover, counter-productive behaviors, undermining of self-confidence/sense of worth, degradation of personal/home life, illness and depression

performance.[32] A great deal of research in positive psychology indicates that those who are positively disposed are more optimistic and satisfied with life, experience greater psychological well-being, feel more connected to others and less socially anxious, have a greater sense of self-worth, are more understanding and less critical of their own mistakes, and tend to be more forward-thinking and motivated.[33] It is understandable, then, how sound management practices can instill the right frame of mind for optimal performance. People who are positive do not think the same way as those who are negative.[34] People who experience positive emotions in the workplace (and elsewhere) are more open to new experiences, attentive to a wider field of stimuli, and have a broader behavioral repertoire in responding. That is, people who are satisfied have a more extensive range of observations, thoughts, and actions than those who are less satisfied. Specifically, they find it easier to muster the resources they need to grow and flourish. Because they are more open to new experiences and knowledge, they tend to adaptively cope with stressors. Because their social relations are sounder, they find it easy to reach out to others for support. Because they are willing to stray from well-trodden paths and experiment with new thoughts and behaviors, they tend to live more exhilarating and intellectually engaging lives. Overall, the upbeat lives of those who are satisfied become self-reinforcing and enduring across the domains of work and home. This conveys a simple formula: the better the management, the more people will thrive and the better they will perform.[35]

Many theories exist about the attributes that make a superb leader. We have summarized several of these in box 11.1 and applied a rudimentary classification to distinguish among these theories. These theories have both distinct and overlapping characteristics and have slightly different organizational aims and functions. Some of these theories concentrate on personality and some focus on facets of leadership that are believed to directly influence employee motivation.

Years ago, we interviewed twenty-five CEOs known for their kindness—and effectiveness—and distilled the text of those conversations into six traits: compassion, integrity, gratitude, authenticity, humility, and humor.[36] These are not all-inclusive traits but are traits that make superior leadership possible. For example, we list humility as one of our virtues. As it happens, humble leaders are more likely than less-than-humble leaders to stimulate innovation by creating an environment in which people more readily help one another and process information in more balanced, unbiased ways.[37] Indeed, a recent meta-analysis shows that these leaders who are quite literally grounded (*humus*—the root for *humility*—is Latin for *earth*) significantly reduce counterproductive work behaviors—behaviors that are contrary to the interests of the organization.[38] All of the traits we list have concomitant research that connects the importance of the trait to the outcome measures of import to organizations—mediated by what the trait enables leaders to do. Again, our original set of traits was incomplete, and we have since enlarged the set to include other traits with clear links to performance, such as conscientiousness,[39] which is one of the main factors on the Big Five personality inventory that assesses achievement motivations and self-discipline, and is one of the most consistent predictors of leadership effectiveness.[40] (Energy, self-confidence, and decisiveness rounds out our current list of leadership traits.)

In returning to the Burke-Litwin model, a major, overlooked feature of their model is that they separate the leader from leadership. Several organizational experts have since made the same point: leadership is not possessed by an individual but rather is a social construction of the leader.[41] Leadership has a "thing-ness" that emerges from a host of social relations in which the leader is engaged and the multiplicity of decisions that they make by which leadership is materialized.[42] Character counts, but only insofar as it enables followers to see what a leader has to offer. A leader with odious dispositions or indecent inclinations would prohibit others from appreciating what leaders have to say no matter how good they otherwise are. A person's true character, if known, can either create a barrier to communications or facilitate the flow.

This raises the question, "What exactly is the materiality of leadership?" Stated differently, "How will we know good leadership when we see it?" Our answer hinges on our view of leadership as an open concept.[43] This notion is borrowed from Wittgenstein's idea of family resemblances, in which he claims that the necessary and sufficient conditions for some concepts cannot be specified. He used games as an example: there are many different kinds of games that have common properties that allow us to categorize them as "games, but none have the exact same features."[44] We believe that, like games, a precise definition of leadership cannot be stated. Any one definition will leave something out that another theorist will believe central. This is readily seen in the list of competing theories we provided in box 11.1.

Theories of Leadership

Traits and Motives

Great Person: Leaders are genetically endowed with special traits that set them apart from others.

Achievement Motivation: Leaders' effectiveness is dependent on the appropriate mix of underlying motives.

Trait Theories: Leaders have particular traits that enable them to emerge as leaders.

Skills and Practices

Skills and Capability/Competencies: Leaders' effectiveness grows over time through experience and the acquisition of skills and abilities.

Complexity: Leaders' central task is to effectively manage large amounts of diverse and rapidly changing information to sustain organization-wide meaning, focus, and clarity of goals.

Exemplary Leadership: Leaders enact a set of practices that, taken together, generate the best outcome.

Role Set/Competing Values: The leader's job is to expertly manage competing demands and skillfully handle trade-offs in the workplace in pursuit of goals.

Path Goal: Leaders' central responsibility is to motivate employees and, therefore, to focus on those things that instill motivation and remove barriers that can get in the way of employees' goal achievement.

Integrity

Authentic Leadership: Leaders form connections with others by building a common purpose in which the leader has personal conviction.

Ethical Leadership: Leaders carry out the organizational mission while exhibiting right conduct through personal actions and interpersonal relations.

Benevolent Leadership: Leaders who pursue actions and produce results aimed toward the common good.

Leader-Staff Relations

Contingency/Situational Leadership: Effective leaders adjust their styles to accommodate the situation.

Servant Leadership: Leaders attend to the needs and interests of employees with the aim of developing employees' full potential and helping them to be successful.

Leader-Member Exchange: Leadership fundamentally is a relationship with employees; the better the relationships, the greater the sense of mutual obligation and reciprocity, the better the results.

Emotional Intelligence: Leaders are able to motivate others by having the ability to "read," understand, and respond to social or emotional cues.

Purpose

Visionary Leadership: Leadership involves the expression and application of ideals throughout the organization.

Charismatic Leadership: Leaders produce an alluring vision for the organization and, through presence and persuasiveness, gain the intellectual and emotional allegiance of the workforce.

Change

Transformational Leadership: Leaders are able to subjugate employees' personal interests in favor of collective ones, and engender the belief among employees that they can accomplish more than they thought possible.

Adaptive Leadership: Leaders help others to be successful in their environment by helping them to make quality decisions in response to the challenges they face.

The best we can do, therefore, is name the criteria that would qualify a person as a leader and to render an opinion about the quality of their leadership based on those criteria. This is similar to the way we evaluate other things in our lives. By way of example, say you go to a movie with friends. Afterward, each person renders an opinion on what they just watched. Experienced movie-goers will back their opinions by appealing to certain aspects of the movie, such as character development, plot, costume design, and sound. The informed viewer is equipped with a set of criteria that they apply to render an opinion to which similarly informed viewers will, mostly, agree. Additionally, although we use the same criteria to evaluate movies, not all criteria will be equally relevant to each movie or weighted in precisely in the same manner by every critic. We would not apply the criteria as stringently to the maker of a student film as an experienced director.

The criteria we developed is based on our knowledge of the leadership literature as well as criteria that have been developed in other evaluative domains, mainly the arts.[45] These criteria provide the foundation for a sensible discussion about who is good and who is not. This set of criteria allows informed observers to distinguish the exceptional from the ordinary and provides a language to communicate the differences. On the positive side, for example, leadership may be described as inspiring, consistent, creative, unique, passionate, and engaging. Alternatively, leadership may be perceived as unpleasant, phony, inept, unfocused, boorish, and pedestrian. Evaluative terms like these serve as the bases for some consensus about what constitutes greatness.

So, let us suggest the following twelve criteria for judging the artistry of leaders:

Aligns: Able to see the organization as a systemic whole and to logically, coherently, and effectively combine its many parts and processes

Builds: Builds a closely knit community and sense of team based on common values and purposes; is invested in the success of the group

Communicates: Eloquently and thoughtfully conveys complex meanings to different audiences in a manner that allows them to understand what is occurring, and why, and what must happen next or get done

Engages: Captures the intellectual interests and curiosities of others and elicits their active, thoughtful participation in the life of the organization

Enlightens: Serves as a model for ethical behavior and right conduct, helping people to reflect on what is most important when making complex decisions

Expresses: Sincerely and authentically voices and acts upon personal beliefs and convictions—expresses what they believe in and stands for in all they say and do

Focuses: Keeps people's attention focused on what is most important as opposed to what is secondary or of inconsequential value in the scheme of things and directs people accordingly

Imagines: Offers novel, creative ways of looking at issues and problems and in thinking about markets, products, and services

Inspires: Gives others confidence in themselves as capable, effective individuals, and inspires and motivates them to excel in their discipline or craft

Instructs: Possesses deep domain expertise and business skills, and acts as an astute teacher and mentor to others through words and deeds

Intends: Articulates a compelling and alluring vision and demonstrates a commitment to its realization, persisting and seeing things through to their logical conclusions (without prematurely giving up)

Rewards: Creates a work environment that is pleasurable, stimulating, and rewarding

Succeeding on all these criteria is difficult, and not even the best leaders do so routinely. Leaders have their strengths and stand out in unique ways. Leadership deficits become apparent when a person resembles a leadership caricature: when they possess only a couple of criteria to the exclusion of all others. For example, the *humanistic* types never miss a birthday, sponsor team dinners at the house, and go out of their way to make the workplace pleasurable, enriching, and fun. The *traditionalists* do only what is prescribed by "the book" and never would contemplate deviating from what a businessperson is supposed to wear, say, or do. The skilled and bureaucratic *technicians* manage numbers and sheets of paper, and attempt to orchestrate every conceivable employee behavior through a carefully planned and rigid set of rules, compensation designs, policies, and organizational structures. Some wildly imaginative but nondirective *shape-shifters* hop from one idea and initiative to the next, dragging befuddled employees along in their wake.

Perhaps the best exemplary case of an incomplete leader involves charisma, a term introduced into the leadership lexicon by Max Weber.[46] Charismatic leaders exude confidence; however, not all charismatic leaders are good and effective. They all have a knack for invigorating employees through their colorful visions of the future and motiving them toward a common goal.[47] There are, however, two types of charismatic leaders. Some are focused on the social good and the welfare of people, whereas others have a strong strain of Machiavellianism and narcissism who craftily advocate outlooks best suited to their personal interests—combined with severe deficits in competence.[48] In fact, studies show that these latter charismatics become so enamored with their inspiring ideas that they are completely out of touch with operational demands.[49] The differences between competent and incompetent charismatics are hard to detect at first. Without keen discernment, both kinds of leaders initially are believable, often giving the ersatz leader time to flee before discovered. In fact, people frequently overweight leaders' confident message delivery over content (judge a book by its cover) when determining their competence, and erringly mistake glibness for leadership.[50] For example, Billy McFarland was twenty-five when he convinced people to partake in a stupendous party in the Bahamas called Fyre Festival. Like Elizabeth Holmes of Theranos, he convinced investors to chase his dream and employees to keep working despite their reservations. Ultimately, the gourmet cuisine Billy promised was a slice of cheese on bread (with rudimentary side salad) and the luxury accommodations he assured were leftover tents from a hurricane relief cache.[51]

Notably absent from our list of leadership criteria is results. Our point is that, yes, we expect good leaders to win against rivals and have a tangible product to show for their efforts, but we would not appreciate them as leaders unless their process had some identifiable quality that made them and their work worthy of our admiration. To succeed as a leader, they must orchestrate the company's activities and create a relationship with their people in ways that demand respect for the skill involved. That is, the evidence must show that the results were achieved through genuine strengths attributable to the leader.

The twelve criteria we outlined would allow us to differentiate the relentless cost cutter whose exploits over a three-year span dramatically increase earnings from the leader who prudently and artistically reshapes a company while minimizing the detrimental effects on its future—and makes money doing so. The former creates a wasteland bereft of focused, forward energy and employee engagement, whereas the latter shepherds people through the trials of a troubled organization while enlarging their interests and their capacities to perform.

This "cluster" approach to leadership we advocate makes the work of the assessor more challenging because there are no simple cutoff criteria, two-by-two boxes to fit people into, or infamous red lines to delineate the good from the bad and ugly. No prepackaged outputs describe people as a homogeny to whom we assign labels. There is a person who must meet the strenuous requirements of being a leader: a person who has strengths and liabilities and who others look at with a circumspect eye in the hope that this person somehow embodies qualities that make him or her special and worthy of our attention, who will enrich our work, and change our lives. The best leaders give us perspective on our social condition (good or bad) and a greater appreciation of our world, ourselves, and our choices. Moreover, they challenge, excite, comfort, and motivate. They bring us closer together by providing a forum for shared experiences and by forging a sense of community. Leadership animates our social encounters and can change our lives in ways that are as invigorating and real as being hit by a wave.

Once again, the items on our list are traceable to research that support their inclusion. For example, *engagement* captures the intellectual stimulation dimension of transformational leadership.[52] leaders who encourage others to reflect on their work, to think of new approaches to nagging problems, and to participate in innovative projects inspire greater effort through the intellectual challenge.[53] Transformational leaders simply convey greater intrinsic meaning to the work and elicit more creativity from followers. In essence, good leaders invite people to throw themselves into their work, emotionally and intellectually.[54]

The concept of engagement is ubiquitous in organizations, although efforts to promote and measure engagement have not always met expectations. Initially called on to fight in the war for talent and armed with a seductive business rationale that promised better business results, the concept of engagement has been a staple of organizational thought for twenty years. Yet what if we discovered our methods for measuring engagement all these years have been wrong? Can we identify a better way that is consistent with psychological principles and imparts more practical applications in the workplace?

Historically, organizations have conceived of engagement as the energizing sum of what employees like and do not like about the policies and practices of their employers, often as relayed through their managers. Employee engagement, however, may not be as dependent on *what* people like and dislike as much as the relative *balance* between their likes and dislikes. The idea that individuals' satisfaction depends on the ratio of their positive to negative experiences has been around

252 Foster a Leadership Culture

for some time, as popularized by researcher John Gottman's analysis of married couples. He showed that couples were likely to stay married if their positive experiences and feelings about each other outnumbered their negative experiences and feelings. Observational and diary studies showed that couples with "positivity ratios" of 5:1 were almost certain to weather the inevitable storms and stay together, and almost certain to divorce or separate as these ratios approached 1:1. These positivity ratios, then, were found to predict both relationship quality and durability.[55]

Researchers extended work on positivity ratios to other facets of life, showing that people with higher positive to negative experiences report better relationships, greater personal satisfaction, and higher work satisfaction. Studies also show that people with higher positivity ratios are more likely to "flourish," defined as striving toward one's potential, withstanding normal everyday stresses, working productively, and contributing to one's community.[56] When the positives in the workplace increase, people think more expansively and flexibly, are more willing to undertake novel activities and experiment, are more resilient, exhibit greater self-control, are more self-efficacious, and see their environments as more supportive and encouraging. Positivity is like the proverbial perpetual motion machine that fuels itself: positive people can generate their own resources to persevere and succeed.

Research generally has found that people with ratios of greater than 3:1 are significantly more satisfied with their employers and more likely to stay. These results demonstrate that ratios of positive to negative attitudes are indicative of potential turnover. The fact that more positive experiences are required to offset negative experiences is consistent with what is known as the *negativity bias*. Negative experiences weigh more heavily on people than corresponding positive experiences. The good things that happen to us are less potent and decay faster than negative experiences so that it takes approximately three goods to equal one bad.[57]

This new formulation for engagement dramatically changes how we approach employee motivation and intervene in the workplace. This revised definition suggests that many things may make work life more satisfying and worthwhile and that any number of changes may make the workplace more appealing and increase engagement. We need not hunt for the one program improvement that will change everything. Creating a more experientially invigorating workplace in its myriad manifestations will go a long way. This new view more aptly represents an index of organizational health that is highly contingent on the aptitude of leaders. This is not an index of happiness or prescription for escape from hard work—far from it. Most of what people do at work is work, and they would prefer to derive a robust sense of purpose and satisfaction in doing just that. Therefore, we are in search of something more substantive than pleasure when we invoke a new and different era for engagement. Let's call it fulfillment.

Data also support our inclusion of *enlightened* on our list (again, rather than justify the inclusion of all twelve leadership criteria, we have selected two for illustration). People who are enlightened are able to see situations and themselves in new ways. Experts have written about the importance of self-awareness for leaders. We think, however, it is more important for leaders to make other people—employees—self-aware so that they can tune into their principles, attitudes, and beliefs. For much of the time, we see the world from our points of view without a whole lot of nuance and refection. We see and act from the inside looking out. At times our brains need to tell us to stop and look and think about ourselves in a different way—to see ourselves as others might, or to figuratively step out of our bodies and look at ourselves objectively from the outside in. Rather than allowing others to act on impulse, the leader's chore is to get followers to probe their thoughts and feelings so that they will act deliberately and prudently.

Getting people to focus inwardly on themselves is called objective self-awareness, and this focus can be achieved rather simply in experimental settings.[58] Looking in a mirror does it. As does listening to a recording of one's voice, hearing one's own heartbeat, and writing a story about oneself. Researchers found that simply putting an image of human eyes ("watchful eyes") and recommended pricing (pricing was posted in all conditions) over an honor-system coffee dispenser and collection container produced almost three times the monetary contributions. This effect presumably occurs because the eyes induce people to look inwardly and reflect on the right standard of conduct.[59] Art, too, elicits self-awareness, as in the "museum effect," in which studies have shown that people perusing museums become more mindful of who they are, where their lives are going, the way they interact with others, and the future of society and the planet.[60] Reflection on, and group discussion about, works of art have the same effect of increasing participants' (in this case, managers') self-awareness.[61]

Instructure views self-awareness as one of three critical attributes that employees need to develop (self-esteem and sound judgment are the other two), and it finds interesting ways to instill this quality in the workforce. Using the artistic form of film as a mirror, one group showed us an example of how this can be done. Recently, at the annual all-employee meeting, the marketing department presented video reenactments of employee suggestions and complaints that it had gathered throughout the year. One complaint concerned the bulk ordering of Pop-Tarts, which distributors ship without identifying the flavors on the foil wrappers. Employees presented this as a problem; apparently, it is difficult to sniff out the flavors through the wrappers. Marketing's video showed the CEO and CFO standing in a dimly lit basement labeling packages of Pop-Tarts. It was very funny. More important, the company demonstrated its ability to laugh at itself and not take itself too seriously. Instructure also is putting problems in perspective by vividly depicting the triviality of many concerns and thereby suggesting that there are more important matters to worry about and attend to. It is an open invitation for people to examine what really matters.

Most studies that investigate culture use values as the proxy for culture for two reasons. First, values are the deepest measurable facet of culture—as opposed to superficial artefacts such as mode of dress.[62] Second, values represent guiding principles that profoundly influence how we think and act.[63] That is, values describe what people view as important and shape their goals.

Many different scales measure values (see box 11.2 for a list of several of these).[64] No single cultural profile emerges from this literature to suggest a given set of values that are diagnostic of success. More generally, compendiums of values are typed as constructive or destructive depending on whether the values are normatively sound and consistent, or are inconsistent, with the organization's mission. For example, a destructive culture is one in which the first concern is productivity, with ethics and safety trailing far behind in importance.[65] A constructive culture is one in which the company has adopted a more balanced outlook of business in society. We trust you know what we mean. The press is filled with examples of cultures gone terribly wrong in cases in which falsified or defective products and services are knowingly passed off to consumers or deleterious financial results meticulously disguised and hidden from investors. Fortunately, most organizations

BOX 11.2
Representative Value Scales

Level of Analysis	Name of Scale
National	GLOBE
	World Values Survey
Organizational	Competing Values Model
	Denison Organizational Culture Survey
	Organizational Culture Profile
	Organizational Culture Inventory
	Organizational Culture Assessment Instrument
Individual	Rokeach Values Survey
	Schwartz Values Survey
	Chinese Values Survey

do not make it into the press for those reasons. Most companies try to inculcate values to live by with easily recalled mnemonics. Instructure has as their value system, COOTIES (customer experience, openness, ownership, trust, integrity, excellence, simplicity).

Again, no list will conclusively relate to organizational success, however, we believe a minimum number of cultural traits are necessary for success. Several of these have been discussed throughout the book and are aptly supported by the research evidence as essential. We provided our suggested list of values in the first two columns of table 11.3. The first column represents the basics: cultural attributes that are required for success. The second column represents cultural values that are more action-oriented and add to or accentuate the basic cultural values. We view the latter as depending more on the preferences of the company. For reference, the third and fourth columns are a summary of the most recurring values in a study of the S&P 500.[66]

The thing about culture is that every place has one. All cultural voids are filled. In the absence of intentional forces, cultural compositions will form—rightly or wrongly—that favor certain behaviors over others. In a similar vein, without adequate controls, the wrong people often are promoted and obtain power—or more power. In many organizations the people who tend to rise frequently are those who most crave power, control, wealth, or other forms of idolatry. This "cream"

TABLE 11.3
List of cultural values

Our List		Summary Values	
Basic	*Basic+*	*Theme*	*Sample Adjectives*
Cooperation	Conscientiousness	Communication	Rewarding, fun,
Fairness	Diversity	Community	energetic
Life satisfaction	Innovation	Hard Work	Openness
Purpose	Learning	Innovation	Trust, honesty,
Respect	Openness	Integrity	fairness
Security	Optimism	Quality	Customer, commit-
Trust	Quality/Service	Respect	ment, dedication
Truthfulness	Responsibility	Safety	Collaboration,
	Sportspersonship	Teamwork	cooperation
	Standards		Environment,
	Sustainability		caring
	Urgency		Diversity, empower-
			ment, dignity
			Health, work–life
			balance, flexibility
			Creativity,
			excellence,
			improvement

at the top, described in its biological form, is a lightweight, fatty globule with little substance that needs to be skimmed off. The void that allows the proliferation of bad management includes a failure to set standards and limits on conduct. These "chaotic" organizations are typified by laissez-faire leadership that has abdicated responsibility for establishing ethical ground rules and social order. Planning is poor, information flows are poor, role clarity is poor, and the cleanliness and orderliness of the work environment is poor. Inadequate and hostile strains of management reproduce because corporate decision making is scattered, poorly constrained, and loosely watched, allowing managers throughout the company to decide for themselves the best way to administer business.[67]

It is remarkable how easily and quickly cultures can deteriorate. Yet it is a well-known phenomenon in psychology. The spontaneous acquisition of a behavioral repertoire is perhaps most fatefully illustrated by the Stanford University prison experiment.[68] The experiment randomly separated participants into prisoners and guards in a simulated prison environment. Although the prison guards had prescribed duties, experimenters did not instruct them on how those duties should be carried out. The experiment was prematurely stopped because of mounting aggressive behaviors displayed by the guards. This demonstration of behavioral change showed that people who we would regard as ordinary on the street might act in unusual and alarming ways under certain circumstances. For many student participants, nothing especially revealing in their character would have predicted their treatment of the prisoners—and fellow students. Researchers have offered different explanations for the results of the prison experiment. One explanation posits a capacity to objectify others as categories, as opposed to seeing them as individuals and to impute to a group certain characteristics that make members seem less than human—deserving of, or impervious to, harsh treatment.[69] When in groups, people tend to adopt the prevailing norms of the group. If the norms of the guards are to be tough with the prisoners, then that is the way they will behave.[70] This interpretation, however, does not explain why a norm of intimidation should form.

Recent work by Keltner and associates suggests that differential power may play a role.[71] He finds that more powerful individuals are more likely to engage in rude, selfish, and unethical behavior. Moreover, very little is required to elicit the differential authority of leaders over others. Imagine three people who just met, one of whom is casually selected as the designated leader by the experimenter. Although the trio are working on a presumed writing task, the experimenter places a plate of four freshly baked cookies in front of the subjects for a snack. Guess who eats the extra cookie?

Keltner suggests that the indulgences and abuses of the more advantaged and powerful are significant. Evidence unequivocally supports his claim, as bullying disproportionately occurs between people at different organizational ranks and with differential power.[72] Part of the reason for this may be that people of rank can exert control over others; however, they also seem to be less sympathetic to and distressed by others' predicaments than those without similar authority: the social distance between people appears to widen their emotional distance.[73]

We have seen power's hammer enough times to realize that the phenomenon is real. On several occasions we have seen friendly, charming

258 Foster a Leadership Culture

employees transformed into fiends once they were promoted into managerial positions. Malice lies dormant until released through the disinhibiting effects of power. Power acts as an amplifier that reveals people for who they really are.[74]

One of the primary ways to control the incursion of the obscene into the workplace is to put a premium on leadership and on leaders who enforce respectful relations among members of the workforce. We get the people we deserve as leaders in our governments and organizations when we do not take our commitments to values and to each other seriously, and when we allow those who care about neither to fill the void.

Not everyone who goes to work each day will find meaning and personal satisfaction in what they do. Yet everyone should find respect and safety. Showing respect is not so hard. It entails expressing interest in what employees want for themselves, listening to what they say, sincerely considering their perspectives, figuring out ways to use and grow their talents, and showing appreciation for what they do. When we swaddle our blue- and pink-capped babies, we wish simply for their future happiness; we do not expect that there will be those, similarly born, who will prevent that from happening. The best chance for our institutions is to mobilize our greatest weapon: a mission-driven community based on the governing premise of quality leadership. It is a community that thrives on the energies and abilities of people and that resists giving in to those whose motives reduce purpose to daily survival.

If companies want better management, they will need to pay more attention to those whom they have entrusted to lead. In our estimation, companies remain too accommodating of managerial abominations who take their organizations perilously close to new-age sweatshops. Without changes in our attitudes toward the way people should conduct themselves and relate to others in the workplace, our fear is that institutions will linger longer in an aged form, and on the wrong side of history. When it comes to people, companies seem out of step. Despite the known value of leadership in improving employee welfare and productivity, most of the glory for gains in corporate productivity are attributed to capital improvements, financial maneuvers, and technological advances. We credit the efficiencies of new machines, the facility of intelligent systems, the advances of momentous innovations, and the accretion of smart investments for corporate progressiveness. In contrast, we attend too little to our management practices, which, sans soot and grime, remain archaically mired in an age of "dark satanic mills" (as decried by William Blake). Unvarnished capitalism seems well past its prime. But we do not need a new economic system; we need a variation on a theme that is more just and responsive to the human condition. We need more talk about quality of life alongside GDP, productivity, cost containment, and jobs, for better financial results do not ensure better lives. To enhance human welfare, we need institutions that are prepared to refute an ethos of selfishness and survival and that boldly embrace corporate communities that are more receptive to human virtues.

We have heard it said that the ideal way to increase national GDP, improve corporate profits, and lower healthcare costs is to improve the quality of leaders. In this chapter, we have provided a vocabulary for companies to begin or continue informed discussions about leadership in their institutions. Thus, a leadership culture begins by giving leadership its due. In every survey of management, executives say that leadership and leadership succession are top priorities, but compared with the ruminations given to monthly financial results, it would be hard for us to say that assertion is factual. Relatively speaking, too much attention is given to the ends and too little to the means. We falsely assume that leadership merely entails performing a function well, when in fact we count on our leaders to do, and be, so much more.

In that regard, let us close with a thought experiment. Imagine you are in an audience and we, on stage, place before you an ordinary looking chair and say, "This is a chair." You would likely shrug and begin to wonder why you signed up for the event. Suppose, however, we brought out the same chair and this time said, "This is a work of art." You ultimately may conclude that it seems no more remarkable than a common chair but not before exploring what value this object may hold as a work of art. Therefore, you look at it in a different way than an ordinary chair trying to see that special value it may hold. This chair demands your attention in ways in which a purely functional object does not. We think, "This is your leader," requires the same pause and reflection. It is a big statement to make. It is about value and effect. The statement serves as an invitation to see what else beyond the merely useful may be there, thereby commanding attention that the ordinary does not. We have become too accepting of the commonplace, the merely functional, when in actuality people deserve more and our institutions could use more.

Notes

1. Organization Development Basics

1. Freedman AM. The history of organization development and the NTL institute: What we have learned, forgotten, and rewritten. *Psychologist Manager Journal* 1999; **3**(2): 125–41; French WL, Bell CH, Jr., Zawacki RA. *Organization development: Theory, practice, and research*. New Delhi: Universal Book Stall, 1978.

2. Burke WW. A perspective on the field of organization development and change: the Zeigarnik effect. *Journal of Applied Behavioral Science* 2011; **47**(2): 143–67; Burke WW, Noumair DA. *Organization development: A process of learning and changing*, 3rd ed. Indianapolis, IN: Pearson, 2015.

3. Strogatz SH. Exploring complex networks. *Nature* 2001; **410**(6825): 268–76.

4. Chapman J. Unintended consequences. *Nursing Management* 2005; **12**(4): 30–4; Ben-Jacob E, Levine H. The artistry of nature. *Nature* 2001; **409**(6823): 985–6.

5. Chapman. Unintended consequences.

6. Ben-Jacob, Levine. The artistry of nature.

7. Skaburskis A. The origin of "wicked problems." *Planning Theory and Practice* 2008; **9**(2): 277–80.

8. Leavitt HJ. Big organizations are unhealthy environments for human beings. *Academy of Management learning and Education* 2007; **6**(2): 253–63; Miller D. The Icarus paradox: How exceptional companies bring about their own downfall. *Business Horizons* 1992; **35**(1): 24–35.

9. Appelbaum SH. Socio-technical systems theory: An intervention strategy for organizational development. *Management Decision* 1997; **35**(6): 452–63.

10. Emery FE. Democratization of the work place: A historical review of studies. *International Studies of Management and Organization: The Goals of Economic Organizations* 1971; **1**(2): 181–201.

11. Mills T. Altering the social structure in coal mining: A case study. *Monthly Labor Review* 1976; **99**(10): 3–10.

12. *I Love Lucy.* https://www.youtube.com/watch?v=WmAwcMNxGqM.

13. McClure PK. "You're fired," says the robot: The rise of automation in the workplace, technophobes, and fears of unemployment. *Social Science Computer Review* 2018; **36**(2): 139–56.

14. Binder AJ, Bound J. The declining labor market prospects of less-educated men. *Journal of Economic Perspectives* 2019; **33**(2): 163–90.

15. Taylor, Winslow F. *The principles of scientific management.* New York: Harper, 1919; Parkhurst, Augustus F. *Applied methods of scientific management.* New York: Wiley, 1912.

16. Carey A. The Hawthorne studies: A radical criticism. *American Sociological Review* 1967; **32**(3): 403–16; Bramel D, Friend R. Hawthorne, the myth of the docile worker, and class bias in psychology. *American Psychologist* 1981; **36**(8): 867–78; Adair JG. The Hawthorne effect: A reconsideration of the methodological artifact. *Journal of Applied Psychology* 1984; **69**(2): 334–45.

17. Hsueh Y. The Hawthorne experiments and the introduction of Jean Piaget in American industrial psychology, 1929–1932. *History of Psychology* 2002; **5**(2): 163–89; Lee RM. "The most important technique . . .": Carl Rogers, Hawthorne, and the rise and fall of nondirective interviewing in sociology. *Journal of the History of the Behavioral Sciences* 2011; **47**(2): 123–46.

18. Massarik F. The humanistic core of industrial/organizational psychology. *Humanistic Psychologist* 1992; **20**(2–3): 389–96.

19. Argyris C. The next challenge for TQM—taking the offensive on defensive reasoning. *Journal for Quality and Participation* 1999; **22**(6): 41–43.

20. Argyris C. Double-Loop Learning, Teaching, and Research. *Academy of Management learning & education* 2002; **1**(2): 206-18.

21. Senge PM. The leaders new work—building learning organizations. *Sloan Management Review* 1990; **32**(1): 7–23.

22. Kezar A. What campuses need to know about organizational learning and the learning organization. *New Directions for Higher Education* 2005; **2005**(131): 7–22.

23. Suchy Y. Executive functioning: Overview, assessment, and research issues for non-neuropsychologists. *Annals of Behavioral Medicine* 2009; **37**(2): 106–16.

24. Kantrow A. *The constraints of corporate tradition.* New York: Harper and Row, 1987.

25. Kelloway EK, Day AL. Building healthy workplaces: What we know so far. *Canadian Journal of Behavioural Science* 2005; **37**(4): 223–35.

26. Korkmaz M. The effects of leadership styles on organizational health. *Educational Research Quarterly* 2007; **30**(3): 23–55; Miles MB. Planned

change and organizational health—figure and ground. In Carlson, RO et al. (Eds.) *Change processes in the public schools* (pp. 11–34). Eugene, OR: Center for the Advanced Study of Educational Administration, University of Oregon, 1965.

27. Sorohan EG. Healthy companies. *Training and Development* 1994; **48**(3): 9–10; Quick JC, Macik-Frey M, Cooper CL. Managerial dimensions of organizational health: The healthy leader at work—Introduction. *Journal of Management Studies* 2007; **44**(2): 189–205.

28. Highhouse S. A history of the T-group and its early applications in management development. *Group Dynamics* 2002; **6**(4): 277–90; Burnes B, Cooke B. The Tavistock's 1945 invention of organization development: Early British business and management applications of social psychiatry. *Business History* 2013; **55**(5): 768–89.

29. Fraher AL. Systems psychodynamics: The formative years of an interdisciplinary field at the Tavistock Institute. *History of Psychology* 2004; 7(1): 65–84.

30. Highhouse. A history of the T-group.

31. Snyder M. In the footsteps of Kurt Lewin: Practical theorizing, action research, and the psychology of social action. *Journal of Social Issues* 2009; **65**(1): 225–45.

32. Boog BWM. The emancipatory character of action research, its history and the present state of the art. *Journal of Community and Applied Social Psychology* 2003; **13**(6): 426–38.

33. Burnes B. Reflections: Ethics and organizational change—time for a return to Lewinian values. *Journal of Change Management* 2009; **9**(4): 359–81.

34. Novotna T. Hastily arranged marriage: political attitudes and perceptions in Germany twenty years after unification. *German Politics and Society* 2010; **28**(4)): 19–40; Silver H. The social integration of Germany since unification. *German Politics and Society* 2010; **28**(1)): 165–88; Hogwood P. 'How happy are you . . .?' Subjective well-being in east Germany twenty years after unification. *Politics* 2011; **31**(3): 148–58; Behrend H. Viewpoints on German partition and reunification. *Social Semiotics* 2011; **21**(1): 55–65.

35. Zimmerman DK. Participative management: a reexamination of the classics. *Academy of Management Review* 1978; **3**(4): 896–901.

36. Kopelman RE, Prottas DJ, Falk DW. Further development of a measure of theory x and y managerial assumptions. *Journal of Managerial Issues* 2012; **24**(4): 450–70; McGregor D, Nord WR, Jacobs D. The human side of enterprise. *Academy of Management Review* 2004; **29**(2): 293–6.

37. Blake RR, Mouton JS. Management by grid® principles or situationalism: Which? *Group and Organization Management* 1981, **6**(4): 439–55.

38. Chemers MM. Leadership research and theory: A functional integration. *Group Dynamics: Theory, Research, and Practice* 2000; 4(1): 27–43.

39. Baumrind D. Current patterns of parental authority. *Developmental Psychology* 1971; 4(1, Pt.2): 1–103; Darling N, Steinberg L. Parenting style as context: An integrative model. *Psychological Bulletin* 1993; 113(3): 487–96.

40. Likert R. From production- and employee-centeredness to systems 1–4. *Journal of Management* 2016; 5(2): 147–56.

2. Organize for Change

1. Olson MS, Bever DV. *Stall points: Most companies stop growing—yours doesn't have to.* New Haven, CT: Yale University Press, 2008;

2. Olson and Bever, *Stall Points*; Pettigrew AM. *The awakening giant: Continuity and change in Imperial Chemical Industries.* London: Routledge, 2013.

3. Ribeiro Serra F, Portugal Ferreira M, Isnard Ribeiro de Almeida M. Organizational decline: A yet largely neglected topic in organizational studies. *Management Research: Journal of the Iberoamerican Academy of Management* 2013; 11(2): 133–56.

4. Van de Ven, AH, Poole MS. Explaining development and change in organizations. *Academy of Management Review* 1995; 20(3): 510–40; Chandler AD, Jr. *Strategy and structure: Chapters in the history of the industrial enterprise.* Philadelphia: Beard Books, 1962.

5. Hambrick DC, D'Aveni RA. Large corporate failures as downward spirals. *Administrative Science Quarterly* 1988; 33(1): 1–23.

6. Gill RB, Mayewski PA, Nyberg J, Haug GH, Peterson LC. Drought and the maya collapse. *Ancient Mesoamerica* 2007; 18(2): 283–302.

7. Foster-Fishman PG, Nowell B, Yang H. Putting the system back into systems change: A framework for understanding and changing organizational and community systems. *American Journal of Community Psychology* 2007; 39(3–4): 197–215.

8. Enzmann DR, Feinberg DT. The nature of change. *Journal of the American College of Radiology* 2014; 11(5): 464–70.

9. Gladwell M. *The tipping point.* New York: Little, Brown, 2004.

10. Boin A, Kofman C, Kuilman J, Kuipers S, van Witteloostuijn A. Does organizational adaptation really matter? How mission change affects the survival of U.S. federal independent agencies, 1933–2011. *Governance* 2017; 30(4): 663–86.

11. Deegan T, Reeves M, Whitaker K. Fighting the gravity of average performance. *MIT Sloan Management Review* eBook; 2020.

12. Trahms CA, Ndofor HA, Sirmon DG. Organizational decline and turnaround: A review and agenda for future research. *Journal of Management* 2013; **39**(5): 1277–307.

13. Nutt PC. Organizational de-development. *Journal of Management Studies* 2004; **41**(7): 1083–103.

14. Bedeian AG, Armenakis AA. The cesspool syndrome: How dreck floats to the top of declining organizations. *Academy of Management Executive* 1998; **12**(1): 58–67.

15. Brockner J, Grover S, O'Malley MN, Reed TF, Glynn MA. Threat of future layoffs, self-esteem, and survivors' reactions: Evidence from the laboratory and the field. *Strategic Management Journal* 1993; **14**(S1): 153–66; Brockner J, Grover S, Reed T, DeWitt R, O'Malley M. Survivors' reactions to layoffs: We get by with a little help for our friends. *Administrative Science Quarterly* 1987; **32**(4): 526–41.

16. Tainter JA. *The collapse of complex societies.* Cambridge: Cambridge University Press. 1988.

17. Raeff C. Distinguishing between development and change: Reviving organismic-developmental theory. *Human Development* 2011; **54**(1): 4–33.

18. Taleb N. *Antifragile: Things that gain from disorder.* New York: Random House, 2012.

19. Sternberg RJ. A theory of adaptive intelligence and its relation to general intelligence. *Journal of Intelligence* 2019; **7**(4): 23–39.

20. Akgün AE, Lynn GS, Byrne JC. Organizational learning: A socio-cognitive framework. *Human Relations* 2016; **56**(7): 839–68.

21. Albrecht K. *Power of minds at work: Organizational intelligence in action.* New York: AMACOM, 2003.

22. Alvesson M, Spicer A. A stupidity-based theory of organizations. *Journal of Management Studies* 2012; **49**(7): 1194–220.

23. Beer M, Nohria N. Cracking the code of change. *Harvard Business Review* 2000; **78**(3): 133–41; Burnes B. Introduction: Why does change fail, and what can we do about it? *Journal of Change Management* 2011; **11**(4): 445–50.

24. McDonald C. Western Union's failed reinvention: The role of momentum in resisting strategic change, 1965–1993. *Business History Review* 2012; **86**(3): 527–49.

25. Mellert LD, Scherbaum C, Oliveira J, Wilke B. Examining the relationship between organizational change and financial loss. *Journal of Organizational Change Management* 2015; **28**(1): 59–71.

26. Erwin DG, Garman AN. Resistance to organizational change: Linking research and practice. *Leadership and Organization Development Journal* 2010; **31**(1): 39–56.

27. Ford JD, Ford LW, D'Amelio A. Resistance to change: The rest of the story. *Academy of Management Review* 2008; **33**(2): 362–77.

28. Armenakis AA, Harris SG, Mossholder KW. Creating readiness for organizational change. *Human Relations* 2016; **46**(6): 681–703.

29. Rusly FH, Sun PY-T, Corner JL. Change readiness: Creating understanding and capability for the knowledge acquisition process. *Journal of Knowledge Management* 2015; **19**(6): 1204–23.

30. Stevens GW. Toward a process-based approach of conceptualizing change readiness. *Journal of Applied Behavioral Science* 2013; **49**(3): 333–60.

31. Steinmetz H, Knappstein M, Ajzen I, Schmidt P, Kabst R. How effective are behavior change interventions based on the theory of planned behavior? A three-level meta-analysis. *Zeitschrift für Psychologie* 2016; **224**(3): 216–33; Fishbein M, Ajzen I. Attitudes, norms, and control as predictors of intentions and behavior. In Fishbein M, Ajzen I. (Eds.) *Predicting and changing behavior: The reasoned action approach.* New York: Psychology Press, 2010: 44–88.

32. Trosten-Bloom A, Whitney DD, Cooperrider D. *The power of appreciative inquiry: A practical guide to positive change.* Oakland, CA: Berrett-Koehler, 2010.

33. Raelin JA. The manager as facilitator of dialogue. *Organization* 2013; **20**(6): 818–39 Gunnlaugson O. Generative dialogue as a transformative learning practice in adult and higher education settings. *Journal of Adult and Continuing Education* 2006; **12**(1): 2–19.

34. Newcomb TM, Turner RH, Converse PE. *Social psychology: The study of human interaction.* New York: Holt, Rinehart and Winston, 1965.

35. Costanza DP, Blacksmith N, Coats MR, Severt JB, DeCostanza AH. The effect of adaptive organizational culture on long-term survival. *Journal of Business and Psychology* 2016; **31**(3): 361–81; Schwaninger M. Intelligent organizations: An integrative framework. *Systems Research and Behavioral Science* 2001; **18**(2): 137–58.

36. Gully SM, Incalcaterra KA, Joshi A, Beaubien JM. A meta-analysis of team-efficacy, potency, and performance: Interdependence and level of analysis as moderators of observed relationships. *Journal of Applied Psychology* 2002; **87**(5): 819–32.

37. Wigfield A, Eccles JS. Expectancy–value theory of achievement motivation. *Contemporary Educational Psychology* 2000; **25**(1): 68–81.

38. Chung GH, Choi JN, Du J. Tired of innovations? Learned helplessness and fatigue in the context of continuous streams of innovation implementation. *Journal of Organizational Behavior* 2017; **38**(7): 1130–48.

39. Probst G, Raisch S. Organizational crisis: The logic of failure. *Academy of Management Executive* 2005; **19**(1): 90–105.

40. Deming WE. *Out of the crisis.* Cambridge, MA: MIT Press, 2000; Ford JK, Lauricella TK, Van Fossen JA, Riley SJ. Creating energy for change: The role of changes in perceived leadership support on commitment to an organizational change initiative. *Journal of Applied Behavioral Science* 2021 Jun;57(2):153–73.

41. Burnes B. Understanding resistance to change—Building on Coch and French. *Journal of Change Management* 2015; **15**(2): 92–116.

42. Parry W, Kirsch C, Carey P, Shaw D. Empirical development of a model of performance drivers in organizational change projects. *Journal of Change Management* 2014; **14**(1): 99–125.

43. Burnes B, Cooke B. Kurt Lewin's field theory: A review and re-evaluation. *International Journal of Management Reviews* 2013; **15**(4): 408–25.

44. Dawkins R. Universal Darwinism. In Bedau MA, Cleland CE. (Eds.) *The nature of life.* Cambridge: Cambridge University Press, 2010: 360–373.

45. Teece DJ. Explicating dynamic capabilities: The nature and micro-foundations of (sustainable) enterprise performance. *Strategic Management Journal* 2007; **28**(13): 1319–50.

46. Al-Haddad S, Kotnour T. Integrating the organizational change literature: A model for successful change. *Journal of Organizational Change Management* 2015; **28**(2): 234–62.

47. Rudolph JW, Repenning NP. Disaster dynamics: Understanding the role of quantity in organizational collapse. *Administrative Science Quarterly* 2002; **47**(1): 1–30; Perrow C. *Normal accidents: Living with high risk technologies.* Princeton, NJ: Princeton University Press, 2011.

48. Kuhn TS, Hacking I. *The structure of scientific revolutions.* Chicago: University of Chicago Press, 1962; Klammer A, Grisold T, Gueldenberg S. Introducing a "stop-doing" culture: How to free your organization from rigidity. *Business Horizons* 2019; **62**(4): 451–8.

49. *Don't get Netflixed: Your current business model isn't going to last much longer.* Hoboken, NJ: Wiley, 2012.

50. Snihur Y. Responding to business model innovation: Organizational unlearning and firm failure. *Learning Organization* 2018; **25**(3): 190–8.

51. Wason PC. On the failure to eliminate hypotheses in a conceptual task. *Quarterly Journal of Experimental Psychology* 1960; **12**(3): 129–40; Johnson-Laird PN, Legrenzi P, Legrenzi MS. Reasoning and a sense of reality. *The British Journal of Psychology* 1972; **63**(3): 395–400.

52. Scott P. Rethinking business models in the Great Depression: The failure of America's vacuum cleaner industry. *Business History Review* 2019; **93**(2): 319–48; Christensen CM, Bartman T, Van Bever D. The hard truth about business model innovation. *Sloan Management Review* 2016; **58**(1): 31–40.

268   2. Organize for Change

53. Schreyögg G, Sydow J. Organizational path dependence: A process view. *Organization Studies* 2011; **32**(3): 321–35.

54. Zhao L, Yang G, Wang W, et al. Herd behavior in a complex adaptive system. *Proceedings of the National Academy of Sciences* 2011; **108**(37): 15058–63.

55. Janis IL. *Groupthink*. Boston: Houghton Mifflin, 1983.

56. Rook L. An Economic Psychological approach to herd behavior. *Journal of Economic Issues* 2016; **40**(1): 75–95.

57. Chen Y-F. Herd behavior in purchasing books online. *Computers in Human Behavior* 2008; **24**(5): 1977–92.

58. Asch SE. Opinions and social pressure. *Scientific American* 1955; **193**(5): 31–35; Asch SE. Studies of independence and conformity: A minority of one against a unanimous majority. *Psychological Monographs* 1956; **70**(9): 1–70.

59. Kundu P, Cummins DD. Morality and conformity: The Asch paradigm applied to moral decisions. *Social Influence* 2013; **8**(4): 268–79.

60. Griskevicius V, Goldstein NJ, Mortensen CR, Cialdini RB, Kenrick DT. Going along versus going alone: When fundamental motives facilitate strategic (non)conformity. *Journal of Personality and Social Psychology* 2006; **91**(2): 281–94.

61. Manning K. How many saints are there? *The Guardian*. May 13, 2013.

62. Lorenz KZ. The evolution of behavior. *Scientific American* 1958; **199**(6): 67–82.

63. Stinchcombe AL, Baum JAC, Dobbin F. (Ed.) *Economics meets sociology in strategic management. Vol. 17, Advances in strategic management.* Stamford, CT: JAI Press, 2000; Simsek Z, Fox BC, Heavey C. What's past is prologue: A framework, review, and future directions for organizational research on imprinting. *Journal of Management* 2015; **41**(1): 288–317.

64. Johnson V. What is organizational imprinting? Cultural entrepreneurship in the founding of the Paris Opera. *American Journal of Sociology* 2007; **113**(1): 97–127.

65. Baumol WJ, Bowen WG. On the performing arts: The anatomy of their economic problems. *American Economic Review* 1965; **55**(1/2): 495–502.

66. Schwarz GM, Yang K-P, Chou C, Chiu Y-J. A classification of structural inertia: Variations in structural response. *Asia Pacific Journal of Management* 2018; **37**(1): 1–31; Hannan MT, Freeman J. Structural inertia and organizational change. *American Sociological Review* 1984; **49**(2): 149–64.

67. Kahneman D, Tversky A. Prospect theory: An analysis of decision under risk. *Econometrica* 1979; **47**(2): 263–92.

68. Miller D. The architecture of simplicity. *Academy of Management Review* 1993; **18**(1): 116–38; Miller D. What happens after success: The perils of excellence. *Journal of Management Studies* 1994; **31**(3): 325–58.

69. Staw BM. Knee-deep in the big muddy: A study of escalating commitment to a chosen course of action. *Organizational Behavior and Human Performance* 1976; **16**(1): 27–44.

70. Brockner J. The escalation of commitment to a failing course of action: Toward theoretical progress. *Academy of Management Review* 1992; **17**(1): 39–61.

71. Lofquist EA, Lines R. Keeping promises: A process study of escalating commitment leading to organizational change collapse. *Journal of Applied Behavioral Science* 2017; **53**(4): 417–45.

72. Kahneman D, Knetsch JL, Thaler RH. Anomalies: The endowment effect, loss aversion, and status quo bias. *Journal of Economic Perspectives* 1991; **5**(1): 193–206; Inzlicht M, Shenhav A, Olivola CY. The effort paradox: Effort is both costly and valued. *Trends in Cognitive Sciences* 2018; **22**(4): 337–49.

73. Brewer N, Wells GL. The confidence-accuracy relationship in eyewitness identification: effects of lineup instructions, foil similarity, and target-absent base rates. *Journal of Experimental Psychology Applied* 2006; **12**(1): 11–30.

74. Moore DA, Healy PJ. The trouble with overconfidence. *Psychological Review* 2008; **115**(2): 502–17.

75. Greenberg S, Stephens-Davidowitz S. You underestimate yourself. Opinion. *New York Times*. April 6, 2019.

76. Van Zant AB, Moore DA. Avoiding the pitfalls of overconfidence while benefiting from the advantages of confidence. *California Management Review* 2013; **55**(2): 5–23.

77. Johnson DDP, Fowler JH. The evolution of overconfidence. *Nature* 2011; **477**(7364): 317–20.

78. Jones N. The underdog might win the day. NewScientist. August 2, 2002.

79. Charness G, Rustichini A, van de Ven J. Self-confidence and strategic deterrence. Tinbergen Institute, Tinbergen Institute Discussion Papers: 11-151/1; 2011.

80. Beer M, Eisenstat RA. The silent killers of strategy implementation and learning. *Sloan Management Review* 2000; **41**(4): 29–40.

81. Glor ED. Assessing organizational capacity to adapt. *Emergence* 2007; **9**(3): 33–46.

82. Gassmann O, Enkel E, Chesbrough H. The future of open innovation. *R&D Management* 2010; **40**(3): 213–21; Johnson MW, Christensen CM, Kagermann H. Reinventing your business model. *Harvard Business Review*. December 2008.

83. Huang H-C, Lai M-C, Lin L-H, Chen C-T. Overcoming organizational inertia to strengthen business model innovation: An open innovation perspective. *Journal of Organizational Change Management* 2013; **26**(6): 977–1002.

84. Agarwal N, Grottke M, Mishra S, Brem A. A systematic literature review of constraint-based innovations: State of the art and future perspectives. *IEEE Transactions on Engineering Management* 2017; **64**(1): 3–15.

85. Leliveld A, Knorringa P. Frugal innovation and development research. *European Journal of Development Research* 2017; **30**(1): 1–16.

86. Lévi-Strauss, Claude (1966). *The Savage Mind.* Chicago: University of Chicago Press.

87. Witell L, Gebauer H, Jaakkola E, Hammedi W, Patricio L, Perks H. A bricolage perspective on service innovation. *Journal of Business Research* 2017; **79**: 290–8; Engelen E, Erturk I, Froud J, Leaver A, Williams K. Reconceptualizing financial innovation: Frame, conjuncture and bricolage. *Economy and Society* 2010; **39**(1): 33–63.

88. Peirson LJ, Boydell KM, Ferguson HB, Ferris LE. An ecological process model of systems change. *American Journal of Community Psychology* 2011; **47**(3): 307–21.

89. Buchanan D, Claydon T, Doyle M. Organisation development and change: The legacy of the nineties. *Human Resource Management Journal* 1999; **9**(2): 20–37.

90. Buchanan D, Fitzgerald L, Ketley D, et al. No going back: A review of the literature on sustaining organizational change. *International Journal of Management Reviews* 2005; **7**(3): 189–205.

91. Felin T, Powell TC. Designing organizations for dynamic capabilities. *California Management Review* 2016; **58**(4): 78–96.

92. Murray A, Skene K, Haynes K. The circular economy: An interdisciplinary exploration of the concept and application in a global context. *Journal of Business Ethics* 2015; **140**(3): 369–80.

93. Daou A, Mallat C, Chammas G, Cerantola N, Kayed S, Saliba NA. The ecocanvas as a business model canvas for a circular economy. *Journal of Cleaner Production* 2020; **258**: 120938.

94. Sovacool BK, Ali SH, Bazilian M, et al. Sustainable minerals and metals for a low-carbon future. *Science* 2020; **367**(6473): 30–3; Lee J, Bazilian M, Sovacool B, Greene S. Responsible or reckless? A critical review of the environmental and climate assessments of mineral supply chains. *Environmental Research Letters* 2020; **15**(10): 103009.

95. Stalinski S. Organizational intelligence: A systems perspective. *Organization Development Journal* 2004; **22**(2): 55.

3. Anticipate the Future

1. Daepp MIG, Hamilton MJ, West GB, Bettencourt LMA. The mortality of companies. *Journal of the Royal Society Interface* 2015; **12**(106): 20150120.

2. Graham JR, Harvey CR, Rajgopal S. The economic implications of corporate financial reporting. *Journal of Accounting & Economics* 2005; **40**(1): 3–73.

3. Napolitano MR, Marino V, Ojala J. In search of an integrated framework of business longevity. *Business History* 2015; **57**(7): 955–69.

4. Barton D, Manyika J, Koller T, Palter R, Godsall J, Zoffer J. Measuring the economic impact of short-termism. *McKinsey Quarterly*. February 2017; 1–16.

5. Bereskin FL, Hsu PH, Rotenberg W. The real effects of real earnings management: Evidence from innovation. *Contemporary Accounting Research* 2018; **35**(1): 525–57.

6. Junni P, Sarala RM, Taras V, Tarba SY. Organizational ambidexterity and performance: A meta-analysis. *Academy of Management Perspectives* 2013; **27**(4): 299–312.

7. Barton D, Wiseman M. Perspectives on the long term. *McKinsey Quarterly*. March 1, 2015; 98–107.

8. Rahmandad H, Henderson R, Repenning NP. Making the numbers? "Short termism" and the puzzle of only occasional disaster. *Management Science* 2018; **64**(3): 1328–47.

9. Karlgaard R. Ahead of their time: Noble flops. *Forbes*. April 14, 2013; 1.

10. Hadhazy A. Ahead of its time, gutsy biofuel firm goes bust. *Discover Magazine*. May 15, 2014.

11. Teece D, Peteraf M, Leih S. Dynamic capabilities and organizational agility: Risk, uncertainty, and strategy in the innovation economy. *California Management Review* 2016; **58**(4): 13–35; Czisnik M. Admiral Nelson's tactics at the Battle of Trafalgar. *History* 2004; **89**(296): 549–59; Welsh WE. Nelson at Trafalgar: He did his duty. *Military History* 2005; **22**(7): 38–72.

12. Moore GA. To succeed in the long term, focus on the middle term. *Harvard Business Review* 2007; **85**(7/8): 84–90.

13. Tushman ML, O'Reilly CA. The ambidextrous organizations: Managing evolutionary and revolutionary change. *California Management Review* 1996; **38**(4): 8–30.

14. Danneels E. Trying to become a different type of company: Dynamic capability at Smith Corona. *Strategic Management Journal* 2011; **32**(1): 1–31; Frieswick K. The turning point. CFO.com. April 1, 2005.

15. Denrell J, March JG. Adaptation as information restriction: The hot stove effect. *Organization Science* 2001; **12**(5): 523–38; March JG. Continuity and change in theories of organizational action. *Administrative Science Quarterly* 1996; **41**(2): 278–87.

16. Denrell J, Le Mens G. Revisiting the competency trap. *Industrial and Corporate Change* 2020; **29**(1): 183–205.

17. Arkes HR, Blumer C. The psychology of sunk cost. *Organizational Behavior and Human Decision Processes* 1985; **35**(1): 124–40.

18. Thaler RH. Mental accounting matters. *Journal of Behavioral Decision Making* 1999; **12**(3): 183–206; Thaler RH. From cashews to nudges: The evolution of behavioral economics. *American Economic Review* 2018; **108**(6): 1265–87.

19. Thaler. Mental accounting matters.

20. Harvey JB. The Abilene paradox: The management of agreement. *Organizational Dynamics* 1974; **3**(1): 63–80.

21. Goode E. The "sunk cost fallacy" claims more victims. *New York Times*. July 17, 2018; Sect. D6.

22. Sweis BM, Abram SV, Schmidt BJ, et al. Sensitivity to "sunk costs" in mice, rats, and humans. *Science* 2018; **361**(6398): 178–81.

23. Arkes HR, Ayton P. The sunk cost and Concorde effects: Are humans less rational than lower animals? *Psychological Bulletin* 1999; **125**(5): 591–600.

24. Eswaran M, Neary HM. the evolutionary logic of honoring sunk costs. *Economic Inquiry* 2016; **54**(2): 835–46; Nozick R. *The nature of rationality*. Princeton, NJ: Princeton University Press, 2001.

25. Fox S, Bizman A, Huberman O. Escalation of Commitment: The effect of number and attractiveness of available investment alternatives. *Journal of Business and Psychology* 2009; **24**(4): 431–9.

26. Anderson CJ. The psychology of doing nothing: Forms of decision avoidance result from reason and emotion. *Psychological Bulletin* 2003; **129**(1): 139–67.

27. Magen E, Gross JJ. Harnessing the need for immediate gratification: Cognitive reconstrual modulates the reward value of temptations. *Emotion* 2007; **7**(2): 415–28.

28. McKerchar TL, Renda CR. Delay and probability discounting in humans: An overview. *Psychological Record* 2012; **62**(4): 817–34.

29. MacGregor KE, Carnevale JJ, Dusthimer NE, Fujita K. Knowledge of the self-control benefits of high-level versus low-level construal. *Journal of Personality and Social Psychology* 2017; **112**(4): 607–20.

30. Baum JR, Locke EA, Kirkpatrick SA. A longitudinal study of the relation of vision and vision communication to venture growth in entrepreneurial firms. *Journal of Applied Psychology* 1998; **83**(1): 43–54.

31. Lemmon K, Moore C. The development of prudence in the face of varying future rewards. *Developmental Science* 2007; **10**(4): 502–11.

32. Read D, Frederick S, Orsel B, Rahman J. Four score and seven years from now: The date/delay effect in temporal discounting. *Management Science* 2005; **51**(9): 1326–35.

33. Amir O, Ariely D. Resting on laurels: the effects of discrete progress markers as subgoals on task performance and preferences. *Journal of Experimental Psychology Learning, Memory, and Cognition* 2008; **34**(5): 1158–71.

34. Mischel W. *The marshmallow test: Mastering self-control.* New York: Little, Brown, 2014; Mischel W, Shoda Y, Rodriguez M. Delay of gratification in children. *Science* 1989; **244**(4907): 933–8.

35. Souder D, Shaver JM. Constraints and incentives for making long horizon corporate investments. *Strategic Management Journal* 2010; **31**(12): 1316–36.

36. Frieswick K. The turning point: What options do companies have when their industries are dying? *CFO.* April 1, 2005.

37. Schwenke D, Dshemuchadse M, Vesper C, Bleichner MG, Scherbaum S. Let's decide together: Differences between individual and joint delay discounting. *PLoS One* 2017; **12**(4): e0176003.

38. Kleymann B, Malloch H. The rule of Saint Benedict and corporate management: employing the whole person. *Journal of Global Responsibility* 2010; **1**(2): 207–24.

39. Brettel M, Greve GI, Flatten TC. Giving up linearity: Absorptive capacity and performance. *Journal of Managerial Issues* 2011; **23**(2): 164–89; Daspit JJ, D'Souza DE. Understanding the multi-dimensional nature of absorptive capacity. *Journal of Managerial Issues* 2013; **25**(3): 299–316; Kranz JJ, Hanelt A, Kolbe LM. Understanding the influence of absorptive capacity and ambidexterity on the process of business model change: The case of on-premise and cloud-computing software. *Information Systems Journal* 2016; **26**(5): 477–517.

40. McGovern T. Why do successful companies fail? A case study of the decline of Dunlop. *Business History* 2007; **49**(6): 886–907.

41. Josephson BW, Johnson JL, Mariadoss BJ. Strategic marketing ambidexterity: Antecedents and financial consequences. *Journal of the Academy of Marketing Science* 2016; **44**(4): 539–54.

42. Osvath M. Putting flexible animal prospection into context: Escaping the theoretical box. *Wiley Interdisciplinary Reviews Cognitive Science* 2016; **7**(1): 5–18; Wilkins C, Clayton N. Reflections on the spoon test. *Neuropsychologia* 2019; **134**: 107221.

43. Turner N, Swart J, Maylor H. Mechanisms for managing ambidexterity: A review and research agenda. *International Journal of Management Reviews* 2013; **15**(3): 317–32.

44. Cantarello S, Martini A, Nosella A. A multi-level model for organizational ambidexterity in the search phase of the innovation process: Organizational ambidexterity. *Creativity and Innovation Management* 2012; **21**(1): 28–48.

45. Taylor A. *Sixty to zero: An inside look at the collapse of General Motors—and the Detroit auto industry.* New Haven, CT: Yale University Press, 2010.

46. Markides CC. Business model innovation: What can the ambidexterity literature teach us? *Academy of Management Perspectives* 2013; **27**(4): 313–23.

47. Beer M, Walton E. Developing the competitive organization: Interventions and strategies. *American Psychologist* 1990; **45**(2): 154–61.

48. Stoll JD. Corporate America's most underrated innovation strategy: 3M's 15% rule. *Wall Street Journal.* May 15, 2020.

49. Gunther M, Adamo M, Feldman B. 3M's innovation revival. CNN Money. September 24, 2010.

50. Madden BJ. The purpose of the firm, valuation, and the management of intangibles. *Journal of Applied Corporate Finance* 2017; **29**(2): 76–86.

51. Rahrovani Y, Pinsonneault A, Austin RD. If you cut employees some slack, will they innovate? *MIT Sloan Management Review* 2018; **59**(4): 47–51.

4. Encourage Cooperation

1. Dawes RM. Social dilemmas. *Annual Review of Psychology* 1980; **31**(1): 169–93; Komorita SS, Parks CD. Interpersonal relations: Mixed-motive interaction. *Annual Review of Psychology* 1995; **46**(1): 183–207; Van Lange PAM, Joireman J, Parks CD, Van Dijk E. The psychology of social dilemmas: A review. *Organizational Behavior and Human Decision Processes* 2013; **120**(2): 125–41.

2. Hardin G. The tragedy of the commons. *Science* 1968; **162**(3859): 1243–8.

3. Milinski M, Sommerfeld RD, Krambeck H-J, Reed FA, Marotzke J. The collective-risk social dilemma and the prevention of simulated dangerous climate change. *Proceedings of the National Academy of Sciences* 2008; **105**(7): 2291–4.

4. Attari SZ, Krantz DH, Weber EU. Reasons for cooperation and defection in real-world social dilemmas. *Judgment and Decision Making* 2014; **9**(4): 316–34.

5. Rand DG, Greene JD, Nowak MA. Spontaneous giving and calculated greed. *Nature* 2012; **489**(7416): 427–30; Tenbrunsel AE, Messick DM. Sanctioning systems, decision frames, and cooperation. *Administrative Science Quarterly* 1999; **44**(4): 684–707.

6. Greenbaum RL, Bonner JM, Mawritz MB, Butts MM, Smith MB. It is all about the bottom line: Group bottom-line mentality, psychological safety, and group creativity. *Journal of Organizational Behavior* 2020; **41**(6): 503–17.

7. Kollock P. Social dilemmas: The anatomy of cooperation. *Annual Review of Sociology* 1998; **24**(1): 183–214.

8. Moisan F, ten Brincke R, Murphy RO, Gonzalez C. Not all prisoner's dilemma games are equal: Incentives, social preferences, and cooperation. *Decision* 2018; **5**(4): 306–22.

9. Efferson C, Roca CP, Vogt S, Helbing D. Sustained cooperation by running away from bad behavior. *Evolution and Human Behavior* 2016; **37**(1): 1–9.

10. Milinski M. Reputation, a universal currency for human social interactions. *Philosophical Transactions Biological Sciences* 2016; **371**(1687): 20150100; Nowak MA, Sigmund K. Evolution of indirect reciprocity by image scoring. *Nature* 1998; **393**(6685): 573–7.

11. Heider F. *The psychology of interpersonal relations*. Hove, England: Psychology Press, 1958; Gross J, De Dreu CKW. The rise and fall of cooperation through reputation and group polarization. *Nature communications* 2019; **10**(1): 776–10.

12. Balliet D, Van Lange PAM. Trust, conflict, and cooperation: A meta-analysis. *Psychological Bulletin* 2013; **139**(5): 1090–112; Holmes JG. Interpersonal expectations as the building blocks of social cognition: An interdependence theory perspective. *Personal Relationships* 2002; **9**(1): 1–26.

13. Balliet, Van Lange. Trust, conflict, and cooperation.

14. Putnam RD. Bowling alone: America's declining social capital. *Journal of Democracy* 1995; **6**(1): 65–78.

15. Kramer RM. Trust and distrust in organizations: Emerging perspectives, enduring questions. *Annual Review of Psychology* 1999; **50**(1): 569–98.

16. Klapwijk A, Van Lange PAM. Promoting cooperation and trust in "noisy" situations: The power of generosity. *Journal of Personality and Social Psychology* 2009; **96**(1): 83–103; Reinders Folmer CP, Wildschut T, De Cremer D, van Lange PAM. Coping with noise in social dilemmas: Group representatives fare worse than individuals because they lack trust in others' benign intentions. *Group Processes and Intergroup Relations* 2019; **22**(2): 200–14.

17. O'Malley MN, Schubarth G. Fairness and appeasement: Achievement and affiliation motives in interpersonal relations. *Social Psychology Quarterly* 1984; **47**(4): 364–71.

18. Lange F, Eggert F. Selective cooperation in the supermarket. *Human Nature* 2015; **26**(4): 392–400.

19. Zaki J, Mitchell JP. Intuitive prosociality. *Current Directions in Psychological Science* 2013; **22**(6): 466–70.

20. Rand DG, Nowak MA. Human cooperation. *Trends in cognitive sciences* 2013; **17**(8): 413–25; Chiong R, Kirley M. Promotion of cooperation in social dilemma games via generalised indirect reciprocity. *Connection Science* 2015; **27**(4): 417–33; Simpson B, Harrell A, Melamed D, Heiserman N, Negraia DV. The roots of reciprocity: Gratitude and reputation in generalized exchange systems. *American Sociological Review* 2018; **83**(1): 88–110.

21. Horita Y, Takezawa M, Kinjo T, Nakawake Y, Masuda N. Transient nature of cooperation by pay-it-forward reciprocity. *Scientific Reports* 2016; 6(1): 19471.

22. Chancellor J, Margolis S, Bao KJ, Lyubomirsky S. Everyday prosociality in the workplace: The reinforcing benefits of giving, getting, and glimpsing. *Emotion* 2018; 18(4): 507–17.

23. Paternotte C. The epistemic core of weak joint action. *Philosophical Psychology* 2015; 28(1): 70–93.

24. Ostrom E. *Governing the commons: The evolution of institutions for collective action.* Cambridge: Cambridge University Press, 2015; Parsons T. *The structure of social action.* New York: McGraw-Hill, 1937.

25. Kelley HH, Thibaut JW. *Interpersonal relations. A theory of interdependence.* New York: Wiley, 1978.

26. Brodbeck FC, Kugler KG, Reif JAM, Maier MA. Morals matter in economic games. *PLoS One* 2013; 8(12): e81558.

27. Irwin K, Mulder L, Simpson B. The detrimental effects of sanctions on intragroup trust: Comparing punishments and rewards. *Social Psychology Quarterly* 2014; 77(3): 253–72.

28. Bailey C, Shantz A. Creating an ethically strong organization. *MIT Sloan Management Review* 2018; 60(1): 1–10.

29. Denant-Boemont L, Masclet D, Noussair CN. Punishment, counterpunishment and sanction enforcement in a social dilemma experiment. *Economic Theory* 2007; 33(1): 145–67.

30. Irwin, Mulder, Simpson. The detrimental effects of sanctions on intragroup trust.

31. Festinger L, Carlsmith JM. Cognitive consequences of forced compliance. *Journal of Abnormal and Social Psychology* 1959; 58(2): 203–10.

32. Aronson E, Carlsmith JM. Effect of the severity of threat on the devaluation of forbidden behavior. *Journal of Abnormal and Social Psychology* 1963; 66(6): 584–8.

33. Simpson B, Willer R, Harrell A. The enforcement of moral boundaries promotes cooperation and prosocial behavior in groups. *Scientific Reports* 2017; 7(1): 42844; Fehr E, Gächter S. Altruistic punishment in humans. *Nature* 2002; 415(6868): 137–40.

34. Ellingsen T, Johannesson M. Anticipated verbal feedback induces altruistic behavior. *Evolution and Human Behavior* 2008; 29(2): 100–5.

35. Pruitt DG, Kimmel MJ. Twenty years of experimental gaming: Critique, synthesis, and suggestions for the future. *Annual Review of Psychology* 1977; 28(1): 363–92; Columbus S, Münich J, Gerpott FH. Playing a different game: Situation perception mediates framing effects on cooperative behaviour. *Journal of Experimental Social Psychology* 2020; 90: 104006.

36. Goette L, Huffman D, Meier S. The impact of group membership on cooperation and norm enforcement: Evidence using random assignment to real social groups. *The American Economic Review* 2006; **96**(2): 212–6; Ames K, Majolo B, Hall K, Wilson N, Brumpton R, Garratt R. Human friendship favours cooperation in the iterated prisoner's dilemma. *Behaviour* 2006; **143**(11): 1383–95.

37. Chierchia G, Coricelli G. The impact of perceived similarity on tacit coordination: Propensity for matching and aversion to decoupling choices. *Frontiers In Behavioral Neuroscience* 2015; **9**(JULY): 202.

38. Van Vugt M, Hogan R, Kaiser RB. Leadership, Followership, and Evolution: Some lessons from the past. *The American Psychologist* 2008; **63**(3): 182–96.

39. Rossano MJ. The essential role of ritual in the transmission and reinforcement of social norms. *Psychological Bulletin* 2012; **138**(3): 529–49; Briody EK, Berger EJ, Wirtz E, Ramos A, Guruprasad G, Morrison EF. Ritual as work strategy: A window into organizational culture. *Human Organization* 2018; **77**(3): 189–201.

40. Durkheim, É. *The elementary forms of the religious life. A study in religious sociology.* Oxford: Oxford University Press, 2008.

41. MacCormick N. Norms, institutions, and institutional facts. *Law and Philosophy* 1998; **17**(3): 301–45; Schmitt BH, Dubé L, Leclerc F. Intrusions into waiting lines: Does the queue constitute a social system? *Journal of Personality and Social Psychology* 1992; **63**(5): 806–15.

42. Thoits PA, Hewitt LN. Volunteer work and well-being. *Journal of Health and Social Behavior* 2001; **42**(2): 115–31; Weinstein N, Ryan RM. When helping helps: Autonomous motivation for prosocial behavior and its influence on well-being for the helper and recipient. *Journal of Personality and Social Psychology* 2010; **98**(2): 222–44.

43. Sherif CW, Harvey OJ, Sherif M, Hood WR, White J. *Robbers cave experiment: Intergroup conflict and cooperation.* Middleton, CT: Wesleyan University Press, 2010; Perry G. Real-life lord of the flies. *Guardian.* April 16, 2018.

44. Deutsch M. Constructive conflict resolution: Principles, training, and research. *Journal of Social Issues* 1994; **50**(1): 13–32.

45. Campbell DT. Common fate, similarity, and other indices of the status of aggregates of persons as social entities. *Systems Research and Behavioral Science* 2007; **3**(1): 14–25.

46. Bass B. The inspirational processes of leadership. *Journal of Management Development* 1988; **7**(5): 21–31.

47. Bartleby. Mission implausible. *Economist* August 4, 2018; **414**(9100).

48. Rafferty AE, Griffin MA. Dimensions of transformational leadership: Conceptual and empirical extensions. *Leadership Quarterly* 2004; **15**(3): 329–54.

49. Heath C, Heath D. *Made to stick.* New York: Random House 2007.

50. Benkler Y. The unselfish gene. *Harvard Business Review.* August 2011.

51. Grueneisen S, Tomasello M. Children use rules to coordinate in a social dilemma. *Journal of Experimental Child Psychology* 2019; **179**: 362–74; Simpson B, Willer R. Beyond altruism: Sociological foundations of cooperation and prosocial behavior. *Annual Review of Sociology* 2015; **41**(1): 43–63.

52. Schein EH, Schein P. *Organizational culture and leadership,* 5th ed. New York: Wiley, 2017.

53. North D, Field AJ. *Institutions, institutional change and economic performance.* Cambridge: Cambridge University Press, 1991.

54. Curry O, Dunbar RIM. Do birds of a feather flock together?: The relationship between similarity and altruism in social networks. *Human Nature* 2013; **24**(3): 336–47.

55. Tajfel H. Social psychology of intergroup relations. *Annual Review of Psychology* 1982; **33**(1): 1–39; Turner JC, Oakes PJ. Self-categorization theory and social influence. In Paulus PB. (Ed.) *Psychology of group influence.* Mahwah, NJ: Erlbaum,1989: 233–75; Hogg MA, Terry DJ, White KM. A Tale of two theories: A critical comparison of identity theory with social identity theory. *Social Psychology Quarterly* 1995; **58**(4): 255–69.

56. Bavel JJV, Baicker K, Boggio PS, et al. Using social and behavioural science to support COVID-19 pandemic response. *Nature Human Behaviour* 2020; **4**(5): 460–71.

57. Balliet D, Wu J, De Dreu CKW. Ingroup favoritism in cooperation: A meta-analysis. *Psychological Bulletin* 2014; **140**(6): 1556–81.

58. Dunham Y. Mere membership. *Trends in Cognitive Sciences* 2018; **22**(9): 780–93.

59. Lee E-S, Park T-Y, Koo B. Identifying organizational identification as a basis for attitudes and behaviors: A meta-analytic review. *Psychological Bulletin* 2015; **141**(5): 1049–80.

60. Callahan SP, Ledgerwood A. On the psychological function of flags and logos: Group identity symbols increase perceived entitativity. *Journal of Personality and Social Psychology* 2016; **110**(4): 528–50; Keblusek L, Giles H, Maass A. Communication and group life: How language and symbols shape intergroup relations. *Group Processes and Intergroup Relations* 2017; **20**(5): 632–43.

61. Wiltermuth SS, Heath C. Synchrony and cooperation. *Psychological Science* 2009; **20**(1): 1–5.

62. Garrett HJ. The kernel of human (or rodent) kindness. Opinion. *New York Times.* December 28, 2018.

63. Shellenbarger S. Why perks no longer cut it for workers.. Journal Reports: Leadership. *Wall Street Journal.* December 3, 2018.

64. Ansberry C. What to do about that awful parent at the game. Life & Arts: Turning Points. *Wall Street Journal.* June 3, 2019.

65. Worrell FC, Knotek SE, Plucker JA, et al. Competition's role in developing psychological strength and outstanding performance. *Review of General Psychology* 2016; **20**(3): 259–71.

66. Tsai W. Social structure of "coopetition" within a multiunit organization: coordination, competition, and intraorganizational knowledge sharing. *Organization Science* 2002; **13**(2): 179–90.

67. Evans RB, Prado MP, Zambrana R. Competition and cooperation in mutual fund families. *Journal of Financial Economics* 2020; **136**(1): 168–88.

68. Roux C, Goldsmith K, Bonezzi A. On the psychology of scarcity: When reminders of resource scarcity promote selfish (and generous) behavior. *Journal of Consumer Research* 2015; **42**(4): 615–31.

69. Kilduff GJ, Galinsky AD, Gallo E, Reade JJ. Whatever it takes to win: Rivalry increases unethical behavior. *Academy of Management Journal* 2016; **59**(5): 1508–34.

5. Remain Flexible

1. Feldman MS, Pentland BT. Reconceptualizing organizational routines as a source of flexibility and change. *Administrative Science Quarterly* 2003; **48**(1): 94–118; Pentland BT, Feldman MS. Organizational routines as a unit of analysis. *Industrial and Corporate Change* 2005; **14**(5): 793–815.

2. Gebauer J, Schober F. Information system flexibility and the cost efficiency of business processes. *Journal of the Association for Information Systems* 2006; 7(3): 122–46.

3. Au S-Y, Dong M, Tremblay A. Employee flexibility, exogenous risk, and firm value. *Journal of Financial and Quantitative Analysis* 2021 May;56(3):853-84.

4. Burns T, Stalker GM. Mechanistic and organic systems. In Cameron KS. (Ed.) *Organizational effectiveness: The international library of critical writings on business and management.* Northampton, MA: Elgar, 2010: 3–8.

5. Lawrence PR, Lorsch JW. Differentiation and integration in complex organizations. *Administrative Science Quarterly* 1967; **12**(1): 1–47; Hage J. An axiomatic theory of organizations. *Administrative Science Quarterly* 1965; **10**(3): 289–320.

6. Kessler SR, Nixon AE, Nord WR. Examining organic and mechanistic structures: Do we know as much as we thought? *International Journal of Management Reviews* 2017; **19**(4): 531–55; Sherehiy B, Karwowski W, Layer JK. A review of enterprise agility: Concepts, frameworks, and attributes. *International Journal of Industrial Ergonomics* 2007; **37**(5): 445–60; Brown A. Organisational paradigms and sustainability in excellence. *International*

Journal of Quality and Service Sciences 2014; 6(2/3): 181–90; Burns T, Stalker GM. *The management of innovation*. New York: Oxford University Press (rev. ed.), 1994.

7. Huang X, Kristal MM, Schroeder RG. The impact of organizational structure on mass customization capability: A contingency view. *Production and Operations Management* 2010; **19**(5): 515–30.

8. Wright PM, Snell SA. Toward a unifying framework for exploring fit and flexibility in strategic human resource management. *Academy of Management Review* 1998; **23**(4): 756–72.

9. Jain A, Jain PK, Chan FTS, Singh S. A review on manufacturing flexibility. *International Journal of Production Research* 2013; **51**(19): 5946–70; Mendes L, Machado J. Employees' skills, manufacturing flexibility and performance: a structural equation modelling applied to the automotive industry. *International Journal of Production Research* 2015; **53**(13): 4087–101.

10. Westrum R. A typology of organisational cultures. *Quality and Safety in Health Care* 2004; **13**(2): ii22–ii7.

11. Roberts KH, Bea R. Must accidents happen? Lessons from high-reliability organizations. *Academy of Management Executive* 2001; **15**(3): 70–8; Weick KE, Sutcliffe KM. Mindfulness and the quality of organizational attention. *Organization Science* 2006; **17**(4): 514–24.

12. Nonaka I. A dynamic theory of organizational knowledge creation. In Starbuck WH, Whalen PS. (Eds.) *Organizational learning and knowledge management. Vol. 2, Learning by organizations*. Northampton, MA: Elgar, 2008: 106–29.

13. Bamel UK, Bamel N. Organizational resources, KM process capability and strategic flexibility: A dynamic resource-capability perspective. *Journal of Knowledge Management* 2018; **22**(7): 1555–72.

14. Yan Z, Gao SY, Teo CP. On the design of sparse but efficient structures in operations. *Management Science* 2018; **64**(7): 3421–45.

15. Roberts G. Honda introduces "flowing cell" production system in Thailand. *JustAuto*. April 21, 2016.

16. Duncker K. *On problem-solving*. Psychological Monographs, No. 270. Washington, DC: American Psychological Association, 1945; Georgsdottir AS, Getz I. How flexibility facilitates innovation and ways to manage it in organizations. *Creativity and Innovation Management* 2004; **13**(3): 166–75.

17. Mason S, Mountain G, Turner J, et al. Innovations to reduce demand and crowding in emergency care; a review study. *Scandinavian Journal of Trauma, Resuscitation and Emergency Medicine* 2014; **22**: 55–61.

18. Nagarajan M, Shechter S. Prospect theory and the newsvendor problem. *Management Science* 2014; **60**(4): 1057–62; Long X, Nasiry J. Prospect theory explains newsvendor behavior: The role of reference points.

Management Science 2015; **61**(12): 3009–12; Vipin B, Amit RK. Describing decision bias in the newsvendor problem: A prospect theory model. *Omega* 2019; **82**: 132–41.

19. Ashby WR. *An introduction to cybernetics.* Oxford: Wiley, 1956.

20. Kashefi M. Work flexibility and its individual consequences. *Canadian Journal of Sociology* 2007; **32**(3): 341–69; Oke A, Idiagbon-Oke M. Implementing flexible labour strategies: Challenges and key success factors. *Journal of Change Management* 2007; 7(1): 69–87.

21. Sullivan TA. Greedy institutions, overwork, and work-life balance. *Sociological Inquiry* 2014; **84**(1): 1–15; Beckers DGJ, van der Linden D, Smulders PGW, et al. Voluntary or involuntary? Control over overtime and rewards for overtime in relation to fatigue and work satisfaction. *Work and Stress* 2008; **22**(1): 33–50; Board TE. Working less can save lives. *New York Times.* May 30, 2021.

22. Rabenu E, Aharoni-Goldenberg S. Understanding the relationship between overtime and burnout. *International Studies of Management and Organization* 2017; **47**(4): 324–35.

23. Wheatley C. Nursing overtime: Should it be regulated? *Nursing Economics* 2017; **35**(4): 213–7.

24. Nicol A-M, Botterill JS. On-call work and health: A review. *Environmental Health* 2004; **3**: 15–7; Ziebertz C, van Hooff MLM, Beckers DGJ, et al. The relationship of on-call work with fatigue, work-home interference, and perceived performance difficulties. *BioMed Research International* 2015; **2015**: 1–10.

25. Carson ED. Disney, Zumiez among 6 retailers ending "on call" work schedules. *Investor's Business Daily.* December 20, 2016.

26. Henly JR, Lambert SJ. Unpredictable work timing in retail jobs: Implications for employee work-life conflict. *ILR Review* 2014; **67**(3): 986–1016.

27. Kamalahmadi M, Yu Q, Zhou Y-P. Call to duty: Just-in-time scheduling in a restaurant chain. *Management Science.* In press.

28. Dunn M. Who chooses part-time work and why? *Monthly Labor Review.* U.S. Bureau of Labor Statistics, March 2018: 1–25.

29. Künn-Nelen A, De Grip A, Fouarge D. Is part-time employment beneficial for firm productivity? *ILR Review* 2013; **66**(5): 1172–91; Kesavan S, Staats BR, Gilland W. Volume flexibility in services: The costs and benefits of flexible labor resources. *Management Science* 2014; **60**(8): 1884–906.

30. Costa G, Sartori S, Åkerstedt T. Influence of flexibility and variability of working hours on health and well-being. *Chronobiology International* 2006; **23**(6): 1125–37; Baltes BB, Briggs TE, Huff JW, Wright JA, Neuman GA. Flexible and compressed workweek schedules: A meta-analysis of their effects on work-related criteria. *Journal of Applied Psychology* 1999; **84**(4): 496–513;

Dizaho EK, Salleh R, Abdullah A. Achieving work life balance through flexible work schedules and arrangements. *Global Business and Management Research* 2017; 9: 455–65.

31. Mas A, Pallais A. Valuing alternative work arrangements. *The American economic review* 2017; 107(12): 3722–59.

32. Lee BY, DeVoe SE. Flextime and profitability. *Industrial Relations* 2012; 51(2): 298–316; Contreras F, Baykal E, Abid G. E-Leadership and teleworking in times of COVID-19 and beyond: what we know and where do we go. *Frontiers in Psychology* 2020; 11. 3484.

33. Gajendran RS, Harrison DA. The good, the bad, and the unknown about telecommuting: meta-analysis of psychological mediators and individual consequences. *Journal of Applied Psychology* 2007; 92(6): 1524–41; Virick M, DaSilva N, Arrington K. Moderators of the curvilinear relation between extent of telecommuting and job and life satisfaction: The role of performance outcome orientation and worker type. *Human Relations* 2010; 63(1): 137–54.

34. Golden TD, Eddleston KA. Is there a price telecommuters pay? Examining the relationship between telecommuting and objective career success. *Journal of Vocational Behavior* 2020; 116 103348; Allen TD, Golden TD, Shockley KM. How effective Is telecommuting? Assessing the status of our scientific findings. *Psychological Science in the Public Interest* 2015; 16(2): 40–68.

35. Get used to it: The internet and covid-19. *The Economist* 2020; 435(9190): 73.

36. Could a four-day working week become the norm? *The Economist* explains, July 8, 2021.

37. Bartleby. Working hard for the money. *The Economist*, June 12, 2021: 61.

38. Lindström J. Does higher energy intake explain weight gain and increased metabolic risks among shift workers? *Scandinavian Journal of Work, Environment and Health* 2016; 42(6): 455–7; Knutsson A, Bøggild H. Gastrointestinal disorders among shift workers. *Scandinavian Journal of Work, Environment and Health* 2010; 36(2): 85–95.

39. de Cordova PB, Bradford MA, Stone PW. Increased errors and decreased performance at night: A systematic review of the evidence concerning shift work and quality. *Work: Journal of Prevention, Assessment and Rehabilitation* 2016; 53(4): 825–34.

40. Atkinson J, Meager N. Is flexibility just a flash in the pan? *Personnel Management* 1986: 26–9.

41. Hyman L. Temps, consultants, and the rise of the precarious economy. *Hedgehog Review* 2016; 18(1): 17–32.

42. Davis-Blake A, Broschak JP. Outsourcing and the changing nature of work. *Annual Review of Sociology* 2009; **35**: 321–40.

43. Saleh JH, Mark G, Jordan NC. Flexibility: A multi-disciplinary literature review and a research agenda for designing flexible engineering systems. *Journal of Engineering Design* 2009; **20**(3): 307–23.

44. Chan TCY, Fearing D. Process flexibility in baseball: The value of positional flexibility. *Management Science* 2018; **65**(4):1642–66.

45. Akşin OZ, Çakan N, Karaesmen F, Örmeci EL. Flexibility structure and capacity design with human resource considerations. *Production and Operations Management* 2015; **24**(7): 1086–100; Iravani SM, Van Oyen MP, Sims KT. Structural flexibility: A new perspective on the design of manufacturing and service operations. *Management Science* 2005; **51**(2): 151–66.

46. Allwood JM, Lee WL. The impact of job rotation on problem solving skills. *International Journal of Production Research* 2004; **42**(5): 865–81; Park PS. The examination of worker cross-training in a dual resource constrained job shop. *European Journal of Operational Research* 1991; **52**(3): 291–9; Nembhard DA. Cross training efficiency and flexibility with process change. *International Journal of Operations and Production Management* 2014; **34**(11): 1417–39.

47. Campion MA, Cheraskin L, Stevens MJ. Career-related antecedents and outcomes of job rotation. *Academy of Management Journal* 1994; **37**(6): 1518–42.

48. Eriksson T, Ortega J. The adoption of job rotation: Testing the theories. *ILR Review* 2006; **59**(4): 653–66.

49. Moorman C. Organizational improvisation and organizational memory. *Academy of Management Review*, **23**(4): 698–723.

50. Kossek EE, Piszczek MM, McAlpine KL, Hammer LB, Burke L. Filling the holes: Work schedulers as job crafters of employment practice in long-term health care. *Industrial and Labor Relations Review* 2016; **69**(4): 961–90; Kossek EE, Rosokha LM, Leana C. Work schedule patching in health care: Exploring implementation approaches. *Work and Occupations* 2020; **47**(2): 228–61.

51. De Bruecker P, Van den Bergh J, Beliën J, Demeulemeester E. Workforce planning incorporating skills: State of the art. *European Journal of Operational Research* 2015; **243**(1): 1–16.

52. Nohria N, Gulati R. Is Slack good or bad for innovation? *Academy of Management Journal* 1996; **39**(5): 1245–64.

53. Guo J, Zhou B, Zhang H, Hu C, Song M. Does strategic planning help firms translate slack resources into better performance? *Journal of Management and Organization* 2018; **26**(4): 1–13.

6. Create Distinctive Spaces

1. Rosen D, Santesso A. The panopticon reviewed: Sentimentalism and eighteenth-century interiority. *ELH* 2010; 77(4): 1041–59; Manokha I. Surveillance, panopticism, and self-discipline in the digital age. *Surveillance and Society* 2018; 16(2): 219–37.

2. Santesso DR. The panopticon reviewed: Sentimentalism and eighteenth-century interiority. *ELH* 2010; 77(4): 141.

3. Manokha. Surveillance, panopticism, and self-discipline.

4. Mims, C. The Bezos school of management is changing the way we work. *Wall Street Journal.* September 11–12, 2021.

5. Nieuwenhuis M, Knight C, Postmes T, Haslam SA. The relative benefits of green versus lean office space: Three field experiments. *Journal of Experimental Psychology Applied* 2014; 20(3): 199–214.

6. Zhong C-B, House J. Hawthorne revisited: Organizational implications of the physical work environment. *Research in Organizational Behavior* 2012; 32: 3–22.

7. Sadatsafavi H, Walewski J, Shepley M. Physical work environment as a managerial tool for decreasing job-related anxiety and improving employee-employer Relations. *Journal of Healthcare Management* 2015; 60(2): 114–31.

8. Yorks L, Whitsett DA. Hawthorne, Topeka, and the issue of science versus advocacy in organizational behavior. *Academy of Management review* 1985; 10(1): 21–30.

9. Tarantini M, Pernigotto G, Gasparella A. A co-citation analysis on thermal comfort and productivity aspects in production and office buildings. *Buildings* 2017; 7(2): 36.

10. Wickhorst V, Geroy G. Physical communication and organization development. *Organization Development Journal* 2006; 24(3): 54–63.

11. Proshansky HM, Fabian AK. *Psychological aspects of the quality of urban life.* Boston: De Gruyter, 1986: 19–30; Jensen PA, van der Voordt TJM. Healthy workplaces: What we know and what else we need to know. *Journal of Corporate Real Estate* 2019; 22(2): 95–112.

12. Chan JK, Beckman SL, Lawrence PG. Workplace design: A new managerial imperative. *California Management Review* 2007; 49(2): 22–3; Budie B, Appel–Meulenbroek R, Kemperman A, Weijs–Perrée M. Employee satisfaction with the physical work environment: The importance of a need based approach. *International Journal of Strategic Property Management* 2019; 23(1): 36–49; van der Voordt TJM. Productivity and employee satisfaction in flexible workplaces. *Journal of Corporate Real Estate* 2004; 6(2): 133–48.

13. Jensen JL. Designing for profound experiences. *Design Issues* 2014; 30(3): 39–52.

14. Gjerland A, Søiland E, Thuen F. Office concepts: A scoping review. *Building and Environment* 2019; 163: 106294; Ashkanasy NM, Ayoko OB,

Jehn KA. Understanding the physical environment of work and employee behavior: An affective events perspective. *Journal of Organizational Behavior* 2014; **35**(8): 1169–84.

15. MacNaughton P, Satish U, Laurent JGC, et al. The impact of working in a green certified building on cognitive function and health. *Building and Environment* 2017; **114**: 178–86.

16. Delmas MA, Pekovic S. Environmental standards and labor productivity: Understanding the mechanisms that sustain sustainability: environmental standards and labor productivity. *Journal of Organizational Behavior* 2013; **34**(2): 230–52.

17. Vischer JC. The effects of the physical environment on job performance: Towards a theoretical model of workspace stress. *Stress and Health* 2007; **23**(3): 175–84; Choi H-H, van Merriënboer JJG, Paas F. Effects of the physical environment on cognitive load and learning: Towards a new model of cognitive load. *Educational Psychology Review* 2014; **26**(2): 225–44.

18. Thach T-Q, Mahirah D, Sauter C, et al. Associations of perceived indoor environmental quality with stress in the workplace. *Indoor Air* 2020; **30**(6): 1166–77.

19. Pfeffer J. The hidden costs of stressed-out workers. Life & Arts. *Wall Street Journal.* February 28, 2019.

20. Roberts AC, Yap HS, Kwok KW, Car J, Soh C-K, Christopoulos GI. The cubicle deconstructed: Simple visual enclosure improves perseverance. *Journal of Environmental Psychology* 2019; **63**: 60–73.

21. Anderson CA, Anderson DC. Ambient temperature and violent crime: Tests of the linear and curvilinear hypotheses. *Journal of Personality and Social Psychology* 1984; **46**(1): 91–7; Baron RA, Bell PA. Aggression and heat: The influence of ambient temperature, negative affect, and a cooling drink on physical aggression. *Journal of Personality and Social Psychology* 1976; **33**(3): 245–55.

22. Ulrich RS. A theory of supportive design for healthcare facilities. *Journal of Healthcare Design: Proceedings from the Symposium on Healthcare Design Symposium on Healthcare Design* 1997; **9**: 7–24.

23. Salamé P, Baddeley A. Disruption of short-term memory by unattended speech: Implications for the structure of working memory. *Journal of Verbal Learning and Verbal Behavior* 1982; **21**(2): 150–64; Kraus, N. Hearing too much in a noisy world. *Wall Street Journal.* September 11–12, 2021.

24. Ribeiro FS, Santos FH, Albuquerque PB. How does allocation of emotional stimuli impact working memory tasks? An overview. *Advances in Cognitive Psychology* 2019; **15**(2): 155–68; Konstantinou N, Bahrami B, Rees G, Lavie N. Visual short-term memory load reduces retinotopic cortex response to contrast. *Journal of Cognitive Neuroscience* 2012; **24**(11): 2199–210.

25. Kim J, de Dear R. Workspace satisfaction: The privacy-communication trade-off in open-plan offices. *Journal of Environmental Psychology* 2013; **36**:

18–26; Skuballa IT, Xu KM, Jarodzka H. The impact of co-actors on cognitive load: When the mere presence of others makes learning more difficult. *Computers in Human Behavior* 2019; **101**: 30–41.

26. Klitzman S, Stellman JM. The impact of the physical environment on the psychological well-being of office workers. *Social Science and Medicine* 1989; **29**(6): 733–42; Pejtersen J, Allermann L, Kristensen TS, Poulsen OM. Indoor climate, psychosocial work environment and symptoms in open-plan offices. *Indoor Air* 2006; **16**(5): 392–401.

27. Lamb S, Kwok KCS. A longitudinal investigation of work environment stressors on the performance and wellbeing of office workers. *Applied Ergonomics* 2016; **52**: 104–11.

28. James O, Delfabbro P, King DL. A comparison of psychological and work outcomes in open-plan and cellular office designs: a systematic review. *SAGE open* 2021; **11**(1).

29. Fuhrmans V. CEOs want their offices back: Some bosses pushing back against open-floor plans. Management & Careers. *Wall Street Journal.* May 22, 2017.

30. Cawood S. How employee experience will change in the new office model. *Employee Benefits News.* June 29, 2020.

31. Open office can lead to closed minds. *Economist* July 28, 2018; **428**(9102): 47.

32. Otterbring T, Pareigis J, Wästlund E, Makrygiannis A, Lindström A. The relationship between office type and job satisfaction: Testing a multiple mediation model through ease of interaction and well-being. *Scandinavian Journal of Work, Environment and Health* 2018; **44**(3): 330–4.

33. Allen TJ. *Managing the flow of technology: Technology transfer and the dissemination of technological information within the R and D organization.* Boston: MIT Press, 1977; Waber B, Magnolfi J, Lindsay G. Workspaces that move people. *Harvard Business Review.* October 2014.

34. Margolies J. Escaping the din of the open office. *New York Times.* February 19, 2020; Sect. B6.

35. Gibson JJ. The theory of affordances. In Gieseking JJ, Mangold W. (Eds.) *The People, Place, and Space Reader.* London: Routledge, 2014: 90–94.

36. Menatti L, Casado da Rocha A. Landscape and health: Connecting psychology, aesthetics, and philosophy through the concept of affordance. *Frontiers in Psychology* 2016; **7**(May): 571; Pepper GL. The physical organization as equivocal message. *Journal of Applied Communication Research* 2008; **36**(3): 318–38.

37. Kelling GL, Wilson JQ. Broken windows. *Atlantic.* March 1982.

38. Keizer K, Lindenberg S, Steg L. The spreading of disorder. *Science* 2008; **322**(5908): 1681–5.

39. Ramos J, Torgler B. Are academics messy? Testing the broken windows theory with a field experiment in the work environment. *Review of Law NS Economics* 2012; **8**(3): 563–77.

40. Shellenbarger S. Use your seat to get ahead at work. Life & Arts. *Wall Street Journal.* August 8, 2017.

41. Haapakangas A, Hongisto V, Varjo J, Lahtinen M. Benefits of quiet workspaces in open-plan offices: Evidence from two office relocations. *Journal of Environmental Psychology* 2018; **56**: 63–75.

42. Morrison RL, Smollan RK. Open plan office space? If you're going to do it, do it right: A fourteen-month longitudinal case study. *Applied Ergonomics* 2020; **82**: 102933.

43. Evans J. The dark side of hip office design. *Financial Times.* January 5, 2020.

44. Laing A, Craig D, White A. High-performance office space. *Harvard Business Review.* September 1, 2011.

45. Wells M, Thelen L. What does your workspace say about you? The influence of personality, status, and workspace on personalization. *Environment and Behavior* 2002; **34**(3): 300–21.

46. De Paoli D, Sauer E, Ropo A. The spatial context of organizations: A critique of "creative workspaces." *Journal of Management and Organization* 2017; **25**(2): 1–22.

47. Knight C, Haslam SA. The relative merits of lean, enriched, and empowered offices: An experimental examination of the impact of workspace management strategies on well-being and productivity. *Journal of Experimental Psychology Applied* 2010; **16**(2): 158–72.

48. Moskaliuk J, Burmeister CP, Landkammer F, Renner B, Cress U. Environmental effects on cognition and decision making of knowledge workers. *Journal of Environmental Psychology* 2017; **49**: 43–54.

49. Tuan Y-F. *Topophilia: A study of environmental perceptions, attitudes, and values.* New York: Columbia University Press, 1990.

50. Masterson VA, Enqvist JP, Stedman RC, Tengö M. Sense of place in social–ecological systems: From theory to empirics. *Sustainability Science* 2019; **14**(3): 555–64; Calvard TS. Integrating organization studies and community psychology: A process model of an organizing sense of place in working lives. *Journal of Community Psychology* 2015; **43**(6): 654–86.

51. Choudhury P, Crowston K, Dahlander L, Minervini MS, Raghuram S. GitLab: Work where you want, when you want. *Journal of Organization Design* 2020; **9**(1): 1–17.

52. Gajendran RS, Harrison DA. The good, the bad, and the unknown about telecommuting: meta-analysis of psychological mediators and individual consequences. *Journal of Applied Psychology* 2007; **92**(6): 1524–41.

53. Choudhury et al. GitLab: Work where you want, when you want.

54. Bindley K. A cubicle in the cloud: Some founders opt to forgo physical workplaces entirely, for now, at least. Exchange. *Wall Street Journal.* February 26, 2021.

55. Kuruzovich J, Paczkowski WP, Golden TD, Goodarzi S, Venkatesh V. Telecommuting and job outcomes: A moderated mediation model of system use, software quality, and social Exchange. *Information and Management* 2021; **58**(3): 20–24.

56. Craven VD. The future of open office. *Buildings* 2020 **114** (1).

57. Hot desk, cold comfort. *Economist.* September 26, 2019; **432**(9162): 60.

58. Taskin L, Parmentier M, Stinglhamber F. The dark side of office designs: towards de-humanization. *New Technology, Work, and Employment* 2019; **34**(3): 262–84.

59. Oakman J, Oakman J, Kinsman N, Kinsman N, Briggs AM, Briggs AM. Working with persistent pain: an exploration of strategies utilised to stay productive at work. *Journal of Occupational Rehabilitation* 2017; **27**(1): 4–14.

60. Boutillier S, Capdevila I, Dupont L, Morel L. Collaborative spaces promoting creativity and innovation. *Journal of Innovation Economics and Management* 2020; **31**(1): 1–9.

61. Hoff EV, Öberg NK. The role of the physical work environment for creative employees: A case study of digital artists. *International Journal of Human Resource Management* 2015; **26**(14): 1889–906; McCoy JM. Linking the physical work environment to creative context. *Journal of Creative Behavior* 2005; **39**(3): 169–91.

62. Lee YS. Creative workplace characteristics and innovative start-up companies. *Facilities* 2016; **34**(7/8): 413–32.

63. Schell E, Theorell T, Saraste H. Workplace aesthetics: Impact of environments upon employee health? *Work* 2011; **39**(3): 203–13; Mintz NL. Effects of esthetic surroundings: II. Prolonged and repeated experience in a "beautiful" and an "ugly" room. *Journal of Psychology* 1956; **41**(2): 459–66.

64. Wilson EO. *Biophilia.* Cambridge, MA: Harvard University Press, 1986.

65. Cutter C, Feintzeig R. New offices seek comfort, fewer distractions. *Wall Street Journal.* November 25, 2019.

66. Margolies J. Making a day at the office like a walk in the park. *New York Times,* January 16, 2019; Higgins A. Designs for Amazon HQ2's garden focus on a connection to nature. *Washington Post.* July 7, 2021.

67. Jo H, Song C, Miyazaki Y. Physiological benefits of viewing nature: A systematic review of indoor experiments. *International Journal of Environmental Research and Public Health* 2019; **16**(23): 4739.

68. Park S-H, Mattson RH. Therapeutic influences of plants in hospital rooms on surgical recovery. *HortScience* 2009; **44**(1): 102–5.

69. Kaplan R. The nature of the view from home: psychological bene-fits. *Environment and Behavior* 2001; **33**(4): 507–42; Kaplan R. The role of nature in the context of the workplace. *Landscape and Urban Planning* 1993; **26**(1–4): 193–201.

70. Sheikh K. Enjoy 2 hours a week in nature, doctors say. *New York Times.* June 13, 2019; Sect. D4.

71. Brown, DK, Barton, JL, Pretty, J, and Gladwell, VF. Walks4work: Assessing the role of the natural environment in a workplace physical activity intervention. *Scandinavian Journal of Work, Environment and Health* 2014; **40**(4): 390–9.

72. Morris B. For better health, just head outdoors. Health & Wellness. *Wall Street Journal.* February 14, 2021.

73. Hartig T. Where best to take a booster break? *American Journal of Preventive Medicine* 2006; **31**(4): 350.

74. Webb CE, Rossignac-Milon M, Higgins ET. Stepping forward together: Could walking facilitate interpersonal conflict resolution? *American Psychologist* 2017; **72**(4): 374–85.

75. Razani N. Nature and health in practice. *Parks Stewardship Forum* 2021; **37**(1): 17–23.

76. An M, Colarelli SM, O'Brien K, Boyajian ME. Why we need more nature at work: Effects of natural elements and sunlight on employee mental health and work attitudes. *PLoS One* 2016; **11**(5): e0155614; Largo-Wight E, Chen WW, Dodd V, Weiler R. Healthy workplaces: The effects of nature contact at work on employee stress and health. *Public Health Reports* 2011; **126**(Suppl 1): 124–30.

77. Madeddu M, Zhang X. Harmonious spaces: the influence of Feng Shui on urban form and design. *Journal of Urban Design* 2017; **22**(6): 709–25; Whedon GA. Frames of reference that address the impact of physical environ-ments on occupational performance. *Work* 2000; **14**(2): 165–74.

78. Stellar JE, Gordon AM, Piff PK, et al. Self-transcendent emotions and their social functions: compassion, gratitude, and awe bind us to others through prosociality. *Emotion Review* 2017; **9**(3): 200–7; Keltner D, Haidt J. Approaching awe, a moral, spiritual, and aesthetic emotion. *Cognition and Emotion* 2010; **17**(2): 297–314.

79. Piff P, Keltner D. Why do we experience awe? *New York Times.* May 22, 2015; Zhang JW, Piff PK, Iyer R, Koleva S, Keltner D. An occasion for unselfing: Beautiful nature leads to prosociality. *Journal of Environmental Psychology* 2014; **37**: 61–72; Bai Y, Ocampo J, Jin G, et al. Awe, daily stress, and elevated life satisfaction. *Journal of personality and social psychology* 2021; **120**(4): 837–60.

80. Miller L, Balodis IM, McClintock CH, et al. Neural correlates of per-sonalized spiritual experiences. *Cerebral Cortex* 2019; **29**(6): 2331–8.

81. Shusterman R. Art as dramatization. *Journal of Aesthetics and Art Criticism* 2001; **59**(4): 363–72.

82. Klotz AC. Creating jobs and workspaces that energize people: *MIT Sloan Management Review* 2020; **61**(4): 74–8.

7. Diversify and Inclusify the Workforce

1. Roberson QM. Diversity in the workplace: A review, synthesis, and future research agenda. *Annual Review of Organizational Psychology and Organizational Behavior* 2019; **6**(1): 69–88.

2. Lynch FR. Corporate diversity. *Society* 2005; **42**(3): 40–7; Oswick C, Noon M. Discourses of diversity, equality and inclusion: Trenchant formulations or transient fashions? *British Journal of Management* 2014; **25**(1): 23–39.

3. Grant RM. Toward a knowledge-based theory of the firm. *Strategic Management Journal* 1996; **17**(S2): 109–22.

4. Nielsen S, Huse M. The contribution of women on boards of directors: Going beyond the surface. *Corporate Governance* 2010; **18**(2): 136–48; Nielsen S, Huse M. Women directors' contribution to board decision-making and strategic involvement: The role of equality perception. *European Management Review* 2010; **7**(1): 16–29.

5. Amabile TM, Conti R, Coon H, Lazenby J, Herron M. assessing the work environment for creativity. *Academy of Management Journal* 1996; **39**(5): 1154–84.

6. Mayer RC, Warr RS, Zhao J. Do pro-diversity policies improve corporate innovation? *Financial Management* 2018; **47**(3): 617–50.

7. Hector A. Ecology: Diversity favours productivity. *Nature* 2011; **472**(7341): 45–6.

8. Lilienfeld DE, Beekman N. The imperative for gender diversity on boards. *Corporate Governance Advisor* 2014; **22**(3): 19–22.

9. Sarhan AA, Ntim CG, Al-Najjar B. Board diversity, corporate governance, corporate performance, and executive pay. *International Journal of Finance and Economics* 2018; **24**(2): 761–86.

10. White G. Promoting gender parity on boards: A holistic diversity and inclusion strategy. *Cost Management* 2020; **34**(3): 20–24.

11. Sabatier M. A women's boom in the boardroom: effects on performance? *Applied Economics* 2015; **47**(26): 2717–27.

12. Kim D, Starks LT. Gender diversity on corporate boards: Do women contribute unique skills? *American Economic Review* 2016; **106**(5): 267–71.

13. Khatib SFA, Abdullah DF, Elamer AA, Abueid R. Nudging toward diversity in the boardroom: A systematic literature review of board diversity

of financial institutions. *Business Strategy and the Environment* 2021; **30**(2): 985–1002.

14. Eagly AH. When passionate advocates meet research on diversity, does the honest broker stand a chance? *Journal of Social Issues* 2016; **72**(1): 199–222; Benkraiem R, Hamrouni A, Lakhal F, Toumi N. Board independence, gender diversity and CEO compensation. *Corporate Governance* 2017; **17**(5): 845–60.

15. Creek SA, Kuhn KM, Sahaym A. Board diversity and employee satisfaction: The mediating role of progressive programs. *Group and Organization Management* 2017; **44**(3): 521–48.

16. Herring C. Is diversity still a good thing? *American Sociological Review* 2017; **82**(4): 868–77.

17. Talke K, Salomo S, Kock A. Top management team diversity and strategic innovation orientation: The relationship and consequences for innovativeness and performance. *Journal of Product Innovation Management* 2011; **28**(6): 819–32.

18. Ruiz-Jiménez JM, Fuentes-Fuentes MdM, Ruiz-Arroyo M. Knowledge combination capability and innovation: The effects of gender diversity on top management teams in technology-based firms. *Journal of Business Ethics* 2014; **135**(3): 503–15.

19. Li J, Meyer B, Shemla M, Wegge J. From being diverse to becoming diverse: A dynamic team diversity theory. *Journal of Organizational Behavior* 2018; **39**(8): 956–70.

20. Fenwick GD, Neal DJ. Effect of gender composition on group performance. *Gender, Work, and Organization* 2001; **8**(2): 222–5; Hoogendoorn S, Oosterbeek H, van Praag M. The impact of gender diversity on the performance of business teams: Evidence from a field experiment. *Management Science* 2013; **59**(7): 1514–28.

21. Gompers P, Kovvali S. The other diversity dividend. *Harvard Business Review.* July 1, 2018.

22. Levine SS, Apfelbaum EP, Bernard M, Bartelt VL, Zajac EJ, Stark D. Ethnic diversity deflates price bubbles. *Proceedings of the National Academy of Sciences* 2014; **111**(52): 18524–9.

23. Pennekamp F, Pontarp M, Tabi A, et al. Biodiversity increases and decreases ecosystem stability. *Nature* 2018; **563**(7729): 109–12.

24. Page SE. Where diversity comes from and why it matters? *European Journal of Social Psychology* 2014; **44**(4): 267–79.

25. Greene RR. Resilience as effective functional capacity: An ecological-stress model. *Journal of Human Behavior in the Social Environment* 2014; **24**(8): 937–50.

26. Ives AR, Carpenter SR. Stability and diversity of ecosystems. *Science* 2007; **317**(5834): 58–62.

27. Folke C, Carpenter S, Walker B, et al. Regime shifts, resilience, and biodiversity in ecosystem management. *Annual Review of Ecology, Evolution, and Systematics* 2004; **35**(1): 557–81.

28. Bonabeau E. Understanding and managing complexity risk. *MIT Sloan Management Review* 2007; **48**(4): 62–91.

29. MacDougall AS, McCann KS, Gellner G, Turkington R. Diversity loss with persistent human disturbance increases vulnerability to ecosystem collapse. *Nature* 2013; **494**(7435): 86–9.

30. Deller S, Watson P. Spatial variations in the relationship between economic diversity and stability. *Applied Economics Letters* 2016; **23**(7): 520–5.

31. Leslie P, McCabe JT. Response diversity and resilience in social-ecological systems. *Current Anthropology* 2013; **54**(2): 114–44; Schoen C, Rost K. What really works?! Evaluating the effectiveness of practices to increase the managerial diversity of women and minorities. *European Management Journal* 2021; **39**(1): 95–108.

32. Fugère MA, Cathey C, Beetham R, Haynes M, Schaedler RA. Preference for the diversity policy label versus the affirmative action policy label. *Social Justice Research* 2016; **29**(2): 206–27.

33. Surowiecki J. Valley boys. *New Yorker*. November 17, 2014.

34. O'Brien KR, Scheffer M, van Nes EH, Van Der Lee R. How to break the cycle of low workforce diversity: A model for change. *PLoS One* 2015; **10**(7): e0133208; Kogut B, Colomer J, Belinky M. structural equality at the top of the corporation: mandated quotas for women directors. *Strategic Management Journal* 2014; **35**(6): 891–902.

35. Miller C. Affirmative action and its persistent effects: A new perspective. *California Management Review* 2019; **61**(3): 19–33.

36. Schlachter SD, Pieper JR. Employee referral hiring in organizations: An integrative conceptual review, model, and agenda for future research. *Journal of Applied Psychology* 2019; **104**(11): 1325–46; Pieper JR, Trevor CO, Weller I, Duchon D. Referral hire presence implications for referrer turnover and job performance. *Journal of Management* 2019; **45**(5): 1858–88.

37. Agarwal S, Qian W, Reeb DM, Sing TF. Playing the boys game: Golf buddies and board diversity. *American Economic Review* 2016; **106**(5): 272–6.

38. Shellenbarger S. The perils of "cultural fit": Efforts can veer into a ditch if hires look, think and act alike. Life & Arts. *Wall Street Journal*. September 23, 2019.

39. Byrne D. Interpersonal attraction and attitude similarity. *Journal of Abnormal and Social Psychology* 1961; **62**(3): 713–5; Alves H. Sharing rare attitudes attracts. *Personality and Social Psychology Bulletin* 2018; **44**(8): 1270–83.

40. Hackett JD, Hogg MA. The diversity paradox: When people who value diversity surround themselves with like-minded others. *Journal of Applied Social Psychology* 2014; **44**(6): 415–22.

41. Almandoz J, Tilcsik A. When experts become liabilities: Domain experts on boards and organizational failure. *Academy of Management Journal* 2016; **59**(4): 1124–49.

42. Park G. Blizzard president Brack allowed toxicity to fester, according to lawsuit. *Washington Post*. July 22, 2021.

43. Sommers SR. On racial diversity and group decision making: Identifying multiple effects of racial composition on jury deliberations. *Journal of Personality and Social Psychology* 2006; **90**(4): 597–612; Triana MdC, Jayasinghe M, Pieper JR. Perceived workplace racial discrimination and its correlates: A meta-analysis. *Journal of Organizational Behavior* 2015; **36**(4): 491–513.

44. Dhanani LY, Beus JM, Joseph DL. Workplace discrimination: A meta-analytic extension, critique, and future research agenda. *Personnel Psychology* 2018; **71**(2): 147–79.

45. Kline PM, Rose EK, Walters CR. Systemic discrimination among large U.S. employers. National Bureau of Economic Research, August, 2021.

46. Hangartner D, Kopp D, Siegenthaler M. Monitoring hiring discrimination through online recruitment platforms. *Nature* 2021; **589**(7843): 572–76.

47. Phillips KWP, Lount JRB, Sheldon O, Rink F. The biases that punish racially diverse teams. *Harvard Business Review*. February 22, 2016; Phillips KW. How diversity works. *Scientific American*. October 2014: 43–7; Hebl M, Cheng SK, Ng LC. Modern discrimination in organizations. *Annual Review of Organizational Psychology And Organizational Behavior* 2020; **7**(1): 257–82.

48. Hoyt CL, Burnette JL. Gender bias in leader evaluations: Merging implicit theories and role congruity perspectives. *Personality and Social Psychology Bulletin* 2013; **39**(10): 1306–19.

49. Henry A. What to do when you feel marginalized? Business/Financial Desk. *New York Times*. October 7, 2019; Sect. B7.

50. Heilman ME, Haynes MC. No credit where credit is due: Attributional rationalization of women's success in male-female teams. *Journal of Applied Psychology* 2005; **90**(5): 905–16.

51. Foschi M. Double standards for competence: Theory and research. *Annual Review of Sociology* 2000; **26**(1): 21–42.

52. Pasquerella L, Clauss-Ehlers CS. Glass cliffs, queen bees, and the snow-woman effect: Persistent barriers to women's leadership in the academy. *Liberal Education* 2017; **103**(2): 6.

53. Williams MT. Microaggressions: Clarification, evidence, and impact. *Perspectives on Psychological Science* 2019; **15**(1). 3–26; Pierce CM, Carew

JV, Pierce-Gonzalez D, Wills D. An experiment in racism: TV commercials. *Education and Urban Society* 1977; **10**(1): 61–87.

54. Sue DW, Capodilupo CM, Torino GC, et al. Racial microaggressions in everyday life: Implications for clinical practice. *The American Psychologist* 2007; **62**(4): 271–86.

55. Crespo G. Doctor says she was racially profiled while trying to help fellow passenger. CNN. November 1, 2018.

56. Goldberg E. It can cause you to shrink. *New York Times*. 2020; Sect. D4.

57. Leslie LM. Diversity initiative effectiveness: A typological theory of unintended consequences. *Academy of Management Review* 2019; **44**(3): 538–63; Koch AJ, D'Mello SD, Sackett PR. A meta-analysis of gender stereotypes and bias in experimental simulations of employment decision making. *Journal of Applied Psychology* 2015; **100**(1): 128–61.

58. Kalev A, Dobbin F, Kelly E. Best practices or best guesses? Assessing the efficacy of corporate affirmative action and diversity policies. *American Sociological Review* 2016; **71**(4): 589–617.

59. McDonald ML, Westphal JD. Access denied: Low mentoring of women and minority first-time directors and its negative effects on appointments to additional boards. *Academy of Management Journal* 2013; **56**(4): 1169–98.

60. Wolgast S, Bäckström M, Björklund F. Tools for fairness: Increased structure in the selection process reduces discrimination. *PLoS One* 2017; **12**(12): e0189512.

61. Axt JR, Lai CK. Reducing discrimination: A bias versus noise perspective. *Journal of Personality and Social Psychology* 2019; **117**(1): 26–49.

62. Goldin C, Rouse C. Orchestrating impartiality: The impact of "blind" auditions on female musicians. *American Economic Review* 2000; **90**(4): 715–41.

63. Kahneman D. *Thinking, fast and slow*. New York: Farrar, Straus and Giroux, 2011.

64. Amodio DM, Swencionis JK. Proactive control of implicit bias: A theoretical model and implications for behavior change. *Journal of Personality and Social Psychology* 2018; **115**(2): 255–75; Bugg JM, Crump MJC. In support of a distinction between voluntary and stimulus-driven control: A review of the literature on proportion congruent effects. *Frontiers in Psychology* 2012; **3**: 367.

65. Miller CC. Why mothers' choices often feel like no choice. *New York Times*. January 19, 2020; Sect. BU1.

66. Andrews H. Who will defend the American family? *New York Times*. April 28, 2019; Sect. SR1; Hirko C. Women did everything right. Then work got greedy. *New York Times*. April 28, 2019.

67. Pasquerella et al. Glass cliffs, queen bees, and the snow-woman effect.

68. Groysberg B, Bell D. Dysfunction in the boardroom. *Harvard Business Review.* June 2013.

69. Simons SM, Rowland KN. Diversity and its impact on organizational performance: the influence of diversity constructions on expectations and outcomes. *Journal of Technology Management and Innovation* 2011; 6(3): 171–83.

70. Bertrand O, Lumineau F. Partners in crime: The effects of diversity on the longevity of cartels. *Academy of Management Journal* 2016; 59(3): 983–1008; Harrison DA, Klein KJ. What's the difference? diversity constructs as separation, variety, or disparity in organizations. *Academy of Management Review* 2007; 32(4): 1199–228.

71. Solanas Pérez A, Selvam RM, Navarro Cid J, Leiva Ureña D. Some common indexes of group diversity: upper boundaries. *Psychological Reports* 2012; 111(3): 777–96; Maturo F, Migliori S, Paolone F. Measuring and monitoring diversity in organizations through functional instruments with an application to ethnic workforce diversity of the U.S. federal agencies. *Computational and Mathematical Organization Theory* 2018; 25(4): 357–88.

72. Blau PM. *Inequality and heterogeneity: A primitive theory of social structure.* New York: Free Press, 1977.

73. Danbold F, Unzueta MM. Drawing the diversity line: Numerical thresholds of diversity vary by group status. *Journal of Personality and Social Psychology* 2020; 118(2): 283–306.

74. Forman L. Critical mass is key for women in business: Companies and boards with many women, not just token females, may outperform their peers. Markets. *Wall Street Journal.* August 14, 2019.

75. Elstad B, Ladegard G. Women on corporate boards: Key influencers or tokens? *Journal of Management and Governance* 2010; 16(4): 595–615.

76. Garcia Martinez M, Zouaghi F, Garcia Marco T. Diversity is strategy: The effect of R&D team diversity on innovative performance. *R&D Management* 2017; 47(2): 311–29.

77. Downey SN, van der Werff L, Thomas KM, Plaut VC. The role of diversity practices and inclusion in promoting trust and employee engagement. *Journal of Applied Social Psychology* 2015; 45(1): 35–44.

78. Reagans R, Zuckerman EW. Networks, diversity, and productivity: The social capital of corporate R&D teams. *Organization Science* 2001; 12(4): 502–17.

79. Svyantek DJ, Mahoney KT, Brown LL. Diversity and effectiveness in the Roman and Persian empires. *International Journal of Organizational Analysis* 2002; 10(3): 260–83; Svyantek DJ, Bott J. Received wisdom and the relationship between diversity and organizational performance. *International Journal of Organizational Analysis* 2004; 12(3): 295–317.

80. Reed H. Corporations as agents of social change: A case study of diversity at Cummins Inc. *Business History* 2017; **59**(6): 821–43.

81. Highhouse S. A history of the T-Group and its early applications in management development. *Group Dynamics: Theory Research and Practice* 2002; **6**(4): 277–90.

82. Brown CB, Orr D. Influential DNA: A study of prominent women and their impact on the field of organization development. *Organization Development Journal* 2010; **28**(3): 27–40; Waclawski J, Church AH, Burke WW. Women in organization development: A profile of the intervention styles and values of today's practitioners. *Journal of Organizational Change Management* 1995; **8**(1): 12–22.

83. Hajro A, Gibson CB, Pudelko M. Knowledge exchange processes in multicultural teams: Linking organizational diversity climates to teams' effectiveness. *Academy of Management Journal* 2017; **60**(1): 345–72; Devine PG, Ash TL. Diversity training Goals, limitations, and promise: a review of the multidisciplinary literature. *Annual Review of Psychology* 2022; **73**(1).

84. Anand R, Winters M-F. A Retrospective view of corporate diversity training from 1964 to the present. *Academy of Management Learning and Education* 2008; **7**(3): 356–72; Lipman J. How diversity training infuriates men and fails women. *Time.* January 25, 2018.

85. Bezrukova K, Spell CS, Perry JL, Jehn KA. A meta-analytical integration of over 40 years of research on diversity training evaluation. *Psychological Bulletin* 2016; **142**(11): 1227–74; Onyeador IN, Hudson S-kTJ, Lewis NA. Moving beyond implicit bias training: Policy insights for increasing organizational diversity. *Policy Insights from the Behavioral and Brain Sciences* 2021; **8**(1): 19–26.

86. Murrar S, Campbell MR, Brauer M. Exposure to peers' pro-diversity attitudes increases inclusion and reduces the achievement gap. *Nature Human Behaviour* 2020; **4**(9): 889–97.

87. Pearsall MJ, Ellis APJ, Evans JM. Unlocking the effects of gender faultlines on team creativity: Is activation the key? *Journal of Applied Psychology* 2008; **93**(1): 225–34.

88. van Peteghem M, Bruynseels L, Gaeremynck A. Beyond diversity: A tale of faultlines and frictions in the board of directors. *Accounting Review* 2018; **93**(2): 339–67.

8. Promote Personal Growth

1. Chambers EG, Foulton M, Handfield-Jones H, Hankin SM, Michaels III EG. The war for talent. *McKinsey Quarterly* 1998; (3): 44–57.

2. O'Connor S. World will have 13 'super-aged' nations by 2020. *Financial Times.* August 6, 2014.

3. Perez Arce F, Prados MJ. The decline in the U.S. labor force participation rate: a literature review. *Journal of Economic Surveys* 2021; **35**(2): 615–52.

4. Abbott B. At 30-year low, U.S. birth rate shows striking differences between states. *Wall Street Journal.* January 10, 2019.

5. Jain N, Bhatt P. Employment preferences of job applicants: Unfolding employer branding determinants. *Journal of Management Development* 2015; **34**(6): 634–52.

6. *2017 Training industry report.* Excelsior, MN: Lakewood Media Group, 2017.

7. Nguyen TN, Truong Q, Buyens D. The relationship between training and firm performance: A literature review. *Research and Practice in Human Resource Management* 2010; **18**(1): 36–45.

8. Dostie B. The impact of training on innovation. *ILR Review* 2018; **71**(1): 64–87; Sung SY, Choi JN. Effects of training and development on employee outcomes and firm innovative performance: Moderating roles of voluntary participation and evaluation. *Human Resource Management* 2018; **57**(6): 1339–53.

9. Jacobs RL, Washington C. Employee development and organizational performance: A review of literature and directions for future research. *Human Resource Development International* 2003; **6**(3): 343–54.

10. Crook TR, Todd SY, Combs JG, Woehr DJ, Ketchen DJ. Does human capital matter? A meta-analysis of the relationship between human capital and firm performance. *Journal of Applied Psychology* 2011; **96**(3): 443–56; Xu J, Liu F. The impact of intellectual capital on firm performance: A modified and extended VAIC model. *Journal of Competitiveness* 2020; **12**(1): 161–76.

11. Dumay J, Garanina T. Intellectual capital research: a critical examination of the third stage. *Journal of Intellectual Capital* 2013; **14**(1): 10–25; Pedro E, Leitão J, Alves H. Back to the future of intellectual capital research: A systematic literature review. *Management Decision* 2018; **56**(11): 2502–83.

12. Bagdadli S, Gianecchini M. Organizational career management practices and objective career success: A systematic review and framework. *Human Resource Management Review* 2018; **29**(3): 353–70.

13. Martin BO, Kolomitro K, Lam TCM. Training methods: A review and analysis. *Human Resource Development Review* 2014; **13**(1): 11–35.

14. Whyte WH. *The organization man.* Oxford: Simon and Schuster; 1956.

15. Carnevale AP, Smith N. Workplace basics: The skills employees need and employers want. *Human Resource Development International* 2013; **16**(5): 491–501.

16. Erdogan B, Bauer TN, Truxillo DM, Mansfield LR. Whistle while you work: A review of the life satisfaction literature. *Journal of Management* 2012; **38**(4): 1038–83; Haar JM, Roche MA. Family supportive organization perceptions and employee outcomes: The mediating effects of life satisfaction. *International Journal of Human Resource Management* 2010; **21**(7): 999–1014; McNall LA, Nicklin JM, Masuda AD. A meta-analytic review of the consequences associated with work–family enrichment. *Journal of Business and Psychology* 2010; **25**(3): 381–96.

17. Greenhaus JH, Powell GN. When work and family are allies: A theory of work-family enrichment. *Academy of Management Review* 2006; **31**(1): 77–92.

18. Eldor L, Westring AF, Friedman SD. The indirect effect of holistic career values on work engagement: A longitudinal study spanning two decades. *Applied Psychology: Health and well-being* 2020; **12**(1): 144–65.

19. Leung ASM, Cheung YH, Liu X. The relations between life domain satisfaction and subjective well-being. *Journal of Managerial Psychology* 2011; **26**(2): 155–69.

20. Cho E, Tay L. Domain satisfaction as a mediator of the relationship between work-family spillover and subjective well-being: A longitudinal study. *Journal of Business and Psychology* 2016; **31**(3): 445–57; Heidemeier H, Göritz AS. Individual differences in how work and nonwork life domains contribute to life satisfaction: Using factor mixture modeling for classification. *Journal of Happiness Studies: An Interdisciplinary Forum on Subjective Well-Being* 2013; **14**(6): 1765–88; Ilies R, Liu X-Y, Liu Y, Zheng X. Why do employees have better family lives when they are highly engaged at work? *Journal of Applied Psychology* 2017; **102**(6): 956–70; Judge TA, Watanabe S. Another look at the job satisfaction: Life satisfaction relationship. *Journal of Applied Psychology* 1993; **78**(6): 939–48; Wolfram HJ, Gratton L. Spillover between work and home, role importance and life satisfaction. *British Journal of Management* 2014; **25**(1): 77–90.

21. Ferreira P, Gabriel C, Faria S, Rodrigues P, Sousa Pereira M. What if employees brought their life to work? The relation of life satisfaction and work engagement. *Sustainability* 2020; **12**(7): 2743.

22. Greenbaum RL, Babalola M, Quade MJ, Guo L, Kim YC. Moral burden of bottom-line pursuits: How and when perceptions of top management bottom-line mentality inhibit supervisors' ethical leadership practices. *Journal of Business Ethics* June 2020, 1–15; Babalola MT, Mawritz MB, Greenbaum RL, Ren S, Garba OA. Whatever It Takes: How and When Supervisor Bottom-Line Mentality Motivates Employee Contributions in the Workplace. *Journal of Management* 2021; **47**(5): 1134–54.

23. Babalola MT, Greenbaum RL, Amarnani RK, et al. A business frame perspective on why perceptions of top management's bottom-line mentality

result in employees' good and bad behaviors. *Personnel Psychology* 2020; **73**(1): 19–41.

24. Sirgy MJ, Lee D-J. Work-life balance: An integrative review. *Applied Research in Quality of Life* 2017.

25. Butts MM, Casper WJ, Yang TS. How important are work–family support policies? A meta-analytic investigation of their effects on employee outcomes. *Journal of Applied Psychology* 2013; **98**(1): 1–25; Fiksenbaum LM. Supportive work–family environments: Implications for work–family conflict and well-being. *International Journal of Human Resource Management* 2014; **25**(5): 653–72; Renaud S, Morin L, Béchard A. Traditional benefits versus perquisites: A longitudinal test of their differential impact on employee turnover. *Journal of Personnel Psychology* 2017; **16**(2): 91–103.

26. Drobnič S, Beham B, Präg P. Good job, good life? Working conditions and quality of life in Europe. *Social Indicators Research* 2010; **99**(2): 205–25.

27. Greenhaus JH, Powell GN. When work and family are allies: A theory of work-family enrichment. *Academy of Management Review* 2006; **31**(1): 72–92.

28. Cherrstrom CA, Bixby J. *Construct of expertise within the context of HRD: Integrative literature review.* Los Angeles, CA: SAGE, 2018.

29. André D, Fernand G. Sherlock Holmes: An expert's view of expertise. *British Journal of Psychology* 2008; **99**(1): 109–25.

30. Ullén F, Hambrick DZ, Mosing MA. Rethinking expertise: A multifactorial gene-environment interaction model of expert performance. *Psychological Bulletin* 2016; **142**(4): 427–46.

31. Dweck CS. Mindsets and human nature: Promoting change in the Middle East, the schoolyard, the racial divide, and willpower. *American Psychologist* 2012; **67**(8): 614–22.

32. Ericsson KA, Krampe RT, Tesch-Römer C. The role of deliberate practice in the acquisition of expert performance. *Psychological Review* 1993; **100**(3): 363–406; Ericsson KA, Towne TJ. Expertise. *WIREs Cognitive Science* 2010; **1**(3): 404–16.

33. Heslin PA, VandeWalle D. Managers' implicit assumptions about personnel. *Current Directions in Psychological Science* 2008; **17**(3): 219–23.

34. Lyons PR, Bandura RP. Apprehending mindsets in employee development. *Human Resource Management International Digest* 2017; **25**(3): 4–7.

35. Miller AG, Jones EE, Hinkle S. A robust attribution error in the personality domain. *Journal of Experimental Social Psychology* 1981; **17**(6): 587–600.

36. Han SJ, Sticha V. *Growth mindset for human resource development: A scoping review of the literature with recommended interventions.* Los Angeles, CA: SAGE, 2020.

37. Yeager DS, Hanselman P, Walton GM, et al. A national experiment reveals where a growth mindset improves achievement. *Nature* 2019; 573(7774): 364–9; Murphy F, Gash H. I can't yet and growth mindset. *Constructivist Foundations* 2020; 15(2): 83–94.

38. Gladwell M. *Outliers: The story of success.* New York: Little, Brown, 2008.

39. Weiss DJ, Shanteau J. Who's the best? A relativistic view of expertise. *Applied Cognitive Psychology* 2014; 28(4): 447–57.

40. Vaci N, Edelsbrunner P, Stern E, Neubauer A, Bilalić M, Grabner RH. The joint influence of intelligence and practice on skill development throughout the life span. *Proceedings of the National Academy of Sciences* 2019; 116(37): 18363–9.

41. Hambrick DZ, Burgoyne AP, Macnamara BN, Ullén F. Toward a multifactorial model of expertise: Beyond born versus made. *Annals of the New York Academy of Sciences* 2018; 1423(1): 284–95.

42. Ullén, Hambrick, Mosing. Rethinking expertise.

43. Burns ST. Validity of person matching in vocational interest inventories. *Career Development Quarterly* 2014; 62(2): 114–27; Van Iddekinge CH, Roth PL, Putka DJ, Lanivich SE. Are you interested? A meta-analysis of relations between vocational interests and employee performance and turnover. *Journal of Applied Psychology* 2011; 96(6): 1167–94.

44. Harrington T, Long J. The history of interest inventories and career assessments in career counseling. *Career Development Quarterly* 2013; 61(1): 83–92; Holland JL. A theory of vocational choice. *Journal of Counseling Psychology* 1959; 6(1): 35–45; Holland JL. *Making vocational choices: A theory of vocational personalities and work environments*, 3rd ed. Odessa, FL: Psychological Assessment Resources, 1997; Dik BJ, O'Connor WF, Shimizu AB, Duffy RD. Personal growth and well-being at work: Contributions of vocational psychology. *Journal of Career Development* 2019; 46(1): 31–47.

45. Strauss K, Griffin MA, Parker SK. Future work selves: How salient hoped-for identities motivate proactive career behaviors. *Journal of Applied Psychology* 2012; 97(3): 580–98.

46. Peterson C, Seligman MEP. *Character strengths and virtues: A handbook and classification.* Washington, DC: American Psychological Association, 2004.

47. Bakker AB, van Woerkom M. Strengths use in organizations: A positive approach of occupational health. *Canadian Psychology* 2018; 59(1): 38–46; Douglass R, Duffy R. Strengths use and life satisfaction: A moderated mediation approach. *Journal of Happiness Studies* 2015; 16(3): 619–32; Littman-Ovadia H, Lavy S, Boiman-Meshita M. When theory and research collide: Examining correlates of signature strengths use at work. *Journal of Happiness*

Studies 2017; **18**(2): 527–48; Woerkom M, Meyers MC. Strengthening personal growth: The effects of a strengths intervention on personal growth initiative. *Journal of Occupational and Organizational Psychology* 2018; Josefina Pelaez M, Coo C, Salanova M. Facilitating work engagement and performance through strengths-based micro-coaching: A controlled trial study. *Journal of Happiness Studies* 2020; **21**(4): 1265–84.

48. Allen TD, Eby LT, Poteet ML, Lentz E, Lima L. Career benefits associated with mentoring for protégés: A meta-analysis. *Journal of Applied Psychology* 2004; **89**(1): 127–36; Jones RJ, Woods SA, Guillaume YRF. The effectiveness of workplace coaching: A meta-analysis of learning and performance outcomes from coaching. *Journal of Occupational and Organizational Psychology* 2016; **89**(2): 249–77.

49. Wrzesniewski A, Dutton JE. Crafting a job: Revisioning employees as active crafters of their work. *Academy of Management Review* 2001; **26**(2): 179–201.

50. Rossi MA, Yin HH. Methods for studying habitual behavior in mice. *Current Protocols in Neuroscience* 2012; **60**(1): 8.29.1–8.29.9; Hilario MRF. High on habits. *Frontiers in Neuroscience* 2008; **2**(2): 208–17; Yin HH, Knowlton BJ. The role of the basal ganglia in habit formation. *Nature Reviews Neuroscience* 2006; **7**(6): 464–76.

51. Mayer JD, Caruso DR, Salovey P. The ability model of emotional intelligence: Principles and updates. *Emotion Review* 2016; **8**(4): 290–300.

52. O'Boyle EH, Jr., Humphrey RH, Pollack JM, Hawver TH, Story PA. The relation between emotional intelligence and job performance: A meta-analysis. *Journal of Organizational Behavior* 2011; **32**(5): 788–818.

53. Nelis D, Kotsou I, Quoidbach J, et al. Increasing emotional competence improves psychological and physical well-being, social relationships, and employability. *Emotion* 2011; **11**(2): 354–66.

54. van Rooij SW, Merkebu J. Measuring the business impact of employee learning: A view from the professional services sector. *Human Resource Development Quarterly* 2015; **26**(3): 275–97.

55. Marsick VJ, Volpe M. The nature and need for informal learning. *Advances in Developing Human Resources* 2016; **1**(3): 1–9; Marsick VJ, Watkins KE. *Facilitating learning organizations: making learning count.* Aldershot, UK: Gower, 1999.

56. Onken-Menke G, Nüesch S, Kröll C. Are you attracted? Do you remain? Meta-analytic evidence on flexible work practices. *Business Research* 2018; **11**(2): 239–77.

57. Paik SJ, Gozali C, Marshall-Harper KR. Productive giftedness: A new mastery approach to understanding talent development. *New Directions for Child and Adolescent Development* 2019; **2019**(168): 131–59.

9. Empower People

1. Argyris C. Empowerment: The emperor's new clothes. *Harvard Business Review* 1998; **76**(3): 98–105; Maynard MT, Gilson LL, Mathieu JE. Empowerment: Fad or fab? A multilevel review of the past two decades of research. *Journal of Management* 2012; **38**(4): 1231–81; Maynard MT, Luciano MM, D'Innocenzo L, Mathieu JE, Dean MD. Modeling time-lagged reciprocal psychological empowerment–performance relationships. *Journal of Applied Psychology* 2014; **99**(6): 1244–53.

2. Maynard, Gilson, Mathieu. Empowerment—fad or fab?; Maynard et al. Modeling time-lagged reciprocal psychological empowerment; Seibert SE, Wang G, Courtright SH. Antecedents and consequences of psychological and team empowerment in organizations: A meta-analytic review. *Journal of Applied Psychology* 2011; **96**(5): 981–1003.

3. Raub S, Liao H. Doing the right thing without being told: Joint effects of initiative climate and general self-efficacy on employee proactive customer service performance. *Journal of Applied Psychology* 2012; **97**(3): 651–67.

4. Lorinkova NM, Pearsall MJ, Sims Jr HP. Examining the differential longitudinal performance of directive versus empowering leadership in teams. *Academy of Management Journal* 2013; **56**(2): 573–96.

5. Maynard et al. Modeling time-lagged reciprocal psychological empowerment.

6. Seibert, Wang, Courtright. Antecedents and consequences; Raub, Liao H. Doing the right thing; Lorinkova, Pearsall, Sims Jr. Examining the differential longitudinal performance; Grealish A, Tai S, Hunter A, Emsley R, Murrells T, Morrison AP. Does empowerment mediate the effects of psychological factors on mental health, well-being, and recovery in young people? *Psychology and Psychotherapy: Theory, Research and Practice* 2017; **90**(3): 314–35; Koontz H. Making theory operational: the span of management. *Journal of Management Studies* 1966; **3**: 229–43.

7. Frazier ML, Fainshmidt S. Voice climate, work outcomes, and the mediating role of psychological empowerment: A multilevel examination. *Group and Organization Management* 2012; **37**(6): 691–715.

8. Prasad P, Eylon D. Narrating past traditions of participation and inclusion: Historical perspectives on workplace empowerment. *Journal of Applied Behavioral Science* 2001; **37**(1): 5–14.

9. O'Connor ES. Back on the way to empowerment: The example of Ordway Tead and industrial democracy. *Journal of Applied Behavioral Science* 2001; **37**(1): 15–32.

10. O'Connor. Back on the way to empowerment; Kaufman BE. The theory and practice of strategic HRM and participative management. *Human Resource Management Review* 2001; **11**(4): 505–33.

11. Kaufman B. Divergent fates: Company unions and employee involvement committees under the railway labor and national labor relations acts. *Labor History* 2015; **56**(4): 423–58.

12. DeStefanis AR. The road to Ludlow: breaking the 1913–14 southern Colorado coal strike. *Journal of the Historical Society* 2012; **12**(3): 341–90; Deutsch S. *Making an American workforce: The Colorado Fuel & Iron Company's construction of a workforce during the Rockefeller years.* Boulder: University of Colorado Press, 2014.

13. Likert R. *New patterns of management.* New York: McGraw-Hill; 1961.

14. Miller KI, Monge PR. Participation, satisfaction, and productivity: a meta-analytic review. *Academy of Management Journal* 1986; **29**(4): 727–53.

15. Mowbray PK, Wilkinson A, Tse HHM. An integrative review of employee voice: Identifying a common conceptualization and research agenda. *International Journal of Management Reviews* 2015; **17**(3): 382–400.

16. Wilkinson A, Fay C. New times for employee voice? *Human Resource Management* 2011; **50**(1): 65–74.

17. Cavendish R. *Henry Hudson sails into Hudson Bay.* London: History Today, 2010; Drabelle D. *Mutiny on the Hudson. Washington Post.* August 23, 2009; McCoy RM. *Henry Hudson has a very bad day, 1607, 1608, 1609, 1610.* New York: Oxford University Press, 2012; Miller J. *Accidental explorer.* Peterborough, NH: Carus, 2007.

18. Deming WE. Opportunities in mathematical statistics, with special reference to sampling and quality control. *Science* 1943; **97**(2514): 209–14.

19. Lawler III EE, Mohrman SA. Quality circles after the fad. *Harvard Business Review* 1985; **63**(1): 64–71.

20. Pereira GM, Osburn HG. Effects of participation in decision making on performance and employee attitudes: A quality circles meta-analysis. *Journal of Business and Psychology* 2007; **22**(2): 145–53.

21. Bernstein E, Bunch J, Canner N, Lee M. Beyond the holacracy hype. *Harvard Business Review* 2016; **94**(7/8): 38–49; Mintzberg H, McHugh A. Strategy formation in an adhocracy. *Administrative Science Quarterly* 1985; **30**(2): 160–97.

22. Moss Kanter R. Power failure in management circuits. *Harvard Business Review* 1979; **57**(4): 65–75; Kanter RM. *When giants learn to dance: Mastering the challenge of strategy, management, and careers in the 1990s.* New York: Simon and Schuster, 1989.

23. Jaehoon R, Seo Dae S, Bozorov F, Dedahanov AT. organizational structure and employees' innovative behavior: the mediating role of empowerment. *Social Behavior and Personality* 2017; **45**(9): 1523–36; Dust SB, Resick CJ, Mawritz MB. Transformational leadership, psychological empowerment, and the moderating role of mechanistic–organic contexts. *Journal of Organizational Behavior* 2014; **35**(3): 413–33.

24. Fayol H. *General and industrial management*. London: Pitmin 1949.

25. Guadalupe M, Li H, Wulf J. Who Lives in the C-Suite? Organizational structure and the division of labor in top management. *Management Science* 2014; **60**(4): 824–44.

26. Meier KJ, Bohte J. Ode to Luther Gulick. *Administration and Society* 2000; **32**(2): 115–137; Orth U, Robins RW, Widaman KF. Life-span development of self-esteem and its effects on important life outcomes. *Journal of Personality and Social Psychology* 2012; **102**(6): 1271–88; Urwick LF. V. A. Graicunas and the span of control. *Academy of Management Journal* 1974; **17**(2): 349–54; Van Fleet DD, Bedeian AG. A history of the span of management. *Academy of Management Review* 1977; **2**(3): 356–72.

27. Wulf J. The flattened firm: Not as advertised. *California Management Review* 2012; **55**(1): 5–23.

28. Drucker PF. The knowledge society. *New Society* 1969; **13**(343): 24–631.

29. Spreitzer GM. Psychological, empowerment in the workplace: Dimensions, measurement and validation. *Academy of Management Journal* 1995; **38**(5): 1442–65; Conger JA, Kanungo RN. The empowerment process: Integrating theory and practice. *Academy of Management Review* 1988; **13**(3): 471–82.

30. Hackman JR, Oldham GR. Motivation through the design of work: Test of a theory. *Organizational Behavior and Human Performance* 1976; **16**(2): 250–79.

31. Spreitzer GM. Psychological empowerment in the workplace: dimensions, measurement, and validation. *Academy of Management Journal* 1995; **38**(5): 1442–65.

32. Grant AM. How customers can rally the troops. *Harvard Business Review* 2011; **89**(6): 96–103.

33. Cameron KS, Spreitzer GM. *The Oxford handbook of positive organizational scholarship*. New York: Oxford University Press, 2012.

34. Bacon TR, Pugh DG. Ritz-Carlton and EMC: The gold standards in operational behavioral differentiation. *Journal of Organizational Excellence* 2004; **23**(2): 61–76; Yeung A. Setting people up for success: How the Portman Ritz-Carlton hotel gets the best from its people. *Human Resource Management* 2006; **45**(2): 267–75.

35. Reece A, Yaden D, Kellerman G, et al. Mattering is an indicator of organizational health and employee success. *Journal of Positive Psychology* 2021; **16**(2): 228–48.

36. Bandura A. Human agency in social cognitive theory. *American Psychologist* 1989; **44**(9): 1175–84.

37. Kirkman BL, Rosen B. Powering up teams. *Organizational Dynamics* 2000; **28**(3): 48–66.

38. McNatt DB. Ancient Pygmalion Joins contemporary management: A meta-analysis of the result. *Journal of Applied Psychology* 2000; **85**(2): 314–22.

39. Babad EY, Inbar J, Rosenthal R. Pygmalion, galatea, and the golem: Investigations of biased and unbiased teachers. *Journal of Educational Psychology* 1982; **74**(4): 459–74.

40. Menon ST. Employee empowerment: An integrative psychological approach. *Applied Psychology* 2001; **50**(1): 153–80; Li Y, Wei F, Ren S, Di Y. Locus of control, psychological empowerment and intrinsic motivation relation to performance. *Journal of Managerial Psychology* 2015; **30**(4): 422–38; Huang X. Helplessness of empowerment: The joint effect of participative leadership and controllability attributional style on empowerment and performance. *Human Relations* 2012; **65**(3): 313–34.

41. Maier SF, Seligman MEP. Learned helplessness at fifty: Insights from neuroscience. *Psychological Review* 2016; **123**(4): 349–67.

42. Kim M, Beehr TA, Prewett MS. Employee responses to empowering leadership: A meta-analysis. *Journal of Leadership and Organizational Studies* 2018; **25**(3): 257–76; Pigeon M, Montani F, Boudrias J-S. How do empowering conditions lead to empowered behaviours? Test of a mediation model. *Journal of Managerial Psychology* 2017; **32**(5): 357–72.

43. Schultz JR. Creating a culture of empowerment fosters the flexibility to change. *Global Business and Organizational Excellence* 2014; **34**(1): 41–50.

44. Pratto F. On power and empowerment. *British Journal of Social Psychology* 2016; **55**(1): 1–20.

45. Treviño LK, Brown ME. Ethical leadership. In Day DV. (Ed.) *The Oxford handbook of leadership and organizations.* New York: Oxford University Press, 2014: 524–38; Bass BM. From transactional to transformational leadership: Learning to share the vision. *Organizational dynamics* 1990; **18**(3): 19–31.

46. Greenleaf RK. The servant as leader. In Vecchio RP. (Eds.) *Leadership: Understanding the dynamics of power and influence in organizations.* Notre Dame, IN: University of Notre Dame Press, 2007: 407–15.

47. Zhang X, Bartol KM. Linking empowering leadership and employee creativity: The influence of psychological empowerment, intrinsic motivation, and creative process engagement. *Academy of Management Journal* 2010; **53**(1): 107–28; Wong SI, Giessner SR. The thin line between empowering and laissez-faire leadership: An expectancy-match perspective. *Journal of Management* 2018; **44**(2): 757–83; Lee A, Willis S, Tian AW. Empowering leadership: A meta-analytic examination of incremental contribution, mediation, and moderation. *Journal of Organizational Behavior* 2018; **39**(3): 306–25; Zhang Y, Zheng Y, Zhang L, Xu S, Liu X, Chen W. A meta-analytic review of the consequences of servant leadership: The moderating roles of cultural factors. *Asia Pacific Journal of Management* 2019; **38**(1): 371–80.

48. Chanhoo S, Kwangseo Ryan P, Seung-Wan K. Servant leadership and team performance: The mediating role of knowledge-sharing climate. *Social Behavior and Personality* 2015; **43**(10): 1749–60.

49. Liden RC, Wayne SJ, Chenwei L, Meuser JD. Servant leadership and serving culture: Influence on individual and unit performance. *Academy of Management Journal* 2014; **57**(5): 1434–52.

10. Reward High Performers

1. Baumard N, Mascaro O, Chevallier C. Preschoolers are able to take merit into account when distributing goods. *Developmental Psychology* 2012; **48**(2): 492–8.

2. Brosnan SF, de Waal FBM. Monkeys reject unequal pay. *Nature* 2003; **425**(6955): 297. Brosnan SF, de Waal FBM. Evolution of responses to (un)fairness. *Science* 214; **346**(6207): 314

3. Camerer CF. *Behavioral game theory: Experiments in strategic interaction.* New York: Russell Sage, 2003.

4. Bridge M, Mark B. Musk: Tesla worker has sabotaged our systems. *Times* (London). June 20, 2018.

5. Ogbonnaya C, Daniels K, Nielsen K. Does contingent pay encourage positive employee attitudes and intensify work? *Human Resource Management Journal* 2017; **27**(1): 94–112.

6. Combs J, Liu Y, Hall A, Ketchen D. How much do high-performance work practices matter? A meta-analysis of their effects on organizational performance. *Personnel Psychology* 2006; **59**(3): 501–28; Messersmith JG, Patel PC, Lepak DP, Gould-Williams JS. Unlocking the black box: Exploring the link between high-performance work systems and performance. *Journal of Applied Psychology* 2011; **96**(6): 1105–18; Gittell JH, Seidner R, Wimbush J. A relational model of how high-performance work systems work. *Organization Science* 2010; **21**(2): 490–506; Shin D, Konrad AM. Causality between high-performance work systems and organizational performance. *Journal of Management* 2017; **43**(4): 973–97.

7. Maslow AH. *Toward a psychology of being*, 2nd ed. Oxford: Van Nostrand; 1968.

8. Ryff CD. Well-being with soul: Science in pursuit of human potential. *Perspectives on Psychological Science* 2018; **13**(2): 242–8; Ryff CD, Singer BH. Know Thyself and Become What you are: A eudaimonic approach to psychological well-being. In Delle Fave A. (Ed.) *The exploration of happiness: present and future perspectives.* Happiness Studies Book Series. New York: Springer, 2013: 97–116.

9. Deci EL, Ryan RM. Self-determination theory: A macrotheory of human motivation, development, and health. *Canadian Psychology* 2008;

49(3): 182–5; Seligman MEP, Parks AC, Steen T. A balanced psychology and a full life. *Philosophical Transactions Biological Sciences* 2004; **359**(1449): 1379–81.

10. Williams G. Management millennialism: Designing the new generation of employee. *Work, Employment and Society* 2020; **34**(3): 371–87.

11. Sruk B. How millennials are changing organizations and business models: New values, new principles, new culture. *Dubrovnik International Economic Meeting* 2020; **5**(1): 101–8.

12. Lepper MR, Greene D. Turning play into work: Effects of adult surveillance and extrinsic rewards on children's intrinsic motivation. *Journal of Personality and Social Psychology* 1975; **31**(3): 479–86.

13. Ryan RM, Deci EL. *Self-determination theory: Basic psychological needs in motivation, development, and wellness.* New York: Guilford Press, 2017.

14. Frick BJ, Goetzen UTE, Simmons R. The hidden costs of high-performance work practices: Evidence from a large German steel company. *ILR Review* 2013; **66**(1): 198–224.

15. Kim JH, Gerhart B, Fang M. Do financial incentives help or harm performance in interesting tasks? *Journal of applied psychology*, September, 2021 (advance on-line publication).

16. Cerasoli CP, Nicklin JM, Ford MT. Intrinsic motivation and extrinsic incentives jointly predict performance: A 40-year meta-analysis. *Psychological Bulletin* 2014; **140**(4): 980–1008.

17. Byron K, Khazanchi S. Rewards and creative performance: A meta-analytic test of theoretically derived hypotheses. *Psychological Bulletin* 2012; **138**(4): 809–30.

18. Park S, Sturman MC. Evaluating form and functionality of pay-for-performance plans: The relative incentive and sorting effects of merit pay, bonuses, and long-term incentives. *Human Resource Management* 2016; **55**(4): 697–719; Pohler D, Schmidt JA. Does pay-for-performance strain the employment relationship? The effect of manager bonus eligibility on nonmanagement employee turnover. *Personnel Psychology* 2016; **69**(2): 395–429.

19. Lazear EP. Performance pay and productivity. *American Economic Review* 2000; **90**(5): 1346–61.

20. Hinds PJ, Carley KM, Krackhardt D, Wholey D. Choosing work group members: Balancing similarity, competence, and familiarity. *Organizational Behavior and Human Decision Processes* 2000; **81**(2): 226–51; Chiaburu DS, Harrison DA. Do peers make the place? Conceptual synthesis and meta-analysis of coworker effects on perceptions, attitudes, OCBs, and performance. *Journal of Applied Psychology* 2008; **93**(5): 1082–103.

21. Groysberg B, Lee L-E. The effect of colleague quality on top performance: The case of security analysts. *Journal of Organizational Behavior* 2008; **29**(8): 1123–44.

22. Rossman G, Esparza N, Bonacich P. I'd like to thank the academy, team spillovers, and network centrality. *American Sociological Review* 2010; 75(1): 31–51.

23. Weber B, Hertel G. Motivation gains of inferior group members: A meta-analytical review. *Journal of Personality and Social Psychology* 2007; 93(6): 973–93.

24. Osborn KA, Irwin BC, Skogsberg NJ, Feltz DL. The Köhler effect: Motivation gains and losses in real sports groups. *Sport, Exercise, and Performance Psychology* 2012; 1(4): 242–53.

25. Aiello JR, Douthitt EA. Social facilitation from Triplett to electronic performance monitoring. *Group Dynamics: Theory, Research, and Practice* 2001; 5(3): 163–80.

26. Gerhart B, Fang M. Pay for (individual) performance: Issues, claims, evidence and the role of sorting effects. *Human Resource Management Review* 2014; 24(1): 41–52.

27. Nyberg A. Retaining your high performers: Moderators of the performance–job satisfaction–voluntary turnover relationship. *Journal of Applied Psychology* 2010; 95(3): 440–53.

28. Tervio M. Superstars and mediocrities: Market failure in the discovery of talent. *Review of Economic Studies* 2009; 76(2): 829–50.

29. Colquitt JA, Jackson CL. Justice in teams: The context sensitivity of justice rules across individual and team contexts. *Journal of Applied Social Psychology* 2006; 36(4): 868–99.

30. Nederhand M, Tabbers H, Rikers R. Learning to calibrate: Providing standards to improve calibration accuracy for different performance levels. *Applied Cognitive Psychology* 2019; 33(6): 1068–79.

31. Kruger J, Dunning D. Unskilled and unaware of it: How difficulties in recognizing one's own incompetence lead to inflated self-assessments. *Journal of Personality and Social Psychology* 1999; 77(6): 1121–34.

32. Nederhand et al. Learning to calibrate.

33. Kawall J. On complacency. *American Philosophical Quarterly* 2006; 43(4): 343–55; Rhodes MG. Metacognition. *Teaching of psychology* 2019; 46(2): 168–75; McIntosh RD, Fowler EA, Lyu T, Della Sala S. Wise up: Clarifying the role of metacognition in the Dunning-Kruger effect. *Journal of Experimental Psychology General* 2019; 148(11): 1882–97.

34. Dunning D, Johnson K, Ehrlinger J, Kruger J. Why people fail to recognize their own incompetence. *Current Directions in Psychological Science* 2003; 12(3): 83–7.

35. Cappelen C, Dahlberg S. The law of Jante and generalized trust. *Acta Sociologica* 2018; 61(4): 419–40.

36. Reh S, Tröster C, Van Quaquebeke N. Keeping (future) rivals down: Temporal social comparison predicts coworker social undermining via future

status threat and envy. *Journal of Applied Psychology* 2018; **103**(4): 399–415; Campbell EM, Liao H, Chuang A, Zhou J, Dong Y. Hot shots and cool reception? An expanded view of social consequences for high performers. *Journal of Applied Psychology* 2017; **102**(5): 845–66; Kim E, Glomb TM. Get smarty pants: Cognitive ability, personality, and victimization. *Journal of Applied Psychology* 2010; **95**(5): 889–901; Kim E, Glomb TM. Victimization of high performers: The roles of envy and work group identification. *Journal of Applied Psychology* 2014; **99**(4): 619–34; Jensen JM, Patel PC, Raver JL. Is it better to be average? High and low performance as predictors of employee victimization. *Journal of Applied Psychology* 2014; **99**(2): 296–309.

37. Hermanowicz J. The culture of mediocrity. *Minerva* 2013; **51**(3): 363–87.

38. Kim, Glomb. Victimization of high performers.

39. Pieper JR. Uncovering the nuances of referral hiring: How referrer characteristics affect referral hires' performance and likelihood of voluntary turnover. *Personnel Psychology* 2015; **68**(4): 811–58.

40. Burks SV, Cowgill B, Hoffman M, Housman M. The value of hiring through employee referrals. *Quarterly Journal of Economics* 2015; **130**(2): 805–39; Ekinci E. Employee Referrals as a screening device. *RAND Journal of Economics* 2016; **47**(3): 688–708; Stockman S, Van Hoye G, Carpentier M. The dark side of employee referral bonus programs: Potential applicants' awareness of a referral bonus and perceptions of organisational attractiveness. *Applied Psychology* 2017; **66**(4): 599–627.

41. Young M. *The rise of the meritocracy, 1870–2033*. London: Thames & Hudson, 1958; Young M. Interview by Dench G. Looking back on meritocracy. *Political Quarterly* 2006; **77**(s1): 73–77; Chang-Hee K, Yong-Beom C. How meritocracy is defined today? Contemporary aspects of meritocracy. *Economics and Sociology* 2017; **10**(1): 112–21.

42. Gallardo-Gallardo E, Dries N, González-Cruz TF. What is the meaning of "talent" in the world of work? *Human Resource Management Review* 2013; **23**(4): 290–300; Adamsen B. Do we really know what the term "talent" in talent management means? And what could be the consequences of not knowing? *Philosophy of Management* 2014; **13**(3): 3–20.

43. Weber M. *The protestant ethic and the spirit of capitalism*, repr. ed. Translated by Talcott Parsons. With a foreword by RH Tawney. Mineola, NY: Dover, 2003.

44. Christopher AN, Zabel KL, Jones JR, Marek P. Protestant ethic ideology: Its multifaceted relationships with just world beliefs, social dominance orientation, and right-wing authoritarianism. *Personality and Individual Differences* 2008; **45**(6): 473–7; Mudrack PE. An outcomes-based approach to just world beliefs. *Personality and Individual Differences* 2005; **38**(4): 817–30.

45. Day JW, Holladay CL, Johnson SK, Barron LG. Organizational rewards: Considering employee need in allocation. *Personnel Review* 2014; **43**(1): 74–95.

46. Gilboa S, Shirom A, Fried Y, Cooper C. A meta-analysis of work demand stressors and job performance: examining main and moderating effects. *Personnel Psychology* 2008; **61**(2): 227–71.

47. Fuller S, Cooke LP. Workplace variation in fatherhood wage premiums: Do formalization and performance pay matter? *Work, Employment and Society* 2018; **32**(4): 768–88.

48. Deutsch M. Cooperation, competition, and conflict. In Coleman PT, Deutsch M, Marcus EC. (Eds.) *The handbook of conflict resolution: Theory and practice*, 3rd ed. San Francisco, CA: Jossey-Bass, 2014: 3–28.

49. Ingham AG, Levinger G, Graves J, Peckham V. The Ringelmann effect: Studies of group size and group performance. *Journal of Experimental Social Psychology* 1974; **10**(4): 371–84; Simms A, Nichols T. Social loafing: A review of the literature. *Journal of Management Policy and Practice* 2014; **15**(1): 58–67.

50. Adler S, Campion M, Colquitt A, et al. Getting rid of performance ratings: Genius or folly? A debate. *Industrial and Organizational Psychology* 2016; **9**(2): 219–52; Cappelli P, Tavis A. The performance management revolution. *Harvard Business Review* 2016; **94**(10): 58–67.

51. Feintzeig R. The trouble with grading employees. Management & Careers. *Wall Street Journal*. April 21, 2015.

52. Cappelli P, Conyon MJ. What do performance appraisals do? *ILR Review* 2018; **71**(1): 88–116.

53. Aguinis H, Bradley KJ. The secret sauce for organizational success: Managing and producing star performers. *Organizational Dynamics* 2015; **44**(3): 161–8; Aguinis H, O'Boyle E, Gonzalez-Mulé E, Joo H. Cumulative advantage: Conductors and insulators of heavy-tailed productivity distributions and productivity stars. *Personnel Psychology* 2016; **69**(1): 3–66; Joo H, Aguinis H, Bradley KJ. Not all nonnormal distributions are created equal: Improved theoretical and measurement precision. *Journal of Applied Psychology* 2017; **102**(7): 1022–53.

54. Green BG, Dalton P, Cowart B, Shaffer G. Evaluating the "labeled magnitude scale" for measuring sensations of taste and smell. *Chemical Senses* 1996; **21**(3): 323–34; Green BG. Derivation and evaluation of a semantic scale of oral sensation magnitude with apparent ratio properties. *Chemical Senses* 1993; **18**(6): 683–702.

55. Haines VY, St-Onge S. Performance management effectiveness: Practices or context? *International Journal of Human Resource Management* 2012; **23**(6): 1158–75.

56. Gorman CA, Rentsch JR. Evaluating frame-of-reference rater training effectiveness using performance schema accuracy. *Journal of Applied Psychology*

2009; **94**(5): 1336–44; DeNisi AS, Murphy KR. Performance appraisal and performance management: 100 years of progress? *Journal of Applied Psychology* 2017; **102**(3): 421–33; MacDonald HA, Sulsky LM. Rating formats and rater training redux: A context-specific approach for enhancing the effectiveness of performance management. *Canadian Journal of Behavioural Science* 2009; **41**(4): 227–40.

57. Bradler C, Dur R, Neckermann S, Non A. Employee recognition and performance: A field experiment. *Management Science* 2016; **62**(11): 3085–99; Neckermann S, Yang X. Understanding the (unexpected) consequences of unexpected recognition. *Journal of Economic Behavior and Organization* 2017; **135**: 131–42.

58. Li N, Zheng X, Harris TB, Liu X, Kirkman BL. Recognizing "me" benefits "we": Investigating the positive spillover effects of formal individual recognition in teams. *Journal of Applied Psychology* 2016; **101**(7): 925–39.

59. Heidemeier H, Moser K. Self–other agreement in job performance ratings: A meta-analytic test of a process model. *Journal of Applied Psychology* 2009; **94**(2): 353–70.

60. Kim KY, Atwater L, Patel PC, Smither JW. Multisource feedback, human capital, and the financial performance of organizations. *Journal of Applied Psychology* 2016; **101**(11): 1569–84.

61. Evans TR, Dobrosielska A. Feedback-seeking culture moderates the relationship between positive feedback and task performance. *Current Psychology* 2019; **40**(7): 3401–8.

62. Lee WR, Choi SB, Kang S-W. How leaders' positive feedback influences employees' innovative behavior: the mediating role of voice behavior and job autonomy. *Sustainability* 2021; **13**(4): 1901.

63. DeLong TJ, Vijayaraghavan V. Let's hear it for B players. *Harvard Business Review* 2003; **81**(6): 96–102.

64. King WC, Miles EW, Day DD. A test and refinement of the equity sensitivity construct. *Journal of Organizational Behavior* 1993; **14**(4): 301–17.

65. Gilley JW, Gilley AM, Jackson SA, Lawrence H. Managerial practices and organizational conditions that encourage employee growth and development. *Performance Improvement Quarterly* 2015; **28**(3): 71–93; Gilley A, Gilley JW, Ambort-Clark KA, Marion D. Evidence of managerial malpractice: An empirical study. *Journal of Applied Management and Entrepreneurship* 2014; **19**(4): 24–42.

11. Foster a Leadership Culture

1. Janicijevic N. business processes in organizational diagnosis. *Management* 2010; **15**(2): 85–106.

2. Uhl-Bien M. Relational leadership theory: Exploring the social processes of leadership and organizing. *Leadership Quarterly* 2006; **17**(6): 654–76; Barge JK. Pivotal leadership and the art of conversation. *Leadership* 2014; **10**(1): 56–78.

3. Deal TE, Kennedy AA. *Corporate cultures: the rites and rituals of corporate life*. Reading, Mass.: Addison-Wesley, 1982; Ouchi WG. *Theory Z: How American business can meet the Japanese challenge*. Reading, Mass.: Addison-Wesley, 1982; Peters TJ, Waterman RH. *In Search of Excellence: lessons from America's best-run companies*. New York: Warner, 1982; Porras, Collins. *Built to Last: Successful habits of visionary companies*. London: Random House, 2000; Tan B-S. In search of the link between organizational culture and performance: A review from the conclusion validity perspective. *Leadership and Organization Development Journal* 2019; **40**(3): 356–68.

4. Levering R. The 100 best companies to work for. *Fortune* 2016; **173**(4): 142–165.

5. Harvey CR, Graham J, Grennan J, Rajgopal S. Corporate culture: Evidence from the field. National Bureau of Economic Research Paper, 2017.

6. O'Reilly CA, Chatman J, Caldwell DF. People and organizational culture: A profile comparison approach to assessing person-organization fit. *Academy of Management Journal* 1991; **34**(3): 487–516.

7. Eric Van den S. Culture clash: The costs and benefits of homogeneity. *Management Science* 2010; **56**(10): 1718–38.

8. Anonymous. The caring company: Corporate culture and performance by John Kotter and James Heskett. *The Economist*. June 1992.

9. Sackmann SA. Culture and performance. In Ashkanasy NM, Wilderom CPM, and Peterson, MF. (Eds.) *The handbook of organizational culture and climate*. Thousand Oaks, CA: SAGE, 2011: 188–224.

10. O'Reilly CA, Caldwell DF, Chatman JA, Doerr B. The promise and problems of organizational culture: CEO personality, culture, and firm performance. *Group and Organization Management* 2014; **39**(6): 595–625.

11. Schneider WE. Productivity improvement through cultural focus. *Consulting Psychology Journal* 1995; **47**(1): 3–27; Denison DR, Mishra AK. Toward a theory of organizational culture and effectiveness. *Organization Science* 1995; **6**(2): 204–23.

12. Mushtaq AL. Organizational culture in the hotel industry: Perceptions and preferences among staff. *Advances in Management* 2013; **6**(5): 55–60.

13. Warrick DD. What leaders need to know about organizational culture. *Business Horizons* 2017; **60**(3): 395–404.

14. Klein AS, Wallis J, Cooke RA. The impact of leadership styles on organizational culture and firm effectiveness: An empirical study. *Journal of Management and Organization* 2013; **19**(3): 241–54; Giberson TR, Resick CJ, Dickson MW, Mitchelson JK, Randall KR, Clark MA. Leadership and

organizational culture: Linking CEO characteristics to cultural values. *Journal of Business and Psychology* 2009; **24**(2): 123–37.

15. Block L. The leadership-culture connection: an exploratory investigation. *Leadership and Organization Development Journal* 2003; **24**(6): 318–34; Tsai Y. Relationship between organizational culture, leadership behavior and job satisfaction. *BMC Health Services Research* 2011; **11**(1): 98–106.

16. Gibbons R, LiCalzi M, Warglien M. What situation is this? shared frames and collective performance. *Strategy scien$ce* 2021; **6**(2): 124–40.

17. Christensen CM, Alton R, Rising C, Waldeck A. The new M&A playbook. *Harvard Business Review.* March 2011.

18. Selling Chrysler: Putting the shine back on. *The Economist.* May 14, 2007.

19. Steigenberger N. The challenge of integration: A review of the M&A integration literature. *International Journal of Management Reviews* 2017; **19**(4): 408–31; Monin P, Noorderhaven N, Vaara E, Kroon D. Giving sense to and making sense of justice in postmerger integration. *Academy of Management Journal* 2013; **56**(1): 256–84.

20. Schat ACH, Frone MR. Exposure to psychological aggression at work and job performance: The mediating role of job attitudes and personal health. *Work and Stress* 2011; **25**(1): 23–40; Caza BB, Cortina LM. From insult to injury: Explaining the impact of incivility. *Basic and Applied Social Psychology* 2007; **29**(4): 335–50.

21. Riskin A, Erez A, Foulk TA, et al. The impact of rudeness on medical team performance: A randomized trial. *Pediatrics* 2015; **136**(3): 487–95.

22. Shin Y, Hur W-M. Supervisor incivility and employee job performance: The mediating roles of job insecurity and amotivation. *Journal of Psychology* 2019; **154**(1): 38–59; Priesemuth M, Schminke M, Ambrose ML, Folger R. Abusive supervision climate: A multiple-mediation model of its impact on group outcomes. *Academy of Management Journal* 2014; **57**(5): 1513–34.

23. Edmondson AC, Lei Z. Psychological safety: The history, renaissance, and future of an interpersonal construct. *Annual Review of Organizational Psychology and Organizational Behavior* 2014; **1**(1): 23–43; Newman A, Donohue R, Eva N. Psychological safety: A systematic review of the literature. *Human Resource Management Review* 2017; **27**(3): 521–35.

24. Kim S, Lee H, Connerton TP. How psychological safety affects team performance: Mediating role of efficacy and learning behavior. *Frontiers in Psychology* 2020; **11**: 1581; Nellen LC, Gijselaers WH, Grohnert T. A meta-analytic literature review on organization-level drivers of team learning. *Human Resource Development Review* 2019; **19**(2): 152–82; Hennel P, Rosenkranz C. Investigating the "socio" in socio-technical development: The case for psychological safety in agile information systems development. *Project Management Journal* 2020; **52**(1): 11–30.

25. Wang H-j, Lu C-q, Siu O-l. Job insecurity and job performance: The moderating role of organizational justice and the mediating role of work engagement. *Journal of Applied Psychology* 2015; **100**(4): 1249–58; Abolade DA. Impact of employees' job insecurity and employee turnover on organisational performance in private and public sector organisations. *Studies in Business and Economics* 2018; **13**(2): 5–19.

26. Foulk T, Woolum A, Erez A. Catching rudeness is like catching a cold: The contagion effects of low-intensity negative behaviors. *Journal of Applied Psychology* 2016; **101**(1): 50–67.

27. Lim S, Cortina LM, Magley VJ. Personal and workgroup incivility: Impact on work and health outcomes. *Journal of Applied Psychology* 2008; **93**(1): 95–107; Porath CL, Erez A. Does rudeness really matter? The effects of rudeness on task performance and helpfulness. *Academy of Management Journal* 2007; **50**(5): 1181–97.

28. Farh CIC, Chen Z. Beyond the individual victim: Multilevel consequences of abusive supervision in teams. *Journal of Applied Psychology* 2014; **99**(6): 1074–95.

29. Andersson LM, Pearson CM. Tit for tat? The spiraling effect of incivility in the workplace. *Academy of Management Review* 1999; **24**(3): 452–71; Tepper BJ. Abusive supervision in work organizations: Review, synthesis, and research agenda. *Journal of Management* 2007; **33**(3): 261–89.

30. LeBreton JM, Shiverdecker LK, Grimaldi EM. The dark triad and workplace behavior. *Annual Review of Organizational Psychology and Organizational Behavior* 2018; **5**(1): 387–414; Paulhus DL, Buckels EE, Trapnell PD, Jones DN. Screening for dark personalities: The short dark tetrad (SD4). *European Journal of Psychological Assessment* 2021; **37**(3): 208–22.

31. Palmer JC, Holmes RM, Perrewé PL. The cascading effects of CEO dark triad personality on subordinate behavior and firm performance: A multilevel theoretical model. *Group and Organization Management* 2020; **45**(2): 143–80.

32. Youssef CM, Luthans F. Positive organizational behavior in the workplace: The impact of hope, optimism, and resilience. *Journal of Management* 2007; **33**(5): 774–800; Avey JB, Reichard RJ, Luthans F, Mhatre KH. Meta-analysis of the impact of positive psychological capital on employee attitudes, behaviors, and performance. *Human Resource Development Quarterly* 2011; **22**(2): 127–52.

33. Otake K, Shimai S, Tanaka-Matsumi J, Otsui K, Fredrickson BL. Happy people become happier through kindness: A counting kindnesses intervention. *Journal of Happiness Studies* 2006; **7**(3): 361–75; Thielmann I, Hilbig BE. The traits one can trust: Dissecting reciprocity and kindness as determinants of trustworthy behavior. *Personality and Social Psychology Bulletin* 2015; **41**(11): 1523–36.

34. Fredrickson BL. The broaden-and-build theory of positive emotions. In Csikszentmihalyi M, Csikszentmihalyi IS. (Eds.) *A life worth living: Contributions to positive psychology.* New York: Oxford University Press, 2006: 85–103.

35. Gerbasi A, Porath CL, Parker A, Spreitzer G, Cross R. Destructive de-energizing relationships: How thriving buffers their effect on performance. *Journal of Applied Psychology* 2015; **100**(5): 1423–33; Kleine AK, Rudolph CW, Zacher H. Thriving at work: A meta-analysis. *Journal of Organizational Behavior* 2019; **40**(9–10): 973–99.

36. Baker WF, O'Malley M. *Leading with kindness: How good people consistently get superior results.* Saranac Lake, NY: American Management Association, 2008.

37. Mallén F, Domínguez-Escrig E, Lapiedra R, Chiva R. Does leader humility matter? Effects on altruism and innovation. *Management Decision* 2019; **58**(5): 967–81; Rego A, Cunha MPe, Simpson AV. The perceived impact of leaders' humility on team effectiveness: An empirical study. *Journal of Business Ethics* 2016; **148**(1): 205–18.

38. Lee Y, Berry CM, Gonzalez-Mulé E. The importance of being humble: A meta-analysis and incremental validity: Analysis of the relationship between honesty-humility and job performance. *Journal of Applied Psychology* 2019; **104**(12): 1535–46.

39. Frieder RE, Wang G, Oh I-S. Linking job-relevant personality traits, transformational leadership, and job performance via perceived meaningfulness at work: A moderated mediation model. *Journal of Applied Psychology* 2018; **103**(3): 324–33.

40. McCrae RR, Costa PT. Discriminant validity of NEO-PIR facet scales. *Educational and Psychological Measurement* 2016; **52**(1): 229–37; Derue DS, Nahrgang JD, Wellman NED, Humphrey SE. Trait and behavioral theories of leadership: An integration and meta-analytic test of their relative validity. *Personnel Psychology* 2011; **64**(1): 7–52.

41. Cunliffe AL, Eriksen M. Relational leadership. *Human Relations* 2011; **64**(11): 1425–49.

42. Hawkins B. Ship-shape: Materializing leadership in the British Royal Navy. *Human Relations* 2015; **68**(6): 951–71; Allen S. Exploring Quaker organising to consider the possibilities for relational leadership. *Quaker Studies* 2019; **24**(2): 249–69.

43. Weitz M. Open concepts. *Revue Internationale De Philosophie* 1972; **26**(99/100 (1/2)): 86–110.

44. Ma L, van Brakel J. Revisiting Wittgenstein on family resemblance and Colour(s). *Philosophical Investigations* 2016; **39**(3): 254–80.

45. Dutton D. A naturalist definition of art. *Journal of Aesthetics and Art Criticism* 2006; **64**(3): 367–77; Bond EJ. The essential nature of art. *American Philosophical Quarterly* 1975; **12**(2): 177–83.

46. Weber M. *Economy and society: A new translation.* Cambridge, MA: Harvard University Press; 2019.

47. Tskhay KO, Zhu R, Zou C, Rule NO. Charisma in everyday life: Conceptualization and validation of the general charisma inventory. *Journal of Personality and Social Psychology* 2018; **114**(1): 131–52.

48. Rogoza R, Fatfouta R. Decoding the narcissism-charisma link: A facet approach. *Personality and Individual Differences* 2020; **156**: 109774.

49. Vergauwe J, Wille B, Hofmans J, Kaiser RB, De Fruyt F. The double-edged sword of leader charisma: Understanding the curvilinear relationship between charismatic personality and leader effectiveness. *Journal of Personality and Social Psychology* 2018; **114**(1): 110–30.

50. Caspi A, Bogler R, Tzuman O. "Judging a book by its cover": The dominance of delivery over content when perceiving charisma. *Group and Organization Management* 2019; **44**(6): 1067–98.

51. The grinch that sold charisma. Bartleby. *Economist* 2019; **430**(9136): 67.

52. Bass BM. Leadership: Good, better, best. *Organizational Dynamics* 1985; **13**(3): 26–40.

53. Vandenberghe C, Stordeur S, D'Hoore W. Transactional and transformational leadership in nursing: Structural validity and substantive relationships. *European Journal of Psychological Assessment* 2002; **18**(1): 16–29.

54. Kahn WA. Psychological conditions of personal engagement and disengagement at work. *Academy of Management Journal* 1990; **33**(4): 692–724.

55. Gottman JM. *What predicts divorce? The relationship between marital processes and marital outcomes.* Hove, England: Psychology Press 1993.

56. Fredrickson BL. Updated thinking on positivity ratios. *American Psychologist* 2013; **68**(9): 814–22; Palgi Y, Bodner E, Shrira A. Positivity ratio of flourishing individuals: Examining the moderation effects of methodological variations and chronological age. *Journal of Positive Psychology* 2016; **11**(2): 109–23; Schutte NS. The broaden and build process: Positive affect, ratio of positive to negative affect and general self-efficacy. *Journal of Positive Psychology* 2014; **9**(1): 66–74; Moroń M. Perceived emotional intelligence and life satisfaction: the mediating role of the positivity ratio. *Current Issues in Personality Psychology* 2018; **6**(3): 212–23.

57. Baumeister RF, Bratslavsky E, Finkenauer C, Vohs KD. Bad is stronger than good. *Review of General Psychology* 2001; **5**(4): 323–70.

58. Silvia PJ, Duval TS. Objective self-awareness theory: Recent progress and enduring problems. *Personality and Social Psychology Review* 2001; **5**(3): 230–41.

59. Bateson M, Nettle D, Roberts G. Cues of being watched enhance cooperation in a real-world setting. *Biology Letters* 2006; **2**(3): 412–4; Pfattheicher S, Keller J. The watching eyes phenomenon: The role of a sense of being seen and public self-awareness. *European Journal of Social Psychology* 2015; **45**(5): 560–6.

60. Smith JK. Art as mirror: Creativity and communication in aesthetics. *Psychology of Aesthetics, Creativity, and the Arts* 2014; **8**(1): 110–8.

61. Romanowska J, Larsson G, Theorell T. An art-based leadership intervention for enhancement of self-awareness, humility, and leader performance. *Journal of Personnel Psychology* 2014; **13**(2): 97–106.

62. Rousseau DM. Normative beliefs in fund-raising organizations: Linking culture to organizational performance and individual responses. *Group and Organization Management* 1990; **15**(4): 448–60.

63. Arieli S, Sagiv L, Roccas S. Values at work: The impact of personal values in organisations. *Applied Psychology* 2020; **69**(2): 230–75; Rokeach M. *The nature of human values.* New York: Free Press 1973.

64. Giberson et al. Leadership and organizational culture; Ralston DA, Russell CJ, Egri CP. Business values dimensions: A cross-culturally developed measure of workforce values. *International Business Review* 2018; **27**(6): 1189–99.

65. Hald EJ, Gillespie A, Reader TW. Causal and corrective organisational culture: A systematic review of case studies of institutional failure. *Journal of Business Ethics* September 2020: 1–27.

66. Guiso L, Sapienza P, Zingales L. The value of corporate culture. *Journal of Financial Economics* 2015; **117**(1): 60–76.

67. Hodson R, Roscigno VJ, Lopez SH. Chaos and the abuse of power: Workplace bullying in organizational and interactional context. *Work and Occupations* 2006 **33**(4), 382–416; Roscigno VJ, Lopez SH, Hodson R. Supervisory bullying, status inequalities and organizational context. *Social Forces* 2009; **87**(3): 1561–89.

68. Zimbardo PG. *The pathology of imprisonment. Down to earth sociology: Introductory readings.* New York: Free Press, 2001.

69. Castro SA, Zautra AJ. Humanization of social relations: Nourishing health and resilience through greater humanity. *Journal of Theoretical and Philosophical Psychology* 2016; **36**(2): 64–80.

70. Postmes T, Spears R. Deindividuation and antinormative behavior: A meta-analysis. *Psychological Bulletin* 1998; **123**(3): 238–59.

71. Keltner D. Don't let power corrupt you. *Harvard Business Review* 2016; **94**(10): 112–5.

72. Formanowicz M, Goldenberg A, Saguy T, Pietraszkiewicz A, Walker M, Gross JJ. Understanding dehumanization: The role of agency and communion. *Journal of Experimental Social Psychology* 2018; **77**: 102–16; Tuckey MR, Dollard MF, Hosking PJ, Winefield AH. Workplace bullying: The role of psychosocial work environment factors. *International Journal of Stress Management* 2009; **16**(3): 215–32.

73. Magee JC. Power and social distance. *Current Opinion in Psychology* 2020; **33**: 33–7.

74. Grant A. Power doesn't corrupt. It exposes your real self. *Washington Post.* 2019 Feb 24.

Index

Page numbers in *italics* indicate figures or tables.

ability, *64*
abundance, 102–3, 224
abuse, 257–58
accountability, 156, 157
ACER, *68*
action research, 25–26
adaptation: to change, 58; with intelligence, 35–36; by leadership, *247*; by organization, 35–36
affirmative action, 151
agility, 202
aging, *167*
Alice in Wonderland (Carroll), 1
Allen curve, *133*, 133–34
Amazon, 42, 59
ambidexterity, 60, 65, 75–76
American Psychological Association, 22
American Telephone and Telegraph (AT&T), 16
anatomy, 181
A&P. *See* Great Atlantic and Pacific Tea Company
Apple headquarters, 127–28, *128*
appreciative inquiry, 38
architecture, 139–40, 141–42
Argyris, Chris, 19

Arkadium, 236
Armenakis, Achilles, 35
Aronson, E., 89
art, 253
Asch, Solomon, 46
Assembly Revolution Cell Line, 110
AT&T. *See* American Telephone and Telegraph
attitudes, 38
authority: decentralization of, 202; of employees, 192; empowerment and, 193; freedom and, 211–12; servant leadership and, 210–11
automation, 14
autonomy, 89, 202, 205

balance, 251–52
Bartleby's Law, 119
Baumol, W. J., 48
Beckhard, Richard, 4, *15*
Bedeain, Arthur, 35
Beer, Michael, 52
behavior: culture deteriorating with, 256–57; employee reengaging in, 188; empowerment changing, 206; goal-directed, 187–88; habits contrasted with, 187–88;

behavior (*continued*)
    herd, 45–48; measurement of,
    231, 231–32; OD and, 25–30,
    28; performance improving with,
    208, 240; principles of, 25–30,
    28; self-maximizing, 86; Stanford
    University prison experiment
    changing, 257; for success, 255–
    56, *256*; supervisory, 241–42;
    surveillance impacting, 128; trust
    betrayed by, 86; unfreezing of,
    40–41
beliefs, 38, 45
Bentham, Jeremy, 127–28, *128*
Bentham, Samuel, 128
Berlin Wall, *28*
Bethlehem Steel, 16
bias: accountability reducing, 156;
    confirmation, *43*; in hiring,
    151–53; merit misshapen
    by, 221, *222*; with natural
    selection, 51; negativity, 252;
    with overconfidence, 50; with
    performance, *222*; in recruitment,
    157; sunk costs as, 70; in
    workplace, 252
Big Ass Fans (BAFs), 173
Biggest Little Farm, The, 150–51
Bion, Wilfred, 23
biophilia, 141
Blake, Robert, 4, *15*, 29
Blau Index, *160*
blood flow, 54–55
boom-and-bust cycle, 61–62
Borders, 42
Bowen, W. G., 48
Brandeis, Louis, 195
bricolage, 52–54
British Leyland, 75
Brockner, Joel, 35
Burke-Litwin model, 238–40, *239*,
    245

burnout, 39, 115
Burns, T., 106
bürolandshaft (office landscaping),
    142

calibration, 222
capability, 166, 183, 186–87
capacity, 74–75, 112–13, *113*
capital, 86, 169
Caporaso, Tom, *210*
career, 171, *182*, 186
Carlsmith, J. M., 89
Carroll, Lewis, 1
CEO, 201
CF&I. *See* Colorado Fuel & Iron
change, *247*; adaptation to, 58;
    appreciative inquiry in, 38;
    autonomy influenced, 89;
    barriers to, 39; with behavior,
    45–48; commitment to, 49–51;
    complexity of, 5; as constant,
    32; constraint-based, *53*; in
    culture, 27; as developmental,
    35; *Doctor Who* demonstrating,
    18; employees feigning, 39;
    environment and, 33, 36, 55;
    feedback guiding, 10–11; forms
    of, 52, *53*; as futile, 39; future of,
    54–57; imprinting and, 48–49;
    improvement evaporation in,
    54; with innovation, 51–54, *53*;
    leadership required for, 37–38;
    locked-in process of, 43–45;
    messiness of, 6; methodologies
    of, 41, *41*; OD with, 18–22, *19*,
    26–27; in organization, 18–22,
    19, 34, 35, 37, 40, 43–44, 55;
    organize for, 32–57; process of,
    40–45, *41*, *43*, *44*; programmatic,
    52; to relationships, 89–90; self-
    examination in, 19; simplicity
    and, 41–42; social identity and,

95–101, *98*; in specialization, 13; with structural inertia, 49; sunk costs and, 66–68, *67–68*; in systems, *19*, 27; transaction cost of, 34; ups and downs of, 6, *7*
Changing World Technologies, 62
charisma, 249
Chesbrough, H., 52
childcare, 158
Child Welfare Research Station, 27
Chrysler, 241
Clarus Commerce, *210*
Clockwork Universe, 16
coal mines, 13, 14
Coates, Josh, 99
Coch, Lester, 40
Cochran-Siegle, Ryan, 183–84
collaboration, *15*, 15–18, 133
Collins, Suzanne, 226
Colorado Fuel & Iron (CF&I), *196*
commitment, 49–51
communication, 135; in coordination, 94; with open office, *133*, 133–34, *134*
company: diversity reduced by, 151–52; employees sponsored by, 177; job shadowing in, 172–73; management declining with, 236–37
competency trap, *44*, 44–45, 66
competition, 101–3; abundance tempering, 224; in social identity, 98, *98*
complexity, 7–8; of change, *5*; of systems, *9*
conflict, 162
conformity, 45–47
connection, 137–38
consistency, 61
Constraints of Corporate Tradition, The (Kantrow), 21–22
consultants, of OD, 2, 18

control, spans of, *201*. *See also* perceived control
Control Data, 20
cooperation: abundance and, 102–3; as contagious, 86–87; dissonance in, 89; employees preferred with, 88; encouragement of, 81–103, *83*, *85*, *87*, *92*, *98*; etiquette encouraging, 91–92; exploitation and, 85; fairness promoting, 214; leadership facilitating, 90–91; OD centralizing, 87–88; organization built on, 85–86; in pay-it-forward reciprocity, 86–87, *87*; payout and, 88; positive interdependence in, 93–95; with rationality, 82–83; rewards and punishments undermining, 89; self-interest contrasted with, 82–84, *83*; with social affinity, 90–93, *92*; social identity with, 95–100, *98*
coordination, 94–95, 108
corporations, 59
cost, 115, 119–20. *See also* sunk costs
cost disease, 48
Covid-19, 96, 138, 158
creativity, 96–97, 141, 142–43
cross-training, 122–25, *123*
culture: behavior deteriorating with, 256–57; change in, 27; coordination impacted by, 94–95; Eastern *versus* Western, 61; with efficiency, 107–8; employees fitting, 224; feedback in, 206; generative, *107*, 107–8; generative and pathological, *107*, 107–8; in Germany, *28*; job candidate attracted to, 168; leadership fostered in, 238–59; Mayan, 33; merger undermined by, 241–42, norms shaping, 38;

culture (*continued*)
OD and, 27; paralysis of, *28*;
performance impacted by, 212,
240–41; relationship, 108;
of self-interest, 88–89; social
identity influenced by, 96;
strategy contrasted with, 95; time
influenced by, 61; values used by,
254–55, *255*, *256*; women and
minorities obstructed by, 154,
155, 158–59
Cummings Engines, 162
Cunningham, Billy, 101
Curie, Marie, 190–91
curiosity, 190–91
cycle, 61–62, 63

Daimler, 241
Darwin, Charles, 147
decentralization, 202
de-developing, 34
defector, 84–85
demand, 111–12
Deming, W. E., 39, 199
democratization, 197
Descartes, René, 16
Deutsch, Morton, 93
Devil's Advocate, 47
devolution, 33–34
Dewey, John, 195
Digital Equipment Computers
(DEC), 20
direct report, 201
discrimination, 153–54, 156
dissonance, 89
distinction, 127–44, *128*, *133*, *134*,
137, *144*
distinctiveness, 98–99
diversity: with affirmative action,
151; Blau Index balancing, *160*;
company reducing, 151–52;

conflict reduced by, 162;
definition of, 159–60;
discrimination with, 153;
distinctiveness contrasted with,
99; efficacy improving with,
147; faultlines and, 160–61,
163–64, *164*; gender, *148*; of
group, 164–65; inclusivity and,
145–65, *148*, *155*, *160*, *161*,
164; job satisfaction influenced
by, 145; mentoring bolstering,
156; performance impacted by,
149–50; practitioners prioritizing,
165; productivity improving with,
161, 161–62; racial, *148*; R&D
and, 147; referral programs and,
151–52; simplicity complicated by,
159; system stabilized with, 149;
training for, 163; in workforce,
145–65, *148*, *155*, *160*, *161*, *164*
Doctor Who, 18
Drucker, Peter, 95, 202
drug usage, 7
dumb organization, 20
Duncker, K., *111*
Dunlop, 75
Dunning-Kruger effect, 223
durability, 23, 59
Durkheim, É., 91

East Africa, 150
Ebbinghaus illusion, *134*
economy, 54–55, 57
Edison, Thomas, 141
Edmunds, 172, 206
efficacy, 38–39, 147; leadership
developing, 207. *See also*
self-efficacy
efficiency, 106, 107–8, 117
Electrolux, *44*, 44–45
emergency rooms, 111–12

Emperor's New Clothes, 66
employees: authority of, 192; balance
for, 251–52; behavior reengaged
in by, 188; capability of, 166;
change feigned by, 39; company
sponsoring, 177; competition
among, 102; cooperation
preferred in, 88; culture fit by,
224; empowerment of, 192–212,
196, 198, 201, 204, 209, 210;
environment influencing,
130–32, 141; flexibility impacting,
114–15, 118; formal performance
appraisal of, 229; human
relations movement valuing,
17; independent contractors
contrasted with, 121–22;
information withheld by, 81;
involvement in, 28; job rotation
of, 124–25; leadership improving,
258–59; lighting influencing,
17; with management, 193;
mentoring of, 185–86; merit of,
237; nature befitting, 143–44;
on-call work confining, 116;
participation of, 29; part-time,
116–17; performance and, 105,
130–32, 180–81; personal growth
of, 166–91, *167, 170, 174, 182*;
personal office preferred by,
136–37; reward attracting,
218–19; satisfaction of, 221,
222; shift work by, 119–20; as
successors, *174*; temporary, 120,
121; training attracting, 168–69;
value of, 229; Valve Corporation
guided by, 54; vilifying of, 37;
wholeness of, 175–76
employer–employee representation,
196
employers, 178–79

empowerment: authority and,
193; behavior changed by, 206;
Clarus Commerce enabled by,
210; of employees, 192–212,
196, 198, 201, 204, 209, 210;
flexibility with, 200; with job
satisfaction, 202–12, *204, 209,
210*; by leadership, 208, 209;
management using, 209–10;
performance influenced by,
194–95; at Ritz Carlton, *204*; of
workforce, 192–93
engagement, 251
environment: change and, 33,
36, 55; communication with,
135; of competition, 101–2;
creativity contributed to by, 141;
employees influenced by, 130–32,
141; human relations movement
prioritizing, 129; indoor, 130;
job satisfaction influenced by,
129, 131; mining impacting,
56; Patagonia supporting, 56;
performance influenced by,
130–32, 137; of personal office,
136; productivity impacted by,
130; sick building syndrome
caused by, 132; as social
construction, *134*, 134–35;
technology prioritizing, 55–56;
temperature-aggression and, 131
equality, 228–29
equifinality, 11
equity, 228–29
Esso's Bayway Refinery, 4
Estonian folktale, 76, *76*
etiquette, 91–92
evidence, 26
executive functioning, 21
executives, 65–66
expectations, 207–8

expertise, 178–79; experience
compared with, 181; resistance
with, 183–84; success with,
184–85
exploitation, 71, 77–78, 85
exploitation and exploration: growth
with, 61–62; in hive, 73–74;
Newton demonstrating, 62;
practical considerations of, 63; in
recession, 63; short-term interests
and, 63; of Smith Corona, 77
exploration, 64–65, 76–78, 77

factory lines, 162
failure, 224–25
fairness, 214
Family and Medical Leave Act,
158
family relations, 29–30
faultlines, 160–61, 163–64, *164*
feedback, 232; change guided
by, 10–11; in culture, 206;
job satisfaction with, 205–6;
performance and, 235–36
feng shui, 143–44, *144*
Festinger, L., 89
fixed mindset, 180
flexibility: agility contrasted
with, 202; cost of, 115; with
cross-training, *123*, 123–24;
efficiency with, 106; employees
impacted by, 114–15, 118;
with empowerment, 200; with
flextime, 118; forms of, 106–7;
functional, 114; geographic,
119; of labor, 114; newsvendor
problem influenced by, 112;
numeric, 114–15; organization
remaining, 104–26, *106, 107,*
111, 113, 121, 123; performance
influenced by, 104–5;
profitability contrasted with, 105;

telecommuting offering, 138–39;
wage, 114; of work, 118–19
flexible scheduling, 117–18
flextime, 118
foragers, 74
force, 16
Ford, Henry, 36
formal performance appraisal, 229,
234
fountain, 135
freedom, 211–12, 216
French, John, 40
full-time equivalent (FTE), 114–15
future: anticipation of, 58–80,
64, 67–68, 76, 78; of change,
54–57; of organization, 71–72;
prospection of, 72; short-
term interests contrasted with,
59–60; sunk costs and, 70; of
telecommuting, 139

Galton, Francis, 179
Gardner, David, 47
Gardner, Tom, 47
General Mills, 4
Germany, 25, 27, *28*, 218
Gerstner, Lou, Jr., 20
Gibson, James, 134–35
Gilley, A. M., 237
Gilley, J. W., 237
Gladwell, Malcolm, 34, 181
Glass Ceiling, *155*
goals, 3, *7*
golem effect, 207–8
Gore, W. L., 12
Gottman, John, 252
Grant, R. M., 203
Great Atlantic and Pacific Tea
Company (A&P), 20
Greene, D., 217
gross domestic product (GDP),
158, 259

group: behaviors influencing, 241–42; diversity of, 164–65; information utilized by, 108; leadership of, 220; recognition benefiting, 234; women influencing, 146. *See also* Training Groups

groupthink, 45–46

growth: of capability, 183; with exploitation and exploration, 61–62; regulation impacting, 186; stalling of, 32; of systems, 12–13; of wholeness, 177–78. *See also* personal growth

growth mindset, 180

habits: behavior contrasted with, 187–88; hiring for, 188–89; of learning, 190; into routines, 187

Hackman, J. R., 202

Hambrick, David Z., 33

Hardin, Garrett, 82

Hartig, T., 143

Harvey, William, 54–55

Harwood Manufacturing Corporation, 28

Hawthorne effect, 17

health, 22–25; faltering of, 58–59; leader impacting, 252–53; mental, 185; nature and, 142–43; practitioners focusing on, 30

Health Catalyst, 225

Hebl, M., 153

Heider, F., *85*

helplessness, *209*

Heraclitus, 32

herd behavior, 45–48

Herodotus, 223, *224*

Hertzberg, Frederick, 215–16

Heskett, James, 240

heterogeneity, *148*, 148–49

hiring: bias in, 151–52, 153; for habits, 188–89; information refining, 236; at Instructure, 171; organization loosening, 225–26

Hitler, Adolf, 25

hive, 61, 73–74

Holland, *182*

Holmes, Elizabeth, 250

home, 175

honeybee (*Apis mellifera*), 61, 74, 75–76

Hoover Dam, 16

Hoover Vacuum Cleaner, *44*, 44–45

Hudson, Henry, *198*

human body, 8, 13

human concerns, 140

human relations movement, 17–18, 129

human resources, 170–71, 172

humility, 244–45

IBM, 20

Icarus, 12–13

identity, 138, 203. *See also* social identity

I Love Lucy, 14

imprinting, 48–49

incivility, 242–43

inclusion: faultlines weakened by, 163–64; incivility contrasted with, 242–43; through military service, *161*, 161–62; trust with, 161; value of, 163–64

inclusiveness, 197

inclusivity, 99; diversity and, 145–65, *148*, *155*, *160*, *161*, *164*; in workforce, 145–65, *148*, *155*, *160*, *161*, *164*

independent contractors, 121–22

indigenous populations, 52–53

indoor environments, 130

industrialization, 16

Industrial Revolution, 128–29, 169
inflows, *9*
information: capacity for, 74–75;
   employees withholding, 81;
   group utilizing, 108; hiring
   refined with, 236; interpretation
   of, 43; as limited, 45; sunk costs
   influencing, 69–70
Information Age, 169
initiation of structure, 29
innovation, 51–54, *53*; fatigue
   from, 39; R&D leading, 79–80;
   sustaining, *44*, 44–45
Instructure, 171, 254
Intel, 65
intelligence, 21–22, 35–36, 189
interest, of employee: performance
   and, 185; RIASEC describing,
   182; work benefited by, *182*,
   182–83. *See also* self-interest
International Systems Institute, 57
internship, *170*, 172
interpretation, 42–43
interventions, *7*, 8
Intuitive Research and Technology
   Corporation (INTUITIVE), 79
irrelevant speech, 131–32
Israel, 242

James, William, 100
Japan, *113*, 115, 199
job candidate, 168, 170, 171
job crafting, 186
job rotation, 124–25, *170*
Jobs, Steve, 62
job satisfaction: with autonomy,
   205; diversity influencing, 145;
   empowerment with, 202–12,
   204, 209, 210; environment
   influencing, 129, 131; with
   feedback, 205–6; formulation of,
   202–12, *204, 209, 210*; identity

with, 203; life in, 176; pay for
   performance increasing, 215;
   with skill variety, 204–5; task and,
   203–4, *204*
job shadowing, *170*, 172–73
job skills, 175
Johnson and Johnson, 136
joint decision-making, 73–74
justice, 214–15

Kahneman, D., 49
Kanter, Rosabeth, 200
Kantrow, Alan, 21–22
Keltner, D., 257
Kim, D., 147
knowledge, 21; consultants
   transferring, 18; criteria
   developed with, 247–49;
   management of, 109
Kohler, Otto, 220
Kongo Kumi, 59
Kotter, John, 240
Kuhn, T. S., 42

labor, 114, *167*, 167–68
labor force, 14
labor market, 166–67
labor reform, 16
language, 99
Law of Effect, 215
leader, 248–49; health impacted by,
   252–53; humility of, 244–45;
   leadership contrasted with, 245;
   self-awareness of, 253
leadership, 237; adaptation by, *247*;
   change requiring, 37–38; with
   charisma, 249; cluster approach
   to, 250–51; common purpose
   conveyed by, 94; cooperation
   facilitated by, 90–91; criteria
   defining, 245–48, *246–47*;
   culture fostering, 238–59;

dark triad of, *243*; directive and empowering, 194; efficacy developed by, 207; employee improving with, 258–59; empowerment by, 208, 209; with engagement, 251; family relations compared with, 29–30; of groups, 220; leader contrasted with, 245; personal issues acted on by, 224–25; productivity impacted by, 27–28; with respect, 258; responsibility taken by, 49–50; servant, 210; skills of, *246*; with success, 238, 240; successors groomed by, *174*; theories of, 244–45, *246–47*; transformational and adaptive, *247*; types of, 210–11; women passed over by, 154. *See also* servant leadership

Leadership Development Simulator, 194

Leadership in Energy and Environment Design (LEED), 130

learning: effective action describing, 19; habit of, 190; of helplessness, *209*; informal, 189–90; of personal growth, 189–90; single- and double-loop, 10, *10*, 19

LEED. *See* Leadership in Energy and Environment Design

Leibniz, Gottfried Wilhelm, 16

Lepper, M.R., 217

Levi-Strauss, Claude, 52, 53

Lewin, Kurt, 25, 27–28, 40–41

life satisfaction, 176, 178

lighting, 17

Lilly, 136, *137*

LinkedIn, 219

long-term interests, 73–74

Lorenz, Konrad, 48

Ludlow Massacre, *196*

MacArthur Foundation, 23

Machiavelli, Niccolò, *243*, 249–50

management: company declining with, 236–37; employees with, 193; empowerment used by, 209–10; formal performance appraisal of, 234; of knowledge, 109; participatory, 198–99; performance and, 232, *239*, 244; succession, 173; of talent, 170–71, 173. *See also* scientific management; total quality management

Manpower, *121*

manufacturing, 48–49

Marrow, Alfred, 40

Marx, Arthur "Harpo," 98

Marx, Julius Henry "Groucho," 98

Maslow, Abraham, 216

Mathew effect, 226, 227

Mayo, Elton, *15*, 17

McFarland, Billy, 250

McGregor, Douglas, 4, *15*, 29

McNeil, William, 97

memory, 131–32

men and whites, 153–55

Mencken, H. L., 7

mentoring, 156, *170*, 185–86

merger, 241–42

merit, 213–14; bias misshaping, 221, *222*; of employees, 237; organization abandoning, 221–22, *222*; with pay for performance, 215; value contrasted with, 226, 227

metacognition, 18

Michelin, 75

microaggressions, 155–56

Miles, M. B., 23

military service, *161*, 161–62

Miller, D., 12–13

minimal group technique, 96
mining, 56
minorities. *See* women and
minorities
Mischel, Walter, 73
money, 216
monitoring, 88–89
Moore, Geoffrey, 65
Moore, Gordon, 65
Moreno, Jacob, 24
Morison, Elting, 22
Motivation to Work, The
(Hertzberg), 215–16
Motley Fool, The, 47, 79
Mouton, Jane, 29
multiplicity, 232
muscular bonding, 97
Music Center, in Los Angeles, 144

Napoleon, *64*
NASA, 11
National Cash Register (NCR),
44, 44–45
National Training Labs, 23, 25
natural selection, 40, 51, 84–85
nature: with architecture, 141–42;
creativity increased by, 142–43;
employee befitting from,
143–44; feng shui integrating,
143–44, *144*; health and,
142–43; productivity with, 142;
prosociality elicited by, 143;
Salesforce utilizing, 144; of work,
200, 202; in workplace, 142
Nazi Party, 25
NCR. *See* National Cash Register
needs, 216–17, 228
Nelson, Horatio, *64*
newsvendor problem, 112–13,
113
Newton (Apple), 62
normative standards, *201*

norms, 38, 45–46
Noyce, Robert, 65
Nutt, P. C., 34

OD. *See* organization development
Oldman, G. R., 202
on-call work, 116
open office, *133*, 133–36, *134*
open spaces, 135
opinions, 45
O'Reilly, C. A., 65
organization: adaptation by, 35–36;
with ambidexterity, 60; change
in, 18–22, *19*, 34–35, 37, 40,
43–44, 55; cooperation building,
85–86; as creative, 96–97;
death of, 59; in decline, 33;
devolution of, 33–34; dumb,
20; expertise honed by, 178–79;
fitness of, 220–37, *222*, *224*,
227, *230*, *231*, *235*; flexibility
remaining in, 104–26, *106*,
107, *111*, *113*, *121*, *123*; future
of, 71–72; goals achieved by,
3; hiring loosened by, 225–26;
intelligence of, 21–22, 35–36;
learning implemented by, 19;
life span of, 33; mechanistic and
organic, *106*; merit abandoned
by, 221–22, *222*; models of, *239*;
past guiding, 21–22; performance
of, 213, 223–24, *224*; personnel
issues addressed by, 224–25;
public goods dilemma in, 81–82;
Red Queen effect suffered by,
151, *155*; routines of, 105; smart,
20; social identity impacting,
96; standards of, 223–24, *224*;
systems and, 5, 8, *9*, 13; weighing
down of, 3
organization development (OD):
basics of, 3–31; behavior and,

25–30, *28*; with change, 18–22, *19*; change reflected by, 26–27; collaboration in, *15*, 15–18; context emphasized by, 40; cooperation central to, 87–88; culture and, 27; definitions of, 4, *5*, 5–6; as democratic process, 27–29; evidence basing, 26; health and, 22–25; human relations movement assimilated into, 17–18; industrialization growing, 16; job candidates differentiated in, 171; job skills prioritized by, 175; planned, 6–14, *7*, *9*, *10*; principles of, 25–30, *28*; selective works from, *15*, 16; sociotechnical system optimized by, 14; success of, 4. *See also* practitioners, of OD

Organization for Economic Cooperation and Development, 14, 158

Ostrom, Elinor, 88

outflows, *9*

Outliers (Gladwell), 181

outsourcing, 120–21

"Overcoming Resistance to Change" (Coch and French), 40

overconfidence, 50–51

overextraction, 82

overwork, *113*

Page, S. E., 149

panopticon, 127–28, *128*, 132

paralysis, *28*

Paris Opera House, 48

Parsons, Talcott, 87–88

participation: of employees, 29; inclusiveness and, 197; in labor, *167*, 167–68; success with, 29; of workforce, 14

part-time employees, 117

part-time work, 117–18

past, 21–22, 65

Patagonia, 56, 227

pattern, 26, 43–45

pay for performance: in Germany, 218; job satisfaction increased with, 215; merit with, 215; productivity influenced by, 218; sorting from, 219

pay-it-forward reciprocity, 86–87, *87*

payout, 88

Pepe's Pizza, 110–11

perceived control, 38–39

performance: behavior improved with, 208, 240; bias with, *222*; calibration standardizing, 222; culture impacting, 212, 240–41; diversity impacting, 149–50; efficacy and, 38–39; of employees, 105, 130–32; employees attributed to, 180–81; empowerment influencing, 194–95; environment influencing, 130–32, 137; faultlines damaging, 160–61; feedback and, 235, 236; flexibility influencing, 104–5; heterogeneity influencing, *148*, 148–49; innovation and, 52; with intelligence, 189; interests and, 185; management and, 232, *239*, 244; measurement of, 229–32, *230*, *231*; as multidimensional, 234–35; normal and pareto distributions for, *230*; open office influencing, 135–36; of organization, 213, 223–24, *224*; overtime impacting, 115–16; paths to, *235*, 235–36; recognition of, 228, 234; as recruitment, 219; reward for, 213–37, *218*,

performance (*continued*)
222, 223, 224, 227, 230, 231,
235; self-efficacy influencing,
206–7; separations and, 225; sick
building syndrome undermining,
132; standards for, 223–24,
224; status rewarding, 103; team
elevated with, 220; training aided
by, 232; trust determining, 139;
victimization and, 223. *See also*
formal performance appraisal; pay
for performance
Persian empire, 161, 161–62
personal growth, 166–91, 167, 170,
174, 182
personal issues, 224–25
personal office, 136–37
Personal Word Processor (PWP), 67
personnel issues, 224–25
Phillips, Katherine, 153
planned organization development,
6–14, 7, 9, 10
Pontiac Aztek, 77
positive interdependence, 93–95
power, 257–58
power lines, 8
practitioners, of OD, 2; action
research with, 25–26; diversity
prioritized by, 165; health
focused on by, 30; interventions
planned by, 8; profitability
weighed by, 56; staff-planning
prioritized by, 125–26;
technology contended with by,
14; trust built by, 162–63
prisoner dilemma, 83, 84
private offices, 138
productivity: with cross-training,
124; decline impairing, 34–35;
diversity improving, 161, 161–62;
environment impacting, 130;
flextime increasing, 118; leadership impacting, 27–28; with

nature, 142; pay for performance
influencing, 218; workplace
impacting, 16–17, 129
profitability: competency trap and,
66; flexibility contrasted with,
105; health contrasted with,
22–23; practitioners weighing, 56
prosociality, 143
prospection, 72
psychopathy, 243
public goods dilemma, 81–82
punctuated equilibrium, 33
punishment. *See* rewards and
punishments
PURE Insurance, 189, 225
PWP. *See* Personal Word Processor
Pygmalion (Shaw), 207

Quality Bicycle Products (QBP), 99
quality circles, 199–200

radial tire technology, 75
Rand, Ayn, 133
rationality, 51, 82–83, 83, 84
RCA, 65
R&D. *See* research and development
recession, 61–62, 63
reciprocity, 86–87, 87
recognition, 228, 232–34
recognition plans, 232–33
recruitment: bias in, 157;
discrimination in, 153–54;
performance as, 219;
representation and, 152
recycling, 7
Red Queen effect, 151, 155
redundancy, 123, 123
referral programs, 151–52, 226
regulation, 42–43, 186
relationship, 89–90, 108, 214–15
reliability, 150–51
remote work, 139–40
replacement, 173

representation: recruitment and, 152; in social identity, 100; of value, *255*; of women, 148; of women and minorities, 160. *See also* employer–employee representation
reputation, *85*
research and development (R&D), 24–25, 60, *67–68*, 68–69, 78–80, 147
resilience, 150–51, 186–87
resistance, 183–84
resource dilemma, 82
resources, 53–54, 68, 76–77
respect, 258
responsibility, 49–50
results, 250
Results Only Work Environment (ROWE), 118
retailers, 42
revenues, 64–65
reward, 103; employees attracted to, 218–19; as extrinsic and intrinsic, 217; needs and, 228; for performance, 213–37, *218, 222, 223, 224, 227, 230, 231, 235*; recognition plans for, 232–33
rewards and punishments, 88–89, 228
risk, 45–46, 50–51
Rittel, Horst, 11
rituals, 91
Ritz Carlton, *204*
Robbers Cave Experiments, *92*, 93–94
Roman empire, *161*, 161–62
routines, 105, 187
ROWE. *See* Results Only Work Environment
Ryff, Carol, 216–17

Salesforce, 144
SAS, 205
satisfaction, 221, 222. *See also* job satisfaction; life satisfaction

scarcity, 102–3
Scheinfeld, Aaron, *121*
scientific management, 16, 128–29
self-awareness, 253, 254
self-efficacy, 206–7
self-examination, 19
self-interest, 82–84, *83*, 88–89
self-sufficiency, 18
Seligman, M. E. P., *209*
Senge, Peter, 19
separations, 225
servant leadership, 210–11
services, 48–49
Shaw, George Bernard, 207
Shepard, Herbert, 4, *15*
shift work, 119–20
short-term interests: executives on, 65–66; with exploitation, 71; exploitation and exploration and, 63; future contrasted with, 59–60. *See also* long-term interests
short-termism, 82
sick building syndrome, 132
simplicity, 7–8, 41–42, 159
skill, 184
skill variety, 204–5
slack resources, 60, 75–76, 126
sleuthing, 60
smart organization, 20
Smith Corona, 66–69, *67–68*, 73, 77
social affinity, 90–93, *92*
social construction, *134*, 134–35
social dilemma, *83*, 84
social identity: categorization in, 97; change and, 95–101, *98*; common experiences in, 97; competition in, 98, *98*; with cooperation, 95–100, *98*; culture influencing, 96; distinctiveness in, 98–99; in language, 99; organizations impacted by, 96; representation in, 100; status and, 99; symbolism in, 100

social movement, 25
social proofs, 54
social traps, 82–83
sociotechnical system, 13, 14
sorting, 219
space, 127–44, *128, 133, 134, 137, 144*
specialization, 13
staff-planning, 125–26
Stalker, G. M., 106
Stanford University prison experiment, 257
Starks, L. T., 147
status, 99, 103
stereotypes, 154
Sticky Floor, *155*
strategy, *64,* 95
strengths-use, 185
Stroop task, 157
structural inertia, 49
success: behavior for, 255–56, *256;* with expertise, 184–85; with interdependence of outcomes, 93; leadership with, 238, 240; of OD, 4; with participation, 29; with R&D, 60; self-sufficiency as, 18
successors, *174*
sunk costs: as bias, 70; change and, 66–68, *67–68;* future and, 70; information influenced by, 69–70; resources trapped by, 68
surveillance, 128
Swift, Jonathan, 72
symbolism, 100
systems: basic elements of, *19;* behavior in, 45; change in, *19,* 27; complexity of, *9;* depictions of, 8, *9;* diversity stabilizing, 149; growth of, 12–13; human body exemplifying, 8, 13; inflows in, *9;* as open or closed, 10–11;

organization and, *5,* 8, *9,* 13; outflows in, *9;* sociotechnical, 13, 14; within system, 13; as whole, 10; wicked problems in, 11. *See also* International Systems Institute

Taleb, Nassim, 35
talent, 166–67, 170–71, 173, 181, *227*
task, 203–4, *204*
Tavistock Institute, 23, 24
Taylor, Frederick, 16, 129
teachers, 1–2
team, 23–24, 220
telecommuting, 138–39
temperature-aggression, 131
temporary agency, *121*
Tesla, 214
T-groups. *See* Training Groups
Thaler, Richard, 69
thinking, 110, 157, 176–77
Three Little Pigs, The, 64
3M, 79
Tobin's Q, 149, 169
topophilia, 137–38
total quality management (TQM), 199–200
tragedy of commons, 82
training: for diversity, 163; employees attracted to, 168–69; performance aided by, 232; skill focused on by, 184; types and methods of, *170*
Training Groups (T-groups), 23, 24, 25
transaction cost, 34
Trist, Eric, 13, *15*
trust: behavior betraying, 86; capital built on, 86; with inclusion, 161; performance determined by, 139; practitioners building, 162–63

Turing, Alan, 11
Tushman, M. L., 65
Tversky, A., 49

Uchino, Kenichi, *113*
underestimation, 152, 153
unions, 196
United Kingdom, 13, 23

values: bottom-line thinking
  undercutting, 176–77; culture
  using, 254–55, *255, 256;* of
  employee, 229; of inclusion,
  163–64; merit contrasted with,
  226, 227; representation of, *255;*
  rituals reaffirming, 91
Valve Corporation, 54
victimization, 223
Vinci, Leonardo da, 203
volunteering, 92

Watson, John, 179
Weber, Max, 249
Wedgewood, Josiah, 129
Welch, Jack, 36
well-being, 92
Western Electric Hawthorne Plant,
  16–17, 129
Western Union, 37
Westrum, R., 107
whites. *See* men and whites
wholeness, 175–76, 177–78
wicked problems, 11–12
Wilson, E. O., 141
Winter, Elmer, *121*
Wm Filene & Sons, 196
women: childcare for, 158; double
  standard for, 154; efficacy
  improved with, 147; groups
  influenced by, 146; leadership

passing over, 154; personal
  choice of, 158; representation of,
  148; work by, 157–58
women and minorities: culture
  obstructing, 154, *155,* 158–59;
  men and whites contrasted
  with, 153–55; microaggressions
  toward, 155–56; representation
  of, 160; stereotypes
  overgeneralizing, 154; in
  workforce, 146
work: autonomy of, 202; Bartleby's
  Law and, 119; curiosity
  engaging, 190–91; home and,
  118–19, 175; interests benefiting,
  182, 182–83; nature of, 200,
  202; on-call, 116; in open spaces,
  135; part-time, 117–18; shift,
  119–20; by women, 157–58
workforce, 14; cross-training of,
  122–23; diversity in, 145–65,
  148, 155, 160, 161, 164;
  empowerment of, 192–93;
  human resources upgrading, 172;
  inclusivity in, 145–65, *148, 155,
  160, 161, 164;* sorting of, 219;
  women and minorities in, 146
Workforce 2000 report, 145–46
workplace: bias in, 252;
  democratization of, 197; human
  concerns prioritized by, 140;
  nature in, 142; productivity
  impacted by, 16–17; productivity
  prioritized by, 129; in Silicon
  Valley, 151
workspace, *137*
World War I, 22, 195
World War II, 16, 22, 195

Young, Michael, 226